INTERNET CO-REGULATION

Chris Marsden argues that co-regulation is the defining feature of the Internet in Europe. Co-regulation offers the state a route back into questions of legitimacy, governance and human rights, thereby opening up more interesting conversations than a static no-regulation versus state regulation binary choice. The basis for the argument is empirical investigation, based on a multi-year, European Commission-funded study and is further reinforced by the direction of travel in European and English law and policy, including the Digital Economy Act 2010. He places Internet regulation within the regulatory mainstream, as an advanced technocratic form of self- and co-regulation which requires governance reform to address a growing constitutional legitimacy gap. The literature review, case studies and analysis shed a welcome light on policy-making at the centre of Internet regulation in Brussels, London and Washington, revealing the extent to which states, firms and, increasingly, citizens are developing a new type of regulatory bargain.

CHRISTOPHER T. MARSDEN is Senior Lecturer at Essex University School of Law, where his research centres on the regulation and management of information technologies. He has twenty years' experience of exploring the Information Society and its regulation with commercial, academic, think tank and government organizations.

INTERNET CO-REGULATION

European Law, Regulatory Governance and Legitimacy in Cyberspace

CHRISTOPHER T. MARSDEN

CAMBRIDGE
UNIVERSITY PRESS

CAMBRIDGE UNIVERSITY PRESS
Cambridge, New York, Melbourne, Madrid, Cape Town,
Singapore, São Paulo, Delhi, Tokyo, Mexico City

Cambridge University Press
The Edinburgh Building, Cambridge CB2 8RU, UK

Published in the United States of America by Cambridge University Press, New York

www.cambridge.org
Information on this title: www.cambridge.org/9781107003484

First published 2011

Printed in the United Kingdom at the University Press, Cambridge

A catalogue record for this publication is available from the British Library

Library of Congress Cataloguing in Publication data
Marsden, Christopher T.
Internet co-regulation : European law, regulatory governance, and
legitimacy in cyberspace / Christopher T. Marsden.
p.   cm.
Includes bibliographical references and index.
ISBN 978-1-107-00348-4 (hardback)
1. Internet–Law and legislation–Europe.   2. Computer networks–Law and
legislation–Europe.   3. Internet–Law and legislation.   4. Computer
networks–Law and legislation.   I. Title.
KJC164.C65M367 2011
343.409′944–dc22
2011017971

ISBN 978-1-107-00348-4 Hardback

CONTENTS

ACKNOWLEDGEMENTS

This book is a revised, edited and very critical update on the body of reports I published for the European Commission in 2004 and 2007–8, especially the Phases 1–3 reports of that second, specifically co-regulatory project. Whereas those reports amount to some 400,000 words and 500 pages, this book is a mere 100,000; moreover, I have not simply reduced those reports to a concise version, and I therefore refer readers to the complete case studies where there are factual queries or questions of brevity.

My acknowledgements for this book go back twenty years, for it is there that my interest in regulation was formed, and those influences underpin my research even today. Though the empirical aspect of this work is dominant, and in particular European Commission projects of 2001–4 and 2007–8, it is to the legacy of research and practice in the 1990s that I owe most thanks. I acknowledged in my recent previous work 'Net Neutrality' many other influences too numerous to mention – to them also many thanks. I grew up and was educated in regulation at the London School of Economics over the period 1986–97, taking LL.B. in 1986–9, LL.M. in International Economic Law 1993–4 and pursuing doctoral studies while teaching and researching in 1994–7. During that time, I received a grounding in both practical and theoretical aspects of regulation that has influenced my approach ever since. This book is overwhelmingly based on empirical case studies, reflecting an Anglo-Saxon pragmatism that was inculcated in me by my work as research assistant on projects run by Dr Mike Hodges at CRUSA (Centre for Research on the USA) and Professor Rob Baldwin on the 'Regulation in Question' project for Merck Sharp Dohme (working a little with Mark Thatcher and Colin Scott on this project, I focused on gas/electricity/water privatization, as well as background literature), both in 1995–6. I also worked with Jonathans Liebenau and Barton on the ill-fated LSE Information Society Observatory in 1995–6, and held the non-job title of legal adviser there. My interest in economic theory of regulation and its human rights relationship was, however, started much earlier, as an undergraduate studying at the time of financial services deregulation, privatization of state utilities and the creation of independent national regulatory agencies (INRAs) in the late 1980s. LSE was a crucible of these changes, and indeed it was the realization of the power of global finance to undermine apartheid in 1987–8 that led me to focus on interdisciplinary and largely theoretical study in my final undergraduate year (firsts in Anthropology of Law, Civil Liberties and Jurisprudence).

Having taken a crash course in practical transactional economics working in advertising sales at Media Week Ltd at the end of boom and start of bust in 1989–91, and start of renewed longer boom at Euromoney Ltd/World Economic Forum joint venture WorldLink in 1993, I returned to LSE in 1993–4 to study the remarkable transformations by then becoming evident in the global economy, driven by financial reform and information networks. At that point, IBM carried more international data than British Telecommunications, at the dawn of the consumer Internet era. China was rising, computing had become ubiquitous in businesses, and multinationals were seen to be losing their territorial moorings. My dissertation in 1994 focused on Rupert Murdoch's skilful changes of nationality for business and person to evade media ownership limits, as well as his corporate restructuring to avoid tax and institute captive insurance companies in such locations as the Cayman Islands. Truly he was 'Ringmaster of the Information Circus' and his adviser's claim that 'civilization is bandwidth' was an evocative image. At LSE that year, while realizing I would spend the next three years in ultimately fruitless pursuit of multimedia multinationals and a theory of regulation, I spent more intellectual time examining continental European regulatory theories, notably systems theory as well as its discontents. In a fairly unique year, the course Law and Social Theory, taught by Tim Murphy and Alain Pottage, was co-taught by visiting professor Gunther Teubner, and my dissertation concerned advertising and systems theory. We also were treated to a three-hour guest seminar by Niklas Luhmann, interrupted by a passionate rant in protest by a fragrant bohemian French professor on behalf of Foucault's opposition to Luhmann's bloodless technocracy, and the following year even the great Žižek, who came to the University of London to treat us to his unique interpretation of Lacan. Lacan and Irigaray, and of course Foucault were of great interest, though ultimately it was Habermas and his theory of the public sphere which I went on to explore in cyberspace. This book contains no reference to these giants,[1] but they sit in the background observing the regulatory games played by

---

[1] But see Froomkin (2003a), p. 749.

the shrinking nation state and rising multinationals, with wry bemuse-
ment. As Žižek states, we are all living in *The Matrix* now, a ubiquitous
information environment in which we are bombarded with falsehoods
by the Big Other and only occasional tears in the firmament remind us
of a reality before globalized multinational corporations, electronic commerce and ceaseless digital media changed our environment. Žižek will
have enjoyed the Hollywood parable of Internet start-ups *The Social
Network* much more than Mark Zuckerberg.[2]

My time at LSE also coincided with the arrival from Oxford of Julia
Black who has done more than any other British academic to explain
the legal implications of self-regulation. My underpinnings in the pragmatic assessment of regulation owe more to Rob Baldwin, Colin Scott
and herself than they will have realized. I was also the 'supervisor' (a
nebulous term meaning mentor and party organizer) for both the LL.M.
students and the new M.Sc regulation students, the latter amounting
to persuading Anthony Giddens to say kind words on behalf of the
university to the incoming cohort. I found myself teaching various
International Business, European Politics and Development Economics
courses at Richmond College through Mike Hodges' friends and associates, and all-in-all had a crash course in basic economic theory as it then
stood. LSE in 1995–6 was an intensive induction to regulation by teaching and publication, but also made me realize the vacuity of the English
legislative process, as I advised both Liberal Democrat and Labour
front benches on the media ownership aspects of the Broadcasting Act
1996 as part of my research interest. I should add my thanks to media
regulation mentors Richard Collins and David Levy in this period and
throughout the late 1990s.

Media convergence was the major regulatory phenomenon of the mid
1990s, inspired by digital satellite broadcasting in the UK as much as
by any nascent 'Information Revolution' (which only arrived in a short
giddy dot-com bubble in 1998–9). While it was established that self-regulation was appropriate for standards, albeit with substantial government
input for interoperability and competition as seen in the Digital Video
Broadcasting standards for set-top box technologies in 1995–7, the creation of a converged regulator that could take a 'light touch' approach to
Internet content was supported by the Labour Party in opposition,[3] though

---

[2] Žižek (2008).
[3] The proposal was most influentially proposed in Collins and Murroni (1995) and adopted
as new media policy by New Labour.

not implemented until 2004 following the 2002 Office of Communications Act. I followed these debates closely, and found myself intimately involved in both the practicalities of regulation in the dying days of Oftel (2001–2 as Regulatory Director of MCI WorldCom UK Ltd), and acting as special adviser to a hopeful for chief executive of the new regulator, then Independent Television Commission head Patricia Hodgson, in 2000. I also wrote a highly influential article on standards and convergence with Campbell Cowie in early 1998, which was cited by European Commission, OECD, ITU and national regulators thereafter. I spent a pleasant winter 'moonlighting' as a visiting Research Fellow at Melbourne University's Law School, thanks to Andrew Kenyon, and Network Insight, the 'Sydney branch' of RMIT, thanks to Mark Armstrong. En route I paid a visit to John Braithwaite, godfather of regulatory law, whose research and example was and remains a great inspiration. All these Australian bases in late 1999 were at the cusp of self-regulation turning into co-regulation, driven by the intransigence of the Telstra and News Corporation monopolies and their implacable enemies in the various communications industries. My time as Research Fellow at Harvard's Kennedy School 1999–2000 both convinced me that public choice was part of the story, but also interested me in Douglass North and institutional economics, as the state is not simply the Mafia! Self-regulation cannot work where the parties will not be in the same room unless with a regulatory 'relationship guidance counsellor'. Moreover, it works less well where government is entirely in thrall to industry's propaganda, as arguably was the case in US Internet regulation at the height of the dot-com bubble, in that heady winter. I finished writing the introduction to *Regulating the Global Information Society* on St Patrick's Day 2000,[4] in the week that the bubble finally burst. The book expresses the more sober critical view that was sorely needed in the late 1990s.

In 2000, I left full-time academia for various industry-regulator roles, but stayed as research associate of first the Centre for the Study of Globalisation and Regionalisation (CSGR) at Warwick, then the Centre for Management Under Regulation (CMUR) at Warwick Business School under direction of Martin Cave in 2001–2, where I had presented a paper when it was under the direction of Catherine Wadhams and Morten Hviid in 1998. I published papers there on WiFi and standards wars, a step beyond the mobile standards debates of the previous several

---

[4] Marsden (ed.) (2000b).

years. The 'standards wars' literature at that time had a boost, not only from Paul David's pioneering work as well as that of Katz and Farrell on network effects and ICT standards, but also by the empirical example of third-generation mobile phone standards, and notably the battle between European GSM and US CDMA standards. My edited collection, *Regulating the Global Information Society* (2000) featured papers by Lemley, McGowan and Gould reflecting on this. I also presented on Internet governance,[5] alongside Hans Klein and Milton Mueller. My work at that time was heavily influenced by then-recently deceased Susan Strange's work on the relations between states and firms, which led me on to co-regulation studies. It also brought me into contact with Jonathan Aronson and his work with Peter Cowhey, and Susan Spar's work on pirates, prophets, pioneers and profits – which established the historical pattern of deregulation, unregulation, self-regulation and re-regulation in communications industries, driven by state–firm relations.

The path-breaking work by Stefaan Verhulst and Monroe Price on self-regulation and its limits was also a significant influence, not least because their selfregulation.info project was awarded by the European Safer Internet Action Plan based in large measure on their insights in that theoretical work. The study on which this work is based was carried out in 2007, and written up in spring 2008. Negotiation with the publishers took the whole of 2009, which I dedicated to writing about the co-regulatory case study of network neutrality. The case studies have been substantially edited and updated in the course of 2010, but of course will be aged by the date of publication. The legitimacy of the very Act of Parliament that led to much rewriting, the Digital Economy Act 2010, is due to be judicially reviewed in spring 2011, as I write. I therefore claim the law as accurate at 1 November 2010, and the case study material as accurate at 1 January 2008 unless stated as later.

The absence of those factors that made my previous book so easy to write conspired to make this an extremely difficult task. I wrote while fully occupied with lecturing, undergraduate admissions, grant applications and other administrative tasks and university business, in the summer of many marriages (I married Kenza in Montreal in August and celebrated with the whole family in Rabat in September), and with a very ill father in hospital for long periods. That I finished the book at all owes much to

---

[5] Marsden (2000b).

my very understanding publishers at Cambridge University Press, Senior Lecturer colleagues at Essex, my wife and family, and the peace and solitude of Cambridge. This book is dedicated to my mother and father, who taught me the vital life lesson that you are remembered for the projects you finish, not those you start.

ABBREVIATIONS

ABA
:   Australian Broadcasting Authority, statutory regulator replaced by Australian Communications and Media Authority

ACCC
:   Australian Competition and Consumer Commission, generic regulator

ACMA
:   Australian Communications and Media Authority, statutory regulator

ATVOD
:   Association for Television On Demand, UK co-regulatory body

AVMS
:   Audiovisual Media Services Directive 2007

BBFC
:   British Board of Film Classification, statutory censoring body

BIS
:   Department for Business, Innovation and Skills, see DTI

CAIC
:   IWF Child Abuse content list of alleged abuse sites blocked using ISP-level filters

CC
:   Creative Commons, commercial royalty-free copyright licensing system

CEOP
:   Child Exploitation and Online Protection Centre, Home Office policing coordinator

DEAct
:   Digital Economy Act 2010, UK legislation

DG INFSO
:   Directorate General Information Society and Media of the European Commission, established by the merger of DG INFOSOC (Information Society) and the Media Directorate of DG Culture in 2004

DNS
:   Domain Name System, 'telephone numbering' for IP addresses, regulated globally by ICANN, nationally by SROs such as Nominet (UK)

DRM
:   Digital Rights Management, method of embedding content standards and policy into computer-readable form, used to enforce copyright conditions

DTI
:   Department for Trade and Industry, UK ministry responsible for Internet and standards development, renamed as Department for Business, Innovation and Skills (BIS)

EC
:   European Commissions, executive body of the EU, responsible for developing and implementing the *acquis communautaire*, the body of EU law

ECD
:   Electronic Commerce Directive, Directive 2000/31/EC

ECHR	European Convention on Human Rights 1950
ECtHR	European Court of Human Rights, highest judicial tribunal for ECHR
ECJ	European Court of Justice, highest judicial tribunal for European Union
ETSI	European Telecommunications Standards Institute, standards body
EU	European Union, as established in the Treaty of Maastricht 1992
European Council	Council of Ministers of EU Member States, representing governments
FCC	Federal Communications Commission, US federal regulator of broadcast and telecommunications
FOSI	Family Online Safety Institute
GPL	General Public Licence, OCL licence, typically for software, version 3.0 released 2007
IA	Impact Assessment, technique within Better Regulation agenda
ICANN	Internet Corporation for Assigned Names and Numbers, California-incorporated not-for-profit organization established in 1998
ICRA	Internet Content Rating Association, an international, non-profit organization of internet leaders working to develop a safer Internet, renamed in 2007 as FOSI
ICSTIS	Independent Committee for the Supervision of Standards of Telephone Information Services, UK co-regulator of Premium Rate Services for telephony, now including mobile telephony, known since 2007 as PhonepayPlus
ICT	Information and Communication Technologies
IETF	Internet Engineering Task Force, technical standards body
IGF	Internet Governance Forum, United Nations multistakeholder discussion forum initially held in Athens 2006, held annually
IIA	Inter-Institutional Agreement of 2003, between European legislative institutions
IMCB	Independent Mobile Classification Board, ratings self-regulator for mobile media
INHOPE	International Association of Internet Hotlines, European association of child sexual content hotlines
IOC	Initial Obligations Code, drawn up by Ofcom in May 2010 to implement DEAct ss.9–18 under direction of government
IP	Internet Protocol
IPR	Intellectual Property Rights

IPTV	Internet Protocol Television; video programming delivered over IP networks rather than broadcast (cable, terrestrial and satellite) networks
ISFE	Interactive Software Federation of Europe, European association of publishers of video and computer games, reference and educational works
ISOC	Internet Society, coordinating mechanism for Internet standards and policy
ISP	Internet Service Provider, company providing access to the Internet for consumers and businesses. The largest ISP in most Member States is provided by the incumbent telco. ISPs often provide content, have 'portal' pages which offer news, weather and video reports, dating, chat, search and other functions. Mobile networks are also ISPs
ITU	International Telecommunication Union
IWF	Internet Watch Foundation, UK 'hotline' for illegal content reporting
JANET	Joint Academic Network, consortium of UK universities and research institutes developing internetworking, including high-speed SuperJANET
KJM	Kommission für Jugendmedienschutz, co-regulatory body for media content in Germany
MP3	File format for digital music from Motion Picture Expert Group (MPEG)
MS	Member State of the EU, twenty-seven in total
NICAM	Netherlands Institute for the Classification of Audiovisual Media, co-regulator
NTD	Notice and Take Down, system for removal by ISPs and content hosts of alleged illegal content
OCL	Open Content Licensing, models include CC and GPL
OECD	Organization for Economic Cooperation and Development, 'think tank' for developed nations: thirty national members; membership is limited by commitment to a market economy and a pluralistic democracy. Formed in 1961 and grew out of the Organization for European Economic Co-operation (OEEC), established in 1947
Ofcom	Converged communications regulator for telecommunications, Internet and broadcasting for UK, established by Office of Communications Act 2002
PEGI	Pan European Game Information, age-rating system
PICS	Platform for Internet Content Selection, W3C website labelling standard implemented by ICRA
RMIT	Royal Melbourne Institute of Technology
SIAP	Safer Internet Action Plan, EC DG INFSO funding for awareness programmes, hotlines and other actions since 1998
SNS	Social Networking Site, such as Facebook or Bebo
SRO	Self or Co-Regulatory Organization, institution designed to provide guidance and/or enforcement of conduct or content standards, in our case including a broad spectrum from 'self-organized' to co-regulatory forms

UGC   User Generated Content, ripped mixed burned from digital files

VoIP   Voice over Internet Protocol, technology to digitize sound in packets sent over the Internet. Its primary advantage is that distance does not affect the cost of the call between two VoIP enabled phones (or PCs attached to the phone or a data system)

W3C   World Wide Web Consortium, standards body established by Tim Berners-Lee in 1994

Web2.0   Compendium description of Ajax-based technologies that permit UGC (pronounced web-two-dot-oh)

WGIG   Working Group on Internet Governance, expert group established in 2005 to report on Internet policy to the United Nations Secretary General

WSIS   World Summit on the Information Society, United Nations Internet regulatory summits formally held in Geneva (2003) and Tunis (2005)

TABLE OF LEGISLATION

Table of Cases

Table of Statutes

1

States, firms and legitimacy of regulation: insoluble issues?

This book aims to answer a simple empirical question in a complex environment. Is Internet regulation a paradigm of constitutionally responsive co-regulation? Within the question, I unpack first what forms of regulation are present in the governance of the Internet, based on case studies. I define and examine what responsive regulation, and specifically co-regulation, entails, and how it contributes to protecting constitutional rights within regulatory organizations.[1] Finally, I assess the extent to which Internet co-regulation is a paradigm of such forms of regulation,[2] as compared to, for instance, financial[3] or environmental regulation.[4]

The book sets out to achieve these objectives with the following structure, based on two multi-year studies for the EC conducted in 2001–4 and 2006–8.[5] This opening chapter identifies how regulation is changing and explains in brief, for the general reader, via mapping, how the Internet has been perceived as being regulated, in terms of self-, co- and state regulation, outlining the methodology adopted, and the substantive case studies.[6] In Chapter 2, I identify more fully what co-regulation is, focusing on its application in European law and regulation. In Chapter 3, I begin with the first of four substantive case study chapters, which both analyze and update the work outlined in Chapter 2, examining self-organizational forms in which organizations establish their own governance form without reference to a wider corporate forum or government involvement. I consider paradigms of emerging regulation including self-organization by social

---

[1] See Klang and Murray (2005); Tambini et al. (2008).
[2] For earlier more theoretical attempts to undertake the same task, see Lessig (1999); Marsden (ed.) (2000b); Murray (2006).
[3] See Black (2009).
[4] Boyle and D'Souza (1992); Hulme and Ong (in press).
[5] Marsden et al. (2008), building on Tambini et al. (2008).
[6] Haddadi et al. (2009) at p. 12 state that they 'observe a move away from a preferential attachment, tree-like disassortative network, toward a network that is flatter, highly-interconnected, and assortative'.

networks. In Chapter 4, I identify the paradigms of technical self-regulation in governing the Internet, a form of relatively pure self-regulation not often encountered in other industries.[7] In Chapter 5, I consider paradigms of content co-regulation in the Internet environment, describing a move towards a form I describe as 'medium law'. In Chapter 6, I explore filtering and removal of content, privatized censorship and co-regulation. In Chapter 7, I summarize the case studies and explore the contribution these exemplars can make towards our understanding of Internet regulation. I summarize the substantive findings, analyze the directions of travel apparent in the case studies over the period 2007–10, and make cross-cutting comparisons with wider regulatory analysis in this period, described as the 'Age of Crises' in both environmental and financial regulation,[8] but also more broadly in advanced market economies subject to the emerging 'long depression' in growth as compared with the earlier 'Golden Age' of regulation in 1982–2007. In Chapter 8, I conclude by examining the prospects for co-regulation to become a more substantial regulatory technique, including via its analysis in Impact Assessment (IA) by government, and for the lessons of Internet co-regulation to be adopted more widely across government. The general heading of 'Better Regulation' lays particular emphasis on the need to assess impacts of proposed changes and specific guidance relating to evaluation and IA.[9] Key aspects are the need to: perform holistic *ex ante* assessment of impacts; consider relevant alternatives; take into account a range of potential impacts (costs, benefits, distributional impacts, administrative requirements); and measure and, where possible, monetize such impacts on the basis of sound data and analytic methods. These general principles are not reflected fully in the state of the art: alternatives are rarely identified, the range of impacts considered is often narrow, and measurement and monetization remain underdeveloped, especially in relation to self- and co-regulatory organizations (henceforth SROs).[10] Thus there is a need to develop further the implications of self- and co-regulation, and to identify clear and consistent principles and practices which can be implemented.

[7] See Price and Verhulst (2000, 2005).
[8] See Campbell (1999), pp. 712–772; Short and Toffel (2007), pp. 1–16; Weiser (2001), pp. 822–846; Kahan (2002), p. 281; Archon Fung, et al. (2004) The Political Economy of Transparency: What Makes Disclosure Policies Effective? Ash Institute for Democratic Governance and Innovation John F. Kennedy School of Government Harvard University OP-03-04, pp. 1-49; Michael (1995), pp. 171–178; CFA Institute (2007); Ofcom (2007); Federal Trade Commission (2007); Pitofsky (1998).
[9] Examples include the EC (2002).
[10] Jacobs (2005, 2006).

The word 'constitutional' is used in two senses in this book. First, it refers to a general adherence to principles of administrative justice, notably fair trial, due process, independence of regulator from regulated, participation by all interested parties, and transparency. Second, it specifically refers to the types of fundamental rights that may be affected by Internet regulation as it affects the specific communications medium,[11] notably the rights to privacy and free expression[12] that may be enhanced or infringed by Internet-based activities. This latter form of constitutional oversight is vital in this context, as Internet regulation affects both economic and social rights to participate in society and economy, but also these more fundamental constitutional rights.[13] It therefore straddles different forms of rights, in much the same manner as environmental regulation.

Much recent scholarship has focused on human rights and the Internet, in three different forms. First, the possibilities the Internet offers for self-publishing has made its use by those seeking more transparency and criticism of governments widespread, through websites such as Wikileaks and IndyMedia. In this sense, the Internet is considered a tool for human rights activists, as the 'world's biggest photocopier'. Second, and associated with the first, much scholarship has focussed on individual and group rights exercised by Internet users against those who offer them services without respecting their constitutional rights, especially concerning censorship of users' speech, and invasions of others' personal privacy, by both the state and private corporations. In this sense, it is the Internet Service Providers' (ISPs') often murky common carrier status which is in question, and the roles of ISP as publisher and user as author. Third, the idea that access to the Internet is a human right in and of itself has emerged, in part from the right to receive and impart communications enshrined in Article XIX of the Universal Declaration of Human Rights 1948.[14] It also stems in part from the ubiquity of the Internet as a means for communications between government and citizen, notably for the conduct of government

---

[11] See Lessig (1999).
[12] For differing US and European conceptions of free speech, see Boyle (2001), pp. 487–521.
[13] On the connection between human security and human rights, notably on the extent to which both can be aligned under what Franklin Roosevelt called the 'Four Freedoms' – freedom of speech and religion, freedom from want and fear – see Boyle and Simonsen (2004).
[14] Also see *International Covenant on Civil and Political Rights* of 16 December 1966; *Rome Statute of the International Criminal Court* of 17 July 1998; *European Convention on Human Rights and Fundamental Freedoms* 1950; *Framework Convention for the Protection of National Minorities* of 1 February 1995; *Council of Europe Convention on Cybercrime* of 23 November 2001 and its *Additional Protocol* of 28 January 2003.

and especially electoral and tax affairs. In this final sense from a rights perspective, the Internet has supplemented universality of telecoms and postal services for communications between individual and state.

These three, often intertwined, senses in which Internet access creates or conveys or transfers human rights are an important element in discussions, especially those surrounding state and private censorship of the Internet. Thus, the right to access the Internet has become an important part of the discussions around network neutrality and the revision of states' telecoms universal service commitments in Europe, with Finland becoming in mid 2010 the first country in the world to enshrine broadband Internet access as a universal human right for its citizens, no matter where they live.[15] Furthermore, the US State Department has set up a unit dealing with innovation,[16] and Secretary Hillary Clinton has given speeches condemning China for its censorship of (notably US-based multinational) ISPs and denying access to the open Internet to Chinese citizens, stating that restrictions on citizens' Internet access and speech:

> contravene the Universal Declaration on Human Rights, which tells us that all people have the right 'to seek, receive and impart information and ideas through any media and regardless of frontiers'. With the spread of these restrictive practices, a new information curtain is descending across much of the world.[17]

The European Parliament has included human rights within its discussions of granting users access to the Internet in legislative amendments to the Electronic Communications Package in 2009.[18] The European Commissioner responsible for fundamental rights has also spoken of Internet access in these terms.

The constitutional position of Internet co-regulation is therefore well established in the fundamental rights debate. Less well established is the basic procedural legitimacy of such arrangements. One could argue that placing the rights principles before the mechanisms to achieve them is a cart-before-horse manner of achieving those ends, but it is inevitable given the paucity of procedural legitimacy in much of the ad hoc governance of the Internet. The case studies will supply plenty of evidence of such policy-making and indeed forum-creation 'on the hoof', and much less evidence of administrative law standards of due process. In making this criticism, one should be careful to distinguish regulatory activities from SROs, and especially so to condemn governments for 'outsourcing'

---

[15] Catacchio (2010).   [16] See Ross (2009).   [17] Clinton (2010).
[18] Directives 2009/136/EC and 2009/140/EC.

activities to an ill-prepared private sector, while avoiding an inappropriate and unsuitably legalistic and governmental approach towards entrepreneurial activities that were never designed to meet formal regulatory
procedural standards in the first place.

The incoming tide of Internet co-regulation

The incoming tide of co-regulation is spreading from Europe into the UK.
As described by Lord Denning,[19] the supremacy of European law means
that the UK is largely a rule-taker not a rule-maker (except as one vote in
twenty-seven members of the Council of Ministers). This tide has had several ebbs and flows, notably an ebb as Thatcherite privatization and regulation flowed out throughout especially Eastern Europe in the late 1980s,
a tide of regulation under the Single European Market in the lead-up to
1992, and further ebbs and flows under various mantras, notably 'Better
Regulation' (which was supposed to be deregulation) in the 2000s. Now
with market failure and sovereignty seen on as spectacular a scale as in
1929, the entire regulatory state is at question.[20] As Sunstein explains, this
leads to new regulatory techniques: 'the strongest arguments for cost-
benefit balancing are based not only on neoclassical economics, but also
on an understanding of human cognition, on democratic considerations,
and on an assessment of the real-world record of such balancing' noting
that cost-benefit analysis 'can protect democratic processes' from interest
groups that are 'pressing for regulation when the argument on its behalf is
fragile'.[21] Writing in 2010, I would suggest that IA is also useful to present
the benefits of auditing self-regulation where industry players claim that
it is more efficient.

This book aims to examine one area in which the excesses of deregulation were sponsored and supported by the UK Government, exposed
to the rest of Europe as a best practice, but are unravelling and being
re-regulated both due to their manifest failings and the tide of European
regulation.[22] Previously, regulation of communications was seen as a sub-
field of either mass media or utilities, depending on whether the issue was
content (particularly professional content for broadcast or print media)

[19] *H.P. Bulmer Ltd* v. *J. Bollinger* S.A. [1974] Ch 401 at p. 418.
[20] See Coglianese and Kagan (2007).
[21] Sunstein (2002a), p. 9.
[22] Recent examples of legal analysis grappling with the role of the EU and the nation state
in the face of globalized markets and regulatory networks, include: Baldwin and Black
(2007); Craig (2009).

or carriage (notably telecommunications, radio, satellite and cable networks). Since approximately 1995, however, communications has seen a
convergence between content and carriage, fostered by digitalization and
particularly the Internet, on which we make Skype telephone calls, read
The Times (behind its paywall), listen to BBC radio and watch some video.
Furthermore, communications infrastructures are so critical to the
knowledge-based economy that this field has grown remarkably in economic importance as well as social pre-eminence. As intellectual property and financial transactions have become 0s and 1s of binary code cut
into packets and fired around the Internet (the amorphous but convenient
geographically metaphorical 'cyberspace' is often used), people appear
locked to their desktop and laptop and mobile smartphone computers
almost all their waking hours. Security, freedom, openness and safety of
this space are seriously important.

There is often a founders' myth associated with 1990s Internet SROs,
which holds that cyberspace would be an anarchic but functional
space.[23] There was just enough truth in that to maintain the fiction that
governments could not enforce their old rules, and normative claims
were established that governments should not enforce such rules, as
well as the practical claim that the technology was so alien, anonymiz-
ing and globalizing that national rule-sets were both damaging to the
legitimacy of nation states that attempted their enforcement and futile
in the face of the technology.[24] This vacuum of rule-enforcing gave
space to the development of the myth of Internet self-organization, a
space for social entrepreneurship that did not even admit of self-regulation, let alone government regulation. However, a flood of private law
also surged into the vacuum, from copyright claims to terms of use for
ISPs and websites, that were absurdly slanted in favour of the large corporate interests that rapidly emerged as the Internet commercialized in
the mid 1990s.

A historical accident, that of unmetered local telephony, meant that US
consumers went online long before Europeans, who were charged by the
minute for access to narrowband Internet services.[25] As a result, it was the
deregulated and aggressively commercial tactics of US ISPs and websites
that predominated, adopted rapidly by the UK market, which was the first

---

[23] Johnson and Post (1996), pp. 1367–1402.
[24] See the critique by Mosco (2004).
[25] The US achieved ten million consumer Internet users about five years before the European
Union, 1994 versus 1999. See Tambini *et al.* (2008), p. 12.

major European Internet adopter,[26] and shortly thereafter by European joint ventures between US and local companies, such as Terra Networks and AOL-Deutschland. The growth, by acquisition, of WorldCom, a US-based ISP that acquired over forty companies in the late 1990s including MCI (second-largest telephony competitor in the US) and UUNet (a pioneering ISP across Europe), led to further infiltration of US regulatory policies into European Internet policy. (I acknowledge that a thumbnail description of consumer Internet access such as this runs twin dangers, that of conflating consumer Internet use with the far more transformative use of the Internet Protocol for business communication, transactions and supply chain management, and of conflating the World Wide Web with other aspects of Internet Protocol-based communication.)

The US Communications Decency Act (CDA) [27] was enacted as part of the Telecommunications Act 1996, but was overturned a year later in the landmark Supreme Court case of *American Civil Liberties Union* v. *Reno* (1997).[28] The Court decided that the virtually unanimous will of Congress to censor the Internet via mandatory filtering was unconstitutionally chilling of speech under the First Amendment to the US Constitution, and that technical filtering as a voluntary option for users was the less intrusive approach from the viewpoint of freedom of speech. This inspired standards experts to attempt to introduce a wide-ranging labelling scheme for Internet content, the PICS (Platform for Internet Content Selection).[29] We examine this connection between technical standards and content, services and applications in some depth in Chapter 4. CDA was then almost immediately replaced by the Child Online Protection Act 1998 (COPA 1998), which established the Commission on Child Online Protection (COPA Commission), whose 2000 COPA Commission report forms the basis for (Family Online Safety Institute) FOSI's educational approach

---

[26] Driven by what was known as the Freeserve model after the subsidiary of Dixons plc that first adopted a revenue-share interconnection model with the incumbent monopoly telephony provider British Telecommunications plc (BT). Freeserve grew rapidly in late 1998, then was absorbed by Wanadoo, a subsidiary of France Telecom, the French monopoly telephony provider. Another leading example was WorldOnline, a Dutch company that used the same business model.

[27] Title V of the Telecommunications Act of 1996, the amendment that became the CDA, was added to the Telecommunications Act in the Senate by an 84–16 vote on 14 June 1995.

[28] *American Civil Liberties Union* v. *Reno* [1997] 21 USC 844 Supreme Court case of 27 June 1997, No. 96–511 suspending parts of CDA by 7–2 majority, Rehnquist and O'Connor dissenting in part.

[29] See www.w3.org/TR/REC-PICS-labels-961031.

to child protection from harmful content.[30] COPA 1998 was suspended and overturned,[31] and the Government's last appeal was refused a hearing by the Supreme Court on 21 January 2009 at the culmination of the George W. Bush Presidency. *Reno* led directly to the Internet Content Rating Association (ICRA) which emerged in 1999 from PICS and the US RSAC system for computer games. ICRA is a not-for-profit company that has been government funded and supported with corporate members. In 2007, ICRA was absorbed into a relaunched advocacy organization for rating, FOSI. The lack of market adoption of ICRA until now has been attributed in part to lack of incentives for websites unless rating can interoperate with other standards, or more radically unless rating is made mandatory. It essentially retreated into becoming an advisory council on online safety after 2007. FOSI itself recently recognized the genesis of its approach.[32]

The collapse of the Internet start-up market in the infamous 'dot-com bubble' of 2000, followed by the technology and telecommunications markets in 2001–2, and finally the collapse of global accountants Arthur Andersen in the wake of the Enron and WorldCom frauds of 2001–2, did not fundamentally change the by-then entrenched self-organizational policies in Internet standards (as readers will appreciate, legislation that is passed in 2002 has its origin years earlier). Legal institutions had embedded the self-regulatory model as their standard for the Internet, in legislative acts such as the Electronic Commerce Directive 2000/31/EC, the European Electronic Communications Package ('ECP') of 2002,[33] the 'Television without Frontiers' Directive 1997 and the UK Communications Act 2003. It was only in 2007–10 that these laws were reviewed, reconsidered and in some cases amended to redress the over-zealous deregulatory intent of those giddy 1990s. As I write in autumn 2010, the E-Commerce Directive is being reviewed, the ECP was amended in November 2009, the Audiovisual Media Services (AVMS) Directive 2007 replaced the 'Television without Frontiers' Directive and was implemented in European Member States in 2009 (see Chapter 5: ATVOD), the Digital Economy Act 2010 amended UK legislation, while the Telecommunications Act 1996

---

[30] Commission on Child Online Protection (2000).
[31] *Ashcroft* v. *ACLU* [2004] 542 U.S. 656, of 29 June, confirming suspension of unconstitutionally broad Internet censorship in COPA, by a 5–4 majority, Rehnquist, Scalia, Breyer and O'Connor dissenting in part.
[32] FOSI (2010).
[33] Five Directives, a Recommendation and a Decision were included within this enormous legislative undertaking. See Marsden (2010), Chapter 6.

was reformed almost beyond recognition by its regulatory agency, the Federal Communications Commission (FCC), and the courts.

Policy-makers retreated from that deregulatory high ground of 1995–2000 as the Internet became a ubiquitous broadband medium. Having recoiled from the futility of their original efforts to regulate, regulators regained their nerve partly because the extent of misuse was becoming so apparent in the early 2000s, partly because the 'dot-com bubble' had demonstrated that the golden goose had choked itself and that therefore there was no alchemy that regulators would disturb by their actions, and partly because Internet markets naturally evolved such that the thousands of early entrepreneurs rapidly consolidated into a few large companies. There was by 2005 a relatively stable constituency of Internet content providers (Yahoo!, Microsoft), of search engines (Google), of electronic commerce providers (Amazon, eBay), and of ISPs (the largest cable and telephone companies and few rivals). Commissioner Kroes has recently stated: 'The lower the costs of entry, the lower the risk to innovators, and the more innovators you get. A time such as this one characterized by a very dynamic environment and a high rate of innovation might not be the best time to close the door to experimentation and private initiative.'[34] The technical standards body, IETF (see Chapter 4), still maintained its original constitutional structure (constitutional in the sense of the basic ground norms and procedural approach), and the body of SROs that mushroomed in the late 1990s was embedded alongside the older telecommunications and electronic engineering SROs on which industry had previously relied.

Internet regulation has been a trailblazer for self-regulation in the 1990s, for re-regulation and state interest in the early 2000s, and now increasingly for co-regulation in the period since about 2005. This is not just because it has 'grown up' and regulators with it – it is obvious that in 1995, very few bureaucrats or politicians had a clue what the Internet would be and it may have appeared attractive to allow it to develop in somewhat of a legislative-regulatory vacuum with minimal enabling of e-commerce and extension of the principle that online behaviour could – with great difficulty – be prosecuted as in offline behaviour. It is certainly true that such Internet exceptionalism ended in the bursting of the post-Cold War deregulatory euphoria with the twin events of the collapse of the dot-com bubble in 2000–2 and the renewed vigour of state security in the period after the 11 September 2001. There is, however, a more important

---

[34]   Kroes (2010). On Internet competition issues, see also Almunia (2010).

narrative than simply the end of the exceptional. Internet regulation has become a testing ground for new forms of regulation, some discarded as too idealistic or naïve in the late 1990s, others tested, adapted and adopted and fitted to new cultures and new practices. This book aims to unpick those practices to explore which have appeared successful – often simply through survival – and those of merit and capable of adoption in other regulatory fora and other industries. The book concludes by noting which practices are indeed 'best of breed' and capable of adoption by the wider regulatory academic and policy community.

Internet regulation was continually declared to be 'light touch' in the UK, notably by its 'super-regulator' Ofcom and sponsoring ministry (the many-named former Department of Trade and Industry), until the collapse of the OECD economies in 2008, after which regulation became briefly fashionable. This short period finished with the election of the deregulatory Conservative Government in May 2010,[35] and the renewed growth of those OECD economies in 2010. The crucible of innovation and enterprise was seen as one in which the alchemy of competition was most likely to produce a successful outcome. 'First do no evil' was the watchword of regulators in the UK, US and many other places. In this, they shared their intellectual inheritance with the Financial Services Authority and other guardians of the information economy. The crashing of financial markets worldwide in 2007–9 had much less effect on the Internet than on many more traditional sectors, not least because it depends on free cash flow for investment in the UK far more than multiples of earnings: the crash of the bubble in 2000–2 was literally a life-changing event for those in Internet industries. Partly through that crunch, partly through the market-concentrating network effects which are such a part of the Internet, much of the industry was very concentrated by 2007, with only two major UK wholesale Internet access providers (Virgin and British Telecom), one major search engine (Google), one UK-owned mobile network operator (Vodafone, the other four being foreign-owned by German, Spanish and French incumbents, and a Hong Kong company), and the largest online content operators being the government-owned BBC and Channel 4. To that extent, oligopoly ensured the survival of the industry, but largely because it had consolidated so rapidly in 2002–7. Social networking sites were US-owned, notably Facebook, MySpace and Bebo. The

---

[35] See Vaizey (2010), stating: 'This government is no fan of regulation, and we should only intervene when it is clearly necessary.' Though his Secretary of State is a Liberal Democrat, this is clearly government policy.

massive influence of US investors on UK Internet markets and therefore policy was arguably somewhat lesser by 2007 than it had been in 2000, but nevertheless Silicon Valley shared its US accent with the deregulatory zeal of Wall Street. There are significant similarities with the financial services industry, therefore, but also significant differences. The most profound of these may be simply that banks are more essential than the Internet unless you trade on eBay for a living. The Internet as a platform is an enabling technology just as is the electricity transmission network (on which it relies), but it is not the lifeblood of the capitalist system. Another difference is perhaps more useful than obvious: the Internet co-regulatory process continues, because the systemic risks in the Internet's self- or un-regulation were held to threaten systemic failure of the system as a whole.

Drake and Wilson aim to reconsider our past paradigms of international communications policy 'to offer the reader non-traditional perspectives on the global governance of global information and communication networks'.[36] That is, the view is not drawn from the 'Washington consensus' of liberalizing globalizers, but 'views the global governance of networks more from the bottom up, and the outside in'. To provide a framework for this, they identify three stages of global communications governance (or the nicely punned 'Net World Orders'), roughly: pre-1990 statist; 1990–8 telecoms and satellite liberalization; and the competitive period since then, when the global Internet took off. Drake tries to isolate what 'governance' actually is. Over the past fifteen years, it has become such a 'weasel word',[37] that Drake's decision to isolate a definition is essential to cynics, and most welcome to sympathizers. Drake examines no less than eighteen different attempts to define by other academic authors, before settling on his own version: 'global governance is the development and application of shared principles, norms, rules, decision-making procedures, and programs intended to shape actors' expectations and practices and to enhance their collective management capacities in world affairs'.[38] He explains that 'programs' is an important addition to the toolset, and that unilateral actors can have global governance impacts, whereas by contrast global chatter is not the same as governance. This draws attention to the need to examine the role of multinational corporate actors in

---

[36] Drake and Wilson (2008).
[37] In the description by one of its foremost proponents: Rhodes (2007), pp. 1243–1264, at p. 1244.
[38] Drake in Drake and Wilson (2008), pp. 8–9.

the processes, where research in political economy and law tends to be either dry technical process descriptions or economists' series of dominant actor war stories over, for instance, 3G telephony or WiFi standards.[39] Balkin states:

> Digital information technologies enmesh individuals, groups, and nations in proliferating networks of power that they neither fully understand nor fully control, and that are controlled by no one in particular … larger forces of technological development and information production are reshaping and possibly even sacrificing human values and human interests to serve goals that no human being in particular seeks.[40]

The regulatory legitimacy gap occasioned by technology and globalization is familiar to regulatory scholars, addressed by Beck,[41] Manuel Castells in his path-breaking work,[42] Mueller[43] and Braithwaite.[44] In legal scholarship, that includes particularly Lessig's canon,[45] Wu and Zittrain.[46]

It is widely claimed that these activities are not regulation in the sense of having binding governmental sanctions and regulated outcomes – they are more properly 'governance', a form of regulation most associated with the pioneering work of Rhodes in political administration. So it is that Chapter 3 will examine self-organizational forms, that is, forms of governance which impose unilateral contracts on consumers, regulated by generic consumer law protections. To these self-organizational forms, we can add 'peer-produced' regulation, or regulatory norms imposed by society itself – a form in which the 'greenfield examples' from the Internet and virtual worlds such as Second Life have been particularly instrumental.

Legal positivists will ask: where is enforcement? The accusation that the 'soft lawyers' amongst us choose to extend definitions of law beyond stretching point in order to have interdisciplinary conversations outside our specialty is common and well founded in international law,[47] but in this European comparative case would be particularly mistaken. As the case studies will show, governments have outsourced constitutionally fundamental regulation to private agents, with little or no regard for the legitimacy claims other than those founded on the avowed deregulatory alchemy of private actors over bureaucrats. The means used are increasingly subject to limited but growing public oversight, whether via judicial review based on human rights legislation or administrative law, or

---

[39] Cowhey and Aronson (2009); Frieden (2010).
[40] Balkin (2010).   [41] Beck (1992).   [42] Castells (1996).
[43] Mueller (2002, 2010a).   [44] Braithwaite (2008).   [45] Lessig (2006, 2008).
[46] Wu (2010); Zittrain (2008).   [47] d'Aspremont (2008).

by means of democratic scrutiny of government spending on support for self- or co-regulation. To take the obvious example, the Safer Internet Action Plan (SIAP) is based on public funding given to hotline activities, which are proposed by the European Commission (EC) and voted on by the European Parliament. That funding has been supported on three occasions, in 1999, 2003 and 2008.[48] In each case, the programme has been evaluated and renewed funding has been sought based on the evaluation of effectiveness, with Article 5(4) of the 2008 Decision stating: 'The Commission shall, by 24 June 2011, report ... on the implementation of the action lines.'[49] Kelsen would surely agree that the legislature has voted on a government measure to support a form of regulation, a case of hard law in authorizing government expenditure.[50] The fact that the regulation supported is largely private does not alter the fact that there is such legitimacy conferred.[51] It is also important to note that the method of legislating for these 'softer' powers is legitimate, and many of the softer law instruments – such as Communications – lead rapidly to harder law powers to remedy perceived regulatory lacunae. Bonnici states that self-

[48] See Decision No.1151/2003/EC of 16 June 2003, amending Decision No. 276/1999/EC adopting a Multiannual Community Action Plan on promoting safer use of the Internet by combating illegal and harmful content on global networks; COM (2001, 2003, 2006).
[49] Decision No. 1351/2008/EC of 16 December 2008 establishing a multiannual Community programme on protecting children using the Internet and other communication technologies 2009–13 (published in the Official Journal L 348/118 of 24.12.2008), at http://ec.europa.eu/information_society/activities/sip/docs/prog_decision_2009/decision_en.pdf
[50] Kelsen (1967).
[51] See COM (2009c). It contains two funding measures aimed specifically at assisting police forces at pp. 19–20: 'Action 2.5 Thematic network: Facilitating cooperation of law enforcement agencies in Europe and internationally ... CIRCAMP will run until October 2010. The 2010 Work Programme calls for proposals to set up a thematic network to facilitate cooperation of law enforcement agencies after this date. The thematic network should stimulate organized and extensive cross-border exchange of best practice between law enforcement agencies in the fight against production and online distribution of child sexual abuse material within Europe and internationally. The thematic network should serve as a point for general exchange of information and best practices, but will not be responsible for police operations ... This coordinated approach will include the establishment of a European list of URLs which contain child sexual abuse images, which is accessible for national Law Enforcement Agencies'. 'Action 2.6 Targeted projects: Enhancing law enforcement agencies' analysis of illegal material within peer-to-peer (p2p) networks. Building upon recommendations received in the Focus Group on "Fighting against online child abuse images" that the Programme organized in March 2009, the Programme invites proposals for a targeted project to support law enforcement agencies in the analysis of child sexual abuse material within p2p networks.'

regulation on the Internet can in part be understood as a form of legal pluralism, with binding rules formed by various groups outside the hierarchical structure of the state. She argues that a regulatory mesh is formed, where 'self-regulation and state regulation intertwine and reciprocally complement each other [and] … are interdependent in the creation, adoption, application, implementation and enforcement of regulation'.[52] I take this to be self-evident, and the case studies provide rich evidence of this regulatory mesh (see Chapters 5–6).

In the following section, I outline the methodological approach adopted and the selection of case studies for examination in later chapters. Those whose interests are not in mapping and methodology may wish to skip ahead to the case study summaries that complete the chapter.

Methodological approach: WGIG and scoping Internet governance

In 2004 the UN Secretary General convened the WGIG (Working Group on Internet Governance), a group of forty experts drawn from all interested stakeholders (public, private, civil society, technical expert), which spent nine months drawing up a comprehensive map of Internet governance.[53] WGIG establishes four broad policy areas at paragraph 13, of which the final one (development and capacity building) is properly an industry support mechanism and therefore not within even the broadest regulatory definition. This leaves three categories, which we use in our mapping. They are: infrastructure and critical resources; issues where global cooperation is ill-defined; and issue areas from offline activities that are converging onto the Internet.

The first is: 'Infrastructure and the management of critical Internet resources … These issues are matters of direct relevance to Internet governance and fall within the ambit of existing organizations with responsibility for these matters.' Its list of areas covered includes those subject to state regulatory control outside what I take to be the ambit of this study, namely telecoms and multilingualism, and one which competition authorities have established has strict commercial secrecy (peering and interconnection for Internet traffic), and therefore would provide insurmountable difficulties in researching for the short case studies provided for by the resources of this study. The remainder form interesting

---

[52] Bonnici (2008), pp. 199–200.
[53] WSIS Declaration of Principles (2005), para. 48.

topic areas: administration of the domain name system (DNS) and IP addresses, administration of the root server system, and generally technical standards. These others are worthy of further examination for self- and co-regulatory practices. Further, there is a web of relationships between key decision-makers and policy advocates involved in the formation of ICANN and other SROs, namely the IETF (the chief international standards body for IP-based standards), ISOC and others.

The second category includes issues which the WGIG states 'are directly related to Internet governance, the nature of global cooperation required is not well defined'. Internet security, including spam, network security and cybercrime are the issues listed. One of the challenges in mapping such SROs is that the organizations of relevance are either state bodies or private bodies and the nature of their interrelationship and co-dependence is ill-defined and non-transparent. This is necessary given their functions in preventing criminal activities. There is a clear and obvious relationship between the nature of public – private cooperation in this field and the standards SROs in key Internet infrastructure. Economic incentives for such deployments and crime fighting activities need to be well aligned in this area.[54]

Third is a category of issues which are by no means exclusive to Internet usage or infrastructure: 'Issues … for which existing organizations are responsible, such as intellectual property rights (IPRs) or international trade.' Here the overlap with regulatory issues as much concerns broader e-commerce issues such as trademark disputes and the regular work of media and content regulatory agencies. WGIG in paragraphs 23–26 lists:

23. **Intellectual Property Rights (IPR)**: While there is agreement on the need for balance between the rights of holders and the rights of users, there are different views on the precise nature of the balance that will be most beneficial to all stakeholders, and whether the current IPR system is adequate to address the new issues posed by cyberspace. On the one hand, intellectual property rights holders are concerned about the high number of infringements, such as digital piracy, and the technologies developed to circumvent protective measures to prevent such infringements; on the other hand, users are concerned about market oligopolies, the impediments to access and use of digital content, and the perceived unbalanced nature of current IPR rules.

---

[54] See Marsden (2010), Chapter 3, pp. 75–81.

24. **Freedom of expression**: Measures taken in relation to the Internet on grounds of security or to fight crime can lead to violations of the provisions for freedom of expression.
25. **Data protection and privacy rights**: There is a lack of national legislation and enforceable global standards for privacy and data-protection rights over the Internet; as a result, users have few if any means to enforce their privacy and personal data-protection rights, even when recognized by legislation.
26. **Consumer rights**: There is a lack of global standards for consumer rights over the Internet, for example in the international purchase of goods through e-commerce.

All these issues arise throughout the case studies, most especially in Chapter 3 (self-organization) and Chapter 6 (filtering).

Mapping the Internet for regulatory innovation

The methodology used included four activities: literature review and documentation collation; expert interview and consultation; synthesis and analysis, including that of gaps in institutional analysis; and reporting. It proceeded from a substantial literature review to analysis of national and international policies and developments and previous studies in the field. This was augmented by consultation with a broad cross-section of experts including field research in 2007–8, with the International Telecoms Union (ITU); EC internal and external experts; ICANN, IETF and W3C participants and experts; and various European and US stakeholders. This interaction was ongoing, with robust debate and analysis over the five-year period 2004–9. I undertook expert interviews with key stakeholders to assess the relative importance and interrelated networks of SROs, in order to assist in establishing which are the 'class leading' or otherwise precedent setting SROs. Both expertise and participation requirements were required of interviewees selected, to ensure that gaps identified in previous studies – namely the ability to integrate the theoretical and practical experiences of regulation – were not duplicated. Case study specific issue areas arose:

• How to introduce greater transparency and dialogue between consumer groups and other civil society stakeholders and standards experts?
• How to ensure the benefits of rapid standards-making are maintained even with the additional scrutiny suggested in increasing multistakeholder arrangements?

I assess the best candidate for the mapping, a considered view of the content sector's position atop a series of technical layers defined by protocols. I map issues using three categories: infrastructure and critical resources; issues where global cooperation is ill-defined; and issue areas from offline activities that are converging onto the Internet. This provides the basis for examination of standards, infrastructure, ISP self-regulation, mass media content, and user-derived content. These form the building blocks for selection of specific case studies in the remainder of the book. The gap analysis incorporates a mapping exercise, and detailed examination of a representative and strategically chosen universe of case studies, to identify the continually emerging environment for new topics and/or sectoral areas of regulatory and/or legislative interest. Mapping the Internet for regulatory purposes can be undertaken via at least five approaches, which I first list and then describe.

(1) Geographical analysis based on national and international boundaries and regulation;
(2) geographical analysis based on the physical nodes in the networks;
(3) temporal analysis based on the type of control based on its success or failure over time;
(4) disciplinary analysis based on the system logic of each 'part' or layer of the Internet – for instance the engineering solutions to transport or economic and legal solutions to copyright;
(5) substantive analysis of the differing systems of regulation 'converging' on the Internet, for instance telecommunications, mass media or information technology law.

Note that none of these approaches is entirely discrete and arguably each has an important perspective on the overall problem. Each has important insights for the overall framework, and it is important to identify the successes and failures of each approach.

Geographical analysis based on national and international boundaries

It is possible to map Internet regulation on a national basis, as a patchwork of national networks where international regulatory discussion centres on areas with overlapping jurisdictions or unclear jurisdiction. This comparison of Internet regulation with the Law of the Sea or mediaeval mercantile law ('Lex Mercatoria'), though attractive to lawyers, is untenable in practice, as unlike maritime transactions, Internet transactions commonly take place in real time in multiple jurisdictions, and the taxation

of e-commerce has proved to be both difficult to implement, and unpopu-
lar politically.[55] There is therefore a far more pervasive 'global' character
to such transactions, and no matter how detailed enveloping and developed international standards may become in substituting norms for those
'sovereignty' gaps, the gaps are broader and more pervasive in Internet
regulation. That is not to say the Internet is 'unregulable', nor that such
a status should be assumed, as with the Law of Space.[56] However, to state
that China can effectively create a wall (like a naval blockade) around
its domestic Internet appears empirically to be an exaggeration. A further difference is in the nature of the goods carried in 'cyberspace' (the
information on the Internet). As information goods, and often media
or 'speech' products which carry a political or ideological message; the
internationalization of Internet content has proved impossible to prevent,
creating very significant enforcement problems, as in the *LICRA* v. *Yahoo!*
case. The court found that by providing access to French citizens, Yahoo!
US was subject to French law; that nothing in the First Amendment pre-
vented Yahoo! from being selective about its auctions; and that blocking
access to French citizens was technically difficult but not impossible.[57]

Geographical analysis based on the
physical nodes in the networks

If Internet transactions cannot be mapped in the same way as physical
goods transactions, a second suggestion is that they be mapped using
their nearest physical analogue: the geography of their routing through
servers. The problem here is significant and can be stated simply: the network is a 'dumb' network, which routes packets without examining their
contents. Though attempts are made to 'see' inside the packets to check
their compliance with the law, governments cannot effectively act as cus-
toms officials and stop, check, deport or import packets. Though this
is a technological possibility in future Internet designs, it would create
a significantly different environment where – for instance – anonymity
of senders was removed or at least penalized. In *LICRA* v. *Yahoo!* court
experts gave evidence that Yahoo! could block French users from auctions
with 70–80 per cent efficacy, as one expert later reasoned:

> I was asked to say to what extent compliance is possible. The best that
> can be achieved is a rather flaky guess at nationality, using IP address

---

[55] Goldsmith (1998), p. 1115; Reidenberg (2005), p. 1951.
[56] Goldsmith and Wu (2006).
[57] Reidenberg (2004), p. 213.

or domain name (we estimated this was around 80 per cent accurate for France, with some obvious huge exceptions, like AOL subscribers). Failing that, one can simply ask the websurfer whether she's French, and, if so, plant a cookie to that effect. Of course, both of these can be trivially circumvented.[58]

French courts did not intend to block all French users from accessing illegal (US-based) content, but to prevent users who did not have the ability or incentive to disguise the IP address on their computer. The idea that one can map Internet regulation based on the location of the bits is therefore superficially attractive but essentially a technologically determined attempt to reintroduce physical jurisdictional boundaries. The ability of police forces to seize physical assets and interrogate that evidence is at the centre of national enforcement. A strong working assumption is that many Internet SROs will not map to geographical boundaries, but rather to sectoral or technical realms. This was borne out by other studies.[59]

Temporal analysis based on the type of control based on its success or failure over time

If one cannot identify the state of self-regulation through geographical mapping, the bounds of temporal mapping form a historical substitute. This history could be considered positively or negatively: regulatory forbearance breached where self-regulation clearly failed to achieve its goals; or a map of successive failed attempts to regulate without success. There are two distinct problems with this historical approach. The first is theoretical: when looking for hidden treasure, one looks for the X on the map, not for an absence of Y. A deductive analysis based on regulatory successes and failures (or statements outlining each) must assume that regulators have surveyed and analyzed all the territory to be mapped, and made decisions based on transparent regulatory objectives whether, how and how much to intervene, and when to withdraw that regulation.

Internet regulation can be discussed from laws relating to copyright, to child protection or to freedom of speech. These are reflected in differing systems of regulation 'converging' on the Internet: telecommunications, mass media or technology law. There are two ideal bases: human rights (for instance child protection and freedom of speech) and economic efficiency (for instance technocratic infrastructure regulation). Though

---

[58] Laurie (2000).
[59] Murray (2006); Thierer (2004); Marsden (2000).

Table 1.1. *Representative regulatory systems and their predominant justification*

Human rights	Economic/Competition
Freedom of expression	DRMs and trusted computing
Fixed/mobile premium content	Personal Internet security
Social networks: new types of user-generated privacy and content concerns	Addressing/domain names
Consumer protection	Trust in e-commerce
Human dignity/child protection	Copyright and associated rights
Data protection and privacy	Infrastructure e.g., ICANN

control over key infrastructure (ICANN and national SROs for DNS) may concern economic issues, it is a fundamental users' rights forum.

While the Internet is no longer a novelty in regulatory discussion,[60] continued relatively fast and technologically dynamic development means that there remains a 'governance gap' between what the technologists and advanced users know of the medium, and political response thereto. Therefore, useful though history proves in individual issue areas, notably ICANN and standard setting, for the most part such history is either oral and partial if not overly partisan (the participants' memories), or incomplete as the issue areas were either neglected by regulators for Internet-specific reasons e.g., as technically forbidding, or because of forbearance based on the desire to avoid harming SROs. This technique provides a partial and incomplete picture of SROs. It cannot form the basis for a map, unless that map contains significant gaps labelled 'Cave! Hic dragones' (Watch out – dragons beyond here).[61]

Disciplinary analysis based on the system logic of each 'part' or layer of the Internet

If neither geography nor history can provide the basis for a map, a more disciplinary determinist view can provide a different perspective. The logic of the infrastructure's design can provide a basis for understanding the particularities of those content types' application to the Internet. This

---

[60] See notably Lessig (1999) and Marsden (ed.) (2000b).
[61] Susan Strange's accusation levelled at academic and government observers of industry self-regulation in the early modern period of globalization in the 1980s. For discussion see Marsden (ed.) (2000b), Chapter 1.

suggests the perspective of standards designers. Internet self-regulation emerges from that technical perspective, with significant policy pronouncements made by the inventor of the Internet Protocol, and the World Wide Web. There are official and unofficial histories of these SROs, and technical mapping of the infrastructure. Problems remain, of both a regulatory and disciplinary nature. The lack of interaction between (most) engineers and (most) social scientists means that the technology design is unsuitable for wider societal goals.

The Treaty of Rome Articles 101, 102 and 106 relate to competition policy and state aid. Returns to scale in digital industries are very high, tending to a high degree of concentration in each industry. Combined with standard settings that give rise to competition concerns, there are economic analyses to be conducted in connection with the manner in which industries self-regulate and otherwise set rules. While different governance traditions give rise to different self-regulatory preferences, backed by differing requirements in co-regulatory fora expressed by both government and other stakeholders, the imposition of high-quality but high-cost SROs may be perceived either positively as a 'dash for quality', or negatively as barriers to entry. Establishing costs and benefits of SROs – especially where not all market entrants take part – can help to determine the extent of free-riding or potentially overelaborate self-regulation.

Converging mapping of the Internet and selection of case studies

Mapping can adopt a hybrid approach incorporating several of these approaches, to extract the benefits of each. There is much from the geographical and historical studies of regulation (both in success and failure) that carries lessons for future developments (for instance in the history of ICANN). A trans-disciplinary approach also offers a more holistic approach to regulatory design. Though economics and human rights approaches have different emphases, there is common ground on, for instance, transparency and end-user/consumer sovereignty.[62]

Holistic approaches mapping technical constraints on regulation

The approach of using interlocking analysis taken from geographical, substantive and disciplinary examination of the Internet is that most commonly used by legal and social scientific analysts of Internet regulation.

---

[62] See Lessig (1999); Ogus (1994).

Technical and geographical challenges to existing regulatory functions were held by early analysts to be insurmountable obstacles to regulation,[63] but there is mutual interdependence between the allegedly 'unregulable' Internet and national rules.[64] Analysis has recently focused on the interdependence of the various national environments, and the question of regulatory divergence or convergence.[65] A nuanced and interdependent (if complex) relationship has emerged.

Technical mapping: horizontal approach to Internet standards

A technical view of Internet mapping would begin with the classic Open Systems Institute (OSI) 'layers model' of the Internet, which represents the 'stack' of protocols that enable end-to-end signalling of Internet traffic. I briefly describe that protocol stack approach, before turning to a more instrumental regulation-led description of the Internet, which nevertheless acknowledges the underlying architecture in the same way as road traffic rules and conventions must acknowledge the environment in which they operate (safety rules do not permit pedal cycling on a motorway at night without lights, for instance). There are cross-cutting issues that affect the stack as a whole, where I suggest that there are rules written into the entirety of the stack which affect the user's perspective of how to receive and share content, or how to ensure the security of their use and enjoyment of that content. Envision content and applications and their regulation sitting atop the Internet's architecture, which is typically represented by the 'Protocol Stack' (at its simplest, this is the technical standards that have been agreed and deployed and enable the Internet to operate successfully as a global medium). Case studies can demonstrate the links between core protocols and content regulation: for instance in filtering.[66] Technical infrastructure underpins the content layer, and design choices in layers that underpin content have a significant influence on content.[67] Case studies chosen have a significant impact on the content layer, including those which may be located lower in the stack and therefore further from the end-user's visibility (technical standards are not described in detail given the legal context). They explain governments' acknowledgement of the futility of attempts to regulate via law alone. In a road traffic

---

[63] Johnson and Post (1996), p. 1367.
[64] Reidenberg (1999), pp. 771–792.
[65] Schulz and Held (2001); Zittrain (2006a), p. 1174.
[66] See Brown and Marsden (in press).
[67] See Wu (2010).

comparison, one cannot enforce fundamental changes in road users' behaviour without the support of manufacturers and transport planners, as well as suppliers and other groups. To implement a content rule, essential expertise is needed to understand system fundamentals.

Vertical or horizontal approach: sectoral descriptions of Internet regulation

The horizontal approach outlined above provides a good technical basis for analyzing the open Internet, which is by definition an interoperable and technically neutral regime. Where different sectors are 'converging' on the Internet, other approaches may be more appropriate. For instance, the mobile industry followed a vertically integrated model, as did broadcasting. Regulatory analysis may not be based on horizontal layers of the Internet but vertical layers of differing inheritances.[68] In content areas, there are three basic objects of regulation, which are represented horizontally.

View content in terms of traditional mass media content, UGC, and content labelled using standardized techniques for various forms of filtering and blocking (see Figure 1.1). The first (see Chapter 5) is regulated by traditional media regulation, commercial communications by both media-specific regulators and general law, applicable to mobile commercial content (1), all premium content (2) and IP television (IPTV, 3). The second is UGC (see Chapter 3), including online games (4), blogs and Wikis (5), virtual worlds (6), invitation-only social networks (14) and public social networks (15). The third (see Chapter 6) extends down into the technical protocol stack, with machine labelling of content (10), for security (13), DRMs (11) and Trusted Computing (12), for removal and reporting via hotlines and ISPs (7, 8) and automated blocking (9). The issue of technical regulation of content is a specific Internet problem, as previous digital media (telecoms and television, for instance) could be regulated by maintaining the closed network.

Conclusion: mapping from an interdisciplinary perspective

The mapping exercise incorporates graphical representation of the multidisciplinary relationship of the technical infrastructure of the Internet architecture to specific SROs. It is clear that there are several different approaches that can be taken to such a map, beginning from sectors, from

---

[68] Werbach (2005), p. 1.

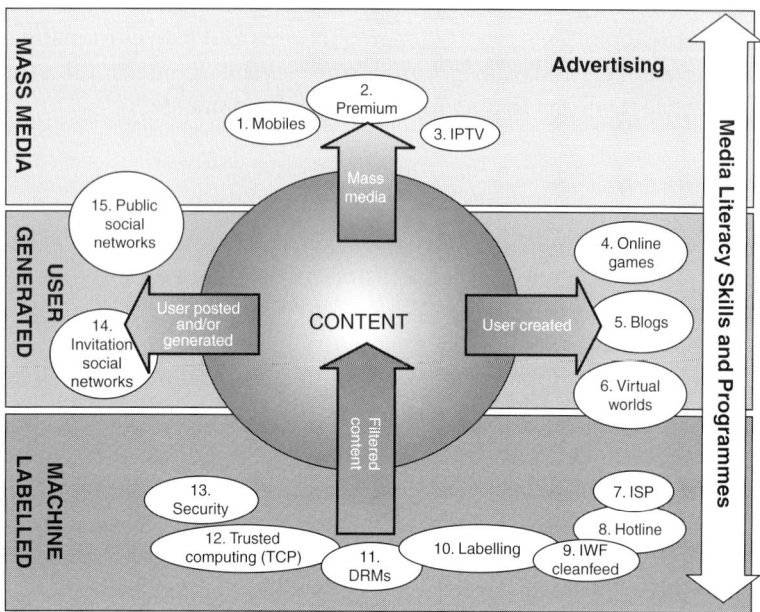

Figure 1.1.   Internet content spectrum from machine-labelled to user-generated to mass media

legal bases for regulatory and policy intervention, or from the architecture of the Internet itself. The latter approach commends itself given my commitment to a holistic approach to Internet co- and self-regulation extending beyond the application of media regulation to Internet content.

Methodology for 'really really responsive regulation'

To understand SROs, it is necessary to put them in a context defined by evolving (existing and emergent) challenges, opportunities and other SROs:

• their internal logic (the specific actor's motivation and role),
• the policy landscape (the theatre) and
• the 'evolutionary play' of overlapping entities and initiatives.

This account could easily become complex – the intention is to make it clear, without losing its complex reality. In other words, while it is not necessary (or possible) to develop a full, unbiased and analytic account of

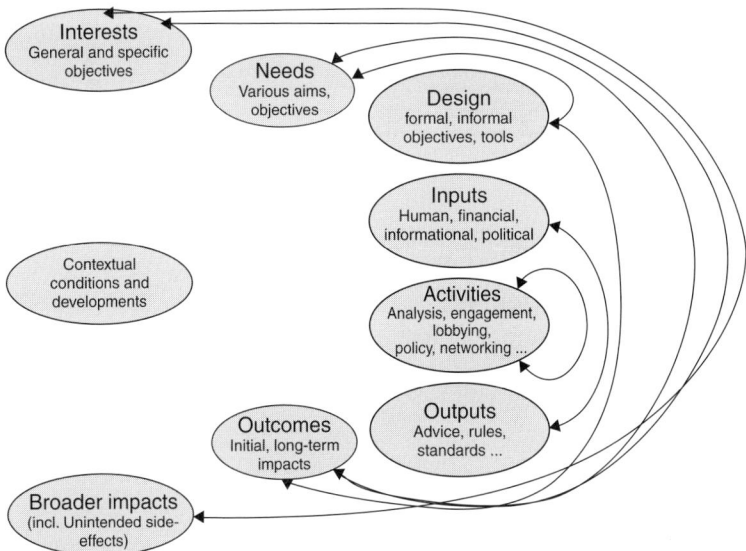

Figure 1.2.   Simple diagram of regulatory interests/needs and their outcomes/
impacts

the deliberate and fortuitous forces behind the organizations, it is necessary to recognize two organizing linkages:

- many organizations arise, change or act in response to a given threat
  (they do not 'take turns' or agree to stay out of each others' way); and
- individual organizations produce benefits by (changes in) their objectives and engagement with key actors as well as through the exercise of
  explicit hard/soft power. Alliance building is an element of importance
  in SRO design.

In the following sections, I show how the dynamic of the organization
interacts with the broader policy environment. First I demonstrate via
two diagrams how the process flow of the institution fits within the environment. Then I unpack the internal workings of the institution and show
how a straightforward log frame analysis can illustrate the organization's
processes. Figure 1.2 illustrates the manner in which interests flow into
needs and then institutional design. The institution then produces outcomes which have broader impacts.

The four processes on the right side of the Figure 1.3 – the real work
of the institution – have been often viewed from outsiders as a 'black

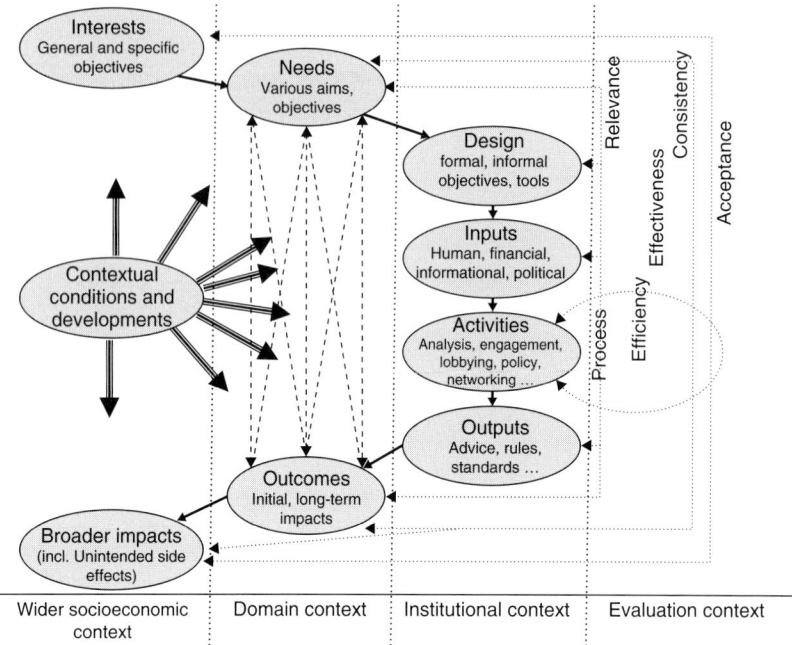

Figure 1.3.   Overall framework including contexts for activities

box' inside the regulatory institution, without transparent process. The methodology is designed to remedy this and make processes more transparent.

'Needs' and 'Outcomes' are found in the arena of daily political public debate, and the 'Interests' and 'Broader Impacts' are of a meta-impact level such that they form a frame around the daily debate: the shifting view of trade-offs between freedom of speech, information security, child protection or family values might form such a context. The more structured perspective that policy analysts in government take of such processes, the more complex the interplay between differing policy agendas, especially in a 'mixed' (economic/technical/social rights-based) environment such as Internet regulation. This may help to explain why constitutional lawyers, institutional economists or technical experts so often develop entirely differing views of self- and co-regulation. The Domain context is where the various institutions overlap. The dotted arrows indicate the overall intervention logic of various institutions, connecting a range of needs (since a given SRO may combine many interest groups) with a range of outcomes (since the members and other stakeholders will be concerned with a range of 'target' outcomes and with others not directly connected to the SRO's constitution). Within this column, there are two types of more detailed map of the organizational ecology. The first is a *process map* showing activities within and among the various stakeholders. Interchanges can include:

- Directive (command and control) influence (hard power);
- Informational flows;
- Promulgation of standards;
- Resource transfers or sharing.

Activities within SROs can include the specific activities exemplified in the 'Institutional context' column of Figure 1.3. It is important to recognize that many of these flows are connected: for instance, an exchange of regulatory forbearance for some form of public activity. In this regard, note also that SROs, in distinction to formal bodies, are not defined by their functions. Thus, an individual firm may fall within the technical, economic or societal regulatory scope of a given formal agency, but belong to an SRO defined along different lines. If the regulator, for instance, has economic regulatory power over the firm, but also has a societal regulatory obligation, it may exchange performance in one area for forbearance in another. These trade-offs can be opaque where, for instance, economic regulation is clearly modelled on transparent public methods, but elements of social regulation (e.g., content or media literacy) are devolved to an SRO.[69]

The second could be a *relational map* showing the relations between organizations in the context of specific domains. These relations could take various forms:

- Hierarchical: one organization reports to or must obey another – and therefore one is more important than the other (in soft or hard power terms);
- Complementary: organizations' activities can advance each others' objectives (as above, this may cross domains);
- Complicating: another organization must be taken into account when formulating strategy or tactics, evaluating outcomes, etc.;
- Cooperating: when organizations act jointly.

---

[69] Examining this 'Gordian knot', through expert interviews and the web survey, may increase the transparency of such trade-offs, and assist in formulating an evaluation agenda that reveals whether the cost-benefit of such implicit trade-offs is increasing or decreasing over time.

Table 1.2. *Oxford five 'C's adapted to Internet SROs*

Oxford five 'C's	Marsden roles	Details on updated categories
Constitution	Constitution	Note conditions of exclusion/ membership/reform
Coverage	Scope	Note expansion of scope/role of SRO
Content	Financing and roles	Activities of SRO critically dependent on resources
Communication	Stakeholders	Importance of civil society/user outreach in legitimacy of SRO
Compliance	Cultural context	Culture (sectoral or national) determines efficacy of sanctions: negative publicity/censure for company, or formal tradition of expulsion

Synthesis and analysis across case studies show the relations between such SROs, as will be shown in Chapter 7. We can analyze each institution much more straightforwardly in inserting evidence into each example, using standard log frame analysis. The Oxford methodology took the five 'C's approach, described as: Constitution, Coverage, Content, Communication and Compliance.[70] I update and adapt the descriptions to more accurately reflect the features of Internet SROs consisting of: constitution, scope, financing, stakeholders/governance and the cultural context, whether sector or nation, in Table 1.2.

In particular, enforcement is a feature that more specifically reflects a legalistic view of explicitly co-regulatory institutions, but has little specific applicability to the institutional case studies. It is therefore an element in 'constitution' (initial membership, censure and potential expulsion conditions and activities) and 'stakeholders/governance' (consideration of, for instance, information-based censure: 'naming and shaming' via tribunals, critical reports on activities and other information-based censure). Further note the acceptance of the integral role of stakeholders rather than as a 'Communication' function.

---

[70] Tambini *et al.* (2008), pp. 50–62.

Table 1.3. Log frame example for SROs: analytical requirements and five 'C's

Analytical	Five 'C's	Constitution	Scope	Finance	Governance	Context
Effectiveness		One member one vote	Definition and measurement	Fit for purpose	Transparent, rapid decision-making	National/ Regional/ Sectoral
Efficiency		Suitability for stakeholders	Problem and resolution	Cost-benefit	Decision, review and appeal process	National/ Regional/ Sectoral
Sustainability		Obedience and enforcement	Responsiveness to market conditions	Duration	Development and legitimacy	National/ Regional/ Sectoral
Innovation		Arrangements for reform	Reform to enlarge	Membership criteria	Reform procedure	National/ Regional
Competitiveness		Flexibility and standing	Comparative international institutions	Comparative costs (v. state regulation)	Comparative and best of breed performance	National/ Regional/ Sectoral
Competition policy		Cartel conditions	Horizontal or vertical issues	Barriers to entry	Transparent and conforming	National/ Regional/ Sectoral

Table 1.4. *Log frame for evidence (I: interviews, S: survey, D: documents and quantitative data)*

Level	Criteria	Evidence: indicators	Assumptions: risks
Design, organization	Relevance, fitness	I, D	Active participation, acceptance, duplication, gaps, conflict
Inputs	Quantity, quality	I, S, D: staff, budget levels	Coordination, resource availability
Activities	Participation, adherence	I, S: coverage, compliance	Enforcement, monitoring
Output	Efficiency	I, S, D: output range, awareness	Dissemination, attention, receptivity
Outcome	Effectiveness	S, D: utilization	Structural, market development
Impact	Competition	S, D (esp. market data): concentration, pricing, sector performance (efficiency)	Antitrust and other regulation – balance between technical, economic, societal regulation.
Sustainability	Innovation, competitiveness	I, D: patent activity, macroeconomic performance	Reconsideration of need, channels, regulatory reform, market changes, e.g., globalization
Evaluation	Quality, transparency, accountability	I, D: management information, self- and external review, link to strategy and design	Systematic compliance, participation, appropriate incentives, information

All these differences are nuances adopted to indicate focus, rather than fundamental distinctions.

The log frame example in Tables 1.3 and 1.4 is in two parts, analytical requirements (effectiveness, efficiency, sustainability, innovation, competitiveness and competition), and analysis against the five 'C's.

Table 1.5. *Structuring case studies*

Section	Subject
1	Policy context
2	Design, organization
3	Inputs
4	Activities
5	Output
6	Outcome
7	Impact
8	Sustainability
9	Reform
10	Evaluation

The second part (see Table 1.4) is a listing of the 'rows' of a conventional log frame for a generic case against the criteria most closely related to this study. The columns representing the measurable indicators (including data and analytic tools) and risk factors are simply sketched because they vary too much with specific types.

To populate the log frames required three types of evidence: interview, documentary was and survey. An expert interview approach was necessary, to supplement documentary evidence and survey research approach. Each individual case study was structured in Table 1.4.

The expert interview approach used the interview protocol in Table 1.6. Note that the interview protocol was based on a template designed to reveal the internal and external dynamics of the institution beyond those facts accessible via annual reports, press interviews or the website. Therefore the protocol focused on the formation and reform of the organization, and the manner in which the original mission and constitution, and reforms thereof, were achieved. In addition, the questions focused on governance, civil society involvement, innovation and competition, and enforcement. Interviewees were also invited to address other matters that they considered relevant.

Case study interviewees comprise more national, pan-European and sector-specific experts.

Documents relevant to each of the examples of SROs include: the Articles of Association, Codes of Conduct and other rules of the body; annual reports; press briefings; parliamentary or regulatory filings;

Table 1.6. *Interview protocol*

Subject	Specific queries
Interests and policy needs	How was the organization formed? What functions does it fulfil? What is its mission? How does the organization fit with formal legal and declared political pressures to regulate its original sector?
Design and organization of the Institution	Is regulation for the SRO a function required by law? Which laws?
	Is the SRO co- or self-regulatory? How does the SRO fit in with government regulations? Are they relevant?
	Are there other organizations with similar missions and regulatory regimes? How are they different?
Inputs	Where is it based? Name of the Chief Executive or Chairman?
	Does the institution file accounts? If so, where? Does it report to a regulator (other than financial)? Approximately what is the budget per annum? Where does the funding come from? How many staff work there?
The board and strategic direction	How independent is the board of directors from the executive of the organization?
	Are there committees independent of the board, for instance for finance or audit?
	How are civil society stakeholders involved in its work? Other stakeholders?
	How is policy made?
Reform	Is it expanding or being reformed? How (new sectors, countries)? Why? How does this affect regulation?
	How is redesign of the institution being carried out? Please state the primary driver for change in the organization's mission or function.*
	Does the organization innovate? Is its regulation model replicable or an exception to other regulatory forms?
	Is the organization responsible for liaison with other Internet SROs?

User knowledge of and participation in SRO	Does the annual general meeting attract a large audience?
	Is there sufficient press coverage of its activities?
	Are its activities well known to its members?
	Is it well known to Internet users?
	Are any reform proposals circulated?
	How transparent is the organization to: board members? ordinary members? Internet users? Governments?
	How accountable is it?
	How accessible is management information?
Enforcing regulations	Is there a tribunal or other enforcement arm?
	• How many enforcement actions occur each year?
	• What types of enforcement actions are undertaken?
	Is there an appeal process or ombudsman?
The market	Do you believe there is competition against this institution and/or its functions? Who are the competitors?
	Is there commercial value in the work of the organization?
	Can you define the market, if any, in which this institution functions?
	What is the impact of this 'market dynamic' on your organization?
	If the institution does perform a market function, how large is the total market?
	What share of the market does the institution take?
	How is the market split (i.e., what share does the largest other institution take)?
	Does the organization impact on economic performance?
Evaluation	Have there been external reviews of the institution? What are they?
	Are you aware of studies into regulation of the SRO or similar organizations?

* Six options were given: Internet usage or design; Government requests or instructions; Competition in the market; Members' suggestions; Civil Society request for greater inclusion; Merger of functions and/or management.

Table 1.7. *Interviewees and dates*

Interviewee	Affiliation	Date in 2007 (location or telephone)	Other affiliation and comments
Archer, Phil	CTO, ICRA/FOSI	13 September	
Banks, Karen	Association for Progressive Communications	London, 28 August	Member, WGIG
Benhamou, Bernard	Senior Lecturer, Paris Pantheon, Sorbonne University	31 August	Former member, ICANN GAC
Borthwick, Rob	Regulatory Affairs, Vodafone UK	10 August	Key negotiator, IMCB and pan-European mobile agreement
Boyle, Martin	Department for Business Enterprise Regulatory Reform	6 September	Formerly IGF negotiator, UK Presidency of the EU (2005)
Callanan, Cormac	Managing Director, INHOPE	10 September	Left INHOPE on 20 September
Carlberg, Ken	Science Applications International Corporation	21 August	IETF expert participant
Carr, John	Coordinator, UK children's charities	London, 8 August	Consultant, MySpace; Former IWF board member
Cecil, Andrew	Regulatory Affairs, Yahoo! Europe, Paris	August 10	
Chazerand, Patrice	Chief Executive, PEGI	Brussels, 26 June	
Christiensen, Per	Regulatory Director, AOL Germany	26 August	Former researcher, Munster University
Clark, David C.	Head, FINE programme, NSF	Washington, DC, 29 September	Interview and paper presentation

Name	Role	Date/Location	Notes
Clayton, Richard	Research Fellow, Cambridge University Computer Laboratory	Cambridge, 28 August	
Delgado, Juan	Yahoo! Europe search engine business unit	26 July	
Eijk, Nico Van	Professor, University of Amsterdam	Istanbul, 3 September	Informal interview and paper presentation
Graham, Sir Alistair	Chair, ICSTIS	London, 25 June	ICSTIS Scope review round table lunch
Guadamuz, Andres	Edinburgh Law School	Edinburgh, 26 October	Creative Common Scotland
Hoff, Ola Kristian	Norway-based independent legal advocate	14 September	Former CTO ICRA and DG INFOSOC
Hutty, Malcolm	Policy Officer, LINX	30 August	Treasurer, INHOPE
Kiedrowski, Tom	Ofcom Strategy Manager	London, 20 September	Head of Ofcom Self- and Co-Regulation Study
Latzer, Michael	Professor, Austrian Academy of Sciences	Leipzig, May and Istanbul, 3 September	Informal interview and paper presentation
Millwood-Hargrave, Andrea	Secretary, ATVOD	London, 26 September	Former Research Director, Broadcasting Standards Commission
O'Connell, Rachel	Chief Safety Officer, Bebo	London, 30 August	Consultant to Council of Europe on Internet child safety
Ondrejka, Cory	Chief Technology Officer, Second Life	Rueschlikon, 14 June (phone), 8 August	Keynote speaker, iSummit, Dubrovnik

Table 1.7. (*cont.*)

Interviewee	Affiliation	Date in 2007 (location or telephone)	Other affiliation and comments
Robbins, Peter	Chief Executive, Internet Watch Foundation	17 August	
Sahel, Jean-Jacques	Department for Business Enterprise Regulatory Reform	London, 24 August	Former Chair, OECD ICCP Committee; Chair, London Action Plan
Swetenham, Richard	DG INFSO	4 July	Head of Unit, SIAP
Taylor, Emily	Legal and Public Policy Director, Nominet	London, 30 June	
Verhulst, Stefaan	Head of Research, Markle Foundation	New York, 26 July	Author, V-chip study, EC DG INFOSOC
Weitzner, Danny	General Counsel, W3C	London, 17 September	Professor of law, MIT
Whiteing, Paul	Director, IMCB	London, 31 August	Director, ICSTIS

minutes of directors'/board meetings; public documents and presentations; member companies' releases, reports and other documents relating to the work of the institution; stakeholder responses and analyses; financial accounts and reports; tribunal and/or other case data, and other forms of dispute resolution permitted under the 'constitution' of the SRO. Where necessary, appropriate and relevant, for instance where there is a lack of transparency and documentation in the public sphere concerning the body, this primary data was supplemented by reviews of the body's work, especially peer-reviewed scientific surveys, but also less authoritative yet indicative coverage in the press, online reportage, journalists' blogs, and the wider 'blogosphere'.[71]

The research included an electronic survey of stakeholder participants, specifically to sample non-participants in expert interviews (i.e., non-enfranchised users) and measure perceptions of and satisfaction with self- and co-regulatory arrangements in terms of specific policy areas and overall transparency, accountability, effectiveness, etc. It was a large-scale survey with over 300 answers, to capture those interests often overlooked in expert studies of Internet governance: civil society stakeholders and Internet users. Due to the voluntary nature of many of the arrangements, insight into the choices and constraints users face is vital to assessment of the current impact and evolution of self- and co-regulatory arrangements. The limitations of surveys are well known and accepted. The objective was to sample the range, not to replicate the statistical distribution. However, these soundings supported some quantitative analysis especially of correlations and patterns of response (and non-response). The survey was carried out with the assistance (in terms of contact details at a minimum) of the civil society groups constituted within the fora. Examples included the Association of Internet Researchers (AoIR), Creative Commons and Association of Progressive Communications (APC). The survey URL distribution was very much a broadcast activity, with the intention of reaching a broad audience of users. It relied on the institutions and personal contacts to distribute the survey. Given the resource limitations, this was not intended to be directly representational of the entire Internet

---

[71] In particular it is acknowledged that the controversy surrounding the work of these SROs often leads to 'slash-dot' type incidents, in which a mass of media-generated user complaints and commentaries are made about a particular judgment or decision from the regulatory body. Such incidents are often illustrative of a particular concern regarding the legitimacy of the activity of the body, though the 'technorati' of educated and often libertarian consumers is by no means the only relevant group. I therefore treat such evidence with the proper caution that it merits.

population: the World Internet Project or Eurobarometer perform such functions. It was intended to be broadly representative of user opinion as a 'best effort' activity. Given the specific nature of the individual surveys for each organization that the survey elicits from users, there is little or no added value in reaching the entire Internet audience without specific knowledge of individual SROs. The stakeholders whose views we captured were participating on an anonymous basis. They included both participants and users of the institutions, and those who bear the consequences, and particularly responded to redistribution of the survey by activists in the Creative Commons movement and W3C.[72]

Based on the three complementary and synergistic evidence types (documentary, expert and broad survey), a comprehensive holistic analysis of the evaluations for each case study produces generalizable conclusions on effectiveness, efficiency and sustainability in co- and self-regulation. It should be emphasized that this went beyond the heavily summative and judgmental character of many evaluations. In addition to its formative character, it examines a set of overlapping public, private and civil society institutions. Therefore it is inappropriate to simply evaluate them as one institution's programme in terms of its stated objectives and terms of reference. Rather, I take account of the multiplicity of institutions, and assess the balance of roles, responsibilities, information, powers to act and incentives. This is essential not least because many of the challenges driving self-and co-regulatory innovation will, if not handled in this way, be dealt with in other ways. Thus the counterfactual is not 'no enforcement' but different enforcement, and the assessment will be integrated to consider the evolution of the ensemble of interacting arrangements on the basis of a suitable evaluation of its components.

Case studies in brief

The following case studies were examined. I summarize each case study briefly.[73]

Chapter 3: Self-organization

Second Life is a virtual world established by Linden Labs from San Francisco, operating since 2003 (as a beta). It claimed nine million residents with about 30,000 concurrent users. There are now many more

---

[72] See announcement of the survey: http://creativecommons.org/weblog/entry/7563.
[73] For full details, see Marsden *et al.* (2008).

Table 1.8. *Grouping case studies by chapter according to scope and interconnectedness*

3: Self-organization	4: Self-regulation and standards	5: Co-regulation and medium law	6: Isps, filtering and co-regulation
Second Life	[ICANN] Nominet	ICSTIS-IMCB	ICRA/FOSI
Bebo	[IETF] W3C	NICAM-PEGI	IWF
Creative Commons		ATVOD	INHOPE-EuroISPA

non-US users, US users only comprise 25 per cent of the total. Its regulatory system works via terms of service and resident self-regulation. Content controversies include the behaviour of avatar personalities: virtual rapes and paedophilia. Economic controversies concern fraud and misuses of the virtual currency – Linden dollar. Bank crashes have resulted, and gambling has been banned from the world. The servers are all US-based, but Linden Labs in 2006 opened offices in the UK. They anticipate strategies to head off future regulatory challenges. Evaluation is thus far mainly academic, where a flourishing industry is developing examining all aspects of Second Life including regulatory options.

Bebo was, in 2007, the largest social network in Ireland, and number three worldwide. It was formed in California in 2005 with European owners, and its core market is European teens. In response to regulatory concerns, especially with regard to child abuse possibilities, a Chief Safety Officer was appointed in 2006. All staff are trained on safety issues. There is a dedicated human interface for profile photos to prevent abuse. As a successful hybrid European/US social network, its pre-emptive regulatory model raises issues: of entry barriers to European (especially youth) markets, of a 'Bill of Rights' for users, and as to whether such safety policies are replicable. It is too recent a phenomenon to have been evaluated externally, though as with Second Life academic and regulatory interest is growing.

Creative Commons (CC) was founded in 2002 as a non-profit based at Stanford, California. It drafts licences for individual content creators to license content on non-commercial terms. It now has over sixty other national CC licences. Lawrence Lessig is its founder Chief Executive, as well as its intellectual leader, in much the same respect as Tim Berners-Lee for the W3C. Early board member and Free Software Foundation head Richard Stallman quit in 2004, criticizing CC for its lack of radical mission. CC licences used on the photo-sharing site Flickr mean over 150 million 'artworks' are licensed. The growth of the CC 'movement' includes iCommons and ccSalon to showcase CC licence use, and CC International (South Africa) and the Creative Commons summit to encourage sharing of best practice. Licence enforcement is controversial as an emerging legal issue for CC in various jurisdictions, as is the relationship between non-commercial content in the public sector and CC licensed content.

Chapter 4: Self-regulation and standards

Internet Engineering Task Force (IETF) was named in 1986, and developed from ARPANet architectural standards committees. Its design is based on extreme radical openness by standards organization traditions – all budgets, contracts, board discussions are published; consensus decisions may only be reached on public working group mailing lists open to all. Most radically, there are no 'members'. The volunteer structure with no corporate entity and low costs ($4m/annum with many thousands of participants) has continued, and it remains the unchallenged pre-eminent Internet standards body. In regulatory discussions, it considers security implications of standards, for instance, but other public policy considerations are driven on a case-by-case basis by participants (e.g., privacy, accessibility) except in extreme circumstances.

World Wide Web Consortium (W3C) was founded by Tim Berners-Lee in 1994. It was founded as an international standards consortium with European and Japanese partner institutions to the US headquarters. The membership organization and director's powers to enforce decisions were adopted with lessons drawn from the IETF. It licenses its patents royalty were free to members, a decision following a complex four-year negotiation to 2002 that illustrates the complex and detailed attention of the corporate members. Its relationship with regulators includes funding by the EC, and standards that include regulatory requirements in design, for instance the P3P (Platform for Privacy Preferences) and PICS. Evaluation has largely been by academic comparisons with other standards bodies.

Internet Corporation for Assigned Names and Numbers (ICANN) was founded in 1998 as a California corporation: this unique arrangement was supervised in a co-regulatory arrangement by the Department of Commerce. Its directors have legal status based on their private law obligations as corporate managers, not as regulators. It has a Government Advisory Council, with differing opinions as to its influence on the Board's decisions. ICANN has invested substantial resources in attempts to achieve broad inclusion and transparency with its international stake-holders, including elections to the Board, which were carried out in 2000 and then abandoned as an experiment. Evaluations have been carried out by One World Trust, LSE and College d'Europe. In 2007, major governance reforms were undertaken, with further reforms in 2009–10, though the same criticisms remain.

Nominet is the UK Top-Level Domain registrar and was founded in 1996. It is a not-for-profit charity with a very large membership. This creates a problem for decision-making: a largely 'inactive' membership creates problems in changing fees for domains. Nominet is growing with the market, and has a large turnover, invests in technical and other staff, and carried a £16m surplus, which it proposes in part to invest in a Foundation for Internet Policy Research. Its current challenges include competition with profit-making and entrepreneurial TLD organizations for back-office services and the ENUM transition, as well as new market developments such as domaining. It underwent major governance reform consultations in 2007–8, and had to lobby hard against governmental co-regulatory oversight that was signalled in the draft Digital Economy Bill 2009 but removed from the Digital Economy Act 2010.

Chapter 5: Co-regulation and medium law

PhonepayPlus/ICSTIS (renamed in October 2007 as PhonepayPlus) was founded in 1986 as the co-regulator of premium telephony services in the UK, recognized by then-regulator Oftel. It commits members to its code of practice which is now in its eleventh edition. It is the paradigmatic regulator of the world's largest premium services market, of about £1.2 billion per annum. In 2007, with its new co-regulatory partner Ofcom (since 2004), a strategic review was launched, with particular attention to the governance structure and regulating the new markets for mobile, broadcast quiz shows and national-local rate (0871) numbers (from 2008). It co-founded the international coordination mechanism: IARN. It is funded by a levy on service providers which is collected by network operators. There are fines and administrative charges collected from service providers who breach the code of practice. Its budget and strategy is approved by Ofcom annually.

Independent Mobile Classification Board (IMCB): In February 2004 UK mobile network operators announced a code of conduct. The code committed them to rating adult (18+) content, backed by a rating body. A tender resulted in the appointment of a subsidiary of ICSTIS established for the purpose, IMCB. After prolonged legal negotiation it began operation in 2005. It is an SRO which for administrative purposes is set up as a subsidiary of ICSTIS (which has a golden share). It has no formal relationship with Ofcom. IMCB follows the NICAM/British Board of Film Classification model. Further European SROs have been rolled out in other jurisdictions (co-regulation in Germany). An agreement for a Pan-European Framework was announced 2007. The codes in place cover adult content providers contracted to the network operators.

Association of Video on Demand: The co-regulator for VOD under Directive 2007/65/EC is ATVOD, which was refounded in 2010 as 'new ATVOD' to replace the former self-regulator.

Nederlands Instituut voor de Classificatie van Audiovisuele Media (NICAM) grew from the 1990s concern with satellite/cable TV growth, leading to a consensus decision on a pan-media system of self-regulation to replace the state regulation model in place. It is mandated by Parliament, and reports to Parliament. It has been widely praised as an entirely transparent and widely adopted system. The training system is also much praised, for its ongoing attention to audit of company classifiers. The consensus and industry/political buy-in to the NICAM system is the result of a long negotiated outcome typical of Dutch politics. This is not necessarily replicable but the system is used elsewhere and NICAM assisted in the creation of pan-European games rating system PEGI. It is evaluated periodically by law.

Pan European Game Information (PEGI): This system is a pan-European video game classification scheme funded by fees for game classification. It emerged from previous UK and US schemes. It merges the Netherlands NICAM system and UK Video Standards Council capabilities in training industry to rate its own content for distributors. Note that legal ratings and decisions not to rate (i.e., refuse licences to distribute) games also exist, and PEGI has no legal force. It does have very broad industry buy-in, including mobile and online game publishers. The latter inspired the recent initiative PEGI Online, which responds to growth of interactive games and was co-funded by the EC SIAP and evaluated by SIAP in 2007. PEGI Online was launched by Commissioner Reding in June 2007. Its coordination can be seen as a type of 'co-regulatory policy-making with self-regulatory implementation'. Note there is a government advisory board.

Chapter 6: Censorship

Internet Watch Foundation (IWF) was founded in 1998 as the UK ISP industry charitable hotline for the removal of child pornographic content.

Hotlines are exemplars of user reporting and ISP removal of illegal content. It is claimed as a success in its core remit: increased number of cases of reported illegal content; driving child pornography out of the UK; involvement in UK government and police initiatives; and international support for INHOPE and coordinated police activities. IWF has broadened its funding base to include mobile networks and search engines, among others, and there is tension between supporters of its original mission and an increasingly independent executive management. IWF has undergone a number of governance reviews during its first ten years, both internal and by government. It has maintained its independence of government despite severe pressure.

INHOPE-EuroISPA: INHOPE is the pan-European hotline association, formed in 1999, based in Dublin and most recently expanding rapidly to twenty-eight members across Europe and worldwide. It has never represented hotlines from all European Union Member States. Its primary role is in training and coordination, and the majority of its funding is guaranteed by the SIAP, as well as Microsoft. It has five full-time staff and a budget of under €1m per annum. In 2007–10, members and governments proposed a pan-European coordinated blocklist similar to the UK CAIC list discussed in the IWF example. This would expand and change the organization's remit, together with a proposed European Directive in 2010 that would refer specifically to its role and this list in establishing mandatory filtering across European Union members. EuroISPA is the pan-European ISP association, formed in 1999, and based in Brussels. It is a very small (three person) organization, has fewer members than INHOPE, and is funded by those members. It opposes any pan-European blocklist, and encourages pan-European ISP cooperation, to which end it signed a Memorandum of Understanding with INHOPE in 2004. Several member associations have adopted filtering as a self-initiative (larger UK ISPs) or under co-regulation (France, Germany, Scandinavia). Nevertheless, with varying technical flaws in filtering, EuroISPA's position is to oppose such ISP-based censorship on principle. There are serious recurring issues about freedom of expression and access to justice, with the original case-by-case take-down notices replaced by the total removal of newsgroups in 2002 and the new initiative, the CAIC blocklist. The implementation of automated filtering based on this list by British Telecom and others encompasses over 90 per cent of consumer Internet users in the UK.

Conclusion: soft law and the Internet

In this chapter, I have explained that the flavours of regulatory theory have extended to the point that we no longer need think of Internet regulation as an exotic outlier to more state-centric regulatory theory. The role of corporations, consumers and states in inter-meshed webs of regulatory activity is now accepted by legal theorists, such that the Internet is more a crucible or even catalyst for regulatory theorizing, rather than an exception that proves the command-and-control rule. Thus we can speak of Internet regulation 'coming home' to mainstream regulatory theory. The wealth of empirical research in Internet regulation lends its weight to existing sectoral and general studies of regulation. I argue it can be seen as something of a 'missing link' between existing studies of financial, industrial and consumer regulation. Information may want to be free, but it also is in need of regulation, and such topics as copyright and data protection invade most areas of society today. Internet regulation is, however, a Janus-faced regulatory subject, showing both the bleeding edge examples of self- and co-regulation, and even technologically led self-organization in which regulatory organization is entirely within a firm (an empire unto itself, such as Second Life or Facebook), but also extraordinarily bad legislation, designed to both fail and signal governmental impotence. Histories of Internet regulation cannot but show the monumental failings of government intervention, as well as some successes.

I analyzed content in terms of traditional mass media content, UGC and content labelled using standardized techniques for various forms of filtering and blocking. The first (see Chapter 5) is regulated by traditional media regulation, commercial communications by both media-specific regulators and general law, applicable to mobile commercial content, all premium content and IP television. The second is UGC (see Chapter 3), including online games, blogs and Wikis, virtual worlds, invitation-only social networks and public social networks. The third (see Chapter 6) extends down into the technical protocol stack, with machine labelling of content, for security, DRMs and Trusted Computing, for removal and reporting via hotlines and ISPs and automated blocking. The issue of technical regulation of content is a specific Internet problem, as previous digital media (telecoms and television, for instance) could be regulated by maintaining the closed network.

Utilizing a broad and holistic approach, I undertook a mapping exercise based, as a first level of classification, on three categories defined by the WGIG: infrastructure and critical resources; issues where global cooperation is ill-defined; and issue areas from offline activities that are converging onto the Internet. This provides the framework for examination of standards, infrastructure, ISP self-regulation, mass media content, user-derived content, personal Internet security, DRM and e-commerce standards. From a revision and mapping exercise undertaken under the WGIG headings, I identified a (limited) number of potential gaps, UGC and copyright, where self-organization rather than regulation seems more common (Chapter 3). I considered the proposition that there can only be an effective regulatory environment if some overt enforcement mechanism operates but found this to be too limiting a viewpoint. Instead, I identified regimes where more subtle mechanisms (peer pressure, moral suasion etc.) do indeed seem to operate effectively, such as the Creative Commons copyright licence explored in Chapter 3. I draw no firm conclusions about the viability of such mechanisms but examine this topic in more precise detail.

Later chapters will elaborate on the many useful SRO examples, but the following chapter explores in depth the development and legal status of co-regulation.

2

Internet co-regulation and constitutionalism

Introduction

The term 'co-regulation' encompasses a range of different regulatory phenomena, which have in common the fact that the regulatory regime is made up of a complex interaction of general legislation and a self-regulatory body. The varying interests of actors result in different incentives to cooperate or attempt unilateral actions at the various points of the value chain. Without regulation responsive to both the market and the need for constitutional protection of freedom of expression and protection of minors at national levels, Internet co- and self-regulatory measures cannot be sufficiently responsive to economic and cultural environments to be self-sustaining. It has enriched conceptions of 'soft law' or 'governance' in the literature in the past ten years, but like those umbrella terms, refers to forms of hybrid regulation that do not meet the administrative and statute-based legitimacy of regulation, yet clearly perform some elements of public policy that cannot be ascribed to self-regulation, in the absence of the nation-state or European law.[1] It is often identified with the rise of the 'new governance' in the late 1990s in environmental and financial regulation, yet its growth can also be traced to the birth of Information Society policy in the mid 1990s.

Co-regulation constitutes multiple stakeholders, and this inclusiveness results in greater legitimacy claims. The state, and stakeholder groups including consumers, are stated to explicitly form part of the institutional setting for regulation. However, direct government involvement including sanctioning powers may result in the gains of reflexive regulation – speed of response, dynamism, international cooperation between ISPs and others – being lost. It is clearly a finely balanced concept. The growing gulf between states' preference for co-regulatory and self-regulatory

---

[1] See Kohler-Koch and Eising (1999).

solutions, and citizens' preferences for greater control if not ownership of vital regulated industries, has led to a crisis of legitimacy. This chapter analyses co-regulation, by defining and exploring its recent institutional history together with that of Internet self-regulation. It then assesses the legal definitions and taxonomies of co-regulation before constructing a twelve-point scale of self- and co-regulation. It explores the possibility for judicial review of co-regulatory arrangements, recent case law that concerns human rights and Internet co-regulation, and regulatory pronouncements.

Examining the origins of Internet co-regulation

It is a commonplace to state that the modern state has faced twin demands for less and better-designed regulation.[2] This argued for an industry-led response to the complexity inherent in many modern regulated industries, notably that associated with globalization of businesses and the rise and ubiquity of modern technology, notably nano-, biomedical, information and communications technologies. These technologies led to spectacular growth in financial and other markets, beyond the reach of individual national regulators, in the period since 1980. The trend towards co-regulation does, however, suggest a rolling back from the spectacular neo-liberal drive towards self-regulation,[3] with an involvement of public interest groups as well as government, to create greater representation in the co-regulatory bodies and therefore (it is hoped) greater transparency, internal democracy and respect for fundamental rights. However, wider re-regulatory optimism may be misplaced, as banking reform has been far more minimal than predicted at the depth of the crisis in early 2009.[4]

Ayres and Braithwaite stated: 'Practical people who are concerned with outcomes seek to understand the intricacies of interplays between state regulation and private orderings … administrative and regulatory practice is in a state of flux in which responsive regulatory innovations are politically feasible.'[5] Responsive regulation reflects a more complex

---

[2] Baldwin *et al.* (1998) at p. 3 explain that: 'At its simplest, regulation refers to the promulgation of an authoritative set of rules, accompanied by some mechanism, typically a public agency, for monitoring and promoting compliance with these rules.' Clearly, we go far beyond this basic definition.

[3] Theories of network governance emerged from the study of the firm in organizational theory; see for instance Williamson (1975, 1985, 1994).

[4] Davies (2010).

[5] Ayres and Braithwaite (1992), p. 4.

dynamic interaction of state and market, a break with more stable previous arrangements.[6] Teubner viewed European conceptions of law as 'moving away from the idea of direct societal guidance through a politically instrumentalised law … Instead, reflexive law tends to rely on procedural norms that regulate processes, organization, and the distribution of rights and competencies.'[7] This applies to globalizing phenomena other than the Internet, for instance financial and environmental law, where negative externalities are highlighted for public concern.[8] Price and Verhulst assert the limits of both government and private action in this sphere, and emphasize the interdependence of both – there is little purity in self-regulation without at least a lurking government threat to intervene where market actors prove unable to agree. They draw on empirical studies demonstrating that in the media, government preference in liberal democracies is for co-regulation.[9]

The Internet developer community has cherished self-regulation based on the codes of conduct and terms of use that early Internet users employed in the scientific institutions that first developed the protocols and social standards.[10] In the Information Society, governments have broadly accepted that a more flexible and innovation-friendly model of regulation is required,[11] particularly in view of the rapid growth, complex interrelationships and dynamic changes taking place in Internet and games development. Though this amounted to an illusory 'article of faith' for the libertarian Internet users at the start of commercial Internet use,[12] for governments it was a pragmatic acceptance that the models used for regulation should be as flexible as possible, to permit significantly greater user innovation and freedom than with other types of communications (notably telecoms and broadcasting). This includes using both hard law and much softer forms of regulation.[13]

---

[6]   See Baldwin and Black (2010), pp. 181–213; Black (2010).
[7]   Teubner (1986), p. 8.
[8]   See for instance Gaines and Kimber (2001), p. 157.
[9]   Price (1995); Price and Verhulst (2000).
[10]   See Helin and Sandström (2007), pp. 253–271; Higgs-Kleyn and Kapelianis (1999), pp. 363–374; Vrielink et al. (2010); Abbott and Snidal (2009), pp. 44–88.
[11]   Gunningham and Grabosky (1998); Gunningham and Rees (1997); Abbott and Snidal (2004), pp. 421–422.
[12]   See Goldsmith and Wu (2006).
[13]   Lemley (2006), p. 459; Senden (2005); Cosma and Whish (2003), pp. 25–56; Hodson and Maher (2004), pp. 798–813.

This self-regulatory paradigm is increasingly challenged by the growth and evolution of the Internet. The forms of technological, social and economic innovation are posing new challenges to regulators, especially in view of the ubiquitous use of broadband connections by domestic consumers in developed nations, creating new security risks, rights and responsibilities for users. Whereas in 1997, when the self-regulatory paradigm was being formed,[14] there were fewer than a million European households connected to the Internet on narrowband speeds, in 2007, there are more than 200 million households, the majority on broadband connections. The cycle of regulation lags behind the apparent pattern of adoption, a technological cycle which has been well recognized in, for instance, the Gartner 'hype cycle' that explains how products are released, their benefits exaggerated resulting in a 'trough of disillusionment', before a later more robust version of the product appears, attracting a more mature mass market, at which point the 'slope of enlightenment' gives way to the 'plateau of improved productivity'.[15]

The development of cheap and reliable broadband access in the middle years of the 2000s replaced the dot-com bubble and its bursting, and by 2011 we are approaching maturity in both plateauing market growth (though speed is constantly increasing) and regulation of many Internet innovations. Fenn sees Internet television, online video and public virtual worlds as occupying various places in the downward slope after early hype, while social networks such as Facebook have been adopted faster, and are approaching maturity.[16]

Spar explains that the circle turns from prophets to pirates to pioneers to politics.[17] The prophet in this case could be seen as John Perry Barlow, the pirate as any number of cyber-criminals in the late 1990s or Napster, the pioneers as early commercial ISPs including Compuserve, AOL and UUNet, and the politics as the events triggering *American Civil Liberties Union* v. *Reno*. She explains from her case studies of radio, satellite television and the telegraph that the noteworthy feature is that anarchy gives way to control and order. This cycle applies to the Internet: 'Governments will impose their laws upon the Internet. This will prove tricky, because

---

[14] See Clinton and Gore, Jr. (1997); Telecommunications Act of 1996, Pub. L. No. 104–104, 110 Stat. 56; Tambini *et al.* (2008) at pp. 2–5, 16–18.

[15] Fenn and Raskino (2008).

[16] The Hype Cycle is updated annually – the September 2010 version will be outdated by the time you read this note, but is found at http://blogs.gartner.com/hypecyclebook/files/2010/09/2010-EmergingTech-HypeCycle.png.

[17] Spar (2001a).

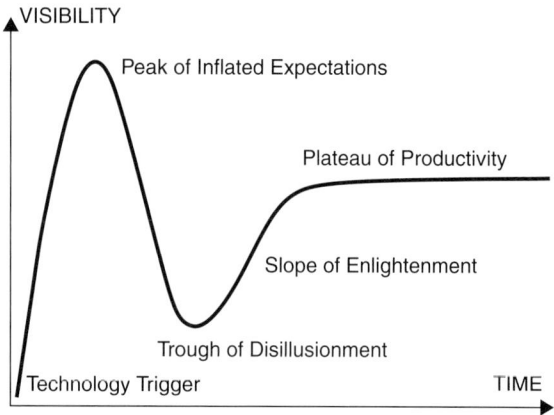

Figure 2.1.   Gartner product hype cycle

the net is still a slippery medium and crosses borders imperceptibly. But governments will nevertheless enforce rules in cyberspace that their citizens are likely to obey.'[18] This regulatory life cycle is clear in the case studies, though the dynamism of the self-regulatory and self-organizational characteristics of the Internet is more adaptable than earlier technologies of radio, television, and the telegraph – not least because the medium itself can be used in a much more informed and distributed networked governance structure.

The baseline for policy-makers deciding on new forms of regulation was described by Samuelson as five key policy challenges:

(1) whether they can apply or adapt existing laws and policies to the regulation of Internet activities, or whether new laws or policies are needed to regulate Internet conduct;

(2) how to formulate a reasonable and proportional response when new regulation is needed;

(3) how to craft laws that will be flexible enough to adapt to rapidly changing circumstances;

(4) how to preserve fundamental human values in the face of economic or technological pressures tending to undermine them; and

(5) how to coordinate with other nations in Internet law and policy-making so that there is a consistent legal environment on a global basis.[19]

The fourth is a vital addition to the 1997 Clinton–Gore 'Framework for global electronic commerce', which had four policy goals: predictability,

---

[18] Spar (2001b).
[19] Samuelson (1999), p. 751.

minimalism, consistency and simplicity.[20] By this extra human rights factor, Samuelson moves towards the European Information Society paradigm and a balance between rights and responsibilities. We can identify various areas in which human rights can be maintained using market-based solutions, and there are bright lines of human rights protection that should not be traded for economic benefit. One such might be thought to be the two-sided coin that is privacy and freedom of expression. Such rights are backed by constitutions from the US and French Bills of Rights forwards to the new European Charter of Fundamental Rights.[21] The Internet environment is a powerful technology for society and individuals to express their rights, as well as an environment in which such rights can be abused and curtailed due to legal, economic, technological, security and other incentives for powerful actors. Consider three shades of sectoral regulatory regime.

(1) *'Heavy' regulation*: a system imposing uniformly high costs such as the broadcast regime.
(2) *'Light-touch' regulation*: in which companies compete freely from a liberalized low-cost base.
(3) *No specific regulation*: general civil and criminal law.

The latter has been the situation for Internet content since its inception, despite a variety of new laws. The application of criminal law in specific European cases has resulted in unintended consequences and content provider losses: consider, for instance, the 1998 German conviction of former CompuServe General Manager Felix Somm,[22] or the *LICRA* v. *Yahoo!* case.[23] There cannot be a 'no regulation' option without reference to national law.

A typology of regulation

Huyse and Parmentier distinguish between the following state/self-regulatory relationships focusing on the role of states: subcontracting in which the state limits its involvement to setting formal conditions for rule-making, but leaves it up to parties to shape the content; concerted action in which the state not only sets the formal but also the substantive conditions for rule-making by one or more parties; and incorporation in which existing but non-official norms become part of the legislative order

---

[20] Clinton and Gore, Jr. (1997) at p. 3.[21] See Peers and Ward (2004).
[22] Bender (1998).   [23] Reidenberg (2001).

by insertion into statutes.[24] Black states that a taxonomy of self-regulation runs from:

- 'mandated private regulation, in which a collective group, an industry or profession for example is required or designated by the government to formulate and enforce norms within a framework defined by the government, usually in broad terms;[25]
- sanctioned private regulation, in which the collective group itself formulates the regulation, which is then subjected to government approval;[26]
- coerced private regulation, in which the industry itself formulates and imposes regulation but in response to threats [of] … statutory regulation; and
- voluntary private regulation, where there is no active state involvement direct or indirect …'[27] [footnotes added].

Cafaggi states, in regard to sanctioned regulation:

> An intermediate hypothesis between delegated private regulation and ex post recognized private regulation is that in which private regulation, produced by the private or self-regulator, has to be approved by a public authority to become effective. Unlike ex post recognition, where private regulation operates in any case in the private sphere, here regulation is subject to approval in order to become effective on regulatees; and, unlike delegation, in such a case no ex ante principles or guidelines are provided.[28]

In other words, the decision on recognition is binary and incapable of negotiation, simply a take-it-or-leave-it option for government. This would apply to many standards, for instance the Institute of Electrical and Electronic Engineers (IEEE) 802.11x standards for WiFi, which were finally approved in Europe but made in the US, whereas a separate European standards process had produced an incompatible solution.[29] By accepting the US standard, European governments knew that they were signing the death warrant of their own standard. In the non-standards environment, such life-or-death decisions are less frequent, and Cafaggi's case is less likely to apply, as the EC and Member States have more flexibility, as for instance in the reshaping of Nominet, PhonepayPlus and ATVOD. Cafaggi points

---

[24] Huyse and Parmentier (1990), p. 260.
[25] As described in Ayres and Braithwaite (1992).
[26] Ogus (1994), p. 96, describes the classic consensual regulation model.
[27] Black (1996), p. 25.   [28] See Cafaggi (2006).
[29] Croxford and Marsden (2001).

out that the recognition is of the standard, not of the process or the regulator, which leaves much greater discretion for both sides. Moreover, he indicates that *Wouters* may prove the basis for the CJEM to decide more minutely the application of competition law to self-regulation.[30]

Within the European context, co-regulation is described by van Scooten and Verschuuren as an element of 'non-state law' backed by 'some government involvement'.[31] They explain that since Hart's *The Concept of Law*,[32] it has been recognized that what is of interest in regulation are generally secondary rules rather than primary legislation, and that what is of interest in this secondary rule-making is how much involvement government actually devolves to private actors.[33] The variety of rules and rule-making in Internet governance describes a law that is about compliance and negotiation rather than a monopoly of force, reflecting Hart's insight. They see co-regulation as one of the emerging forms of smart regulation, alongside certification and audited standard making as an interim step between state-provided regulatory agency action and more self-regulatory forms. OECD has tried to detail the uses of co-regulation.[34] Sinclair states that no clear practical division exists between state and private self-regulation.[35] Latzer further finesses the distinctions between different self-regulatory bodies' establishment and development.[36] Tambini, Leonardi and Marsden state: 'If part of the calculation of industry bodies involves awareness that the state might do something or be compelled to do something should they fail to take responsibility for self-regulation, then we can say that there is at least co-regulatory oversight.'[37]

According to Ofcom, three different forms of regulation can be defined:[38]

---

[30] Case C-309/99 *J.C.J.Wouters et al* v. *Algemene Raad van de Nederlandse Orde van Advocaten* [2002] ECR I-1577, stating that: 'According to its very wording, Article 85 of the Treaty applies to agreements between undertakings and decisions by associations and undertakings. The legal framework within which such agreements are concluded and such decisions taken, and the classifications given to that framework by their various national legal systems are irrelevant as far as the applicability of the Community rules on competition and in particular Article 85 of the Treaty are concerned' (para 66). See the argument that *Wouters* is only a useful precedent for judicial non-activism in licensing rules for the 'liberal professions' rather than wider self-regulation, in Forrester (2004).
[31] Van Scooten and Verschuuren (2008), p. 2.
[32] Hart (1961).
[33] See van Scooten and Verschuuren (2008), p. 65.
[34] OECD (2006a). [35] See Sinclair (1997), pp. 529–559.
[36] Latzer (2007), pp. 399–405; Latzer and Saurwein (2007).
[37] Tambini *et al.* (2008) at p. 43.
[38] Ofcom (2006b), p. 12.

Direct regulation: a statutory body is empowered by law to develop its own regulations, which it maintains, monitors and enforces.

Co-regulation: a body with statutory regulatory authority delegates to the relevant industry responsibility for maintaining and applying a code of practice that the statutory regulator has approved, continuing to oversee the co-regulation, with retained powers to intervene where necessary.

Self-regulation: a group of firms or individuals exert control over their own membership and behaviour. Membership is voluntary and participants draw up their own rules using tools such as codes of conduct as well as technological solutions and standards. Members take full responsibility for monitoring and compliance without reference to a statutory regulatory authority.

Co-regulation is a relatively novel phenomenon, given that state regulation and self-regulation are as old as markets.[39] Co-regulation has been discussed since the late 1980s, in the Australian context as a hybrid of state and self-regulation.[40] By the mid 1990s, it had moved from a proposed technique to a detailed advertising industry rule-making procedure, with the replacement of the industry self-regulatory body by a co-regulatory scheme.[41] This was undertaken by the Australian Competition and Consumer Commission (ACCC) within its powers to exempt collective agreements under the Trades Practices Act 1974.[42] It is explained that:

> Co-regulation is self-regulation in the context of other, external regulation or monitoring – for example, legislative and governmental regulation. Under the co-regulation model, alcohol producers are committed to active and effective self-regulation and, at the same time, are also monitored by independent bodies and/or are expected to comply with codes and regulations established and enforced by outside agencies and authorities.[43]

The key issue here is that federal government and the competition agency were involved in making sure the new codes would be negotiated with their

---

[39] One could argue that the statutory monopolies granted by Royal Charter under Queen Elizabeth I in the sixteenth century were examples of co-regulation, with the East India Company and other trading interests granted wide powers to self-regulate under an authorizing statute. See Imperial Gazetteer of India (1908). Equivalents existed in other states such as Muscovy and the Netherlands. However, we are concerned with the modern conception of self-regulation in the period since 1980.

[40] Beresford Ponsonby Peacocke (1989).

[41] Media Council of Australia (1992, 1993).

[42] ACCC (2007).   [43] Anonymous (2009), p. 3.

involvement, as well as that of the formal federal consumer representation body. The Alcohol Beverages Advertising Code was developed in conjunction with the federal government, the Australian Consumers Association and the ACCC.[44] There is an independent Complaints Adjudication Panel for the code,[45] and a federal bureaucrat sits on the Management Committee. Recent criticisms notwithstanding, which describe the system as 'self-regulation' (note that two of 105 complaints were upheld in 2005), the code has been renewed under the same process until 30 June 2011.[46] At its renewal, it was compared with the UK self-regulatory Portman Code founded in 1989, which was favourably cited as an example of independent self-regulation and which has been praised and cited for its effectiveness by the UK Government and its Better Regulation Executive.[47]

The discussion of co-regulation is unsurprisingly also associated with the rise of discussions of 'governance' as distinct from 'government', which also arose in the late 1980s in political science literature, though earlier in organizational and business studies. The term 'governance' began to be used widely in political science literature in the 1990s, to describe intermediate forms of self-regulation in the post-Cold War globalization literature.[48] Varying definitions of governance have been adopted by practitioners and academics, falling into what might be termed 'minimalist' and 'maximalist' areas.[49] I use the term 'Internet regulation' to refer to the range of public–private interactions covering substantive national and regional-plurilateral rules and practices governing specific Internet topics.[50] Regulation as a rules-based field existing within a wider policy discussion of governance is the approach outlined for legal scholars.[51] Governance is further discussed in much of the political science literature in terms of networks and informal rule-making institutions such as multinational corporations and – particularly relevant for Internet governance – standard-setting organizations.[52] Governance as a concept

---

[44] ACCC (2007) at p. 11 for the background.
[45] According to ACCC (2007) at p. 12, there are five members on the Adjudication Panel, appointed by the Management Committee, who must not be at time of appointment or in the past five years a current employee or member of the alcohol industry.
[46] Science Daily (2009).
[47] Prime Minister's Strategy Unit (2004); Better Regulation Executive (2005), pp. 50–51.
[48] Pierre (2000).
[49] For a maximalist position that places all existing regulation plus informal modes of governance into the over-arching description, see the broad use in Zysman and Weber (2000).
[50] Marsden (ed.) (2000b), and for the broader policy approach Grewlich (1999).
[51] Scott (2004).
[52] See Christou and Simpson (2009).

explains the networked modes of regulating, by the governments concerned, by market actors in collaboration, by civil society stakeholders.[53]
The position adopted in the UN Working Group on Internet Governance
distinguishes direct Internet governance mechanisms from those that
more properly are placed within telecommunications or media law.[54] The
EC 2001 *Governance* White Paper intended to: 'adopt new forms of governance that bring the Union closer to European citizens, make it more
effective, reinforce democracy in Europe and consolidate the legitimacy
of the institutions ... Moreover, the European Union must contribute to
the debate on world governance and play an important role in improving
the operation of international institutions.'[55]

The European adventure in co-regulation in Internet and wider consumer
protection legislation, as well as standards setting, was detailed in 2002,[56]
and became official policy in December 2003, with the Inter-Institutional
Agreement on Better Law-Making which defines co-regulation:

> 18. Co-regulation means the mechanism whereby a Community legisla-
> tive act entrusts the attainment of the objectives defined by the legislative
> authority to parties which are recognized in the field (such as economic
> operators, the social partners, non-governmental organizations, or associ-
> ations). This mechanism may be used on the basis of criteria defined in the
> legislative act so as to enable the legislation to be adapted to the problems
> and sectors concerned, to reduce the legislative burden by concentrating on
> essential aspects and to draw on the experience of the parties concerned.
>
> ...
>
> 20. In the context ... defined by the basic legislative act, the parties
> affected by that act may conclude voluntary agreements for the purpose of
> determining practical arrangements the Commission will verify whether
> or not those draft agreements comply with Community law (and, in par-
> ticular, with the basic legislative act).[57]

Paragraph 21 sets out in some detail the types of monitoring needed:
'The competent legislative authority will define in the act the relevant
measures to be taken in order to follow up its application ... for example,
for the regular supply of information by the Commission ... and, where
necessary ... an amendment to the legislative act.' This suggests substantial work programmes on compliance and adaptation of the legislative
act in the case of co-regulation, an area which the Commission monitors.
The annual report on Better Lawmaking still focuses on legislative acts

---

[53] For forms of regulation far removed from government, see Benkler (2006).
[54] See WGIG (2005) report.   [55] EC (2001).
[56] COM (2002a, b, c).
[57] Inter-Institutional Agreement on Better Law-Making (2003).

and the relationship with national lawmakers.[58] The agreement goes on to define self-regulation:

> 22. Self-regulation is defined as the possibility for economic operators, the social partners, non-governmental organizations or associations to adopt amongst themselves and for themselves common guidelines at European level (particularly codes of practice or sectoral agreements). As a general rule, this type of voluntary initiative does not imply that the Institutions have adopted any particular stance, in particular where such initiatives are undertaken in areas which are not covered by the Treaties or in which the Union has not hitherto legislated. As one of its responsibilities, the Commission will scrutinize self-regulation practices in order to verify that they comply with the provisions of the EC Treaty.
>
> 23. The Commission will notify the European Parliament and the Council of the self-regulation practices which it regards, on the one hand, as contributing to the attainment of the EC Treaty objectives and as being compatible with its provisions and, on the other, as being satisfactory in terms of the representativeness of the parties concerned, sectoral and geographical cover and the added value of the commitments given. It will, nonetheless, consider the possibility of putting forward a proposal for a legislative act, in particular at the request of the competent legislative authority or in the event of a failure to observe the above practices.

Self-regulation is viewed as making standards and practices across industry that the Commission, or a Member State, views agnostically in legislative terms (or pre-legislative, given the focus on areas that are emerging and which are not yet regulated), but which it intends to monitor to analyze the extent to which the self-regulation approaches the standards of 'representativeness' which co-regulation is meant to demonstrate as a best practice. The emphasis on emerging areas that have not yet been subject to regulation does suggest to the cynical commentator that the European spider will eventually trap the self-regulatory fly, but the Commission's insistence that this is not an inevitable journey is backed by its actions in such areas as technical standard setting. The Commission also sets out the circumstances in which forms of regulation short of state regulation will not be appropriate:

> 17. The Commission will ensure that any use of co-regulation or self-regulation is always consistent with Community law and that it meets the criteria of transparency (in particular the publicizing of agreements) and representativeness of the parties involved. It must also represent added value for the general interest. These mechanisms will not be applicable where fundamental rights or important political options are at stake or

---

[58] COM (2009b).

in situations where the rules must be applied in a uniform fashion in all Member States. They must ensure swift and flexible regulation which does not affect the principles of competition or the unity of the internal market.

Academic authors have been somewhat cynical about the legitimacy and representation in co-regulation,[59] especially as regards industry codes of conduct that are supported by government agencies, but Collins maintains that the 'Social Dialogue' has helped create 'labour law [as] the field in which co-regulation has been most successful',[60] explaining its conditionality as 'self-regulation [success] has only been [under] the credible threat of imminent action by the [European] Council'.[61] Moreover, the Court of First Instance has established that co-regulation is only legitimate where the 'representativeness' of relevant stakeholders is well displayed.[62] However, supervision and judicial review is still a necessary fudge in co-regulatory decision-making. Howells asks: 'who will decide what is so unimportant that it can be decided by co-regulation?'[63] This is particularly the case where human rights law is increasingly being applied commercially in various forms. It is self-evident that the more supervision and review resembles that in full state regulation, the less the benefits of flexibility and industry participation.

Towards a typology of self- and co-regulation

The Commission in 2005 analyzed co-regulation in terms of 'better regulation'.[64] This was immediately made part of internal EC practice in the *Impact Assessment Guidelines* which the Commission must follow before bringing forward a new legislative or policy proposal.[65] Ofcom's own managerial and regulatory analysis of co- and self-regulation conducted in 2008 arrives at similar conclusions.[66] The UK Better Regulation Executive has itself described co-regulation in detail, and has broken down eight elements short of 'classic' regulation that can enable regulatory compliance:

- taking no action
- providing information or guidance

---

[59] Scott and Trubek (2002).
[60] Collins (2004), Chapter 1, pp. 1–41.
[61] Collins (2004) at p. 33. See further Joerges *et al.* (2001).
[62] *UEAPME* v. *Council* [1998] Case T-135/96, ECR II-2335.
[63] Howells (2004), Chapter 5, pp. 119–130.
[64] COM (2005a).   [65] SEC (2005).
[66] See Ofcom (2008), largely the work of Tom Kiedrowski.

- using market-based instruments
- co-regulation
- self-regulation
- social partner agreements
- issuing recommendations
- using New Approach Directives (which permit compliance via stand-ards) and flexible Directives (its example being the revised Audio Visual Media Services Directive, an example explored later in this chapter) which permit wide discretion in the manner and form of implementation.[67]

It claims the advantage of co-regulation 'is that it provides a degree of certainty due to the backstop legal provisions whilst also encouraging innovation by allowing a flexible approach to implementation' and claim that 'Co-regulatory initiatives are more likely to be successful as those being regulated have scope to use their experience to design and implement their own solutions.'[68] Case studies suggest that success is mixed and many factors can jeopardize it. Kleinstuber explains 'If the State and the private regulators co-operate in joint institutions, this is called co-regulation. If this type of self-regulation is structured by the State but the State is not involved, the appropriate term is regulated self-regulation.'[69] This follows the nomenclature used by Hoffmann-Riem in his classic study of broadcasting.[70] It has been expanded on by Latzer.[71]

Verhulst and Latzer provide excellent analysis of the types of co-regulation beginning to develop and their institutional path depend-ency.[72] As Latzer explains, SROs form as single issue bodies, often crisis-driven.[73] We should therefore first ask whether they are an emer-gency solution or an ideal solution, and assume the former. He notes that there are different incentives for self-regulation, and economic as well as political analysis is needed, together with attention to the loss of

---

[67] Better Regulation Executive (2005) at p. 6.
[68] Better Regulation Executive (2005) at p. 26.
[69] Kleinstuber (2004), pp. 61–100.   [70] Hoffmann-Riem (2001).
[71] See Latzer et al. (2003), pp. 127–157; (2006), pp. 152–170; Saurwein and Latzer (2010), pp. 463–484.
[72] Note that the interviews with Verhulst and Latzer were carried out at the period in which they were carrying out their survey of co- and self-regulation for Ofcom: Latzer et al. (2007).
[73] Michael Latzer, interview with author, Leipzig, Germany, 25 May 2007.

constitutional guarantees.[74] He identifies five types of regulation short of statutory agency-led regulation:

(1) Co-regulation
(2) State-supported self-regulation
(3) Collective industry self-regulation
(4) Single company self-organization
(5) Self-help/restriction by users including rankings to impose restrictions on access to content.

He notes the direction of travel: both bottom-up transformations from self- into co-regulatory bodies, and top-down delegation from regulation into co- but not self-regulation. He also notes examples of 'zombie' self-regulation – where no-one will declare the patient dead or switch off the life support machine. I describe these as 'Potemkin' self-regulators, where there was a website and the appearance of a regulator but few resources, no physical address containing offices and little or no apparent adjudication or enforcement.[75] Note the gains and losses in the life cycle of regulation: will self-regulation ossify if it stays true to its principles of self-regulation? If ossification would result, does it matter other than to self-regulatory purists if a mature self-regulator is then made into a co-regulator? Price and Verhulst focus on AOL and internal self-organization.[76] They identify increasing realism in recognizing competition problems, emerging monopolies and dominance. Baird suggest that the 'bottom-up' approach from national regulation does not negate the vital role of government – in fact she suggests that they are clearly the leading policy player.[77] Verhulst and Price focus on the scope as well as function of self-regulation, and a grid pattern forming of national, regional and global responses.

Millwood-Hargrave also defines the progress from self- to co- to state regulation. Note that as she is mapping codes of practice, she refers to 'code guardian' rather than SRO. However, the institution is the same. To service provider, we can add content provider.[78]

---

[74] See formal regulatory elaborations at: Ofcom (2004, 2006b); Office of Regulation Review (1998); Oftel (2001).
[75] In the original 'Potemkin' villages, General Potemkin (or Potyomkin) infamously created facades of villages in 1787 to present an image of prosperity to Empress Catherine II of Russia, in which there was no substance to the buildings, a myth for which a website of equally contested veracity provides discussion, http://en.wikipedia.org/wiki/Potemkin_village.
[76] Price and Verhulst (2005).   [77] Baird (2002), p. 81.   [78] Millwood-Hargrave (2007a).

Table 2.1. *Case studies in spatial and regulatory context (from an interview with S. Verhulst, Head of Research, Markle Foundation, New York, with the author on 26 July 2007)*

	Co-regulatory	Self-regulatory	Organizational
Global	ICANN	IETF W3C	Creative Commons
Regional	PEGI INHOPE		Bebo
National	ICSTIS NICAM IWF Nominet ATVOD	IMCB	Second Life

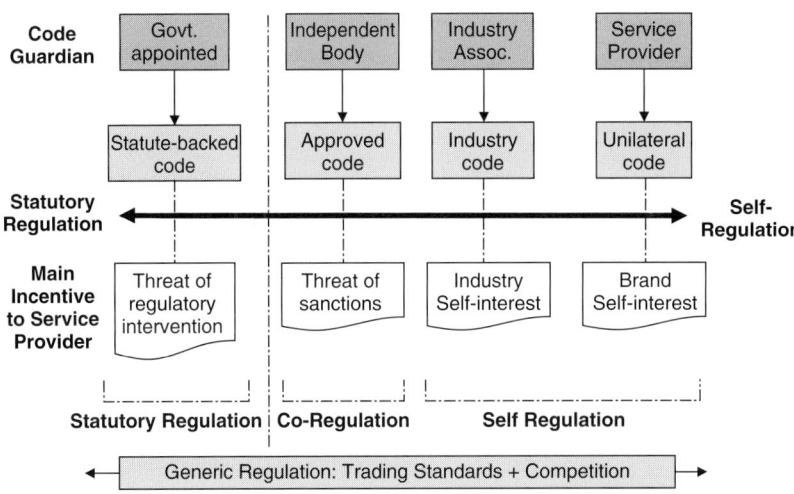

Figure 2.2.   Millwood-Hargrave diagram of SROs, regulatory type and incentive structure[79]

Does the vague legal definition matter? Yes, but legal scholars must admit to the Machiavellian arts that governments use to persuade self- and co-regulators to do their bidding. I have analyzed the previous litera- ture on Internet co- and self-regulation, identified case studies, and then established at least twelve states of regulation from the 'purity' of standard setting self-regulation to a form so close to regulation that the regulator itself internally recognizes the form as effectively regulation. Combining Latzer's approach with Verhulst's leads to Table 2.2.

[79] Millwood-Hargrave (2007a).

Table 2.2. *Twelve ideal types of self- and co-regulation*

Regulatory Scheme	Self-Co	Scale	Government involvement
'Pure' unenforced self-organization	Second Life	0	Informal interchange only – evolving partial industry forum building on players' own terms
Acknowledged self	Bebo, Creative Commons	1	Discussion but no formal recognition/approval
Ex post standardized self	W3C#	2	*Ex post* approval of standards
Standardized self	IETF	3	Formal approval of standards
Discussed self	IMCB	4	*Ex ante* informal consultation – but no sanction/approval/process audit
Recognized self	ISP Associations	5	Recognition of body – informal policy role
Co-founded self	FOSI#	6	*Ex ante* negotiation of body; no outcome role
Sanctioned self	PEGI# Euro mobile	7	Recognition of body – formal policy role (contact committee/process)
Approved self	Hotline#	8	*Ex ante* informal negotiation with government – with recognition/approval
Approved compulsory co-regulatory	ICANN	9	*Ex ante* negotiation with government – with sanction/approval/process audit
Scrutinized co-regulatory	NICAM# ATVOD	10	As 9 with annual budget/process approval
Independent Body (with stakeholder forum)	ICSTIS Nominet	11	Government imposed and co-regulated with taxation/compulsory levy

Hash tag indicates government-funded in whole or part
Source: Cave *et al.* (2008), p. xii.

I recognize that both options 0 and 11 amount to paradigms that are infrequently found in practice – pure self-regulation with no prior or later approval amounts to a self-regulatory body that is close to invisible in practice, and it is certainly the case that only the very 'early-stage' hybrid of self-regulation can be viewed in this space. Its doubtful and contested policy outcomes and processes often reflect a highly politically uncertain environment and it is thus perhaps unsurprising that politicians and bureaucrats do not intervene or even publicly comment on such manoeuvres. Nonetheless, these types are recognizable. Note that these approximate classifications do not relate to degree of government funding – the relationship between direct or indirect government funding is not consistent with policy involvement. For instance, government may choose to support a self-regulatory standard-setting activity as a genuinely deregulatory policy, as in scales 5 and 6. That may include government financial support or co-funding, a policy approached vigorously by the Commission since 1998. One can investigate whether such approaches are consistent with policy support via the failure of proposed policy interventions which sought to extend the role of such bodies.

Judicial review and co-regulation

MacSíthigh states that 'self-regulation retains its allure in some sectors (particularly media and communications), as it neatly side-steps complaints of State interference and keeps the costs of regulation off the public books'[80] even if that incurs costs for private actors dealing with such quasi-public bodies as the Press Complaints Commission (PCC) and Internet Watch Foundation. This is unsatisfactory in the 'Regulatory State'[81] with the devolution of authority from public to private bodies, in which the Internet is a particular exhibit of interest: almost every function in Internet content regulation is 'contracted out' or otherwise left to self-regulation. For instance, Internet Watch Foundation considers itself bound by its constitution as a charity, not by its potential public authority status. Note that private bodies with public functions have proved controversial in tortious liability terms.[82]

---

[80] MacSíthigh (2009), p. 3. See also MacSíthigh (2008), pp. 79–94.
[81] Majone (1999), pp. 1–24.
[82] See Cornford (2008), especially Chapter 2, pp. 9–16.

The nature of a public body, at least in the UK, was extended by the Human Rights Act 1998 (HRA), whose relevant (non-)definition in section 3 is: '(a) a court or tribunal, and (b) any person certain of whose functions are functions of a public nature'. In section 5 it further delimits the definition: 'a person is not a public authority by virtue only of subsection (3)(b) if the nature of the act is private'. Various cases have established that the mere nature of a contract with government authority does not qualify the private body as public, so mere heads of agreement or mutual recognition of a private self-regulatory body with a government agency will not necessarily give grounds for claiming its 'public' nature. While there are moves to designate public bodies more widely under European and UK law, no significant change that would affect the status of such charitable self-regulatory bodies appears likely. The government broadly expects equivalence between definitions of public bodies under HRA,[83] case law on judicial review under the Supreme Court Act 1981, and Freedom of Information Act 2000.[84] MacSíthigh notes that the Information Commissioner was pressed to include the Press Complaints Commission and premium telephone regulator within 'public authorities', and the BBC already has been so designated by the Supreme Court.[85] Horizontal indirect effect is predicted to become more extensive than direct effect, as section 6(1) and section 6(3)(a) HRA provide a limit to review of public bodies, while at least in theory common law is enabled to take an unlimited liability towards human rights for private bodies as well as public.[86] Note the deference paid to public bodies in judicial review still continues, if somewhat weakened since HRA.[87] Section 6(3)(b) also applies to 'any person certain of whose functions are functions of a public nature' within the definition of a public authority, making it unlawful for that body to contravene Convention rights when performing a public function.[88]

[83] On the growth of modern human rights law more generally, and Essex Human Rights Centre's contribution to it, see Boyle (2008), pp. 1–15.

[84] Ministry of Justice (2007) at para. 19.

[85] *BBC* v. *Sugar* [2009] UKHL 9, noting that Part IV of Schedule 1 to the Freedom of Information Act 1998 provides that the BBC is a 'public authority' 'in respect of information held for purposes other than those of journalism art or literature', which in this case meant disclosure under section 50(3) of the Act was required to be always considered. The Commissioner thus must treat hybrid authorities as always being 'public authorities' for the purposes of section 1, irrespective of the nature of the requested information.

[86] Phillipson (1999, 2007); Raphael (2000).

[87] For media and communications regulation to 1996, see Marsden (1996), p. 114.

[88] *Poplar Housing and Regeneration Community Association Limited* v. *Donoghue* (Poplar Housing) [2001] EWCA Civ 595 – wherein a housing association providing the local

European Community law, by contrast, limits the effects on individuals.[89] The distinction drawn in *YL* by the Supreme Court majority is critical,[90] in narrowly defining public function to 'mirror' the European Court of Human Rights (ECtHR) jurisprudence:[91]

> The mere fact that a private body was contractually obliged by a public authority to provide a service that the public authority would otherwise have been required to provide did not mean that the private body in question was performing a public function. A private body would be regarded as performing a public function were it to exercise a governmental function, wielding coercive powers. Nor was it sufficient that the local authority was paying for the service provided by the private body, (although this would indicate the existence of a public function were the local authority to pay for the service as a whole, or to subsidize the provision of this service) or that the function in question was subject to regulation by the government.[92]

Therefore, as the service provided by the care home was that of accommodation, carried out for commercial purposes and subject to commercial regulation through private law, as opposed to the public function of arranging accommodation according to a statutory duty, it was not liable. By contrast, breaches of the tort of privacy have been held to be subject to obligations on private actors in several cases: *Campbell, Murray, McKennitt* and *Von Hannover*.[93] Of course, this only affects

---

authority's duty to provide homeless with shelter was found to be performing the local authority's function and thus subject to review.

[89] Young (2009) states (p. 162) that: 'This contrasts with the position in European Community law, where the obligation to interpret national law in a manner compatible with European Community law does reach a limit when this requires the creation of an obligation in criminal law, or a heightening of a criminal penalty', citing C-80/86 *Kolpinghuis Nijmegen* [1987] ECR 3969 and C-387/02 *Silvio Berlusconi* [2005] ECR I-3565.

[90] *YL (Appellant)* v. *Birmingham City Council and others* [2007] UKHL 27 on appeal from: [2007] EWCA Civ 27, see www.publications.parliament.uk/pa/ld200607/ldjudgmt/jd070620/birm-1.htm.

[91] For the 'mirror principle', see Lewis (2007, 2009).

[92] *YL* (2007) per Lords Scott, Mance and Neuberger, summarized in Young (2009), p. 166. This narrow interpretation was followed in *London and Quadrant Housing Trust v. R. (on the application of Weaver* [2009] EWCA Civ 587; [2009] All ER (D) 179 (Jun), further restricting rights by focusing on the definition of private acts in section 6(5) of the HRA 1998, the nature of the act and the function performed.

[93] *Campbell v. Mirror Group Newspapers plc* [2004] UKHL 22; [2004] 2 AC 457 [15]; *McKennitt v. Ash* 37 [2006] EWCA Civ 1714; [2007] 3 WLR 194; *Murray v. Express Newspapers plc* [2008] EWCA Civ 446; [27]; [2008] 3 WLR 1360; *Von Hannover v. Germany* [2004] ECHR 59320/00 16 BHRC 545.

regulatory organizations inasmuch as they publish details of complaints and cases adjudicated, but *Campbell* in particular is a construction, not a 'mirror' to the ECtHR's jurisprudence,[94] unless one accepts the controversial decision in *Von Hannover* as good authority. Not only have English courts proscribed reporting by private media organizations above and beyond the ECtHR, they have also restricted its alter ego, the right to freedom of expression under Article 10 ECHR in the case of public bodies, in *Pro Life* v. *BBC* and *Animal Defenders International* v. *Secretary of State for Culture, Media and Sport.*[95] This restrictive attitude to free speech – deferring to Parliamentary will – has been noted by several scholars, as Parliament expressly delegated to the BBC judgment in matters of taste and decency, and noted in a Section 19(1)(b) statement that its restrictions on political advertising could be contrary to the ECHR.[96]

Ofcom's use of non-legal instruments, notably the Broadcasting Code for its licensees, has been found reviewable in the recent case of *R. (Gaunt)* v. *Ofcom;*[97] John Gaunt – a wannabe English Rush Limbaugh – was summarily dismissed from his TalkSport radio presenting contract for breaching the Ofcom broadcast code in an abusive rant at an interviewee. Ofcom found that the interview breached regulations 2.1 and 2.3 of the Ofcom Broadcasting Code under the Communications Act 2003. Gaunt claimed that Ofcom's finding was a disproportionate interference with his freedom of expression and an infringement of his human rights. The court found for Ofcom, though finding that proportionality of the code and its enforcement was reviewable.

Sticks not carrots: why Americans don't 'do' co-regulation

Co-regulation is a little-described or understood technique in US literature and regulatory policy, and my approach is based on European literature and policy. The concept of co-regulation is alien to the binary approach to regulation of much US law and economics scholarship,[98]

---

[94] See Moreham (2006), p. 606; Rudolf (2006), p. 533; Hatziz (2005), p. 143.
[95] *R. (ProLife Alliance)* v. *British Broadcasting Corporation* (ProLife) [2003] UKHL 23; [2004] 1 AC 185; *R.(Animal Defenders International)* v. *Secretary of State for Culture, Media and Sport* (ADI) [2008] UKHL 15; [2008] 1 AC 1312.
[96] Barendt (2003), p. 580; Lewis and Cumper (2009).
[97] *R. (Gaunt)* v. *Ofcom (Liberty intervening)* [2010] EWHC 1756 (Admin); [2010] WLR (D) 180, at www.lawreports.co.uk/WLRD/2010/QBD/R(Gaunt)_v_Ofcom.html.
[98] Posner and Posner (1971), p. 22; Noll and Owen (1983).

though governance scholars from political science see the many shades of grey I have described. Joskow and Noll state: 'regulation must accord rights of participation and policy review to anyone substantially affected by its policies, which invites strategies and tactics that, at best, retard the competitive process and, with depressing frequency, invite cartelization'.[99] Competition law is one lens through which to view self-regulation, and therefore co-regulation can be seen to obscure the antitrust case against cartels, and it is clearly the case that the US has historically taken antitrust more seriously than its fast-improving students in the European Union.[100] Newman and Bach state:

> In the US, the government induces self-regulation largely through the threat of stringent formal rules and costly litigation should industry fail to deliver socially desired outcomes. Industry thus views self-regulation as a pre-emptive effort to avoid government involvement. The relationship between the public and private sector is spotty, formal and frequently adversarial. We label the ideal-typical US model legalistic self-regulation.[101]

By contrast to this legalistic self-regulation, they claim that: 'In Europe, public sector representatives meet with industry and agree on a joint course of action. Here, private and public sectors view each other as partners in an often-informal self-regulatory process. Coordinated self-regulation is the term we use to describe the European ideal-typical model.' They explain that in the EU:

> the public sector is generally accepted as a participant in the self-regulatory process, albeit mostly as a facilitator. The EC will make use of its control over R&D funds to sponsor self-regulatory initiatives and to foster the growth of transnational industry networks. The executive branch is also likely to play a role in the creation of intermediary institutions should business alone fail. It will thus play a catalytic role in the process of self-regulation.[102]

---

[99] Joskow and Noll (1999), p. 1252.
[100] Germany's post-1946 ordoliberal rigorous enforcement of antitrust rules has been the European exception.
[101] Newman and Bach (2004), p. 388.
[102] Newman and Bach (2004) at p. 398 continue: 'a stark contrast to the much more hands-off US executive. The judiciary, by contrast, should not play as significant a role in Europe, particularly on the EU level. Yet the more active the courts, agencies, and legislatures on the Member State level are, the more credible the threat of regulatory fragmentation and hence the stronger the incentives for close cooperation between transnationally organized businesses and the Commission in the joint pursuit of coordinated self-regulation.' They cite European approaches as in Duina (1999).

Newman and Bach identify the midway between 'market regulation' (what Latzer calls self-organization) and regulation by 'carrot and stick'; public involvement in self-regulation:

> has greater carrot capacity if it can offer financial and logistical incentives to bring about sustained participation of organized private interests in the regulatory process. Toward the high end of a scale is its ability to formally delegate regulatory authority to organized private interests and/or to make industry rules enforceable in the courts, an arrangement ... aptly called 'private interest government'.[103]

This 'private interest government' is a model readily observable in Internet regulation, and accepted with conditions by the US courts in, for instance, *National Association of Broadcasters* [1976].[104] Law professor and Deputy Assistant Attorney General Philip J. Weiser has proposed co-regulation of network neutrality principles, the control over ISP throttling and blocking of content, while acknowledging that this is a radical and foreign practice for US regulators.[105] Nevertheless, recognizing its useful compromise between legitimacy and flexibility in view of the Ofcom 2008 study, he proposes an adaptation of the European approach that I outlined in a previous monograph.[106]

Newman and Bach explain the variety of regulation as well as co-regulation:

> Just as carrot capacity should not be thought of as a binary variable, stick capacity takes on multiple forms with varying degrees of intensity. For our immediate purpose, stick capacity can be considered higher the easier it is for the public sector to regulate an industry without regard for organized private interests ... Whereas the public sector in the U.S. appears better endowed with stick capacity than with carrot capacity, the opposite is true for Europe.[107]

---

[103] Though they admit different political cultures have different abilities to intervene (Newman and Bach (2004), p. 392): 'Public sector carrot capacity is a critical institutional ingredient for a system of coordinated capitalism. Much attention has been paid in recent years to variation in the extent of business coordination across political economies. The Rhine-ish and Scandinavian economies, for example, are said to be characterized by a high degree of non-competitive interactions among formal competitors within an industry.'

[104] *National Association of Broadcasters* v. *F.C.C.* 180 U.S. App. D.C. 259, 265, 554 F.2d 1118, 1124 [1976]. See also *Writers Guild Of America, West, Inc.* v. *F.C.C.*, 423 F. Supp. 1064 [1976].

[105] Weiser (2009), p. 583, comparing securities with telecoms regulation.

[106] Marsden (2010), repeating and elaborating on conclusions from earlier work.

[107] Newman and Bach (2004), p. 393.

Table 2.3. *Newman/Bach sources and extent of public sector capacity*

	Source	Extent US	Extent EU
Carrot capacity	Conferral of status	Medium	Medium
	Finance and logistics	Weak	Strong
	Ability to delegate	Weak	Strong
Stick capacity	Agencies	Strong	Weak
	Courts/judicial review	Strong	Medium
	Federalism/multi-level governance	Strong	Strong
Resulting form of self-regulation		Legalistic	Coordinated

Source: Newman and Bach (2004), p. 397.

The carrot capacity for the EC has made it pragmatic to fund standards and *ex ante* support self-regulation in cases where the US would simply *ex post* regulate via competition law.

This leads to substantial US–European differences, which may create 'transatlantic competition of standardization philosophies … [in] consumer protection systems'. Data privacy and content filtering have been two such arenas in the 2000s, as case studies reveal.

Newman and Bach state their research questions regarding sectoral self-regulatory effectiveness as: 'How homogenous are stakeholder interests? How influential are existing industry associations? How easily can intermediary institutions be created if such institutions are lacking or insufficient?' Reflecting the overriding US antitrust concern, they state that oligopoly can make self-regulation sustainable, whereas free-riders undermine its effectiveness in more competitive sectors.

European examples of co-regulation now abound in this field, notably in Internet security but also in child safety and filtering, as well as standard setting and social network privacy regulation. President Sarkozy of France has made it clear that government needs to further tighten its grip on the Internet: 'Regulating Internet to correct the excesses and abuses that arise from the total absence of rules is a moral imperative.'[108] It is clear that both soft law and soft enforcement play a vital regulatory role,

[108] Sarkozy (2010).

which legal positivists would be in danger of overlooking or minimizing by a failure to consider the law in its regulatory context.

Conclusion: co-regulation and constitutionalism

The space within which the Commission, Member States and corporations have been able to establish their Internet regulation arrangements without much parliamentary or judicial interference may be drawing to an end.[109] If greater scrutiny results, this is likely to lead to greater use of co-regulation with real accountability and legitimacy, as well as increasing costs of regulation and hence market entry barriers. However, the loss of dynamism that this heralds should not be the cause of great regret: as Wu has suggested,[110] the early dynamic period of Internet market entry has drawn to an end (with incumbent network operators, mobile networks and content behemoths such as Facebook and Google), and the innovation that does take place is in the flourishing standards for self-regulation that takes place in the successful and fully functioning IETF and W3C. The increasing co-regulation of content that is taking place has been postponed for longer than many observers thought likely or credible.

[109] See generally Black (1998).
[110] Wu (2010) discusses the calcification and ossification of previous communications markets and applies this to the Internet.

3

Self-organization and social networks

This first substantive case study chapter begins with forms of self-organization that have not yet become self-regulation. Prior to self-regulation, there is a step that is essentially the relationships within a community, policed by that community.[1] For instance, clubs elect executives and create constitutions (rules) for that club. With the increasing consumer-citizen use of the Internet, new services and new business models have been created for those users.[2] There are many user-created environments in which bottom-up rules have claimed to be set,[3] but I focus on three specific UGC case studies,[4] which were in early 2007 the poster children of self-organization: virtual-world Second Life, copyright reforming Creative Commons and social network Bebo. The first has since declined in popularity and its co-founder has departed, the last has seen sale, decline relative to behemoth Facebook, and resale,[5] but Creative Commons continues to support its functions and has been officially recognized by several governments as a type of copyright licensing system that can support open data sharing.[6] I represent these early-stage organization schemes in the table below, acknowledging that their regulatory effect is voluntary and not supported or recognized by government,[7] the closest approach being 'acknowledgement' that they exist,[8] neither a vote of support nor a condemnation.

Some ISPs display far greater responsiveness to empowering users to create and regulate content, using Social Networking Sites (SNS) and virtual worlds as well as mash-ups and other techniques collectively

---

[1] Suzor (in press) constructs an argument based on private law regimes and the consent of the society member, using doctrines drawn from Dicey (1959), p. 157.
[2] For an early analysis, see Priest (1997), p. 238; Spinello (2002); Mayer-Schönberger and Ziewitz (2007), p. 225.
[3] Wu (2003), pp. 679–751.
[4] See IDATE–TNO–IViR (2008).   [5] BBC (2010a).
[6] See Marsdenand Cave et al. (2006) cited at para. 48 in Mayo and Steinberg (2007).
[7] Posner and Posner (2007); Ellickson (1991), p. 208; Posner (2000), pp. 1781–1819; Murray (2006).
[8] See IDATE–TNO–IViR (2008), at pp. 31, 33.

Table 3.1. *Placing self-organization in the regulatory schematic*

Regulatory scheme	Self-Co	Scale	Government involvement
'Pure' unenforced self	Second Life	0	Informal interchange only
Acknowledged self	Bebo Creative Commons	1	Discussion but no formal rec- ognition/ approval

constituting the Web2.0 phenomenon. Some offer increased security and protection from harmful content for users who desire, or in any case receive, 'walled gardens', less-open Internet experiences. Zittrain states: 'Control over software – and the ability of PC users to run it – rather than control over the network, will be a future battleground for Internet regulation, a battleground primed by an independently moti- vated movement by consumers away from open, generative PCs and toward more highly regulable endpoint platforms.'[9] These platforms are games consoles, mobile handsets, and other 'closed' walled garden networks. Whereas the PC environment is arguably becoming more open, with open source and free programs and applications, peer-to- peer (p2p) distribution,[10] and royalty-free licensing, the mobile and games environments remain subject to vertically integrated network operators.

Difficulties with self-organization include variously: user inertia to default settings; the decision by e-commerce providers to make websites almost impossible to use selectively for average users; and 'The myth of the super-user', the belief that users are technically competent and will self-select.[11] Börzel states: 'A qualitative comparative case study will explore when and how private actors take action for, or against, compli- ance, and to what extent their action facilitates or inhibits compliance. My ultimate aim is to develop a model, which specifies conditions under which private actors are likely to facilitate or inhibit compliance with

---

[9] Zittrain (2006b), p. 254. See also Zittrain (2006a).
[10] Mayer-Schönberger (2003).
[11] See Sunstein (2002b), pp. 106–134; Weinberg (1997), pp. 453–482.

international institutions.'[12] The intention in this chapter is to explore the alternatives.

Web2.0 and alternative content regulation

The economic fundamentals driving Web2.0 are that broadband has become ubiquitous for many. With UGC, the user is enabled to 'pull' content and even adapt and mix content into a 'mash-up'. A mash-up is a combination of existing media reworked into a new and innovative type. 'Data mashing' makes innovative 'recombinant' uses of existing media, e.g., remixed music tracks or the integration of maps with other information. Examples of Web2.0-type applications are varied:

(1) p2p sharing networks (such as *Kazaa* and *BitTorrent*);
(2) Photo-sharing sites (such as *Flickr*);
(3) Video-sharing sites (such as *YouTube* and *Dailymotion*);
(4) Online games (such as *World of Warcraft*);
(5) Public SNS (such as *MySpace, Facebook* and *Bebo*);
(6) Blogs and Wikis, including *Wikipedia*, a user-generated encyclopedia and *WikiLeaks*, a whistleblowers' site; and
(7) Executive SNS (such as *LinkedIn* and *ASMALLWORLD).*

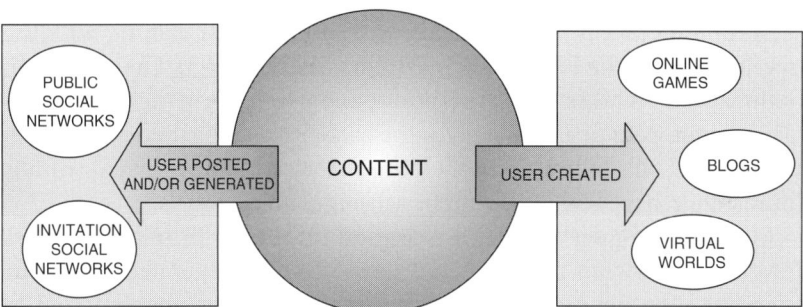

Figure 3.1.   UGC typology

The range of SNS is broad, but easily divided into those that are open to anyone, and exclusive 'walled garden' invitation-only sites. In terms of UGC, we can distinguish online games from the more interactive virtual worlds, the former generally making modifications to a mass media

---

[12] Börzel (2000), p. 2.

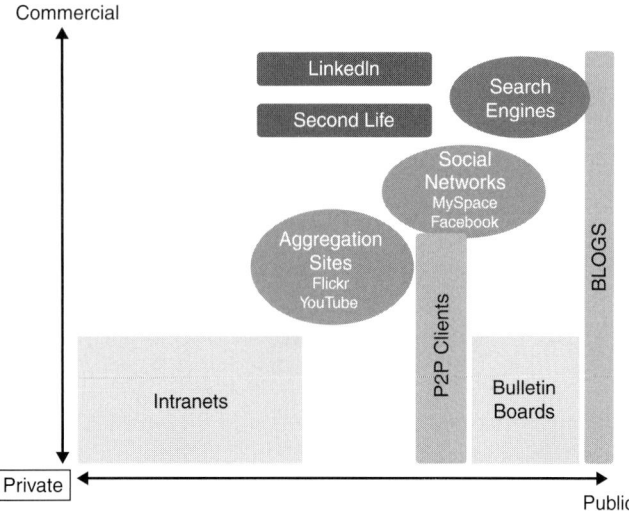

Figure 3.2.   UGC regulation mapped using axes public/private and private/ commercial

gaming software package, the latter involving modification including writing of new code for the 'virtual world'. Blogs and Wikis are collaborative author tools which are largely UGC. Note that there is no cross-sectoral SRO in any of these fields, except for online gaming with the development of the PEGI Online system (see Chapter 5). The regulation of these systems takes place at corporate and user level, in the same way as Usenet sites were first regulated in the early 1990s.[13] That does not mean that there is no innovation in their regulatory structure: virtual worlds, for instance, have built up elaborate self-regulatory models.

Media-sharing services are not communities as such, and there is less interaction between members and therefore little regulated behaviour specific to the networks, except copyright and other unauthorized or inflammatory content that is subject to notice and take-down (NTD). I show the various types of social network modelling against their commercial or public (as opposed to private) characteristics.

Social networking on the Internet did not begin with Web2.0 and note bulletin boards (Usenets, which have a long history, substantially predating the formation of the IETF) and intranets predate the commercial Internet. P2P programmes have carried advertising in the past, notably

---

[13] See Lessig (1999); Goldsmith and Wu (2006).

Kazaa. Note that professional networks such as LinkedIn, and monetized virtual world 'Second Life', are more professional in character than advertising-driven mass market social networks and aggregation sites, such as Bebo or YouTube. Blogs are predominantly non-commercial in character, though those with highest readerships may syndicate advertising. It is clear from the description of the number of users and viewers of SNS that, as a mass phenomenon, it would not be possible to regulate the posters of content directly. On the Internet, as earlier discussed, the content host (typically an ISP but not in these cases) is subject to a NTD regulatory regime. This does not require *ex ante* regulation, but does require content hosts to 'take down' users' content which they have been informed (given 'notice') either breaches law or otherwise offends against their terms of use. There is thus a shift of liability. ECD provides for clarification of the applicable liability regime to Internet intermediaries (with no strict liability), sets out the exoneration conditions for certain types of intermediary activity (transmission and/or storage of third-party content) and does not affect the liability of the actual content provider (which is left to national law). The host's limited liability is to ensure that users are only able to use the service under conditions or terms that explicitly permit the content host to take down material that is illegal, often extending this power to material that is offensive, of an unsuitably adult nature and so on.

Take the example of video-sharing site, YouTube. On YouTube, the editorial controller, if such exists, is the person who posts the content. For regulatory purposes, YouTube users post the content and the YouTube website reacts *ex post* on receiving complaints regarding breaches of copyright or offensive content.[14] This is fundamentally different to traditional broadcast regulation, where the editorial controller (the broadcaster) is responsible for the content *ex ante* – before it is offered to the public. YouTube has claimed that it removes objected-to video within fifteeen minutes.[15] The Child Exploitation and Online Protection Centre claims: 'Web2.0 ... has changed the way children and young people interact online, affording them more creative control over their online experience ... there is a strong positive association between opportunities and risks in this context; increasing opportunities for online interaction also present challenges for those tasked with the regulation of online content, behaviour and offline consequences.'[16] While it is no doubt true that

---

[14] See *Viacom International, Inc. v. YouTube, Inc.* [2010] No. 07 Civ. 2103.
[15] See China People's Daily (2006).
[16] CEOP (2007b), p. 11.

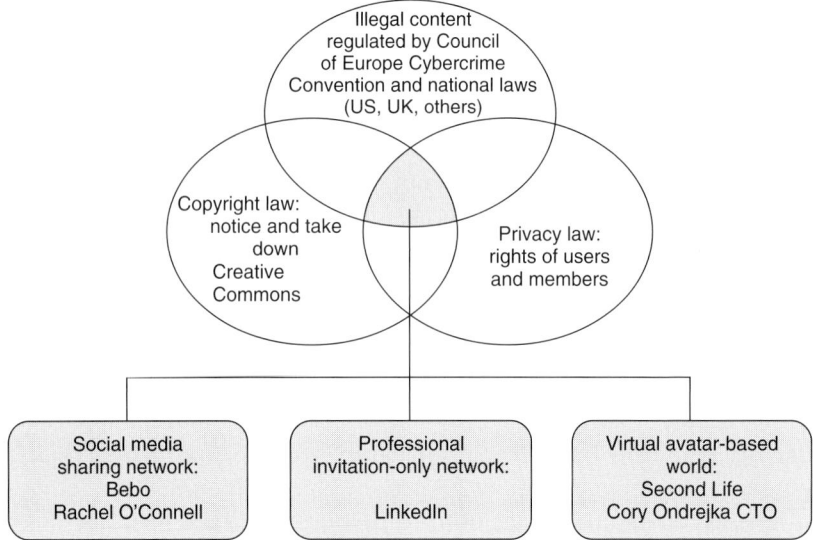

Figure 3.3.   Social networks self-regulate under national and international law

opportunity presents problems and solutions,[17] it also allows for what I term 'Regulation2.0', mass user self-regulation via Web2.0 tools to report abuse, and flag and label content. SNS have membership and usage rules, which entitle them to suspend or expel members accordingly. Members can report and even rate the content or comments of others. There is substantial self-policing by residents of these communities. I illustrate how SNS self-regulate within national and international law frameworks.

DiPerna describes SNS as 'connector' sites and identifies interrelated characteristics, discovery and coordination:

> Connectors make discovery more powerful and accurate through social search and trust-building applications. In terms of coordination, connectors are more efficient than other online community websites because they have the capacity to maneuver (sic), or network, specialized communications and transactions for users in specific situations. Often social search and social networking applications are mixed together on connector websites and previously have been regarded by and large as a single application.[18]

---

[17] European Network Information Security Agency (2007).
[18] DiPerna (2006), p. 7.

Two generations of SNS have been claimed, though in fact most are simply hybrids, and the distinction between pre-Internet 'bubble' (1999) sites and post-'bubble' (2003 onwards) is as much a matter of investor distinction as reflecting techno-socioeconomic changes among users. That is, there is a distinction more based on availability and funding of such sites than necessarily a profound step change in performance or utility. The two generations are:

(1) 'First generation' World Wide Web-based, emphasizing social search applications for online dating (e.g., Match.com), online trading and classifieds (e.g., Craigslist), online auctions (e.g., eBay) and reunion (e.g., Friends Reunited, Classmates.com).
(2) Web2.0 from 2002, using new software functionality and broadband domestic connections, explicit professional (e.g., LinkedIn), elite (e.g., ASMALLWORLD) and social (e.g., Bebo, MySpace, Facebook) networking applications based on referral through mutual friends or interests.

SNS growth reflects a broadening user base from a predominantly teenage and student origin.

SNS and regulatory approaches

Social networks

Bebo

I begin with an examination of a large social network, Bebo, founded by CEO Michael Birch[19] in 2005 and with an estimated 31m members in 2007, which, it claimed, made it the largest SNS in the UK, Ireland and New Zealand in that year.[20] Funding included $15m from Benchmark Capital, which paid back spectacularly in the 2008 sale to AOL.[21] The executive team that ran the organization also set up a number of other organizations such as Birthday Alarm, Ringo and Friendster. Bebo's primary income comes not from subscription fees (subscribing is free to all), but from advertising revenue, with two main sources, traditional online advertising and product placement or sponsorship. Bebo's partnerships with other companies also bring in revenue.

---

[19] Michael Birch (2007) nPost.com (www.npost.com/interview.jsp?intID=INT00160).
[20] http://en.wikipedia.org/wiki/Bebo.
[21] Taken from the Bebo website, 'about us' section (www.Bebo.com/StaticPage.jsp?StaticPageId=2517103831).

Bebo was the most 'European' of the top SNS in 2007, with over 60 per cent of its unique users based in Europe.[22] Although Bebo officially started in January 2005, it was given a major relaunch in July 2005, particularly focusing on schools and universities in English-speaking countries.[23] One of the driving factors for Bebo was that it would be able to have unlimited photo capability and it would be personalizable for individuals who did not have the skills to write their own HTML (through whiteboards and downloadable skins). The Bebo business model evolved to include music, TV and film as part of its remit. Since it partnered with other organizations to provide many of these services, the regulatory pressure was often taken on by the partner, previously supplying the service that requires regulating.[24]

The major regulatory issues that Bebo faces also affect all SNS. Since SNS work in multiple countries they are subject to a number of different regulatory regimes. Bebo responded to this pressure by appointing an expert in Internet safety, to oversee its safety procedures.[25] Child safety depends on age verification, a key aspect for identification.[26] The UK's Children's Charities' Coalition on Internet Safety (UKCCIS) states:

> 12. Far from having an incentive to discover the true ages of their customers, users or web site visitors, far from having an incentive to collect accurate data about them, very many web sites have a material interest in not knowing the real ages.
>
> 13. The foregoing observations are particularly true in relation to the so called 'free internet' i.e., financed largely through advertising.
>
> 21. Consideration should be given to requiring all companies to perform a 'child safety audit' prior to the release of any new product or service on to the internet, particularly if it is going to be made available on the 'free internet'.[27]

Bebo's Chief Safety Officer Rachel O'Connell aimed at the majority (ideally all) staff being trained in safety issues: 'Nothing should go on until it's been through the safety check – and partners should also satisfy that requirement.'[28] It is a challenge to open the environment to third parties

---

[22] ComScore.com at www.comscore.com/press/release.asp?press=1555.
[23] Birch at 'Online Personals Watch', available at http://onlinepersonalswatch.typepad.com/news/2006/03/online_personal_4.html.
[24] See www.Bebo.com/Press.jsp for details of partnerships.
[25] See www.Bebo.com/Press.jsp?PressPageId=1533927716.
[26] Although age verification has many people struggling to identify the best approach: for more details see Thierer (2007).
[27] Children's Charities' Coalition on Internet Safety (2010), p. 3.
[28] O'Connell (2007).

while maintaining those standards, competitively differentiating Bebo from Facebook and Second Life as more third-party facing networks. As the role had only existed for a year at Bebo and is not replicated in the industry over a longer period, the cost-benefit of the chief safety officer role was unclear. The enforcement of safety within Bebo was driven by: policy groups; media and users; law enforcement; and CEO initiative. Bebo staff physically checked all photographs uploaded onto the network for taste and decency. It was hoped that its regulatory type would create precedents for others in the industry to follow, but it represents a practice to which Facebook does not conform. Bebo has also launched safesocial-networking.com to educate schools and add to the curriculum. It follows and showcases the launch of the safety pages. A centre in Bebo called 'Be Well' is aimed at suicide prevention amongst 13–30-year-old men, and with engagement by institutions.

Part of the Bebo equation is that as the market is maturing, ethical responsibility is becoming more ingrained. The substantial resource implications of such a closely monitored system may not be scalable to networks with either more mature (and therefore advertiser friendly) memberships or larger populations. The future of Bebo and the other social network sites is volatile and dynamic.[29] As the market matures, there is consolidation, as seen in South Korea, Japan and Facebook.[30] Bebo was a privately held organization which – typically for a start-up – made it difficult to evaluate its activities and policies. Bebo has not been the subject of any evaluations that are in the public domain. It is important therefore to track the growth and innovation for Bebo through its own corporate website, although this will only provide the 'official' view of growth and innovation within the company.

Police policy on SNS is rapidly developing and preliminary analysis has been undertaken, as discussed in the Second Life case study.[31] Facebook in 2010 found itself forced to push back against CEOP attempts to introduce a 'panic button' on every webpage, which would have overwhelmed both Facebook and the police. Bebo does have a 'report abuse' which exists on every page next to the profile picture – the abuse team sees both people's details on an automated basis. Callanan of INHOPE states that: 'There's no reasonable and proportional debate about what's appropriate and effective

---

[29] Braithwaite (2006).
[30] Joanna Shields, interview with President International for Bebo, in the *Media Guardian*, available at http://media.guardian.co.uk/mediaguardian/story/0,2147332,00.html.
[31] CEOP (2006).

in the modern world.'[32] He argues that as Bebo has direct reporting to Irish police, the latter receive direct reports from kids mainly about other children. As police are under-resourced, other civil society groups are unwilling to push back and state that police are overwhelmed. O'Connell explains that SNS usage cannot be a 'total anonymity/privacy' issue. She believes that fundamentally risk analysis has to encompass the new realities, identifying user behaviour and safety mechanisms as they develop. For O'Connell, the 'approach is about policy guidelines, and risk minimization in product development'. To take a rival example, in Australia: 'Communications Minister Stephen Conroy said [in May 2010] Facebook had a complete disregard for users' privacy ... Mozelle Thompson, Privacy Counsel at Facebook and former Federal Trade Commissioner (US) stated that: "The proposal that they're making is a static proposal for a dynamic problem. And so because of that, I'm not sure it's going to work." '[33]

In the case of privately-owned Facebook, its customers are its advertisers and its shareholders are its investors. Account holders, of whom there were 650 million as I write in November 2010, are merely users of the network, translatable into advertiser dollars. As a California corporation, it owes fealty to European privacy rules only to the extent that its operations may be affected by negative national rulings that would deny it service. As a result, it has taken a very liberal – i.e., minimal – approach to privacy with its users' data,[34] attracting substantial opprobrium over a period of years but little evidence of declining usage. Until and unless privacy commissioners get tough, advertisers are told to boycott or courts issue injunctions preventing business, UK[35] and European parliamentary calls for an Internet Users' bill of rights are not significantly affecting shareholder value, though the company observes due diligence by employing Lord Richard Allan as European Policy Director to engage with regulators. UK Minister Ed Vaizey informed Parliament on 28 October 2010 that:

> I intend to write to the major ISPs and websites, such as Google and Facebook, asking for a meeting ... It is certainly worth the Government brokering a conversation with the internet industry about setting up a mediation service for consumers who have legitimate concerns that their privacy has been breached or that online information about them is inaccurate or constitutes a gross invasion of their privacy to discuss whether there is any way to remove access to that information.[36]

[32] Callanan (2007).   [33] AAP (2010).
[34] See Facebook (2010); see also Constine (2010).
[35] Hansard Westminster Hall (2010b).
[36] Hansard Westminster Hall (2010a).

A mediation service for privacy would be in addition to the NTD regime under the ECD.[37] He expressly compared this to Nominet mediation for consumer issues with registrars (see Chapter 4). A very high proportion of under-13s appear to use Facebook, which is against the website's terms of use. According to EUKidsOnline,[38] from a survey of 23,000 children, by the age of 11–12, 48 per cent of children have a social network profile, rising to 72 per cent by age 13–14. EUKidsOnline states: 'it seems likely that significant numbers of "underage" children are using [SNS]. In its next report in 2011, we will analyse findings in this section for [SNS] separately.'[39]

Carr argues that European concerns for user privacy and child safety can create a new environment in which regulation emerges on an individual company basis. He argues that: 'Our job is not to anguish over the rights of small companies and barriers to competition. If that means making it too expensive for small companies, then that's the cost of being in the business.'[40] This differentiates Europe from US self-regulation, and raises the classic regulatory issue as to whether a race to the top (quality) or the bottom (removing any protections) results, in the absence of government intervention. It may be that recruiting specialists in child safety is an entry barrier to new start-ups – venture capital may neither fully understand the policy environment or invest the money for a start-up. In the US, child safety is a lesser concern than in Europe, but gambling is the exception to any general perception of deregulation. Given the valuation of successful SNS Facebook, the cost of child protection is trivial. York has assessed terms of use and blocking for Facebook, YouTube, Flickr, Blogger and Twitter, and also cites *Marsh* v. *Alabama* [1946], and *New Jersey Coalition Against War in the Middle East* v. *J.M.B. Realty Corp.* [1994][41] holding that shopping malls must permit leafletting on societal issues, subject to reasonable standards set by the malls – taken by York as extending to Facebook in the online environment.[42] New European SNS start-ups may be unable to secure funding, which means there may be a real innovation issue. Note that the child safety issue and associated management costs are borne by individual subsidiaries of even large multinationals. Regulatory fragmentation across Member States, absent of an agreed industry standard, will slow growth of pan-European SNS.

[37] Espiner (2010).   [38] Livingstone *et al.* (2010).
[39] See Livingstone *et al.* (2010) at p. 40.   [40] Carr (2007).
[41] *New Jersey Coalition Against War in the Middle East* v. *J.M.B. Realty Corp.* 650 A.2d 757 (N.J.) [1994].
[42] York (2010).

Virtual worlds

In Asia, Europe and North America, a new type of interactive experience has become increasingly popular, that of online 'virtual worlds'. The self-regulatory approach of these 'virtual worlds' is worth consideration as an alternative to the *ex ante* broadcast/*ex post* Internet regulatory distinction.[43] In an online game, it is possible for the administrator to respond to inappropriate behaviour by a member with the online equivalent of a community punishment.[44] The alternatives to direct enforcement are: to rely on a form of indirect liability against content hosts, and to rely on the media literacy and self-policing of online communities, whether YouTube or Second Life. Enforcement can only be undertaken successfully by the content host. Mayer-Schönberger and Crowley see four scenarios for virtual world regulation:

(1) virtual world providers will serve as regulators by enforcing the terms of their contracts with users to prevent cyber-fraud and ensure proper behaviour;
(2) governments could try to block their citizens from using virtual worlds that don't abide by government restrictions and regulations (although this will never be 100 per cent effective, just as governments have not been able to completely block access to websites);
(3) government may try to minimize the real-world impact of virtual worlds by, for instance, banning the sale of virtual goods for real-world currency; or
(4) 'Real-World Assisted Virtual World Self-Governance': governments provide support for mechanisms whereby users of virtual worlds can agree upon and enforce their own 'community standards' and rules of conduct.[45]

Second Life

The case study is of *Second Life*, the largest Western immersive 'virtual world', i.e., peopled by avatars, established by Linden Labs.[46] Second Life was founded in 2002–3 (alpha and beta versions), with 100,000–150,000 users active to the extent of making transactions, and many more non-US than US users. The servers are all US-based, but Linden Labs in 2006

[43] See Ondrejka (2004); Mayer-Schönberger and Crowley (2006).
[44] Source: www.secondlife.com.
[45] Mayer-Schönberger and Crowley (2006).
[46] Rosedale (2007).

opened offices in the UK. World of Warcraft is a much larger Korean-owned virtual world,[47] and one that has been similarly troubled with the real-life trading of virtual objects between players. Second Life is an immersive 'virtual world' peopled by avatars, see Table 3.2.

Second Life's regulatory system works via terms of service and resident self-regulation. Content controversies include: the behaviour of avatar personalities: virtual rapes and paedophilia. Economic controversies concern fraud and misuses of the virtual currency – called 'Linden Dollars (named after the San Francisco-based owners): bank crashes have resulted, and gambling has been banned from the world. Evaluation has been conducted mainly by academics, where a flourishing industry is developing examining all aspects of Second Life including regulatory options.[48]

Unlike Bebo, the code for Second Life is largely open source,[49] though the technical sophistication (and frequent new version downloads) of the virtual world mean that it requires a broadband connection to use it effectively. Copyright in users' creations on Second Life resides with the users. Second Life is unusual not only for its open source coding and popularity but also for the increasing use of financial transactions by members, using the virtual currency. Its utility for users is therefore directly quantifiable in financial terms, whereas many networks carry reputational, leisure, social or only indirect business value.

Second Life has a 'teen' version of its service for 13–17 year olds, and the authentication of such users is a matter of substantial controversy. The idea behind such teen spaces is to remove the potential for exposure to inappropriate behaviour or content, and elimination of the danger of paedophiles communicating with the young. The authentication of users is an essential element of governance for such large communities with such wide interaction potential.

Founder Philip Rosedale suggested that the drive behind the creation of Second Life was an opportunity to recreate the way people interact on

---

[47] East Asian virtual worlds are vastly more popular than Western versions, partly because the fantasy game-playing is so immersive, partly because broadband connectivity and social acceptance of game-play is so ubiquitous compared to its Western niche. We acknowledge that World of Warcraft is of a different order of magnitude in its popularity and commercial value than Western virtual worlds. An interviewee, Joi Ito, was a very senior member of World of Warcraft.

[48] See generally Balkin and Noveck (2006); Davies and Noveck (2006); Noveck (2006).

[49] Its protocol has been reverse-engineered and its code is moving more towards open source as new versions develop.

Table 3.2. *Social network characteristics of Bebo and Second Life*

Characteristics	Bebo	Second Life
Date founded	2005	2003
Total members[a]	31m	3m
Membership	Open	Open
Primary purpose	Multimedia sharing and social	Immersive virtual world
Identity	User choice	Pseudonymous
Instant messaging	Proprietary	Proprietary
Bandwidth needed	Broadband	Broadband
Teen space	Over-13s only[b]	Yes
Policing	Can report abuse directly to police	User-generated part-moderated
Abuse reporting	Every page	Ubiquitous
Notable user developments	na	Trade in Linden Dollars
Privacy/security	Numerous issues	Some hacking attempts
Other notable networks	MySpace, Classmates, Orkut, Friends Reunited, Windows Live, national variants	Active Worlds, There, Entropia Universe, Dotsoul Cyberpark, Red Light Center

Notes:
[a] Estimated based on media reports – not necessarily active users.
[b] www.bebo.com/TermsOfUse.jsp.

the Internet.[50] The role of Second Life has evolved throughout its short life-span.[51] Businesses have taken to Second Life for a number of reasons,[52] but they have all been facilitated by the ability of Second Life residents to make money in the Second Life economy: Linden Dollars have an exchange rate with US dollars. This is made possible by the intellectual property (IP) laws of Second Life, where individuals can own the IP of their own new script (i.e., objects in Second Life), providing them with an opportunity for transactions in Second Life. Ondrejka estimated the 2007 Second Life GDP as

[50] Maney (2007).
[51] See http://SecondLife.com/whatis/businesses.php for a fuller list of businesses.
[52] See http://en.wikipedia.org/wiki/Businesses_and_organizations_in_Second_Life for a longer list of exemplar companies involved in Second Life.

US$500m.[53] The other key factor for business involvement in Second Life is the ability to own land.[54] Strictly speaking, land is not owned by Second Life residents, since they essentially only rent server space on Second Life's servers. Second Life had a taxation system based on the amount of 'property' owned by residents, very unpopular since taxes stifled innovation (leading to an in-world revolution).[55]

Second Life may eventually move away from its server structure and towards a peer-to-peer (p2p) file sharing network,[56] and it is also working with mobile internet providers, available through mobile phone networks, although connectivity is unreliable.[57] Linden Labs have introduced '3D Voice', to allow avatars to speak to each other within the virtual world, and enable the business use of Second Life for virtual meetings.[58] Technically, it has moved towards 'open source', providing developers with the opportunity to shape their own virtual world.[59] With Second Life becoming open source in 2007, much of the creation of new script has effectively been outsourced to its residents. This does bring regulatory issues in itself, as allowing residents to produce script, and therefore objects, means that there is no longer central control of what people will build in Second Life.[60] Development of international server centres may be sought with partners who would deal with local regulatory issues through their local knowledge – a start-up company is unable to deal with such local regulations in-house outside its own jurisdiction. Second Life has also allowed residents to become stakeholders in the shaping of the virtual world. This power potentially means that were other virtual worlds to open up, then residents could validly take their intellectual property with them to another realm and exit Second Life: although this seems unlikely. In this regard, note the regulatory costs which Google incurred in its ownership of YouTube, without which YouTube may have found compliance overwhelming.

Ondrejka admits that, as a technology start-up company financed by venture capital from Silicon Valley, Second Life is not necessarily well-placed to respond to international regulatory pressure and its transparency, openness and willingness to adapt to such pressures are key tests of the ability of small but rapidly growing Internet service companies to self-regulate or group into SROs;[61] Ondrejka warns against making too many

[53] Figures taken from Second Life Economic Statistics, http://SecondLife.com/whatis/economy_stats.php.
[54] Hof (2006).   [55] Ondrejka (2004).
[56] Mayer-Schönberger and Crowley (2006), p. 50.   [57] Best (2006).
[58] See http://news.cnet.com/Second-Life-to-strengthen-its-voice/2100-1043_3-6178864.html?tag=mncol;9n
[59] Arrington (2007).   [60] Mayer-Schönberger and Crowley (2006), footnote 82.
[61] Ondrejka (2007).

comparisons between regulation for World of Warcraft and for Second Life, since Second Life's economy is more akin to eBay or the Internet in general than to World of Warcraft.[62] A survey by the European Interactive Advertising Association revealed that SNS and video consumption are powerful growing uses for broadband Internet surfers, and that an increasingly female and older profile is emerging as the technology matures from its previous male, youthful demographic.[63] Ondrejka (2007) reported that the median Second Life user was a 38-year-old woman.[64] The Second Life home page (www.second Life.com) on 26 August 2007 showed that the number of residents was over 9.1 million, with 1.6 million residents logging in over the previous sixty days.

In an online 'game' (really more an immersive experience), it is possible for the administrator to respond to inappropriate behaviour by a member by the online equivalent of a community punishment. Nelson and Francis state that: 'Virtual worlds are at a very early phase. In many ways, we are at a stage similar to where the World Wide Web was in 1993, when the first commercial and government Web sites were being created, security was poor, and very few legal and regulatory issues had been adequately addressed.'[65] A key difference is that virtual worlds have to comply with the regulatory agencies and scrutiny which have matured with the public Internet. The number of virtual worlds on the Internet is relatively large, and it is difficult to identify which is the 'most popular'. This is because of the problem with subscriber information versus active user information.

The range of enforcement actions is wide and can lead to expulsion from Second Life.[66] Linden Labs set out six community offences for Second Life: intolerance; harassment; assault; disclosure; indecency; and disturbing the peace.[67] When a report is made of an incident that constitutes breaking one of the community standards, then members of the Second Life abuse team begin an investigation into the incident using screenshots, chat logs and other tools to make sure that the claim is valid. If the claim is valid, then the abuse team can take action against the perpetrator. In April 2007, Linden Labs changed the way that the abuse team worked, by using a pattern-based methodology that allows Linden

---

[62] Ondrejka (2007).
[63] European Interactive Advertising Association (12 November 2007).
[64] See www.foxnews.com/story/0,2933,269690,00.html for more details.
[65] Nelson and Francis (2007).   [66] http://SecondLife.com/community/blotter.php.
[67] Second Life https://secure-web4.Second Life.com/corporate/cs.php.

Labs to identify where abuse occurs and by whom.[68] The aim of this is to speed responses to abuse complaints. It is not clear what the appeals process is for those who feel falsely accused or judged incorrectly. Since Linden Labs only intervenes when a user breaks one of the six community standards or when someone breaks a real world law, there are essentially two types of intervention. Real world illegalities represent less than one percent of the total abuse reports sent to Second Life.[69] For those disputes and complaints that constitute copyright violations, Second Life uses the DMCA (Digital Millennium Copyright Act) NTD procedures. If there are disputes that do not constitute a breach of any of the six community standards or a real world illegal act, Second Life can offer moderators, but these can only help resolve disputes and cannot enforce any agreements between the parties involved.[70]

The most high-profile financial enforcement issues were gambling in Second Life and the collapse of Ginko, a bank in Second Life.[71] This collapse was one for which Second Life denies accountability beyond the fact that it carries all data agnostically. Ginko was an external provider in the Second Life environment and, as a bank, was offering very high rates of interest on Linden Dollars deposited with them. When Ginko's Second Life branch ran out of Linden Dollars there was widespread panic from investors. Ginko owed upward of US$750,000 to clients.[72] This collapse brought the issue of financial regulation in Second Life to the forefront, with financial regulators inquisitive about the role of Second Life as a financial market housed on US servers. For Second Life the best explanation of its position on Ginko is that it was a third party and Second Life terms of service exclude its liability.[73] This prompted SecondLife to set up a Second Life Securities Exchange Act, to provide market stability and investor confidence. John Zdanowsk, CFO of Second Life, was confident in regulation: 'The threat is there, the danger is there. The reality is that unlike the real world, in SecondLife it just so happens that we know everything that happens.'[74]

The gambling issue is one that Second Life chose to address prior to any regulatory pressure,[75] as it was seen as something that would invite US

---

[68] See http://blog.SecondLife.com/2007/04/18/changes-in-abuse-report-resolution/ for further details.
[69] Ondrejka (2007).
[70] Mayer-Schönberger and Crowley (2006), p. 26.
[71] http://blog.SecondLife.com/2007/07/25/wagering-in-second-life-new-policy/.
[72] Rappeport (2007).
[73] http://blog.SecondLife.com/2007/08/14/the-second-life-economy/.
[74] Rappeport (2007).
[75] http://blog.SecondLife.com/2007/08/09/anti-gambling-policy-update-faq/.

government regulation and even threaten the very existence of the environment.[76] Policy changes become rapidly known to residents of Second Life, but the inception of policy is something that is not as well communicated to residents. One resident described the gambling ban as happening 'overnight and without warning'.[77] The impact on Second Life is difficult to estimate, making the withdrawal of gambling within the world difficult to quantify.[78]

Ondrejka has suggested that the lack of a clear regulatory environment leads to increased legal costs as lawyers must be employed by Linden Labs to deal with specific problem cases – such as the 'Families of France' lawsuit to block minors in France using Second Life.[79] Second Life servers are only based in the US, a policy decision to ensure that physically only one national jurisdiction is in a position to enforce against servers. Ondrejka suggests that Second Life would benefit from some form of regulatory certainty to allow Linden Labs to know where they stand on a number of issues.[80] There was no real competitor to Second Life, which is a disappointment for Ondrejka as: 'they could take some regulatory heat off Second Life which is currently a lightning rod for regulatory issues internationally surrounding virtual worlds; there could be competitive differentiation and other useful developer pressures'. Linden Labs employees engaged very broadly with the policy community, including presentations at such events as State of Play conferences (2007 in Singapore),[81] the Harvard-Rueschlikon conference (Zurich 2007),[82] iCommons (Dubrovnik, Croatia 2007)[83] and Aspen Summits.[84] While these are not international regulatory summits, the Aspen Summit for instance brought Linden Labs into discussion with Commissioner Reding, US FCC staff and others.

Ondrejka notes that to apply regulation to such virtual worlds may be counterproductive: 'Completely 100 per cent effective filtering is a

---

[76] Ondrejka (2007).
[77] Comment taken from SciFi Tech, available at http://blog.scifi.com/tech/archives/2007/08/05/peer_review_sec.html.
[78] By banning gambling Second Life's revenue has also dropped, but Ondrejka believes this may be coincidental.
[79] See http://gamepolitics.com/2007/06/04/french-watchdog-organization-targets-second-life for further details (accessed 26 August 2007).
[80] Ondrejka (2007).
[81] www.nyls.edu/pages/3367.asp.
[82] www.rueschlikon-conference.org/r2007/public/public2007.php.
[83] www.icommons.org/isummit07.
[84] www.aspeninstitute.org/site/c.huLWJeMRKpH/b.2628901/k.206B/FOCAS_2007_Participants.htm.

race to unplug your Internet connection.' He also argues that regulatory claims by other UGC sites should be treated with cynicism. The Amazon 'Mechanical Turk' charges US$0.01 a picture for image scanning, and human content is even more expensive – by a factor of perhaps five times, which makes regulating a billion images a day extraordinarily expensive whether by mechanical or human means, if that were the desire of governments. The Bebo solution is not replicable. In Second Life's case, with over three terabytes of UGC generated daily, filtering is not an option. The main regulatory challenges that Second Life will face over the coming years are in scaling internationally, how best to deal with open source development in Second Life and OCL issues. Ondrejka believes that this regulatory pressure should fall onto developers.[85] It has been counter-argued that since virtual world providers can control the code and contracts of residents, the onus is on them to regulate and they are liable for any breach of law.[86] This works relatively well as a model if the provider (in this case Linden Labs) has a server hub that maintains the virtual world. However, if the world moves to a peer-to-peer file sharing style network, in which the architecture of the world is decentralized, as with Napster, the regulatory onus will be on users rather than providers.

Digital copyright

If creativity and intellectual progress involve 'standing on the shoulders of giants', it must be made possible to stand on those shoulders.[87] Access to knowledge is a key driver of social, cultural and economic development, with tangible economic advantages to be gained by sharing.[88] The 'all rights reserved' model of traditional copyright law, with its complex legal concepts and requirement for permission for all uses, does not fit well with an environment which enables sharing and reuse of content by users. In the analogue environment the ability to produce, reproduce, distribute, share and promote creative works was relatively restricted, due primarily to geographic, economic and technological limitations. The emergence of

---

[85] Ondrejka (2007).
[86] Mayer-Schönberger and Crowley (2006), p. 48.
[87] An important related development has been the description of the Free/Open Source development phenomenon in transaction cost theory terms by Benkler (2002), p. 369, as influenced by the work of Moglen (2000). Benkler's model was coined as Commons Based Peer Production and has been exceptionally influential in the way Open Source-like environments are understood in the discourses of law and economics.
[88] See, for a robustly optimistic assessment and for policy-makers of great importance, Weiss (2002).

consumer digital technologies such as Compact Discs and the Internet in the 1990s allowed for increasing levels of functionality, particularly in relation to interactivity. Mobile phone cameras, MP3 encoding for music, rich media applications, video streaming and p2p networking provide simple ways for users to collaborate, communicate and create material, including 'mash-ups'. Pam states: 'it no longer makes sense for the media industry to use the existing producer/publisher/distributor/consumer one-way pipeline business model since a larger proportion of the public are capable, willing and interested to act as producers, publishers and distributors'.[89]

The risk is that copyright law will become a barrier to the realization of the full potential of these technologies. The ease with which material can be converted into digital form, and distributed over the Internet as perfect 'copies', has led to tighter copyright regulation, thus restricting author/creative freedom in the interests of protecting copyright for the publisher – in the US, but also in the European Union and elsewhere. New licensing systems open up access to and use of protected material. Lessig consolidated all these developments in his books.[90] Access to and reuse of materials produced by government and other publicly funded bodies has also emerged as an important issue in recent years. Consumer demand for access to, and reuse of, government information has risen exponentially, driven in part by Web2.0 functionality.

'Open Content Licensing' (OCL) models are based upon and respect copyright while giving permission in advance for the content to be used more broadly than would be permitted under default copyright law. These licences are typically:

- generic (i.e., standard terms apply to all users),
- non-discriminatory (i.e., anyone can access the content) and
- provide the user with the right to reproduce, copy and communicate the content,
- subject to prescribed terms or conditions.

They are designed to be relatively short, simple and easy to read, interoperable with other OCL models, and machine-enabled.

The most popular and widespread of these OCL models in relation to creative material is Creative Commons (CC). CC is an internationally active non-profit organization that aims to promote new copyright management options for creators. CC's launch was by Lessig,[91] CC Chair Joi

---

[89] Pam (2002).   [90] Lessig (2001, 2004).
[91] Lessig (1999).

Ito and cyber-libertarian John Perry Barlow, in 2002. CC claims a staff of 'over thirty in four offices around the world, supporting thousands of volunteers in over seventy jurisdictions'.[92] It set a goal of raising a further $500,000 by end-2007 in order to give the organization 'a solid financial footing'.

CC drafts licences for individual content creators to license content on non-commercial terms. There are over sixty other national CC licences. Lessig was its founder Chief Executive, as well as its intellectual leader, in much the same respect as was Tim Berners-Lee for the W3C. Early board member and Free Software Foundation head Richard Stallman quit in 2004, criticising CC for its lack of radical mission. The growth of the CC 'movement' includes iCommons and ccSalon to showcase CC licence use, and CC International (South Africa) and the CC summit to encourage sharing of best practice.

Licence enforcement is controversial as an emerging legal issue for CC in various jurisdictions, as is the relationship between non-commercial content in the public sector and CC licensed content. CC followed and was stimulated by *Ashcroft* v. *Eldred* [2003],[93] confirming the extension of the copyright term. CC was seen by some copyright holders as potentially a direct threat to their business model, though it is positioned as a 'middle way' between commercial copyright and anarchic free copying. Bill Gates went as far in 2004 as to call CC licence developers 'communists', which led to the memorable rebuttal phrase 'Commonists not communists'.[94]

CC licences allow people to express 'some rights reserved' (or 'no rights reserved') rather than the full protection that the law allows. To work internationally, jurisdiction-specific licences must be developed. The following aspects are of particular interest:

- user-friendly licensing schemes simplify non-commercial licensing, mitigating problems of private regulation (e.g., click-through licences that operate as private regulatory regimes);
- the individual creator/aggregator/curator needs no intermediaries, e.g., lawyers or distributors;
- users receive 'learning through doing' in copyright issues through the licences;
- accountability and transparency are addressed by open source software development.

---

[92] Lessig (2007).
[93] *Eldred* v. *Ashcroft* 537 US 186 [2003].
[94] See variously Benkler (1998a, pp. 183–196; 1998b, pp. 287–400; 2006).

The first CC licences were released in December 2002, with version 3.0 in February 2007. The CC project issues a suite of standardized licences that are made freely available to copyright holders to increase general public access and use of creative material, within copyright. It is a model based on prior permission utilizing private rights for public goods.[95] Licences comes with certain base rights, along with optional 'licence elements' and include:

- attribution (BY): compulsory in each of the core licences since version 2.0; credit must be given to the original author;
- non-commercial (NC): lets others copy, distribute, display and perform the work – and derivative works based upon it – for non-commercial purposes only;
- no derivative works (ND): lets others distribute, display and perform only verbatim copies of a work, not derivative works based upon it;
- share alike (SA): allows others to distribute, display and perform derivative works only under the same licence conditions that govern the original work.

It is important to stress the substantial legal technical problems in constructing a licence set which acts with the artists' interests, and in localizing the CC licences for jurisdictions other than the US. In the UK, for instance, after initial pro bono work by a US law firm's London office, a CC-UK legal licensing team was established with representative copyright lawyers from the Universities of Oxford and Edinburgh, Queen Mary's, London and London School of Economics. It took almost two years to publish licences, split into: CC-EW (England and Wales); CC-Scotland (to reflect the different copyright law tradition) and CC-NI (Northern Ireland). Further complications arose in the UK – by 2003 the CC International (now iCommons) 'flagship' and home territory[96] – in connection with attempts to persuade the British Broadcasting Corporation (BBC) to incorporate the CC-UK licence into its plans to permit licence fee payer reuse of some content in what became its 'Creative Archive'.[97] This is a case study in the problems of combining the concerns of amateur artists with those of a commercially significant and acutely legally conscious organization. Despite the personal visits, meetings, speeches

---

[95] See Coates (2007).
[96] CCInternational was based in Berlin until 2005, then became iCommons and moved to headquarters in Johannesburg, South Africa.
[97] www.bbc.co.uk/creativearchive.

and encouragement of both Lessig and then-BBC Director-General (chief executive) Greg Dyke, the projects could not agree the legal basis for a common licence. Concerns included: ensuring that BBC content was not reused in politically contentious ways which would breach BBC duties of impartiality; value to the UK BBC viewer (television licence fee payer); and no breach of the rights of artists who produced the content for the BBC, notably trades unions' members' concerns and those of collecting societies. As a result, despite the attempts of both BBC Creative Archive lawyers and those of the CC-UK project, agreement could not be reached and the BBC decided on a separate licence which met its concerns. The BBC Creative Archive legal head, Paula LeDieu, resigned to lead iCommons as it became clear the negotiations had reached an impasse. Creative Archive is a repository of content licensed as available for sharing, watching, listening to and reuse by the general public. The Licence Group consisted of the BBC, Channel 4, Open University, the British Film Institute, Teachers' TV, and the Museums, Libraries and Archives (MLA) Council. Content on the archive is freely available to UK citizens only, for viewing and remixing for non-commercial purposes. The licence eventually used by the archive was closely modelled on the CC Attribution-Noncommercial-ShareAlike licence.

Part of this futile UK experience helped in the current iteration of the licences. The version 3.0 licences include a series of changes such as:

- separating the 'generic' (now called unported) licence from the US licence;[98]
- harmonizing the treatment of moral rights[99] and collecting society royalties;[100]
- expressly prohibiting misuse of the attribution requirement to assert or imply association or relationship with the licensor or author;
- inclusion of a mechanism to permit compatibility between CC ShareAlike licences and other similar open content licences; and
- minor language changes to accommodate concerns of key participants Debian[101] and MIT.[102]

---

[98] http://wiki.creativecommons.org/Version_3#Further_Internationalization.
[99] http://wiki.creativecommons.org/Version_3#International_Harmonization_. E2.80.93_Moral_Rights.
[100] http://wiki.creativecommons.org/Version_3#International_Harmonization_. E2.80.94_Collecting_Societies.
[101] http://wiki.creativecommons.org/Version_3#Debian.
[102] http://wiki.creativecommons.org/Version_3#MIT.

Enforcement was not Lessig's primary concern in designing the original licence. CC users are not expected to have a legal background, and its licensing is designed for ease of use, featuring:

- licence generator via the 'License Your Work' button on CC international homepage;[103]
- uniform branding – icons are built into both the Commons Deed and licence buttons;
- the 'Commons Deeds' – a one-page, plain language summary of the licence. This Commons Deed summarizes freedoms afforded to users, terms and conditions on which those freedoms can be exercised and a link to the full legal code of the licence;
- licence buttons – each national CC licence comes with its own 'licence button' which can be embedded on webpages or in digital file formats, making it easy to instantly recognize the material as being under a CC licence.

Government policies increasingly favour use of OCL for material produced by the educational, cultural and research sectors.[104] OECD and the United Nations Educational, Scientific and Cultural Organization (UNESCO) undertook their own open-access initiatives.[105] OECD specifically discussed CC as a way of overcoming obstacles created by legal restrictions that hamper the negotiability of copyright material in the digital environment.[106] MIT launched OpenCourseWare (OCW) in 2002, an online publishing initiative designed to provide free access to virtually all of MIT's undergraduate and graduate course materials. The MIT OCW platform is based on the conviction that "open dissemination of knowledge and information can open new doors to the powerful benefits of education for humanity around the world'.[107] MIT OCW had licensed 1,550 courses under CC across a number of disciplines by 2006. Content within MIT OCW includes course materials such as class plans and study guides as well as supplementary materials and some audio and visual content.

---

[103] http://creativecommons.org/license.
[104] At the extreme, see Maldonado and Tapia (2007).
[105] See OECD (2006b); see also UNESCO (2007) Open Training Platform, at http://open-training.unesco-ci.org.
[106] OECD Centre for Educational Research and Innovation (2007), p. 13.
[107] Massachusetts Institute of Technology (undated), Our Story, http://ocw.mit.edu/OcwWeb/Global/AboutOCW/our-story.htm.

An example of CC licences at work is Flickr,[108] the Yahoo!-operated online photo-management and sharing application. It aims to help people make their photos available to friends, family and the general public, and enable new ways of organizing photos. Flickr directly incorporates CC licensing as an option in its system. Uploaders can choose a CC licence for their photos when they upload, set one as a default for every time they upload, or retroactively change or add a licence for photos they have already uploaded.[109] The page splits up images by licence type, and users can search for specific keywords within that licence type. Coates estimates that 10 per cent of the photos published on Flickr to the end of 2006 were under a CC licence. In the Australian case, there was 'a clear indication that there is a significant lack of understanding of the workings of the CC licensing model among the general community'.[110] There are three main areas where further public awareness and development is needed:

- continued research on issues related to CC and OCL;
- building awareness of CC and expanding the information available about the CC project; and
- providing greater advice and support for projects implementing CC licences.

There was an evident need for better information outlining how to use the CC licensing system, for a range of discrete groups including: individual practitioners looking to license their work; content users looking to utilize CC licensed works; organizations and content providers looking to aggregate content under CC licences; commercial agents; and funding bodies.

The iSummit collaborates with organizations and communities from around the world to demonstrate and share best practice and discuss strategies for continuing the positive impact that 'sharing' practices are having on participation in the cultural and knowledge domains.[111] The ccSalon concept started in San Francisco, and became a monthly event focused on building a community of artists and developers around CC licences, standards and technology. ccSalons have been run in Amsterdam, Beijing, Berlin, Johannesburg, London, Los Angeles, New York, Seoul, Taipei, Toronto and Warsaw.[112]

---

[108] flickr.com.   [109] flickr.com/creativecommons.
[110] Coates (2007), p. 42.
[111] See Bledsoe et al. (2007).
[112] For web addresses for ccSalon see e.g., Toronto: http://wiki.creativecommons.org/ Toronto_Salon.

The decisive break between CC and the more ideological OCL groups came with Richard Stallman's decision to resign from the CC board in 2004. Stallman had founded the 'Copyleft' movement with his Free Software Foundation (FSF) in the 1980s, and his FSF legal counsel, Professor Eben Moglen, is the author of 'Information Communism', the tract which may in part have led to Gates' conflation of the commons with the communist ideal. For many open source advocates, CC is viewed as a non-contentious and relatively uninteresting sideshow experiment, compared to the main discussions about copyright term limits, the uses of open source and controversy over the General Public Licence (GPL) Version 3.0. CC is seen by some as a betrayal of the FSF and 'copyleft' ideals,[113] but given its development by lawyers and wider adoption by industries which survive on copyright payments, that is perhaps inevitable. CC has been criticized as a lawyer's answer to a lawyer's problem, rather than the 'copyleft' rejection of copyright that is characterized by those in the Free Software movement. Berry and Moss question the real influence of the legal solution: 'the legal professor's penchant is to turn to the field of law and lawyers. The GPL has tenacity not due to its legal form alone. The GPL is based on a network of ethical practices that continually (re-)produce its meaning and form. The commons is always more than a formal legal construct. The commons is based on commonalty.'[114]

Critics of CC suggest that a more comprehensive solution to digital copyright would embrace a treaty obligation. In this regard, note the recent UNESCO Cultural Diversity Treaty[115] and the WIPO Broadcast Treaty – though critics claim that the latter may be more a foreclosure of public commons. The UK Office of Public Sector Information found that 87 per cent of the respondents from the general public in the UK did not recognize the CC licence icon, and 59 per cent did not know what a 'commons' was.[116] The licence has a long way to grow in order

---

[113] For a characterization of the type of debate open-source software engenders, see Vance (2007): '"Of course, the open source 'community's' initial response to just about anything tends to veer toward apocalyptic scenarios – in this case a world destroyed by logos. Rather than tempting reality, the members of the never-ending car crash known as the 'license-discuss' mailing list, where all the really important OSI matters are handled, embraced conniption. You know, if you don't like something, give it an evil name and come up with these hypotheticals that don't exist in the real world," Radcliffe said.' See also: http://lawandlifesiliconvalley.blogspot.com/2007/08/open-source-legal-webinar-open-source.html.

[114] Berry and Moss (2006).

[115] www.ictsd.org/weekly/05–10–26/story4.htm.

[116] Gill and James (2009), pp. 32–33, cited in Richter (2010), p. 363, footnote 830.

to perform its function more generally as an alternative to commercial copyright.[117]

Richter has recently compared CC with other types of social entrepreneurship as regulatory techniques,[118] in a pioneering approach to self-organization as a 'solution from outside the regulated environment through entrepreneurship and innovation, and relies on the forces of the market to become effective'.[119] He explains that social entrepreneurs can be more effective and more efficient than regulation (or else go out of business),[120] but that 'Further efforts are required to ensure participation, transparency, and public accountability, and to avoid regulatory fragmentation.'[121] Social entrepreneurship as a tool to regulate has only recently emerged as part of the Third Sector,[122] or Big Society approach to private provision of formerly charitable or state activities.[123] In 2005, the British Government's Office of the Third Sector allowed for the Community Interest Company (CIC) with a regulator.[124] Richter argues that 'the existing framework of social entrepreneurship can be extended to entrepreneurial organizations providing innovative and market-based solutions to environments in which regulation and market self-regulation have failed to provide a social good'.[125] This separates them from non-business policy entrepreneurs.[126] Spear and Bidet state: 'The entrepreneurs are citizens, not the state, the decision-making power is not based on capital ownership, the participatory nature involves those affected by the venture, profit distribution is limited, and finally the venture explicitly aims at benefiting the community.'[127]

Social enterprises can be Type 1 (local) or Type 2 (macro) according to Nicholls,[128] with the Fair Trade movement a classic established example of the latter. Richter states that 'production of social value with market-based solutions and entrepreneurial innovation are sufficient to differentiate social entrepreneurship, profit-maximizing

---

[117] See variously Wiley (2005); Pessach (2010); Linksvayer (2008); Cheliotis *et al.* (2007).

[118] See Giddens (1998), Chapter 5, pp. 69–85; Mulgan and Landry (1995), p. 57: 'This is surely poor public policy' – to remove limited directorial liability while also removing incentives for efficiency in charitable trusteeship. 'The system of oversight … is fragmented and poorly coordinated' (p. 61) associated with the law–tax charitable status link; Kelly *et al.* (2002).

[119] Richter (2010) at p. 3.   [120] Robinson (2006), p. 95.

[121] Richter (2010), p. 3.   [122] Giddens (1998), pp. 81f.

[123] See Nicholls and Albert Hyunbae Cho (2006), p. 102.

[124] CIC Regulator (2008).   [125] Richter (2010), p. 248.

[126] Kingdon (1984); Schneider and Teske (1992), pp. 737–747.

[127] Spear and Bidet (2003), p. 8.   [128] Nicholls (2007).

models of entrepreneurship, from philanthropy, from institutionalized and state-backed forms of civil society engagement, from CSR, and from policy entrepreneurship'.[129] This categorizes CC, though its legal status is as a California corporation. It also may well categorize Nominet as reformed in 2010, should it so choose. As Richter states, there are three governmental approaches to encourage social entrepreneurship, to cooperate in problem and solution definition as might be argued was the case with CC-Brazil and involvement of Minister Gilberto Gil,[130] as a customer for such solutions as in OCL models which I described as 'Regulation2.0',[131] and finally the creation of a market for social entrepreneurship as with the UK CIC, where the 'market regulator should develop and enforce minimum standards for transparency, accountability, and participatory solution design, create an arbitration panel for citizen complaints, encourage independent performance reviews, and push for the interoperability of solutions to preserve competition'.[132] He also argues that in the absence of a CIC regulator, 'legal logic under *Marsh* v. *Alabama* allows the application of basic constitutional rights to private providers of public infrastructure and could also be extended to require transparency and due process rules for the private regulatory activities by … [CC]'.[133]

Through copyright the CC attempts to construct a commons within the realm of private ownership. The CC project appears to be a success. It has generated interest in the issue of intellectual property and the erosion of the 'public domain', and it has contributed to rethinking the role of the 'commons' in the Information Society. CC licences are in the process of being enforced, and a recent Belgian case suggests that this has occurred.[134] In the course of issuing a withering critique of Orlowski's inaccurate reporting of his involvement with Harvard Law School, Lessig offers a summary of the legal position of the iCommons

---

[129] Richter (2010), p. 65, and see pp. 66–68 for definitions.
[130] Richter (2010), p. 403: 'In a co-regulatory model for Socio-Entrepreneurial Regulation, the regulator would similarly support entrepreneurs during the design and implementation process, e.g., by inviting stakeholders to participate in the solution creation phase hearings, by using soft power or threatening adverse regulation when stakeholders do not agree on a mutually beneficial solution.'
[131] See Marsden (2008), pp. 115–132.
[132] Richter (2010), p. 410, following Braithwaite (2008).
[133] Richter (2010), p. 413, citing *Marsh* v. *Alabama* 326 U.S. 501 [1946] as discussed by Zittrain (1999), pp. 1075ff.
[134] Case n° 09–1684-A, *L'ABSL Festival De Theatre De Spa, Tribunal de Premier Instance de Nivelles*, reported in Guadamuz (2010).

organization, as a UK charity with majority non-US citizens on its board.[135]

Conclusion: governance and self-organization as examples of social entrepreneurship

Whether one agrees with Latzer that it is 'self-organization' – there being no multiparty self-regulatory body – or side with Price and Verhulst in terming it self-regulation,[136] there is a particular feature to a single corporate policy negotiated internally rather than through external discussions. First, it is not transparent inasmuch as self-regulation may be so. Second, it is conducted for internally validated reasons: a mixture of profit-maximization via brand enhancement (making the product distinctively better regulated than others), via corporate governance (performing pro bono socially beneficial duties as a means to securing corporate distinction), or because as monopoly or oligopoly player, it is in a position to rule-make rather than rule-take vis-à-vis its competitors i.e., it is not obliged to conduct a 'race to the bottom' in welfare terms. This leaves to one side the unusual category of social entrepreneur, a regulatory actor of such obscurity that few academics have investigated the phenomenon until recently.[137] In a commercial service, such as Facebook, users have terms of use prescribed by the service owner. This is not a new phenomenon, except in the degree to which UGC is generated, and users consider the service owner's brand associated with that third-party content. AOL's branded portal in the mid 1990s was the most successful site on the Internet, as Facebook is in 2011. The type of governance that applies to these organizations is either charitable status or corporate governance rules. For IWF (see Chapter 6) or iCommons, it is the legal status as a charity that its board of directors must observe, which provides a very low baseline of compliance.[138] In the UK, once a charity has been registered with the Charities Commission, it is obliged to follow its own board rules and objectives. In the case of corporate governance, the main obligation on the board of directors is the fiduciary duty to pursue the most beneficial course for shareholders, hence the derision that greeted Google's claim that it would continue to 'do no evil' once its shares were

---

[135] Lessig (2010).
[136] Price and Verhulst (2000) focus on the policies adopted by what was the world's largest ISP, AOL.
[137] Emerson and Twersky (1996); Leadbeater (1997); Thompson (2002), pp. 412–431.
[138] Prakash and Gugerty (2010), pp. 22–47.

floated on the New York Stock Exchange. Henceforth, its duty as a public corporation would be to maximize its commercial opportunities, including in China, had it been able to make profits there without jeopardizing its business model and revenues elsewhere. The November 2010 proposed settlement of a class action suit brought by aggrieved GMail users on the social network Google Buzz (rapidly remedied by Google after public outcry)[139] demonstrates that courts will take action at least in egregious cases of invasion of privacy.[140] The settlement letter states:

> The Action alleges that Google violated (i) the Electronic Communications Privacy Act, 18 U.S.C. §2510 et seq; (ii) the Stored Communications Act, 18 U.S.C. §2701 et seq; (iii) the Computer Fraud and Abuse Act, 18 U.S.C. §1030 et seq; (iv) the common law tort of Public Disclosure of Private Facts as recognized by California common law; and (v) the California Unfair Competition Law, California Business & Professions Code §17200.[141]

Porter and Kramer state that Corporate Social Responsibility (CSR) exists for four reasons:[142]

- Moral obligation: a duty to contribute back to society.
- Sustainability: the obligation to use resources in a manner that sustains resources for future generations, which can be extended beyond physical resources to encompass knowledge.[143] [It is criticized as 'greenwashing', or in the case of Google Books, as hoarding].
- 'Licence to operate': businesses have implicit permission by the state to conduct business, and therefore need to demonstrate social as well as profit utility. In this respect, CSR is a passport to market access.
- CSR is part of corporate reputation-building strategy, much criticized as a token.[144]

Much though we might wish for SNS to conform to these rules as social entrepreneur CC does, it appears that some regulatory action is needed to provoke the many benefits of Regulation (or Self-Organization) 2.0.

---

[139] *In re Google Buzz User Privacy Litigation* (2010) No. 5:10-cv-00672-JW United States District Court for the Northern District of California, San Jose Division.

[140] Darlin (2010). Google is reportedly putting $8.5 million into an independent fund that it says will be used to support organizations promoting education about privacy on the Web. Google said: 'We will also do more to educate people about privacy controls specific to Buzz. The more people know about privacy online, the better their online experience will be.'

[141] Unnamed (2010), p. 3.   [142] Porter and Kramer (2006), p. 80.   [143] Marsden (2008).

[144] Hence efforts are ongoing to create international standards, see International Standards Organization (2009); Pattberg (2005), pp. 589–610.

4

An empire entire of itself? Standards, domain names and government

Introducing Internet standard setting

In this chapter, I consider issues and institutions uniquely designed for the Internet, to provide co- or self-regulatory tools to solve unique problems, and the effect of both technological and government regulation thereon.[1] Though predominantly technical in character, as seen in the previous chapter with UGC, standards define content interoperability.[2] I therefore consider: first, core standards made in the Internet Engineering Task Force (IETF); second, the World Wide Web Consortium (W3C) and its standard setting, including the attempt to introduce labelling standards to enable end-users to filter Internet content; and finally, Internet Corporation for Assigned Names and Numbers (ICANN), which allocates 'addresses' for Internet sites and claims an entirely technical character unrelated to, and entirely agnostic to, content, and the country registrar for the UK, Nominet.[3] The ability of content providers to offer end-users a service ultimately rests on conformance with IETF standards. Understanding the importance of IETF as the basic technical rule-maker of the Internet, and its coordination mechanisms through ISOC to ICANN, and through participation to W3C and content, services and applications, is necessary before considering other SROs.

Government, it is often forgotten, does far more to regulate than simply tax and spend, legislate, rule-make and prosecute. It is also the largest procurer of goods and services, the first adopter of many new technologies, and the commissioner of most new basic research, especially in Europe. It is also frequently overlooked that funding from the US Department of Defense (DoD) developed the Internet in universities, while mobile telephony technology was developed for European and US military uses. In Europe, almost all universities were largely government-funded in

---

[1] Kahin and Abbate (1995).
[2] See variously Braman (2004); DeNardis (2009); Van Schewick (2010).
[3] See a decade ago, a study of these three SROs in Gould (2000).

the twentieth century, and the Internet was a university invention. Most early European experiments with the Internet were also facilitated by the communications experts in the mostly state-owned telecoms companies as well as universities, in the UK by the Post Office and then British Telecommunications. By the time that these networks were tentatively opened to competition, from about 1985 in the US and UK, and later in continental European nations, the Internet had largely been developed and its technical standards became institutionalized in the IETF.[4]

The IETF formalized an ad hoc agreement on standards that had developed throughout the 1970s, and its credo became 'we believe in rough consensus and running code'.[5] That Anglo-Saxon flexibility continues to be both the strength and weakness of the IETF,[6] as compared with the state-centric International Telecommunications Union (ITU) and Committee of European Posts and Telegraphs (CEPT), which were very much formally based on kings and presidents.[7] Note that the two formerly distinct work methods are to some extent converging on the Internet model, though Internet pioneers have often been very harsh critics of telecoms standards. Many previous studies have suggested that standards play an important role in setting the parameters of regulation. Note that as Next Generation Networks (NGNs) are based on the Internet Protocol (IP), IP standards pursue the goal of appropriate interoperability more effectively than previous generations of communications standards.[8] Telecommunications and Internet standards are converging, though governance of ITU, ETSI and IETF remains diverse.[9] Figure 4.1 presents the place of Internet standards in the overall standards environment.

Note that there are telecoms standards bodies based on paid memberships and privately paid published standards with voting mechanisms for formal adoption, as well as secondary and tertiary Internet standards bodies for specific tasks such as email or numbering standards. Some telecoms and Internet standards bodies overlap, as in those for mobile

---

[4] Hafner and Lyon (1996).   [5] Clark (1985), pp. 106–114.
[6] The latest IETF meeting in November 2010 was the first to be held in mainland China, and the first in which a country other than the US had most members in attendance. That country was China. However, standards making remains dominated by Western engineers.
[7] Cowie and Marsden (1999), pp. 53–66; Marsden (2001), pp. 253–285.
[8] See OECD (2006c).
[9] Bob Kahan, co-author of the TCP/IP standard, described the CEPT (Conférence européenne des administrations des postes et télécommunication) as the 'Committee for the Elimination of Competition in Telecoms' in his Marconi Foundation seminar address in 2003.

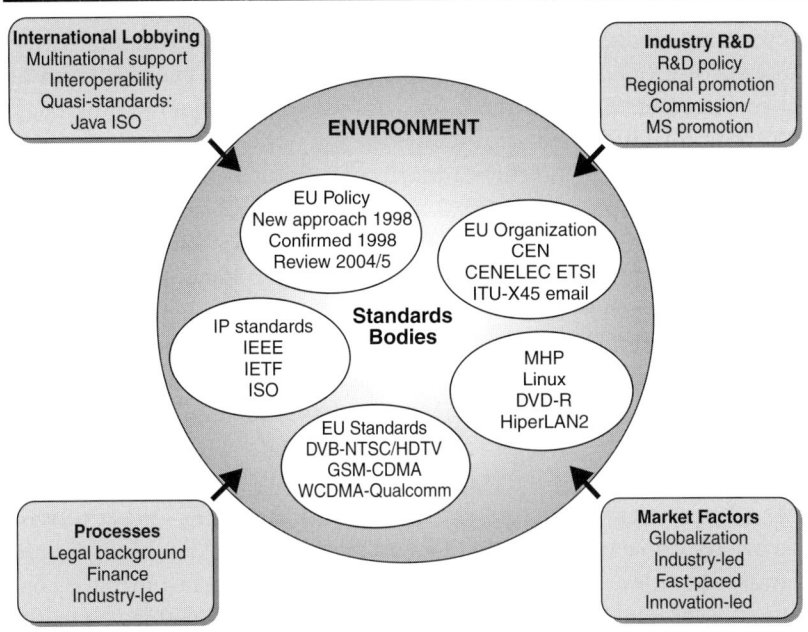

Figure 4.1.   Standard setting and the role of IP standards

standards and ITU standards for emergency IP-based communications.[10]
A revolutionary change in 2010 was that the ITU finally recognized
the IETF and W3C.[11] CEN and CENELEC are long-standing European
standards bodies with governmental approval for their cooperation in the
1998 'New Approach' and earlier, but whose governance standards have
been found wanting in reviews.[12] The industry-led approach also applies

---

[10] Weiser (2001), pp. 822–846.
[11] International Telecommunication Union (2010), p. 53: 'to collaborate closely with the rele-
     vant international recognized partners, including the Internet community (e.g., regional
     Internet registries (RIRs), the Internet Engineering Task Force (IETF) and others), in
     order to encourage the deployment of IPv6 by raising awareness and through capacity
     building' and naming relevant organizations in footnote 1 as: 'Including, but not limited
     to ICANN, the RIRs, the IETF, ISOC and W3C.' It also refers to the IETF at p. 56 and
     (unnumbered p. 217) in Resolution 101 (Rev. Guadalajara, 2010) 'the general cooperation
     agreement between ITU-T and the Internet Society (ISOC)/Internet Engineering Task
     Force (IETF), as referred to in Supplement 3 to the ITU-T Series A recommendations,
     continues to exist'.
[12] General Guidelines (2003); COM (2004a).

to ETSI and even more so to the Digital Video Broadcasting group (DVB). Nevertheless, European standards bodies, including ETSI, maintain their close institutional relationship with European governments, driven by mutual need for European manufacturers to maintain competitiveness with the US and East Asia.[13]

Factors impinging on the standards environment apply to all standards bodies, whether traditional, national, regional or international.[14] Thus processes, lobbying, market factors, and industry research and development efforts affect IP standards much as they do other types of standards, such as those set in Europe for mobile telephony.[15] Subtle institutional shifts in decentralized and privatized regulatory systems afford opportunities for corporate competitiveness advantages by 'gaming' the system of standards.[16] The point here is a simple yet profound one: the IETF is not the 'end of history' in standard setting, and tensions over legitimacy, flexibility, transparency, due process and effectiveness that affect all standards bodies also apply to the IETF.[17] What follows is a brief outline and critique sufficient to contrast IETF with European standards bodies, and the W3C, whereas a more complete outline is contained in the 2008 report.[18]

Internet Engineering Task Force (IETF)

IETF evolved from an earlier, informal body, the Network Working Group (NWG). IETF is the 'original' standards body for the Internet, leading to the famous description of Internet self-regulation as consisting of 'rough consensus and running code'.[19] IETF is a decentralized confederation of equals in its design.[20] Those who participate do so on a volunteer basis, and the trappings of formality – business suits, political posturing and

---

[13] Levy (1997), p. 665 details the policy changes which gave rise to ETSI. For a critical view, see Grindley *et al.* (1999).

[14] See Kerwer (2005), pp. 611–632; Lenox (2006), pp. 677–690; Hilary and Lenox (2005), pp. 211–229.

[15] Standards set in the Global System for Mobile (GSM), in the European Telecoms Standards Institute (ETSI), and in the International Telecommunications Union (ITU) for Universal Mobile Telecommunications System standards (UMTS).

[16] Greenstein and Stango (2008). Also see Blind *et al.* (2010), pp. 165–166.

[17] See Greenstein (2006), pp. 3–4.

[18] See Marsden *et al.* (2008), pp. 45–54, with thanks to Dr Ian Brown who conducted the field research.

[19] See IETF (2002) Request for Comments No. 2418, at http://tools.ietf.org/html/rfc2418.

[20] Huizer and Crocker (1994); IETF (1996).

elaborate hierarchies – are generally rejected. Most of the IETF's work is conducted over email lists with open memberships, so barriers to participation are low and communication is high-speed. The organization has formal meetings three times a year, which are now attended by thousands of participants.[21] The Internet's success to date is a testament to the success of the IETF protocols. One reason for the effectiveness of IETF standards has been that the same researchers who later became the standards' primary users created them.[22] As Van Schewick explains: 'many of the relevant standards [particularly by IETF and W3C] are open standards and their asset specificity is low'.[23] It operates within a 'nest' of coordinating committees and organizations.[24] Note the secretariat of the IETF is, since 2004, the Internet Society (ISOC), which also plays key policy and coordination roles in domain names[25] and Internet governance.

IETF operates on the basis of technical standards papers drafted through working groups and offered as 'Requests for Comments' (RFCs). There have been about 5,000 RFCs. These papers only become standards when adopted by market actors – many RFCs are 'dormant' in that only a few (if any) actors adopted them (this explanation is necessarily simplistic). Once developed, standards are published as RFCs, but other categories of work such as experimental protocols, informational documents, and proposed/draft standards are also included in the RFC series.[26] To avoid confusion, established Internet Standards are now indexed both in the RFC series and in the Standards-only STD series.[27]

---

[21] IETF79 in Beijing, China had 1,388 delegates registered, see www.ietf.org/registration/ietf79/attendance.py. This has led to discussion about holding an equal number of meetings in Asia, as the US and Europe (currently one in six meetings are in Asia, two in Europe, three in North America): see www.mail-archive.com/ietf@ietf.org/msg47870.html.

[22] Davidson, Morris and Courtney (2002). Note that this project was aimed at examining decreasing public policy objectivity and increasing commercial pressure to close Internet standards of concern to privacy and openness advocates, as part of the CDT's 'Standards, Technology, and Policy Project' funded by the Ford Foundation, the Markle Foundation and the Open Society Institute.

[23] Van Schewick (2010) at p. 202.

[24] Note particularly the Internet Architecture Board: 'The IAB is chartered both as a committee of the IETF and as an advisory body of the ISOC. Its responsibilities include architectural oversight of IETF activities, Internet Standards Process oversight and appeal, and the appointment of the RFC Editor.' See www.iab.org/.

[25] Through ICANN and the .org global Top-Level Domain (gTLD).

[26] See for instance Kempf and Austein (2004) [note: written on behalf of the Internet Architecture Board] (discussed in Van Schewick (2010) at p. 523).

[27] IETF (1995) RFC 1792; IETF (2001) RFC 3160. RFCs can be located at www.ietf.org/rfc.html or www.rfc-editor.org/.

IETF's participatory principle is that 'membership in the IETF and its Working Groups is defined to be established solely and entirely by ... individual technical contributors rather than by formal representatives of organizations'.[28] The enormous strategic and commercial importance of IETF standardization, combined with the size of key Internet standards players, has meant that corporations have often sent several hundred such 'individual experts' to meetings.[29] That is not to say that such companies dominate IETF, but the standards process is increasingly contentious and partisan, with commercial realities and consortium-building essential in the major commercial standards. Davidson claims that increased commercialization of the Internet in the 1990s:

> prefigured a significant increase in the number of privately-motivated participants in the standards process. The increase signaled (sic) a subtle change for Internet standards-making ... the extent to which participants can be expected to be in agreement about certain aspects of the network's architecture is diminished. It is a testament to the strength of the standards bodies' deliberative process that 'rough consensus and running code' continues to be a functional way to make technical decisions.[30]

The packing of working groups by engineers from dominant companies has been noted. Companies do not pay for their employees' time and expenses in attending IETF and working on standards because they are entirely paternalistic beneficial charitable organizations.

IETF is a highly successful technical standard setting organization, but cannot avoid the public interest in its workings, particularly as its individual participatory process without formal memberships by corporations is so lauded. Davidson, Morris and Courtney state that: 'Though many technologists within the leading standards bodies are public-minded, few have explicit expertise in policy-making or at interpreting the public interest. Standards organizations have always (appropriately) emphasized technical goals over societal ones, but in the Internet's early history there was a significant overlap between the two.'[31] Avoidance of IETF and use of private standard-setting is of course a less transparent and public-spirited cause, and can also lead to government reaction, as DeNardis states:[32]

---

[28] http://tools.ietf.org/html/rfc2028.
[29] The previous past chairs of the IETF have been Cisco (Fred Baker 1996–2001 and Harald Alvestrand 2001–5) and former IBM employees (Brian Carpenter 2005–7).
[30] Davidson, Morris and Courtney (2002) at p. 5.
[31] Davidson, Morris and Courtney (2002) at p. 4.
[32] DeNardis (2010), p. 11.

> Greater privatization of Internet governance could be, in some environ-
> ments, an invitation for greater government regulation of the Internet, a
> phenomenon that would carry its own set of unintended consequences.[33]
> Another obvious implication is the use of Internet governance techniques
> for competitive advantage. Standards-based patents, search engine trade
> secrecy,[34] and competitively motivated prioritization of traffic can all
> have consequences for competition and innovation. [footnotes added]

The type of regulatory capture described is subtle rather than blatant.[35]
As DeNardis concludes: 'Emerging Internet governance research should
assess the implications of this private ordering and examine the key
issues at stake at the intersection of technical expediency and the public
interest.'[36] That is the task in the next case study, that of the W3C.

IETF rejects procedural legitimacy in favour of efficiency of outcome,
but places its claims for egality in its transparency and lack of hierarchy.
This has worked well, especially in the pre-commercial or disinterested
period in which standards were made in a forum of genuine collaboration and collegiality. By the 1990s, as it became obvious that the Internet
and its standards would soon be of great commercial benefit, the degree
to which an individual could divorce their engineering ideals from the
strategy of their employers obviously became compromised. That is not to
state that no disinterested individuals or indeed standards emerge from
the IETF, as that would clearly be a falsehood. It is to say that organizations with strong ties inside IETF standards-setting can stymie those
standards with which they commercially disagree, should they also find
a legitimate engineering reason for opposition. Much IETF work still fits
the view of disinterested individuals pursuing truth, while the 'rough
veto' of particular sets of interests is overlooked.

World Wide Web Consortium (W3C)

W3C, founded in 1994,[37] is the standards body established by Sir
Tim Berners-Lee, the inventor of the World Wide Web, the hyper-
text protocol-based information standards that provide the most-used

---

[33] See Bendrath (2009). See also Bendrath and Mueller (2010).
[34] She cites Goldman (2006); Pasquale (2006); and Grimmelmann (2007).
[35] Ogus (2004), pp. 329–346.
[36] DeNardis (2010), p. 11. See further Mueller (2010a); Mueller *et al.* (2007).
[37] Sources: www.w3.org/2005/01/timelines/timeline-2500x998.png and www.w3.org/
Consortium/activities.html.

publishing interface (e.g., HTML and HTTP) for the Internet for consumers and non-technical users.[38] W3C is able to interoperate with IETF because it meets RFC standards.[39] It was founded as an international standards consortium with Europe and Japanese partner institutions to the US headquarters.[40] The membership organization and director's powers to enforce decisions were adopted with lessons drawn from the IETF. It licenses its patents royalty-free to members, a decision following a complex four-year negotiation to 2002, which illustrates the complex and detailed attention of the corporate members. Its relationship with regulators includes funding by the EC, and standards that include regulatory requirements in design, for instance the P3P (Platform for Privacy Preferences) and PICS. Evaluation has largely been by academic comparisons with other standards bodies. Particular W3C public policy controversy is detailed later.[41]

It is often overlooked that W3C was launched at the offices of the EC's Information Society Project Office, by then-Commissioner Bangemann. This in part reflected the EC funding for the fledgling W3C, as well as from private industry, resulting in W3C having a tripartite locational spread, from Sophia Antipolis in France to MIT in Massachusetts to Keio University, Japan. Indeed, the careful design of the W3C reflected a determination by its founders not to repeat the national non-membership collectivist formation of the IETF.[42] It is dependent on:

• a broad international corporate and academic membership;
• core teams based in the US, Japan and originally France (now Southampton, UK); and
• a 'benevolent dictator' in its Director, Sir Tim Berners-Lee.

The Membership Agreement, paragraph 4d states:

> Overall direction of the Consortium shall be the responsibility of an MIT-appointed Consortium Director ('Director'), who will act as chief architect

---

[38] See generally Berners-Lee (with Fischetti) (2000); Kahin and Nesson (1997); Kahin and Abbate (1995).

[39] See for instance the work of W3C in IETF standards formation, e.g., IETF (1998a) RFC 2396.

[40] Founded: October 1994. Location: Massachusetts Institute of Technology, 32 Vassar Street, 32-G519, Cambridge, Massachusetts 02139, USA (MIT). European Research Consortium for Informatics and Mathematics, 2004, Route des Lucioles, BP 93, F-06902 Sophia Antipolis, France (ERCIM); Keio University, 5322 Endo, Fujisawa, Kanagawa 252–8520, Japan.

[41] See Cranor (2002).

[42] Weitzner (2007b). Also comments of Tim Berners-Lee, informal interview Southampton, 19 September 2006.

Table 4.1. *Summary of W3C case study*

Was there a government mandate initially?	Not directly: EC funding for French office
What kind of government involvement is there?	None direct
Which other stakeholders are involved and how?	None direct – efforts to achieve interoperability and multilingual/accessible standards
How is transparency ensured?	Web publication of all proceedings
What is the enforcement mechanism; is it effective; at what cost?	Market adoption of standards, rival standards bodies
What is the relative size of administrative burdens?	Risk of exclusion given membership costs.
Is financial independence assured how?	Yes, through growth in size of standards 'market'
Which internal factor most impacts success?	Relation between executive and membership – particularly via potential dominance of larger company representatives
Which external conditions impact success/failure (e.g., competitive situation, technology, etc.)?	Governmental: relationship with national and regional standards bodies, and content regulation. Market: growth of other standards bodies and relation to (especially) IETF. Technology: development of semantic web standards
Lessons for European policy	Membership approach and focused status highly effective; greater efforts to address user community than IETF. Potential competition problems with some standards given closed membership

for all specifications produced by the Consortium and who shall have the ultimate authority for all Consortium activities ... ERCIM and Keio shall each appoint a Deputy Director who report to the Director and manage the development effort at ERCIM and Keio, respectively.[43]

The formal membership model is that of industry standards bodies in, for instance, telecoms, the global organization reflects more traditional

---

[43] www.w3.org/2005/03/Member-Agreement.

United Nations' related bodies which are 'born global', and the 'benevolent dictator' model is related to that of the Free Software Foundation (in which Richard Stallman plays that role). Weitzner stated: 'There are choices that W3C has made that position it between the poles of IETF and European standardisation.'[44] The logic to this organizational structure is that membership ties corporate developers into participating in the standards process very tightly; an intercontinental secretariat provides for the stability and funding of the organizational structure and secretariat; and 'dictatorship' provides for a classical and simple model to overcome any sclerotic impasses dictated by the first two factors. This is also different to a more open source 'dictator' model, such as the Python standards family. W3C chose to be membership-based, with clear funding and transparency impacts. The 'community-governance body' over time had to devote more time to transparency. The Membership Agreement and the Process Document are public.

WWW standards would be a small part of IETF discussion, but the entire focus of the fledgling W3C. Weitzner explains that 'the IETF was not prepared to devote sufficient attention and energy to web architecture as a system' so there was the need for a devoted organization ('It was a question of bandwidth and priorities'). Note, Policy Director Weitzner joined the US Government, his departure from W3C announced 30 July 2009.[45] W3C states:

> The mission of the World Wide Web Consortium (W3C) is to lead the World Wide Web to its full potential by developing common protocols that promote its evolution and ensure its interoperability. The W3C Process Document describes the organizational structure of the W3C and the processes related to the responsibilities and functions they exercise to enable W3C to accomplish its mission.[46]

Its mission is standards- and outreach-based:

> W3C primarily pursues its mission through the creation of Web standards and guidelines. [1994–2007] W3C has published more than ninety such standards, called W3C Recommendations. W3C also engages in education and outreach, develops software, and serves as an open forum for discussion about the Web … By publishing open (non-proprietary)

---

44 Weitzner (2007b).
45 Associate Administrator for Policy at the US Commerce Department's National Telecommunications and Information Administration in the Obama administration: see www.ntia.doc.gov/opadhome/staffbios.htm.
46 www.w3.org/2005/10/Process-20051014/.

standards for Web languages and protocols, W3C seeks to avoid market fragmentation and thus Web fragmentation.[47]

W3C realized early on that having a paying board of directors, one-country-one-vote or one-company-one-vote system would not work. There is no way to legislate against votes and lobbies, but the dictator model allows for the elimination of the worst obstructionist attempts by lobbies. W3C policies are generally broadly adopted by the web development community and the wider market, though not without controversy, for instance the late 1990s 'browser wars' between Microsoft and Netscape. Berners-Lee's role was considered essential in 1994–6 during the Netscape/Microsoft HTML wars, as he alone had the ability to arbitrate between rivals by making independent decisions, which became the default 'final appeal' when all attempts at consensus fail. W3C may have differences from IETF but the critical lesson taken from IETF was technical meritocracy. Weitzner (2007) states: 'If we've done one thing that should be remembered, it's that decisions must have technical merit and engineering substance behind them.'

As an unusually tightly-knit and focused standards body, W3C has maintained a coherence which Weitzner and others argue is unusual in technical standardization in such public standards. It is genuinely international in its approach, with over forty languages used on its website and world offices in eighteen other territories: 'W3C's global initiatives also include nurturing liaisons with national, regional and international organizations around the globe ... W3C operations are jointly administered [at MIT in the USA, France (from 1995) and Japan (from 1996)].'[48]

W3C's more controversial developments such as PICS gave it an unwelcome reputation for attempting technical fixes to what are essentially political problems, as we will see.

In order to promote a diverse membership representing the interests of organizations around the world, W3C fees vary depending on the annual revenues, type and location of headquarters of an organization.[49] For instance, as of 1 April 2007, a small company in India would pay US$ 953 annually, a non-profit in the United States would pay US$ 6,350, and a very large company in France would pay €65,000.[50] Members can

---

[47] www.w3.org/Consortium/.   [48] www.w3.org/International/.
[49] www.w3.org/Consortium/fees.
[50] Members: 439 at 2 November 2007, see www.w3.org/Consortium/Member/List.

put forward one representative to the Advisory Committee which elects the Advisory Board on two-year terms. Its remit is: 'ongoing guidance to the [management] team on issues of strategy, management, legal matters, process, and conflict resolution ... The Advisory Board manages the evolution of the process document. The Advisory Board hears appeals of member submission requests that are rejected for reasons unrelated to web architecture [which are appealed to the TAG]'. Most importantly, the Advisory Board oversees the evolution of the W3C Process Document, the 'constitution' of the W3C.[51] Members also sign an agreement binding them to the process.[52]

W3C follows IETF Best Current Practice as set out in RFC 2119.[53] Standards are described as Recommendations and proceed through the twenty-two W3C activities and sixty-eight working groups (in 2007)[54] with the following steps:[55]

(1) Working drafts
(2) Candidate recommendation (CR): a document that W3C believes has been widely reviewed and satisfies the Working Group's technical requirements. W3C publishes a CR to gather implementation experience.
(3) Proposed recommendation (PR): a mature technical report that, after wide review for technical soundness and implementability, W3C has sent to the W3C Advisory Committee for final endorsement.
(4) W3C r(REC): a specification or set of guidelines that, after extensive consensus-building, has received the endorsement of W3C Members and the Director. W3C recommends their wide deployment.

The Technical Advisory Group charter was added to W3C process in July 2001, and its membership consists of nine people.[56] With the exception of Berners-Lee as chair, all members are elected or appointed by the W3C for two-year terms (four in each year), with the majority elected. Agendas and meeting minutes are publicly available.[57]

[51] www.w3.org/Consortium/process.html.
[52] www.w3.org/2005/03/Member-Agreement.
[53] www.ietf.org/rfc/rfc2119.txt.
[54] www.w3.org/Consortium/activities.html.
[55] Paragraph 7.1.2 of the W3C Process Document at www.w3.org/2005/10/Process-20051014/tr.
[56] www.w3.org/2001/tag/#about.
[57] www.w3.org/2001/tag/2007/09/17-agenda.

The development of patent policy in 1999–2003 is the most challenging case of W3C staff persuading member companies to adopt a new policy. By choosing royalty-free standards, the W3C chose to avoid patent licensing negotiation in favour of wider deployment. Weitzner states that: 'everyone could see that the value was in its universality' and:

> An interesting test of [SRO] robustness is to ask whether it's able to make hard decisions like that. Our decision wasn't a simple democratic decision. It took four years to develop, and a vote at any annual stage before that would have rejected it … An unheralded strength of a well-working [SRO] is that change of attitude works in both directions – from members and staff.

He argues that staff perseverance forced a deliberate and constructive decision, with a huge expenditure in time in order to achieve that result, which came about because of a refusal to follow established 'in the box' thinking by initially staff, and then increasingly closely engaged members such as IBM. A handful of members left in that period (whether through cost-cutting, market turbulence or policy disagreement is not audited), but membership was growing and continues to grow. The Membership Agreement sets out the patent policy at paragraph 7b: 'patentable inventions and copyrighted materials … shall be jointly owned … Member acknowledges that all such jointly owned [information/products/specifications] will be made available to the general public pursuant to the then-current W3C Software Notice and License (www.w3.org/Consortium/Legal/copyright-software)'.

Paragraph 7c continues: 'MIT, ERCIM and Keio agree to grant and hereby grant to Member a non-exclusive royalty-free, irrevocable, right and license to use … throughout the world.'

Platform for Internet Content Selection (PICS)

PICS was an immediate response to the threat of legal classification of indecent content in the United States. As Shah and Kesan explain:

> The history of the PICS begins with proposed legislation to regulate indecent speech on the Internet by Senator Exon in the summer of 1994 … This would eventually become the Communications Decency Act (CDA). The law made it unlawful to transmit indecent material over the Internet to minors. In response, in June 1995, the W3C began setting up a meeting to discuss technical solutions for the regulation of Internet content.[58]

[58] Shah and Kesan (2003), p. 5.

W3C intended to create a viewpoint-independent content labelling system, and thus allow individuals to selectively access or block certain content, without government or content provider censorship.[59] As a scheme, its urgency was somewhat reduced in 1997 by the overturning of the CDA in *American Civil Liberties Union* v. *Reno*. Its scheme was taken up, promoted and adapted by ICRA, which was funded by the EC SIAP, and by 2005 was adapted for use on mobile Internet sites. While support for ICRA included government funding and adoption by some websites, most 'free-riding' websites choose not to label their pages.[60]

Filtering/labelling was the obvious tool to ensure end-users had the choice of which content to view without censorship.[61] Weitzner states that Campaign for Democracy and Technology broadly supported the W3C decision to develop PICS,[62] the Electronic Freedom Foundation was ambivalent, the ACLU against it, but that:

> What was at stake for the industry was their chance to prove they didn't have to be treated like the mass media, and that was the result in the *Reno* decision. It was a different kind of process to the P3P process, where the FTC made clear that regulation was the alternative … The coordination was between the early Internet industry, some part of the civil liberties community and the White House – Gore, Magaziner, Clinton – who gave their blessing right after the *Reno* decision appeared.

This was classic industry-led self-regulation which 'worked in that it was the right approach, but not as regards interoperability with other incentives for individual website owners'. He agrees that co-implementation on child pornography is clearly not a self-regulatory issue. PICS has transparency issues but is in his view the inevitable model. Where real issues existed, there were some differences between the market-driven US approach ('not self-regulatory but technology will provide the tools') and the EU co-regulatory standards-based approach towards ICRA. He concludes: 'I don't think there were ever clear expectations set by policy-makers as to results, nor were there adequate resources provided for deployment. To my mind that is putting a figleaf on the problem.' Tracking the progress of such labelling standards sheds light on the manner in which technical standards can be used to create content classification and ultimately

---

[59] Resnick and Miller (1996), pp. 87–93.
[60] ICRA is considered in depth in Marsden *et al.* (2008), pp. 62–68. See also Archer (2007).
[61] See Berman and Weitzner (1995), p. 1619; Weitzner (2007a), pp. 86–89.
[62] For the end-to-end design, see Saltzer *et al.* (1984), pp. 277–288.

content standards. At this interface, standards bodies are technical fora with clear influence on content standards. It is an excellent example of the influence of technology standards on policy.

W3C Problems Semantic web standards

The failure of the semantic web thus far to develop as its supporters in W3C had predicted is perhaps the most significant lack of impact that W3C standards have sustained. The semantic web is a 'next generation' of web services, which will provide far greater richness and functionality for World Wide Web (web) applications on the Internet.[63] Berners-Lee described the timeframe for such a transformation to take place.[64] There have been various attempts to create electronic records for government data, with the most basic XML data input taking place in about 1998. More recent initiatives label data using Resource Description Framework (RDF), a data standard that enables 'semantic' mixing of data based on the raw data source.[65] This process requires a network effect to become commonplace, in which the RDF standard is used by pilot or 'brochureware' products and projects, leading early adopters to trigger a 'cascade' effect via growing incentives to follow others who have adopted the standard. The resource and adoption curve needs mean that it is at least a medium-term project to move to semantic web standards.

Weitzner argues that the semantic web needs incentives to conform to good privacy practices: 'where there are agreements on data sharing – and where benefits of such data integration are apparent across system boundaries: a database of databases in ever expanding and intersecting circles ... Every link has a cost and they may be too high for certain intersections – financial services and natural sciences for instance.' The turning point for the semantic web was for him that Oracle installed native RDF support for life sciences and geospatial communities. He believes that: 'Governments could have an incredibly positive role in making government information available in open semantic web structures.'[66]

---

[63] See Darlington, J., Cohen, J. and Lee, W. (undated, mimeo), An architecture for a next-generation Internet based on web services and utility computing, London e-Science Centre.
[64] Berners-Lee (2006), presentation to Terra Future conference, 19 September, at www.w3.org/2006/Talks/0919-os-tbl/.
[65] See www.aktors.org/people/.   [66] Weitzner (2007b).

Baron states:

> [Economic] motives lead groups within the W3C to spend significant amounts of time on things that don't help the Web. For example, a company that is using W3C technologies in a non-Web environment may push the issues that arise in their environment to the agendas of working group meetings. Essentially, they're paying the W3C to have experts on the technology (the working group) solve their problems. And those experts are often quite willing, since work to make one's invention used in more places can appeal to the vanity of the inventor.[67]

He argues that the mobile versus computer standards differences are using up the W3C's efforts: 'interoperability between these two worlds is not high enough to make it easy to develop content that works well in both … the Web browser community isn't making much progress on standards relevant to the Web because it's spending all of its time fighting the larger Mobile Web community'.[68]

He adds that: 'Around the same time, there has been concern raised by prominent figures in the Web development community about lack of progress within the W3C [and] its lack of concern for the needs of Web developers.' However, the argument that pre-mobile standards were developed in much greater harmony is claimed to be inventing a Golden Age that never was, by those engaged in the fights between Netscape and Microsoft. W3C continues to receive some criticism for what one might term being a victim of its own success, with the accusation of capture by its corporate clients, and that it is insufficiently focused on developer needs. Baron accepts the need for competing standards to emerge from W3C's activities:

> I used to think that the W3C should focus on things that are compatible … with what is already on the Web and designed primarily to improve the Web … given the breadth of activity within the W3C, we can no longer assume that all the W3C's specifications are part of a single plan … specifications should compete on their own merits among implementers, authors, and users.

Ultimately the fate of W3C standards depends on market adoption, based on both their utility and the technical rigour of the standards development process. As W3C grows, it may be that the type of competitive

---

[67] Baron (2006).
[68] This particularly related to the SVG Tiny 1.2 Working Group advancing the specification to Candidate Recommendation, accused of duplicating features of many other Web standards, failing to clarify basic concepts and not following W3C process, largely duplicating features that already exist in HTML+CSS, and a new script processing model that is incompatible with the one used by HTML on the Web.

behaviour more familiar to the contested standards of ETSI and other standards bodies will become even more routine.

ICANN and addressing infrastructure

The concern regarding the place of the Internet and national sovereignty since 2003 has focused on the World Summit on the Information Society (WSIS) and the reformation of ICANN.[69] ICANN runs the 'telephone numbers' for the Internet and oversees the 246 ccTLDs (country code Top-Level Domains such as .de and .uk) but has retreated from earlier commitments to: a democratic control via direct elections by registered Internet users after the election of 2002, and the removal of supervision by the US Department of Commerce via its National Telecoms and Information Administration (NTIA). It tried to learn from the poster child of bottom-up participation, the IETF, while indulging in public consultation like the best of governmental regulatory agencies, yet with the formal legal apparatus and corporate governance of a California private corporation.[70] ICANN takes its authority from a contract with the US Commerce Department since 1998,[71] and since 2009 from an Affirmation of Commitments (AoC) released 30 September. The AoC replaces the Joint Project Agreement (JPA), under which the Commerce Department exercised supervision of ICANN on a unilateral basis in 1998–2009. As Palfrey states, ICANN itself is such a hybrid that accountability became fraught at its inception: 'ICANN's structure was a compromise in the worst sense of the word. The designers attempted to blend the best parts of a corporation, a standards body, and a government entity, but they ended up with a structure that does not carry the legitimacy or authority or effectiveness of any of its component parts.'[72]

This summary and critique does not assess the overall root system for gTLDs (global Top-Level Domains), but builds upon that work, to examine the impact of global, regional and national governance mechanisms on daily use of the addressing resources. The committee structure of ICANN and its relations with regional and national SROs (e.g., Nominet) appointed to assign IP addresses by ICANN are complex and their reform fraught with interdependencies. ICANN's historical

---

[69] See Peake (2004).
[70] MacSithigh (2010), pp. 274–300 on .xxx and non-alphanumeric domains.
[71] US Government (1998). See further NGO and Academic ICANN Study (2001).
[72] Palfrey (2004), p. 425.

development has been well documented by Mueller,[73] and the competitiveness and European policy challenges identified. ICANN itself acknowledges its reform process is necessarily forced to compromise between its technical mission[74] and the imperatives of good governance, national sovereignty and content regulation, and there are lively ongoing discussions of principle and practice, played out in public in ICANN board meetings.[75] ICANN has in its short history been a lightning rod for concerns regarding the legitimacy of a single nation state (the US) controlling the address space for Internet names, and therefore the ability to locate other users (other options exist at the margins but are not as yet relevant in policy terms). Formal democratic decision-making for the novel ICANN form of co-regulation that the US Government established in 1998, has been subject to severe criticism and proposals for its replacement by international legitimacy.[76]

ICANN signs agreements with national and regional registrars (including .eu for instance), as well as: 'Regional Internet Registries' (RIRs). The RIRs are responsible for allocating and assigning Internet Protocol (IP) resources within a particular geographical region. These resources include IP addresses and autonomous system numbers (commonly referred to as number resources).[77] The European RIR is RIPE NCC (the Réseaux IP Européens Network Coordination Centre). European and East Asian countries have rapidly overtaken the US in absolute numbers of Internet users, especially broadband-enabled consumers and those using the new architecture of IPv6, but this is not yet reflected in a multilateral settlement for the crucial addressing space. New developments promise to remove some of the scarcity constraints on IP address use. First, there are East Asian-led alternatives, which are implementing Unicode and IPv6 addressing. Second, there is the use of subdirectories based on connecting many computers to a single IP address, widely used in China, for instance. Third, there are other proposed non-DNS alternatives, for non-profit purposes. Fourth, there are more or less successful attempts at new gTLDs (e.g., .union or .xxx) and regional TLDs, notably .eu. These would be interesting case studies with a view to gaining greater insight into and analysis of the future potential direction of the

---

[73] See generally Mueller (2002).
[74] See also LSE Public Policy Group and Enterprise (2006).
[75] See one director's blog entry on the issues, at http://joi.ito.com/archives/2007/03/31/icann_board_votes_against_xxx.html.
[76] College of Europe (2005); Froomkin (2003b), pp. 1087–1102.
[77] www.isoc.org/news/2.shtml.

DNS space.[78] A controversial aspect of the Domain Name System (DNS) is the privacy-related problem inherent in the WHOIS database of IP addresses, which was redesigned in 2007.

The 2007 evaluation of ICANN by One World Trust notes that: 'Accountability and transparency featured prominently in the 2006 [JPA] … This agreement provides the mechanisms and procedures that will affect the transition of the Internet domain name and addressing system to the private sector.' It states:

> When benchmarked against other global organisations, the overall level of transparency of the ICANN Board is also high; where ICANN should improve their practice is in explaining more clearly how stakeholder input is used when making decisions. To ensure [volunteer] Directors are able to participate effectively and efficiently in the decision making they need to be provided with additional support by ICANN staff.[79]

International Chambers of Commerce state: 'ICANN should avoid making policy decisions through closed-door discussions. ICANN should also disclose who is involved in discussions, where consensus is achieved, and provide advance notice of how and when decisions are to be made … New ICANN policies should only be established through a defined bottom-up process.'[80]

ICANN has had several recent attempts to improve its accountability,[81] all of which have been initiated by the Board and the executive staff who run the organization. ICANN bylaws require the periodic review of 'each Supporting Organization, each Supporting Organization Council, each Advisory Committee (other than the Governmental Advisory Committee), and the Nominating Committee'. Article IV, section 4 of ICANN's bylaws detail the Board-led process. Each review is conducted by external reviewers selected by the Board following publication of a Request for Proposals (RFP) based on terms of reference (ToR). The

---

[78] Interviewees who participated are: Kieran McCarthy (Public Participation Manager, ICANN); Emily Taylor (Director, Nominet, not-for-profit registrar for .uk); William Drake (academic expert); Martin Boyle (then-DTI UK); and Jeremy Beale (Confederation of British Industry).

[79] One World Trust (2007).

[80] International Chambers of Commerce informal advice to ICANN, 21 June 2007, available on file with author or Ayesha Hassan at ICC file.

[81] An excellent short summary is contained in Mueller (2010b), pp. 8–10. See also Lynn (2002). Accountability and Transparency Frameworks and Principles 2008; the Improving Institutional Confidence consultation in 2008 and 2009, and Accountability and Transparency Review Team (ATRT) consultation closed 14 July 2010, see www.icann.org/en/reviews/affirmation/activities-1-en.htm.

bylaws did not allow for review of the Board itself until amended in 2006, and subsequently the Board was independently reviewed by the Boston Consulting Group in 2008,[82] but in a fifteen-month process 'the Board decided that it should be in the position to review the review of itself. Unsurprisingly the Board decided that it worked much better than the BCG felt it did,[83] and disregarded the most important reforms'.[84]

Responding to criticisms of lack of stakeholder involvement in the SRO's processes, ICANN created the Ombudsman, Reconsideration Committee and Independent Review Panel (IRP) of Board actions.[85] McCarthy,[86] former General Manager of Public Participation 2006–9, left a report on his departure recommending changes to permit more constructive public participation.[87] McCarthy's general view is that ICANN worked better than it previously had, but states that ICANN's accountability mechanisms, including the Ombudsman, the Board reconsideration procedure and the Independent Review Panel do not provide meaningful accountability: 'If anything they are damaging because they give the illusion of accountability while not providing any.' He details the problems, beginning with:

> The Ombudsman's authority was very specifically and purposefully limited by ICANN's staff and does not comply with standard Ombudsman rules. In reality he has extremely limited powers to make or force change. At every step the Board has the ability to ignore the Ombudsman's recommendations and, unfortunately, it has done precisely that whenever he has promoted something that the Board disagrees with. [88]

He provides a solution: to give 'additional powers that other Ombudsmen take for granted'. He goes on to consider the Board Reconsideration Committee: 'Unfortunately this has also been a failure and has only served to reinforce an unhealthy attitude in the Board that they make the right decisions and that attempts to question them stem from a hidden agenda.' He states generally: 'the Board has a long culture and tradition of looking very unfavourably on any questioning of its decisions and as a result the Board reconsideration procedure is actually a damaging process of negative accountability'. In his view, the IRP:

> has been used only once and that proved excessively time-consuming and costly … And, incredibly, when the end result was critical of the ICANN Board's decision, its first response was to stress that the IRP Declaration

---

[82] Boston Consulting Group/Colin Carter & Associates (2008).
[83] ICANN (2010).   [84] McCarthy (2010a).   [85] Komaitis (2010).
[86] McCarthy was previously a technology journalist who investigated and reported on ICANN and domain name registries. See McCarthy (2007).
[87] McCarthy (2009).   [88] McCarthy (2010b).

was non-binding i.e., the Board felt it was able to ignore the entire end result if it didn't like it … And if you read the Declaration, the Panelists make it quite clear that the non-binding nature had been purposefully and deliberately written in by ICANN staff. There is a clear pattern of deliberate and calculated efforts on the part of ICANN staff and Board to avoid as far as possible any accountability as introduced by the IRP process. In that sense, it is also a very poor accountability mechanism. [89]

ICANN bureaucracy maintains the best transparent yet non-accountable method of consulting, by consulting at the last minute and burying policy in unwieldly and enormous documents: 'The biggest problem is a cultural one – ICANN staff maintain a default of not providing [timely accessible] information … For at least five years the community has been calling for every report to come with an executive summary – standard practice in most industries.'[90] When it comes to wider public participation, ICANN appears to ask for too many comments[91] and ignore much of it: 'There is no culture of checking public input against benchmarks, and very little value put on public input – it is seen more as an annoyance than a crucial check and balance.'[92] That latter status has led to severe problems in corporate disclosure, with critics – including former Board members – claiming that ICANN not only fails to serve its wider public but actually fails to disclose correctly to the board that governs it. The overall impression is of a bureaucracy which maintains the semblance of civil society participation without allowing for effective interaction.

Mueller as well as McCarthy has a direct critique of ICANN processes and of what he terms as: '[T]he new participatory evangelists [who] seem more willing to offer people opportunities to get involved than they are willing to offer them real authority or influence over the decisions. There is an important distinction between "making your views known" and "making your views count".'[93] Transparency and consultation without purpose and accountability is the mantra they attack and they particularly target ICANN processes for this critique. They identify ICANN's accountability problems by reference to its hybrid model.[94] Mueller claims that 'ICANN's massive emphasis on public participation can be interpreted as a kind of

---

[89] Article IV, section 3 of the ICANN bylaws defines the Independent Review Procedure. The procedure has only been used once, by ICM Registry in connection with the .xxx top-level domain controversy. At the time of this writing, the results are unknown.
[90] McCarthy (2010b).
[91] See current consultations at: www.icann.org/en/public-comment/.
[92] McCarthy (2010b).
[93] Mueller (2010b).
[94] Klein (2001); Koppell (2005), pp. 94–108; NAIS (NGO and Academic ICANN Study) (2001); Weber (2009).

Table 4.2. *Adapting Mueller's ICANN accountability model – italics indicate adaptation*

Accountability	Corporate	Consensus non-member standards (e.g., IETF)	Governmental
		Organizational models	
Direct	Shareholders (profit); Members (non-profit)	Election of Working Group chairs	Citizenship and voting; Representation
Exit	Competitive choice (profit); Refusal to support (non-profit)	Voluntary adoption of standards (in non-member organiza- tions)	*Emigration, anarchy*
External	Conformity to public law; Government regulation	*Ignorance or non-adoption of standards*	Rule of law; Judicial review
Voice	*Peer production; Crowd-sourcing; Web2.0 and other customer feedback mechanisms*	Open participation	Lobbying, pub-lic hearings, protests, etc.

over-compensation for the glaring absence of Direct, Exit and External forms of accountability'[95] as it is a private corporation that evades all the hybrid models of accountability that would otherwise hold it in check. Transparency without participation is no panacea for private regulation, as can be seen in Table 4.2.

Richter views ICANN as a poorly designed and captured hybrid of cooperation and customer social entrepreneur approaches with limited shareholder support.[96] He does argue that hybrid models can co-exist, as

---

[95] Mueller (2010b) at p. 8.   [96] Richter (2010) at p. 409.

they have done for Creative Commons in Brazil/UK or Nominet in the UK, but that the model is always susceptible to accusations of failure to address constitutional rights absent judicial review, and of transnational arbitrage. This is also the problem with a charity-based approach without the social entrepreneurship element.[97]

As far as the Government Advisory Committee (GAC) is concerned, McCarthy considers that:

> The problem lies not with the GAC, in my view, but with the ICANN Board who seem to have a schizophrenic attitude toward governments – at times being unfairly aggressive, and at times cowering and submissive. The best example of this relationship not working at the moment is the issue of dot-xxx – where the ICANN Board appears to be using the GAC as a shield because it doesn't wish to approve or reject the application itself.[98]

Dot-xxx (or .xxx) is the issue that brings out the worst in ICANN accountability. The issue is fascinating, not least because it is where political concerns over content control meet the monopoly that ICANN maintains in running the DNS system so far as public registries are concerned. It was the main subject of the ICANN meeting I attended as an observer in spring 2007 in Lisbon, Portugal, where I interviewed several key members of ALAC, GNSO and the GAC. The authorization of .xxx would have provided a funding stream for FOSI, as the .xxx domain would have provided a very evident label that could be used for parents to filter out adult content, and the prospective registrar offered to support FOSI with part of the anticipated multimillion dollar annual proceeds. However, the process has continued to be blocked and at the time of writing, in November 2010, still awaits an advisory opinion by the GAC. It may be that the process is complete by the time of publication of this book, but it had looked likely in 2008 during the drafting of the EC report on which the book is based. Such long procedural delays are of course a serious impediment to the business plans of prospective registrar, ICANN itself and of FOSI.

National registrar Nominet

An interesting 'best practice' example of a national registrar is the UK not-for-profit registrar Nominet, acknowledged as a leading actor in multi-stakeholder governance.[99] It is also a particularly transparent example of the type, which is of great importance given both the strategic importance

---

[97] Nicholls (2010).   [98] McCarthy (2010b).
[99] See Marsden et al. (2008), pp. 37–43; Boyle (2007); Clayton (2007); Hutty (2007b); Swetenham (2007); Taylor (2007). Note that Boyle joined Nominet and Taylor left Nominet, in the period since 2008.

of its function and its role as something of a national 'natural monopoly'.[100] Nominet is a non-profit company limited by guarantee, and has members who act as shareholders, but without the right to participate in the profits of the company. Nominet pre-dates ICANN, being established in 1996, and has worked more or less effectively since then, as the UK's domain name market has grown. It allocates addresses to registrars instead of directly allocating them, taking a small fee for each registration. There are at least seven million addresses allocated, making Nominet the fourth-largest registrar globally. This has resulted in a large surplus, which registrars wanted to access by reforming Nominet into a for-profit business that could pay dividends, while government made clear that it wished to see the surplus retained and used for educational and charitable purposes.[101]

The avalanche of changes to ICANN in order to secure its public interest mission against the commercial interests of its domain name registrars is reflected in the controversy over whether Nominet would be made subject to regulation by government within the DEAct.[102] Nominet avoided this fate only by engaging in substantial reforms and an extraordinary general meeting (EGM) in 2010 that resulted in changes to its articles of association, guaranteeing its independence from its member registrars. This process satisfied government, but one should not underestimate the extent to which government threats of regulation were necessary to ensure Nominet made these reforms in the face of much registrar opposition.[103] This frenetic reform activity coincides with the formation of the Digital Britain task team within government in September 2008, and the first House of Commons Reading of the Digital Economy Bill (DEB2009) on 16 March 2010.[104]

David Hendon, Director for the Information Economy in the responsible government department,[105] explains that: 'This is about the development

---

[100] For instance by promoting its best practice challenge, launched by a government minister in Parliament: www.nominet.org.uk/about/bestpracticechallenge/categories/.

[101] See Communications Act 2003, section 124O(7) for definitions.

[102] Note that this refers to its allocation of names to private registrars under .co.uk, .net.uk, .ltd.uk, .plc.uk, .me.uk, .sch.uk as it is not responsible for eleven governmental and other non-profit domains, such as .ac.uk, .nhs.uk, .gov.uk.

[103] Garratt and Garrett (2010) state at p. 4: 'My Board Evaluation Study had interviews in December 2008 and was completed by mid-January 2009. The December interviewees included one recently-resigned director. By late January 2009, another director had resigned and a new director had been appointed. These movements on what is a very small Board made my original analysis obsolete.'

[104] Digital Economy Bill 2009 [HL] was published on 20 November 2009. Digital Economy Act 2010, see www.statutelaw.gov.uk/content.aspx?activeTextDocId=3699621.

[105] The department was known as Department for Business, Enterprise and Regulatory Reform (BERR) 2007–9, and then Department for Business, Innovation and Skills, which it remained after the 2010 General Election.

Table 4.3. *Timetable of Nominet governance reforms 2008–10*

Date	Document	Author
15 October 2008	Letter from BERR	David Hendon at BERR
31 March 2009	1. Governance Review	Professor Bob Garratt
	2. Comparison with 2006 Combined Code of Corporate Governance	Appended to Garratt Report
	3. Mutuo Report: into membership and stakeholder issues	Mutuo – specialist consultants in mutual society activities
	4. Mutuo Parliamentary report	Mutuo review of political opinions
16 April 2009	Nominet letter to BERR	To David Hendon at BERR
12 May 2009	BERR response letter	From David Hendon at BERR
21 May 2009	Shaping the future of .uk	First consultation 21 May–21 August 2009
23 November 2009	Shaping the future of .uk	Second consultation 23 November– 15 December 2009
12 January 2010	Request for feedback on proposals	Member comment 12–25 January 2010
26 January 2010	Chairman's letter to BIS	Nominet Chairman, Bob Gilbert
2 February 2010	BIS response letter	David Hendon at BIS
24 February 2010	Extraordinary General Meeting	Nominet amend Articles of Association

Source: Nominet Governance Review (2010), at www.nominet.org.uk/governance/review/.

of self-regulation and being more responsible. The problem with the Internet is that it evolves so quickly it's impossible for the government to effectively regulate. This is not a fashionable position within government. Many [ministers] are not knowledgeable about how the internet works.'[106] In other words, ministers intended to take over Nominet's functions but

---

[106] Williams (2008).

needed dissuading by Hendon. He further explains: 'It is hard to find another example like the DNS where such a vital aspect of the critical national infrastructure is left in the hands of a private company which is unlicensed and unregulated.' When reserve powers were published in the DEB2009 on 20 November, government explained that: 'There have been reported abuses of the domain name system ... such as cybersquatting, drop-catching, pressure sales of domain names, domain names used for phishing and distributing malware, and instances where foreign-owned (and hosted) websites with a .uk domain dupe people into believing they are British.'[107] This placed additional pressure to act as private policeman for domains as well as ensuring that surplus cash was not returned to registrars (some of whom were of course distributing domains to those bad actors responsible for the mischiefs government discussed). Hendon explains in his letter of 2 February 2010 to Nominet: 'I am particularly pleased to see a specific proposal to amend the Articles of Association to reflect Nominet's public benefit purpose'[108] implementing the Garratt review proposals and blocking members' attempts to distribute the cash surplus to themselves. Special resolutions 1(b)(c) inserted articles 1(a)(b) into the Articles of Association: [109]

> 1a In exercising their duties to promote the success of the company for the benefit of the members as a whole the directors shall have particular regard to the impact of the company's activities on the general public.
> 1b The objects of the company are to undertake activities, particularly (without limitation) as were formerly set out in the company's, memorandum of association, and to do so for the public benefit.

Resolution 1(c) required a super-majority of 90 per cent of votes to be carried, and secured 94.85 per cent.

At the culmination of the reforms, both the Chairman[110] and the Legal and Policy Director[111] resigned after five and ten years' service respectively. The new chair is Baroness Fritchie who explained that: 'I hope to give the government confidence in Nominet but I'm not there for government, I'm there for Nominet.'[112] Coincidentally the UK office of the World Wide Web Consortium moved into Nominet's offices as host, announced 30 September 2010.[113] Baroness Fritchie had chaired the Web

---

[107] Williams (2009a).
[108] Hendon (2010), letter to Bob Gilbert, Chair, Nominet, 2 February 2010, at www.nominet.org.uk/digitalAssets/45073_BIS-BobGilbert020210.pdf.
[109] Popularis Ltd (2010), pp. 1–2.   [110] Williams (2010).
[111] Williams (2009b).   [112] McCarthy (2010b).   [113] Nominet (2010).

Science Research Initiative at Southampton University, where W3C chair Berners-Lee is based.

The DEAct includes requirements for Ofcom to report on domain name allocation, section 1 requiring amendment of the Communications Act 2003 (CA 2003), section 134(c):

> (1) OFCOM must, if requested to do so by the Secretary of State –
> (a) prepare a report on matters specified by the Secretary of State relating to internet domain names, and (b) send the report to the Secretary of State as soon as practicable.

Section 19 of DEAct gives government reserve powers under new section 124O, CA 2003:

> (1) This section applies where the Secretary of State – (a) is satisfied that a serious relevant failure in relation to a qualifying internet domain registry is taking place or has taken place, and (b) wishes to exercise the powers under section 124P or 124R.
> (2) The Secretary of State must notify the internet domain registry, specifying the failure and a period during which the registry has the opportunity to make representations to the Secretary of State.
> (3) There is a relevant failure in relation to a qualifying internet domain registry if – (a) the registry, or any of its registrars or end-users, engages in prescribed practices that are unfair or involve the misuse of internet domain names, or (b) the arrangements made by the registry for dealing with complaints in connection with internet domain names do not comply with prescribed requirements.

Section 20 explains the procedure for the appointment of a manager of the internet domain registry, if government takes over the functions of Nominet.[114] A further amendment is in section 21, explaining how government makes amendments through court order by new section 124R, CA 2003:

> (1) This section applies where – (a) the Secretary of State has given a notification under section 124O to a qualifying internet domain registry specifying a failure, (b) the period allowed for making representations has expired, and (c) the Secretary of State is satisfied that the registry has

---

[114] '(1) After section 124O of the Communications Act 2003 insert – "124P Appointment of manager of internet domain registry (1) This section applies where – (a) the Secretary of State has given a notification under section 124O to a qualifying internet domain registry specifying a failure, (b) the period allowed for making representations has expired, and (c) the Secretary of State is satisfied that the registry has not taken the steps that the Secretary of State considers appropriate for remedying the failure".'

not taken the steps that the Secretary of State considers appropriate for remedying the failure ...

(3) The court may make an order – (a) making alterations of the registry's constitution, and (b) requiring the registry not to make any alterations, or any specified alterations, of its constitution without the leave of the court.

(4) An order under this section may contain only such provision as the court considers appropriate for securing that the registry remedies the failure specified in the notification under section 124O.

It is of note that new section 124R(5), CA2003 specifically explains that: 'constitution means, in the case of a company, the articles of association and, in the case of a limited liability partnership, the limited liability partnership agreement'.

Lessons drawn from the governance arrangements of such a registrar may generate recommendations not only for other national registrars but also as examples of transparency for other Internet-related SROs. Nominet is now formally co-regulated under the DEAct.

Conclusion: 'pure' self-regulation and moving targets

The case studies in this chapter tended towards 'pure' forms of industry self-standardization, though noting that the EC both launched and has constantly supported the W3C. ICANN is the exception – not only is it devolved from the US Government, but it is dependent on political acquiescence for its survival and legitimacy. It therefore tries to emphasize its participatory democracy and transparency, while not fooling anyone. Their approximate place on the Beaufort Scale is shown in Table 4.4, while noting that Nominet and ICANN are 'moving targets'.

Bradner has made the following comments regarding my classification of the IETF:

> The only governmental involvement in the IETF is as individuals. We do not submit our standards to anyone for later approval i.e., the IETF is closer to a 0 (informal interchange only) – from time to time there is some exchange of info with one government or another (note that the IETF does not consider itself a US standards organization); the same is true for the W3C. In both cases various governments may adopt the standards but in neither case does the government have a role in the standards approval process.[115]

---

[115] Bradner (2008), email communication to Chris Marsden, 28 September 2008.

Table 4.4. *Self-regulatory organizations and government*

Regulatory scheme	Self-Co	Scale	Government involvement
Post facto standardized self	IETF	2	Later approval of standards
Recognized self	W3C#	5	Recognition of body – informal policy role
Approved compulsory co-regulatory	ICANN	9	Prior principled discussion with government – with sanction/approval/ process audit
Independent body (with stakeholder forum)	Nominet	11	Government imposed and co-regulated (as reformed) with taxation/ compulsory levy

Hash tag indicates government-funded in whole or part

He is correct in the assessment of IETF, but classification in this table is not binary purity, and options 0–5 are what US commentators might term 'zero' or non-governmental involvement. That governments choose of their own volition to recognize IETF standards demonstrates government faith in the standards, and inherently in the standards organization, rather than IETF courting of 'kings and presidents'.

Government as facilitator has been in some respects a rousing success online. Previous history documented the many miserable failures of 1990s government intervention in the Internet's regulation, from bad legislation driven by moral panic, to ill-considered regulatory intervention, to an entirely hands-off approach. But that is only a clichéd partial account of the story, and this chapter considered the roles in which government has supported Internet development.

The following Chapter 5 considers non-Internet issues converging on the Internet (specifically media content standards). In the final case study Chapter 6, we consider the role of Internet Service Providers (ISPs) and specifically their role in Notice and Take Down (NTD) regimes.

5

Content regulation and the Internet

This chapter analyzes co-regulatory bodies ICSTIS, IMCB, ATVOD, NICAM and PEGI. The rating schemes for mobile phone, video online and computer games content derive from 'purer' forms of self-regulation[1] but have morphed into a much more institutional form, while ICSTIS and NICAM are statute-derived co-regulators.

While standards and critical Internet resources are (at least in their extent) unique self- or co-regulatory institutions, there are many examples in content/applications and services delivered via the Internet which one could say are 'converging' on the Internet. They raise regulatory problems which are created by the differing characteristics of the Internet compared to earlier media for which the regulatory regime was designed. Prior media were largely domestic, closed to interference, and therefore the content was 'certified', protected and complied with cultural standards, norms and laws of the sovereign.[2] In addition, these purely domestic 'receivers' (rather than users) could not generate and mix content themselves, nor send it via p2p networks, nor communicate anonymously, nor send bulk communications virtually without cost. Significant differences exist between broadcast, mass print publishing services and the Internet.

In the case of mass media, which forms the core of this chapter, the regulatory institutions are well known, and their application to the Internet is relatively straightforward where the content provider is a mass media company entering into contractual arrangements with a 'walled garden' ISP, fixed or mobile. Premium content in fixed and mobile telephony has been regulated by SROs over an extensive period (over fifteen years in the case of UK co-regulator ICSTIS with significant recent controversy and scrutiny

---

[1] See case studies by this author in Tambini, Leonardi and Marsden (2008), at Ch. 8 'Self-regulation of the electronic games industry' pp. 190–209, and Ch. 10 'Mobile telephony-delivered Internet services and codes of conduct to protect minors from adult content' pp. 216–268.

[2] Note that satellite television in the 1980s raised many of the problems we associate as novel to the Internet: see Marsden and Verhulst (1999).

Table 5.1. *Co-regulatory schemes for Internet content*

Regulatory scheme	Self-Co	Scale	Government involvement
Discussed self	IMCB	4	*Ex ante* principled discussion – but no sanction/approval/ process audit
Approved compulsory co-regulatory	PEGI Online	9	*Ex ante* principled discussion with government – with sanction/approval/process audit
Scrutinized co-regulatory	NICAM# ATVOD	10	As 9 with annual budget/process approval
Independent body (with stake- holder forum)	ICSTIS#	11	Government imposed and co-regulated with taxation/compulsory levy

Hash tag indicates government-funded in whole or part

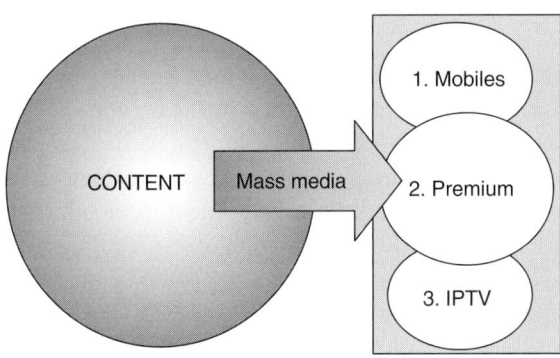

Figure 5.1.   Mass media content categorization

via regulatory audit). While an institution such as the Internet Advertising Bureau can set standards for Internet advertising, it would not be accurate in any respect to describe it as an SRO, when its primary function is as a trade promotion body. Advertising regulation therefore plays a role in this study in terms of known offline examples rather than providing any developments that merit renewed case studies. Lord Currie expresses it thus: 'For pure, internet-delivered content it is difficult to see how any meaningful licensing controls could be imposed and hence how any sanction could be enforced. These problems arise even if the regulatory instrument

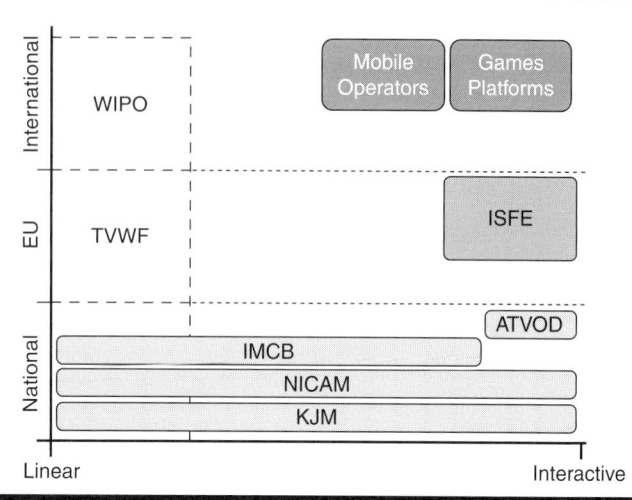

Figure 5.2.   Content regulation from linear to interactive, national to international

of choice is a co-regulatory scheme in which industry operates against a long-stop of possible enforcement action by the regulator.'[3]

The scope and scale of the SRO is important for two reasons: first, how does it fit with formal legal and declared political pressures to regulate its original sector? Second, is it expanding into new sectors (e.g., mobile Internet) or new countries (i.e., pan-European coordination of self-regulation)? Finally, is its model replicable or an exception to other regulatory forms?

The European online content market was surveyed in an independent report for the EC.[4] Holoubek and Damjanovic demonstrate the range of content classifications from offline to online which I have adapted in Figure 5.2.[5] This encompasses a range of classifications with different requirements on intermediaries.

Independent Committee for the Supervision of Standards of Telephone Information Services (ICSTIS)

ICSTIS was founded in 1986 by the telecoms incumbent, BT, the regulator, Oftel (until 2003), and the Government (Department of Trade and

---

[3] Currie (2005).
[4] Screen Digest Ltd, CMS Hasche Sigle, Goldmedia GmbH, Rightscom Ltd (2006).
[5] Holoubek andDamjanovic (2006), p. 8.

Industry (DTI)) to co-regulate premium rate services (PRS). Advertising and PRS substantially pre-date the World Wide Web, and PRS is a long-standing matter of user and regulatory concern.[6] In 1986 there were sixteen service providers using BT's network. Following early scandals (especially related to chat lines, which were banned in 1992 but reintroduced in 2003), the forerunner to the Competition Commission in 1989 recommended that there should be a compulsory code of practice for such services, subject to a single regulator. Oftel delegated ICSTIS to be that regulator.[7]

The premium rate market has seen two substantial changes during its growth since 2002. The first is for mobile services, which are now 33 per cent of the market (total about £1,200m). The second development is broadcast premium services, at 22 per cent or over £270m (typically text message voting). In 2007 the UK PRS industry was the largest in the world – worth €2billion – when controversy emerged as many votes were shown to be badly administered or fraudulent.[8] Further markets were brought inside ICSTIS's remit when 0871 (national calls charged at a local rate) number ranges were passed over from Ofcom: that market size is a further £300m.[9] ICSTIS works with media regulator Ofcom to apply its provisions to mobile networks. With both minors and adults, the intention is to protect customers from overcharging and fraud.[10] In 2007, a strategic review was undertaken, with particular attention to the governance structure and regulating the new markets for mobile, broadcast quiz shows and national-local rate (0871) numbers.

It has been known as PhonepayPlus since October 2007.[11] In this case study, however, ICSTIS is the reference used, as it was for the first twenty-one years of its existence. It is funded by a levy on service providers, which is collected by network operators. Administrative charges are also

---

[6] See further on advertising co-regulation, Dacko and Hart (2005), pp. 2–15.
[7] ICSTIS (2006), pp. 7–8.
[8] ICSTIS (2007).
[9] ICSTIS (2007), p. 15.
[10] See ICSTIS (2005), www.icstis.org.uk/icstis2002/pdf/StakeholderUpdateApril2005.pdf for proposals to withhold payment to potential scammers.
[11] PhonepayPlus (formerly ICSTIS: Independent Committee for the Supervision of Standards of Telephone Information Services): non-profit making company. Clove Building, 4 Maguire Street, London SE1 2NQ. Board: Ten members including chair, with seven independent of the premium rate industry. Formally renamed Board instead of Committee following the eleventh code of practice implementation 4 January 2007. Meets bi-monthly. Non-industry members have further responsibilities in relation to adjudications and special licensed services. Industry Liaison Panel: established 2006. Fifteen members including one ICSTIS member. Budget (£): 2007: 3.459m 2006: 3.612m

collected from service providers and there are fines for those who breach the code of practice of up to £250,000 or disqualification from providing services. Its budget and strategy is ultimately approved by Ofcom, which evaluates the organization annually. ICSTIS established a funding level from the industry (with a levy on turnover introduced in 2003), a compensation scheme and an adjudication procedure, backed from 2001 by an independent appeals tribunal. In 1995, ICSTIS co-founded IARN, the international 'club' of premium rate regulators.

It commits members to its code of practice (11th edition 2007). The code is the cornerstone of ICSTIS regulation, and companies can be investigated and fined for non-compliance. The code applies to any company offering PRS in the UK. These companies are responsible for ensuring that the content and promotion of their premium rate services comply with the code. ICSTIS has a range of sanctions it can impose if it finds that the code has been breached. The code also includes general requirements for network providers to assist ICSTIS in its regulation of companies offering PRS. Ofcom has statutory backstop powers in relation to PRS. It is responsible for approving the code and, under section121 of the Communications Act 2003, for setting the conditions under which PRS providers can operate. Ofcom's stated aims in co-regulation are: 'approving the ICSTIS Code and the ICSTIS budget, where it is satisfied that these enable Ofcom to meet its obligations under the Act; using its powers to ensure compliance with ICSTIS Directions; and carrying out sufficient oversight, and using its backstop powers where necessary, to make sure that regulation is effective'.[12]

The basis on which Ofcom delegates powers under the Communications Act 2003 to ICSTIS are: 'Ofcom will only approve a code if it is satisfied, amongst other things, that there is a person who has the function of administering and enforcing the code. It follows, therefore, that approval of a code effectively signals the approval of an "enforcement authority" to regulate PRS.'

Ofcom's first review of ICSTIS's practices made several recommendations for strengthening ICSTIS's powers: suggesting customer refunds; ICSTIS's investigations; the ICSTIS Code; fines;[13] customer service and

---

[12] Ofcom and ICSTIS (2005).

[13] It suggested the DTI should consider increasing the maximum fine that can be imposed for a breach of the ICSTIS Code of Practice. Under sections 121 and 123 of the Communications Act 2003, the current maximum is £100,000. The Code of Practice

consumer information; and ICSTIS governance: defining ICSTIS and Ofcom roles. On the latter point, it suggested the two organizations should agree a Memorandum of Understanding (MoU) which clarifies the roles of the two organizations in relation to PRS regulation, and ensures appropriate accountability to Ofcom. In August 2005, as an end result of its review for government of ICSTIS begun in 2004, Ofcom announced a revision to the ICSTIS Code to require network operators to retain monies for thirty days following payment.[14] This change is a key recommendation from Ofcom's report to DTI on improving premium rate regulation, and accompanied the MoU, whose terms included new key performance indicators (KPI) for ICSTIS, to be agreed with Ofcom and published every year. Note that changes to the rules require both notification to and consultation with stakeholders under both EU legislative and UK legislative conditions: ICSTIS public consultation on changes to the Code of Practice, including statutory three-month consultation with EC and Member States required under the EU Technical Standards Directive;[15] and Ofcom consultation on amendments to requirements under General Condition 14 and related guidance designed to improve consumer information offered by telecoms companies on premium rate services. Ofcom in 2006 reviewed and approved the eleventh ICSTIS Code:

> 1.4 Section 121(1) of the Act provides that Ofcom may approve a code of practice which has been made by another person for the purpose of regulating PRS. Ofcom approved the ICSTIS Code of Practice (10th edn) on 29 December 2003. On 4 August 2005, Ofcom published its Notification of approval of an emergency code amendment to the ICSTIS Code of Practice (10th edition). The amended Code (10th edn, as amended) ('the approved Code'), and Ofcom's approval of it, remains in force.[16]

The Ofcom Review was undertaken as a result of a formal request from DTI relating to growing concerns about 'rogue' internet diallers which re-routed dial-up Internet connections onto premium rate numbers without customers' knowledge or consent.

ICSTIS handled 131,089 calls to the contact centre in 2006/7 of which 11,000 were complaints and half of the callers were under the impression that they were calling BT not the regulator. ICSTIS also empowers users

---

should also be amended to enable ICSTIS to fine network providers as well as service providers, where the network providers fail to meet their obligations.
[14] Ofcom (2005).
[15] Directive 98/34/EC, as amended by Directive 98/48/EC.
[16] Ofcom (2006a).

to check premium rate numbers – 785,183 checks were made in 2006/7. There were 326,040 unique visitors to the ICSTIS website in 2006/7.[17] New online registration for services has resulted in 617 service providers registering online. ICSTIS also holds a quarterly co-regulatory Forum, for wider engagement with users. It convened the Forum in Manchester and Birmingham as well as two meetings in London in 2006/7. In addition to the website, the industry support team is responsible for consumer and industry outreach.

ICSTIS's strategy is to move from responsive mode (waiting for complaints) to proactive mode (monitoring licensed services and opening own-initiative investigations). In 2003–5 it received 20,000 complaints or more, many related to the 'rogue dialler' issue.[18] The biggest increase in complaints were for adult, text message and dating services, as well as dial-up scams.[19] As a result of the new proactive strategy, ICSTIS opened a record 1,759 new investigations in 2006/7, compared to previous numbers historically between 500 and 1,100 (2000–6). The investigations resulted in 131 cases coming to formal adjudication, with 128 breaches of the code discovered. Of the breaches, 40 per cent related to mobiles. Nine services were shut down using the emergency procedure, which withholds revenues from the network operator, which is instructed not to pass the revenue on to the service provider. This was a very large (90 per cent) drop from the emergency use in 2005/6. Service providers were barred as a result of seventy-three adjudications, with fines issued in a total of 112 breaches. ICSTIS reduced its levy on turnover for service providers from 0.3 per cent to 0.2 per cent, reflecting its policy of setting the levy to reflect ongoing costs. Fine income in proportion to levy income varied between 45 per cent (2007) and 265 per cent (2006), a high variance. Historically, ICSTIS had imposed fines of over £12.5m.[20] The growth of the premium rate market in relation to ICSTIS's fixed costs means that the ICSTIS budget is about 0.25 per cent of the total market, whereas it was about 0.5 per cent in 2000.

The interdependency between ICSTIS and Ofcom is complex, with both broadcasters as service providers and telecoms operators in their network operations responsible to Ofcom. The premium rate industry is complex, with many parties involved in the value chain. Customers pay their telecoms provider for all their calls.[21] The telecoms provider in turn pays

[17] ICSTIS (2007) at pp. 8–9.   [18] ICSTIS (2006) at p. 14.
[19] ICSTIS (2003), p. 7. Note that from 2001, complaints increased by 60 per cent to 11,552.
[20] ICSTIS (2006), p. 4.
[21] For ICSTIS consumer guidance, see www.icstis.org.uk/icstis2002/pdf/consumer_guide. pdf.

other networks to connect the customers' calls, either to the individual or organization they have dialled or to special services such as premium rate. PRS providers collect a share of revenue from their network providers who have in turn been paid by the telecoms provider who is charging the customer. Telecoms operators as wholesalers of premium services to PRS providers are responsible to ICSTIS. The following links in the value chain may be liable:

- Broadcaster as provider of premium phone vote competitions – to Ofcom
- Network operator for integrity of their network – to Ofcom
- Network operator as wholesaler to service providers – to ICSTIS
- Service providers as subcontractors from broadcasters – to ICSTIS.

Until 2006, there was little doubt that the 'first response' regulator should be ICSTIS, as it had powers to fine up to £50,000 for each breach of its Code of Practice. It also has the ability to refer a persistently fraudulent operator to either City of London police or, in the case of a network operator, to Ofcom for removal of its conditions of entitlement.[22] In 2006, the Communications Act was amended to permit Ofcom to fine service providers up to £50,000 for persistent misuse of the network, though its powers to fine broadcast licensees remained unlimited.[23]

ICSTIS and Ofcom faced a crisis of unprecedented proportions in spring/summer 2007, as it emerged that public service broadcasters and their subcontracted service providers had committed fraud on a very widespread basis, by rigging the results of competitions and even awarding prizes to non-entrants. The power to impose unlimited fines on broadcast licensees was exercised in a fine of £2m against the largest breakfast television operator, GMTV. Other broadcasters suspended their competition activities or asked auditors to examine their activities to ensure probity could be restored. Before Parliament the regulators submitted their philosophy of outcome-led regulation:

> Ofcom's view is that detailed prescriptive rules are generally not well suited to matters of content regulation ... Rules based on process may not be applicable in all cases: compliance with a set of rules, no matter how detailed, may still not achieve the desired outcome. The burden

---

[22] In early 2007, representative case bulletins show ICSTIS upheld fines of £45,000 and £50,000 against Zamano and Atlas Interactive Group Ltd respectively.

[23] The maximum financial penalty Ofcom can impose under section 130 of the Act is £50,000 per notification under the Communications Act 2003 (Maximum Penalty for Persistent Misuse of Network or Service) Order 2006.

of compliance, including the editorial processes involved, should rest unambiguously with the broadcaster.[24]

The regulators explain that under the 2005 MoU, Ofcom already 'approves its code of practice, budget and annual activity plan, including an assessment of its performance and the prioritisation of its strategic direction' (at para. 32). They state: 'we do not share the Committee's view that a single point of complaint would be in the best interest of consumers' (at para. 34). They demonstrated their enforcement powers with the £2m fine of GMTV by Ofcom and the £243,000 total fines imposed by ICSTIS on one operator. The regulators explain that ICSTIS set out a range of actions aimed at restoring public trust and confidence in these services and ensuring consumers are protected. This included:

• Asking all broadcasters and their partners to carry out a review of their current and forthcoming participation TV programming to ensure there was no risk of consumer harm.
• Systematic monitoring by ICSTIS and inspections to ensure services are run as they should.[25]

ICSTIS also introduced a licensing regime for all PRS providers operating participation TV services. By autumn 2007, suggestions were made that ITV be fined far above the initial £2m that GMTV was penalized,[26] and then-government minister responsible, James Purnell, asked the head of Ofcom to report back to him on how and where consumer protection might be strengthened in communications regulation.[27] Purnell stated: 'I am writing to [the Ofcom chief executive] Ed Richards today asking him to give us advice on whether the powers at their disposal are sufficient, what the implications for the policy framework are, and whether the regime is stable … The priority has to be viewers.' Concurrently concerns about computer games and Internet safety led to Dr. Tanya Byron's review announced on 20 September 2007. The review examined how to help parents and their children get the best from new technologies while protecting children from inappropriate or potentially harmful material.[28]

The phone-in quiz scandal demonstrates exactly the cracks in the ICSTIS co-regulation model: the regulator Ofcom is seen to have devolved even those powers it retains to the co-regulator. The co-regulator itself is of the view that it should have intervened more aggressively earlier to ensure

---

[24] Ofcom and ICSTIS (2007), para. 16.   [25] Ofcom and ICSTIS (2007), para. 9.
[26] Gibson and Wray (2007).   [27] Tryhorn (2007).
[28] See Marsden (2010), pp. 125–128.

that the industry's own practices were audited more effectively. It invited groups of stakeholders to meetings with the Chair and Chief Executive of ICSTIS for open-ended discussions on the future possibilities for co-regulating the industry, including the most effective means of preventing widespread fraud not simply in the broadcasting area but more widely.[29] The market's rapid growth evidently led broadcasters and their service providers to engage in widespread illegal practices. As a result the market for phone-in quizzes has suffered a substantial amount of damage and retrenchment. Despite this, ICSTIS proved over twenty-one years a 'light touch' co-regulator in a fast-growing liberalized industry sector that rapidly became the largest globally. The extent to which 'light touch' remains an effective philosophy is openly questioned internally as well as externally by the ICSTIS executive, and further changes may be anticipated in response to both its ongoing review with Ofcom, and the ministerial and parliamentary investigation of parts of the market.

Independent Mobile Classification Board (IMCB)

In the most-developed European countries, there was intense pressure on mobile operators to self-regulate Internet-based media content which they or their partners supplied, reflected in its selection as the subject of the EC Safer Internet Forum in 2005.[30] ICSTIS and Vodafone commissioned research in 2003 to identify consumers' attitude to premium rate mobile services. It demonstrates overwhelming approval for child access controls, and own-access controls.[31] The 2007 EC consultation on child protection and mobile phones states that: 'Self-regulation is seen as potentially the most appropriate way to ensure child protection due to the rapidly changing technical environment, but self-regulation still needs to be launched or effectively implemented in some countries … Through their European association GSM Europe, MNOs propose the "development of an EU-wide common Framework for national self-regulation".'[32]

With the growth of the Internet market accessed by mobile devices, the UK mobile network operators (MNOs) announced a code of conduct in February 2004. The case study is particularly instrumental as there are

---

[29] Inviting researcher Marsden to one such meeting: 25 June 2007, chaired by Sir Alistair Graham, Chair, ICSTIS.
[30] http://ec.europa.eu/information_society/activities/sip/si_forum/mobile_2005/agenda/index_en.htm.
[31] Beaufort International (2003), at p. 5.
[32] See EC (2007).

several pan-European MNOs, given the vertical integration of the MNO 'walled garden' model. The code committed them to rating adult (18+) content, backed by a rating body. A tender resulted in the appointment of a subsidiary of ICSTIS established for the purpose, the IMCB.[33] It is a self-regulatory body which for administrative purposes is set up as a subsidiary of ICSTIS. It has no formal relationship with Ofcom. Further European self-regulatory models have been rolled out in other jurisdictions (KJM is co-regulator in Germany). Though ostensibly national in scope, operators' codes regulate content which is likely to overlap contiguous language areas (e.g., Ireland, Austria, Switzerland) given the effects of mobility and roaming. The legal basis remains the E-Commerce Directive (ECD), and there are several national codes of conduct. The regulatory structure is shown in Figure 5.3 (PRS not included). The codes in place cover adult content providers contracted to MNOs. Ahlert, Marsden and Nash conclude: 'Legitimate networks and content owners need to protect "on-net" brand and limit liability from the porn and P2P piracy that "off-net" users and cowboy site operators will create ... They have learnt from the fixed Internet in taking such action early.'[34]

In this case study, I examine the first such scheme, in the UK – driven by pan-European operators – as well as the initiation and drafting of the pan-European Framework. The Irish market has followed the UK example, with RegTel (the premium regulator) launched in 2008, doing the work. The IMCB and UK approach is seen as very much the 'gold standard'. There is no relationship with a type of 'umbrella' international body yet. Borthwick establishes the basis for intervention: 'as you move into offering commercial content, some proportion of content ... is only appropriate to supply to adults ... that general commercial positioning gives rise to wider societal and stakeholder interactions'.[35] Some countries will of course be more developed in either public policy or market or both – he gives as examples the UK, Germany, Ireland, New Zealand and Australia. He confirms an important design issue to eliminate free-riders: 'what is the structure of the underlying industry? The mobile sector characterized as a series of national oligopolies ... for self-regulatory structures, that is a very promising starting point – compared to an industry which is more heterogeneous' such as the fixed ISP market, with thousands of players. Moreover mobile network

---

[33] IMCB: Legal subsidiary of PhonepayPlus, Clove Building, 4 Maguire Street, London SE1 2NQ. Director: Paul Whiteing (ICSTIS Director of Policy and Innovation). Board: four members drawn from ICSTIS Board, meets annually at least.

[34] Ahlert *et al.* (2005); Wright (2005).

[35] Borthwick (2007).

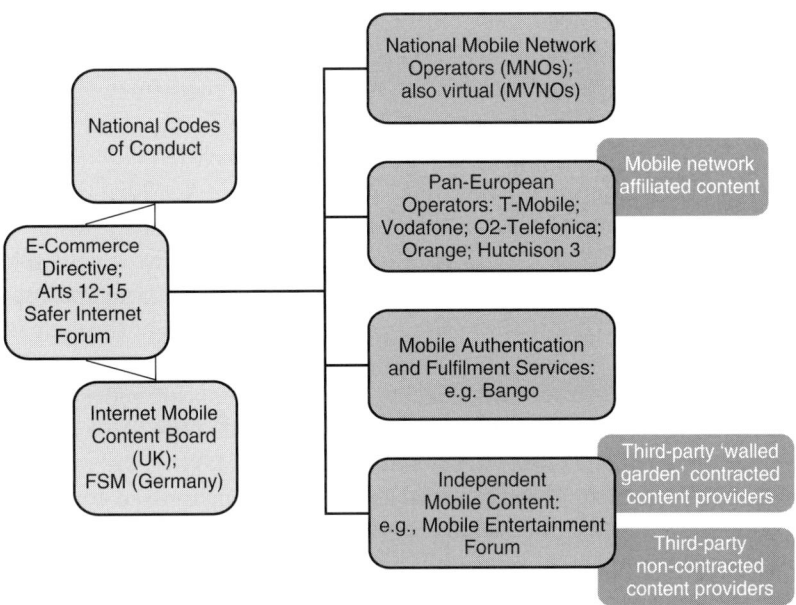

Figure 5.3. Self-regulatory structure in European mobile Internet content regulation

strategies are similar – voice and text moving towards walled garden 'multi-media content services', with a market-driven view that: 'If its legal we want to be able to sell it … even if not in a branded proposition.' Carr, a representative of child safety charities, states that the code was the outcome of long discussions between companies and stakeholders. As Carr explains, the entry barriers create the trivial costs of regulation: 'It's all down to that one single fact: durable consumer-facing oligopoly – there were a lot of arguments we didn't have to have with them.'[36] As to whether the market and incentives for mobile networks are unique he states: 'If you could get MSN, Google, Yahoo!, AOL, Dell, HP to agree on a certain approach to the Internet as a whole, you'd get pretty near … a decisive influence on the Internet as a whole – but they don't because of their competitive nature and fear of antitrust suits.' He argues that ISP initiatives were hampered by this coordination problem.

The UK Code was drafted by a committee including the then-six UK network operators and virtual operators (3, Vodafone, Orange, T-Mobile,

---

[36] Carr (2007).

Virgin Mobile, O2). Informal consultation with content providers, infra-structure and handset suppliers, and government at national and EC levels took place.[37] The code itself was written in the 'regulatory vacuum' of 2003 as Ofcom was being established, against a background of discreet coordinated lobbying by mobile networks, and parliamentary pressure for self-regulation during the Communications Act 2003 debates. There was therefore a combination of regulatory commitment (fostered by cooperation in 2002–3) and political pressure to establish a workable regime prior to the broad 3G launch in 2004. A draft of the code was presented for public consultation prior to the full publication of the code in January 2004.

The code itself is unremarkable, but its *ex ante* adoption reflects high awareness in the sector both of potential harms and of the value of self-regulation. The code observes the same 'notice and take down' requirements with regard to illegal material as those applying to fixed-line ISPs. Thus section 3 of the code states: 'Mobile operators will work with law enforcement agencies to deal with the reporting of content that may break the criminal law.' There are coverage limitations: 'The Code covers new types of content, including visual content, online gambling, mobile gaming, chat rooms and Internet access. It does not cover traditional [PRS]' which remains ICSTIS's co-regulatory responsibility.[38] Nor does it cover wider Internet content not directly supplied by third parties to the mobile operator. Responsibilities here mirror those of fixed-line ISPs. However, the Mobile Entertainment Forum (MEF), a transatlantic grouping of over seventy content providers, issued its own mobile code of conduct, dealing with premium content. This may prove a precedent for a code dealing with adult content.[39] The code also fails to cover issues which have already stimulated media concern such as the use of camera phones and Bluetooth technologies for content creation and distribution that does not require downloading from a website, or other forms of p2p file-sharing.

Borthwick notes that, by billing inclusively for their premium content partners, mobile companies have a point-of-sale chokepoint. Service providers – e.g., Jamba – did join, and there is no principled point why other

[37] Dialogue continued after the launch of the code: European networks, content providers, consumer groups and regulators met in London 29–30 January 2004 for the 'Delivering Adult Mobile Content Responsibly' conference which I chaired for Total Telecom. Network operators were also present at the SIAP's Safer Internet Day event on 6 February.

[38] Code reproduced in full in Tambini *et al.* (2008) at pp. 229–253.

[39] The code was launched in the UK on 19 January 2005, and worldwide on 15 March 2005: see www.m-e-f.org/news032005.html.

third-party transaction specialists such as PayPal could not join, if they wish. There is no joining fee but there are compliance costs, which obviously founder members set as the conditions. Potentially all regulation raises entry barriers – but self-regulation sees itself as a lower-cost option. This group of conditions is adult-oriented and designed to be as low-cost as possible, with broad similarities to other approaches. In his view, self-regulation shares agreed principles with regulation, but implementation is left to the more dynamic flexible market-oriented actors. The six operators include all four of the largest pan-European operators.[40]

The code itself required an SRO to implement decisions regarding adult and age classification of content. Details of the code's implementation were announced on 7 February 2005 with the launch of the IMCB.[41] The contract to run the IMCB was awarded by the mobile networks in open tender. The shadow IMCB board negotiated with Paul Whiteing who led the bid by ICSTIS to establish a separate company, with interesting frictions from the outset in terms of the independence of IMCB, not least because there were six separate legal teams from the six MNOs. Whiteing explain that: 'Its merely a self-regulatory body which for administrative purposes is set up as a subsidiary of ICSTIS (which has a Golden Share).'[42] He claims it 'vigorously defends its independence from government' and claims to be a sort of 'insurance policy' against co-regulation for the mobiles. Board independent members represent the consumer. The UK Code for Content does not have a central arbitrator for disputes: 'Each mobile operator may choose or need to use different organizational and technical solutions to enable it to meet aspects of the Code.' The content scheme is an opt-in self-classificatory scheme overseen by an independent classification body.[43] Content is classified as '18', adult content, or not – with optional interim ratings for younger children (in section 7). Enforcement of the code is formally dependent on individual operators: 'Each mobile operator will enforce the terms of the Code through its agreements with commercial content providers.' IMCB did not enforce any decisions on rating to end-2007. It received forty-nine requests from industry for classification advice in 2006/7, of which eleven referred to

---

[40] Of the 2000 European subscriber market, 56 per cent was O2, Vodafone, T-Mobile and Orange – TIM and Telefonica Moviles, with less significant interest outside their domestic markets, are small in pan-European terms. See Ahlert, Marsden and Nash (2005) at p. 4.

[41] See Classification Framework at www.imcb.org.uk/assets/documents/ ClassificationFramework.pdf

[42] Whiteing (2007).   [43] See www.imcb.org.uk/.

user-generated content, premium rate advertising or access controls, all of which are outside IMCB's scope.

A contractually required labelling system for 'commercial' content coming from third parties should work, because inappropriate content is to be filtered out at the 'gateway' between the network operator and the provider.[44] This approach covers most of the potential areas of concern for parents, and demonstrates to government that the industry has taken its corporate responsibility seriously, but does still leave unanswered some important questions. The code is heavily dependent on age-verification procedures, which are still far from foolproof and are open to fraud. Age-verification procedures applied by the mobile industry are clearly only of use where a phone is being purchased or a new contract established; in so far as many children may just inherit or borrow phones from other family members or friends, it is vital that the code and the child protection measures available are publicized as widely as similar measures for PC-accessed Internet.

The need to ensure brand awareness is not tarnished by adverse press and publicity is likely to make this a central element not only of a minor compliance budget (as with mobile phones and child exposure to radiation) but part of the massive marketing budget of the operators. Borthwick sees the costs of providing adult services, as an element of multimedia content costs, as substantial (perhaps several million euros per operating company, a few percentage points of total content marketing costs). This could create problems arising in that these are fixed costs which become non-trivial in small operating companies/markets (e.g., Malta, Estonia/Cyprus). Is the answer there not to support the adult services? Sometimes to protect wider brands such as Vodafone, that option does not exist, even if it may not be a problem for smaller/less brand-identified companies. However, smaller unaffiliated companies do not always prefer deregulation: GO Mobile in Malta wanted to be in the European framework in order to prevent competitive disadvantage with pan-European MNOs.

The negotiation of the IMCB contract in all occupied May–December 2004. Therefore, the IMCB launched over a year after the code was launched in January 2004. In the year before IMCB was formed, the mobile networks had self-classified content in advance – and had done so since before the code was introduced. Mobiles have since trained with the IMCB and experts in self-rating – there are only occasional problems.

---

[44] See for instance www.orange.co.uk/about/regulatory_affairs.html – the code is the first download item in the middle of the page.

Paul Whiteing explains that the scheme used two key examples, the BBFC and PEGI – particularly the British Board of Film Classification (BBFC). IMCB used BBFC reviewers to train IMCB staff in classification. The IMCB standard talks a great deal about context – and in particular educational context – in deciding on suitability of material. Issues include how to build a relationship of cooperation between mobile operators and commercial content providers, particularly smaller non-MEF members, and raising awareness of the code and the role of retailers.

The pan-European framework for a code developed between MNOs and the EC in 2006–7 is the second part of this case study. Richard Swetenham, of DG INFSO, confirms the coordinating role of the European trade association GSM Europe,[45] though Rob Borthwick of Vodafone led the EU industry scheme set up after the 2005 Safer Internet Forum, with a public consultation finished in January 2007. A high-level group was established with three 'sherpa' (preparatory) meetings. Signature of the agreement occurred in May 2007, which committed signatory companies to national implementation in all twenty-seven countries by February 2008. The problem in instituting the framework is where operators are local, and there are low content concerns, for instance in some Baltic republics, with small markets. Further, child protection at this level of coordination could be perceived as 'Anglo-Saxon regulation' with few grassroots civil society/consumer groups lobbying for this activity (it was even suggested that those concerned might be seen as EC creations, funded by SIAP).

Issues in the negotiation of the agreement appeared to include competition law concerns as an appearance of collusion, and in Ireland, initial proposals that parents check their children's bills, which may be contrary to human rights and data protection legislation. Borthwick states that at European level 'it should be acknowledged that the catalyst was DG INFOSOC'. Competition concerns arose for him only in that there was no mention of Internet access in the agreed framework, whereas it is in several national codes. 'The reason is that industry could not agree on whether Internet access should be available, or device capability, etc.' It is to be expected that 'competitive divergence' will arise on levels of implementation – the role of the framework group was to agree on high-level principles that allow different competitive positions/differentiation. Note the degree to which this makes the framework very much a self-regulatory tool, despite its initiative stemming from the EC and the continuous discussion in its formulation. The approach could be described

---

[45] Swetenham (2007).

as 'enlightened regulatory withdrawal', in that once the Commission was satisfied that the framework achieved its ends in its establishment, it could then adopt an observational rather than direct involvement in the implementation of the framework at national and network operator levels.

Incentives for the pan-European framework can be seen as encompassing broader concerns than simply the SIAP and recommendation, in particular the revised Audiovisual Media Services Directive (AVMS),[46] under which co-regulation of mobile media video content is implemented from the start of 2010. Borthwick states that mobile operators were: 'aiming to use the framework as our implementation tool for the AVMS – we see these two things as quite linked, obviously national legislators and regulators will need to decide … [we are] hoping to prove the effectiveness before the AVMS is implemented'. However, he notes that the timing of the European Framework was prior to final agreement between European institutions on the revised AVMS proposal, and confirms that it never emerged in discussions with the EC. UK interviewees also discuss the self-regulatory 'Cross-Media Content Information Group', a labelling initiative run by the Broadband Stakeholder Group (BSG). BSG is funded by government. It comprises the entire spectrum of content providers: broadcasters, ATVOD, ISPs, BBFC, MySpace, Yahoo!, video games, mobiles and ISPs. It has no public website, and is non-transparent. Its role was apparently to formulate a code of conduct, to be implemented individually.

In Borthwick's view the difference between content regulation such as PEGI and mobile is that mobile access relies on national classification. For mobile, the differences at national level between e.g., Germany and UK need to be respected. Savings in economies of scale for pan-national regulation would be outweighed by different market types and commercial preferences for using descriptor standards – even with different age standards in different markets: 'Where you don't have sensible regulation and effective implementation, [MNOs] turn down the volume of content sold, to manage the risk of discontinuity.' Therefore the value of effective self-regulation is explicitly recognized as a direct addition to the overall market size.

---

[46] Directive 2007/65/EC (AVMS Directive), amending Council Directive 89/552/EEC, on the coordination of certain provisions laid down by law, regulation or administrative action in Member States concerning the pursuit of television broadcasting activities, OJ L332, Brussels: 18 December 2007.

Co-regulation in practice: Association for
Video On Demand (ATVOD)

This introductory case study is an illustration of co-regulation by statutory fiat imposed by European law, and implemented by government and Ofcom in association with the formerly Potemkin self-regulator, ATVOD. In the UK, it was decided not to include VoD or IPTV within the scope of Ofcom under the Communications Act 2003. As a response to this, in 2003, ATVOD was established by five companies then operating in the VoD field, as a private company limited by guarantee.[47] As the industry itself recognized, this was an attempt to pre-empt action on the part of government and until 2009, membership was voluntary. ATVOD had limited resources and no legal requirement for its foundation, simply corporate responsibility on the part of large communications companies, and a 'virtual presence'. Its main function was to provide a consumer protection mechanism via a complaints procedure in respect of VoD services. In 2007, contact with ATVOD was only by post. Government was informed, on an informal basis, of ATVOD's activities, though ATVOD was under no obligation to inform the DCMS or receive its consent of the DCMS for its activities until it became co-regulator under the AVMS. Although it had a secretariat, ATVOD had little in the way of resources or personnel. In 2004, it produced a code of conduct, updated in 2007, as well as a number of practice statements.

In order to implement the AVMS, self-regulatory 'old ATVOD' was scrapped and on 24 March 2010, a new chair and chief executive were appointed and a co-regulatory 'new ATVOD' emerged with an explanation of its difference from the previous 'Potemkin regulator'.[48] To manage its new responsibilities ATVOD has restructured, to ensure independence from the industry's commercial interests. The evolutionary co-regulatory changes are a continuation of this 'taking regulation seriously' by government.

Ofcom's designation powers are granted within amendments of Part 4A of the Communications Act 2003 (on-demand programme services), by regulations passed in 2009 and 2010.[49] Criteria that Ofcom must use

---

[47] For ATVOD's earlier 'Potemkin regulator' phase, see Woods (2008). For broadcast regulation in context, see Feintuck and Varney (2006).
[48] ATVOD (2010a).
[49] Audiovisual Media Services Regulations 2009 No. 2979 at www.legislation.gov.uk/uksi/2009/2979/contents/made; Audiovisual Media Services Regulations 2010 No. 419 at www.legislation.gov.uk/uksi/2010/419/regulation/2/made.

in respect of designation of a co-regulator under section 368B(9) of the Communications Act 2003 are: that the body is a fit and proper body; has consented to designation; has access to adequate financial resources; is sufficiently independent of service providers; and will have regard to a set of principles (transparency, accountability, proportionality, consistency and 'targeted only at cases in which action is needed'). The principles are supported by an earlier Ofcom statement that sets out its decision-making procedures when considering the case for adopting self-regulation or co-regulation in appropriate cases.[50] This work was commissioned partly as a response to wider European co-regulatory adoption, but specifically as a need to transpose the co-regulatory requirements of AVMS by 2009.[51] This is an important step for co-regulation in the UK: firm regulatory control of the high-level principles of co-regulation.

AVMS regulates some Internet video, but it is not unique in so doing. For instance, the areas of harmful and unsuitable communications, racism and xenophobia are addressed by a range of legal measures.[52] An EU report expressly addresses the boundary between freedom of expression and racism and xenophobia, and explains the complex legal situation with regard to international law.[53] Internet video companies were not operating in a legal vacuum, but the possibility of criminal or other court enforcement of general law is at once a less common but more expensive alternative to regulation and self-regulation. Whereas the UK has established an effective co-regulatory solution to block UK-originated child pornography (see Chapter 6), other countries such as the US rely on criminal prosecution.[54] Horlings et al. state that: 'Regulation can only be effective with flanking self-regulation and technological and other instruments to protect viewers.'[55]

The forerunner of the AVMS, the Television without Frontiers Directive (TVWF), affected only licensed broadcasters directly.[56] TVWF had placed every TV broadcaster under the jurisdiction of one Member State, required to impose certain minimum standards on the broadcaster's programming, and all the other Member States were required to ensure reception: the 'Country of Origin Principle'. AVMS will be applied to an industry whose structure is both more complex and more dynamic

---

[50] Ofcom (2008).
[51] See Valcke and Stevens (2007), pp. 285–302. Also Prosser (2008), pp. 99–113.
[52] For an international assessment of the UK, see Council of Europe: European Commission Against Racism and Intolerance CRI (2005).
[53] EU Network of Independent Experts on Fundamental Rights (2005), p. 5.
[54] Williams (2003), p. 469.   [55] Horlings et al. (2006), p. vi.
[56] Directive 89/552/EEC, as amended in Directive 97/36/EC.

than the traditional industries of broadcasting or telecoms, and one in which the effects of regulation may have significant impact on the eventual industry structure that emerges. The single point of control assumed in most broadcasting and telecoms regulation has given way increasingly to clustering, hybridization and agglomeration of skills within virtual organizations. In some cases, the natural response by the market to heavy regulatory burdens and/or increased regulatory risk may be to increase this rate of integration, and hence to make the market structure less competitive and open than would have been the case otherwise.[57] I 'assisted' in the EC 2005 Impact Assessment on AVMS, but cautioned that evidence for impacts on non-linear delivery was lacking.[58]

The EC published the AVMS proposals on 13 December 2005.[59] AVMS encompasses all commercial media services offered over the Internet, mobile networks, telecoms networks, terrestrial, cable and satellite broadcasting networks, or over any other electronic network whose principal purpose is the provision of moving images to the general public. Linear providers are to be regulated according to a revised broadcast regime, and will encompass both traditional broadcasters and providers of Internet Protocol TV (IPTV). Thus streamed 'live' TV over mobiles will be regulated as TV programmes. This regime will apply whether the viewer watches the programme in real time or records (using, for instance, a Personal Video Recorder; PVR) for later playback. Video on-demand (VoD) 'non-linear' services would be subject to less regulation than traditional TV 'linear' services, but to a set of prohibitions on offensive content and forbidden commercially driven content (including inappropriate advertising, racist and xenophobic material, and certain types of sponsorship). This is not dissimilar to the rules in the E-Commerce Directive (ECD)[60] and Recommendation 98/560/EC.[61] AVMS supplants self-regulation by a co-regulatory or regulatory approach. The definition of audiovisual media service is in Article 1(a) of AVMS (Recitals 13–17).

---

[57] The classic article is Stigler (1971), pp. 3–21.
[58] Horlings *et al.* (2006) at p. ii. See further Burri-Nenova (2007), pp. 1689–1725; Collins (2009), pp. 334–361; Ibáñez Colomo (2009).
[59] Formally COM (2005b).
[60] Directive 2000/31/EC on certain legal aspects of information society services, in particular electronic commerce, in the Internal Market, gives consumers clarity about where a company is regulated, and where to pursue any complaints.
[61] Recommendation 98/560/EC on the Development of the Competitiveness of the European Audiovisual and Information Services Industry by Promoting National Frameworks Aimed at Achieving a Comparable and Effective Level of Protection of Minors and Human Dignity.

Table 5.2. *Exclusions from AVMS definitions* [1]

Defining element	Exclusions
Services as defined by Articles 49 and 50 of the Treaty	Non-economic activities, such as *purely private* websites, weblogs (blogs)
The principal purpose of which is	Services where audiovisual element is *only ancillary* (example: travel agency websites, gambling websites)
Delivery of moving images with or without sound	Does not cover audio transmission or radio or *electronic versions of newspapers*
In order to inform, entertain or educate	Audiovisual content *without editorial* – e.g., webcams
To the general public	Private correspondence – e.g., emails
By electronic networks[61]	e.g., DVD rental, cinema

Article 1(b) defines 'media service provider' as those who hold editorial responsibility. Article 1(c) defines a linear audiovisual media service as a service 'where a media service provider decides upon the moment in time when a specific programme is transmitted and establishes the programme schedule'. This equates it with 'television broadcasting' and 'television broadcast'. Linear services include scheduled broadcasting via traditional TV, the Internet or mobile phones, which 'pushes' content to viewers. It also includes all recorded and therefore delayed linear content, whether on PVR or other means. Non-linear services include on-demand films or news, which the viewer 'pulls' from a network. Ultimately, the linear/non-linear (or push/pull) distinction depends upon who decides when a specific programme is transmitted and whether schedules exist. The differing degrees of regulation of content 'pushed' by suppliers or 'pulled' by users reflects differences in user choice and control and the likely impact on society. They also are intended to take account of the principle of proportionality: the costs of regulation should be proportional to the benefits of enforcement.[63] UGC such as YouTube and interactive games are

---

[62] Within the meaning of Article 2(a) of Directive 2002/21/EC.
[63] Heronymi (2006).

excluded.[64] EC's February 2006 Scope 'non-paper' indicated application in practice: 'This definition is intended to regulate as a function of the centre of gravity of the service sector concerned, not as a function of borderline cases. It is binding as to the result to be achieved but leaves to the national authorities the choice of form and methods.'[65]

Until Ofcom designated ATVOD, Ofcom was the regulatory body itself under section 368B(3). Ofcom from 18 March 2010 designated ATVOD as the body for a ten-year period, subject to formal review after two years. Ofcom states at paragraph 1: 'Ofcom in exercise of the powers conferred on it under section 368B of the Act hereby designates ATVOD to be the appropriate regulatory authority (as defined in section 368R of the Act) for the purpose of carrying out the functions set out in paragraph 5 of this Designation in relation to on-demand programme services.'[66] Ofcom also tasked the Advertising Standards Authority with handling all advertising related issues, while ATVOD will deal with all matters pertaining to consumer protection standards and guidelines for taste, decency and sponsorship requirements.[67] Paragraph 6 establishes the enforcement powers for ATVOD:

(viii) where ATVOD has determined that a Service Provider has contravened the requirement in section 368BA of the Act, to issue an enforcement notification in accordance with section 368BB(1)(a);[68]

(ix) to include in such an enforcement notification a requirement to take all such steps for remedying a contravention of the requirement to notify provision of an on-demand programme service in accordance with section 368BA as may be specified in the notification;

(x) (save in cases where Ofcom decides to take enforcement action itself in accordance with its powers under the Act) to enforce compliance with an enforcement notification under s368BB(6) of the Act in civil proceedings.

In paragraph 7, it is given twenty-three separate obligations in order to perform the functions designated by Ofcom. It limits the formal enforcement powers of ATVOD in paragraph 18:

ATVOD is only empowered to carry out the designated functions and exercise the powers specifically designated to them in this designation. Accordingly, and for the avoidance of doubt, ATVOD is not the

[64] See: www.europarl.europa.eu/meetdocs/2004_2009/documents/dt/618/618091/618091en.pdf.
[65] EC (2006).   [66] Ofcom (2010a).
[67] See Ofcom (2009a, b).
[68] Ofcom (2010a), '(except that ATVOD is given no powers under section 368BB(1)(b)'.

appropriate regulatory authority in relation to any function set out in the Act that does not form part of the designated functions (including, in particular, the power to impose financial penalties and to require suspensions or restrictions of on-demand programme services).

ATVOD's July 2010 board meeting minutes paragraph 4.8 state: 'The board discussed what co-regulation means in practice and the definition of co-regulation, as set out in the Communications Act. As further information was needed on the legal definition, DA [Daniel Austin] agreed to research the statutory definition of co-regulation for the next board meeting.'[69] It was hoped that a first draft memorandum and articles would be available for the September board meeting. The size of the task was shown in paragraph 7.2, where 'sixty-seven services were being investigated for not notifying (this is an additional thirty services to last month); ATVOD is in the process of identifying further services that have not notified and at the end of July, it is expected there will be 160 open cases'. In paragraph 7.5, 'DCMS also reminded ATVOD that the EC's two-year review of AVMS implementation is about to commence', and paragraph 10.5, 'The board also discussed the increasing trend for adult broadcasters to have a Dutch (rather than an Ofcom) licence and that this risk may spill over into on-demand services.' ATVOD introduced a flat-rate annual fee of £2,900 on the services of all notified VoD providers in the UK.[70]

As regards potential judicial review, ATVOD 'received feedback from Ofcom that the guidance should make it very clear the difference between the statutory rules and the non-binding guidance'. The various procedures of ATVOD were almost all at that point under review by Ofcom, including complaints and appeals procedures. The complaints procedure took effect from 20 September 2010.[71] At paragraph 21.2, 'it would be advisable for the ATVOD to recruit to the independent director's position a person with experience in child protection'. The expectation must be that ATVOD's functions under the transposition requirements of AVMS will be reviewable, especially given the close involvement of Ofcom in its reform, though this remains untested.

---

[69] ATVOD (2010b). Note these were the latest minutes posted on the website as of 1 November 2010.
[70] Ofcom (2010b).   [71] ATVOD (2010c).

Nederlands Instituut voor de Classificatie
van Audiovisuele Media (NICAM)

NICAM[72] is coordinator of the 'Kijkwijzer' scheme, through which media providers rate their programming according to fixed categories. More than 2,200 companies and organizations are affiliated to NICAM, either directly or through their sector organizations.[73] NICAM was a consensus decision on co-regulation to replace state regulation. It is mandated by, and reports to Parliament. It has been highly praised as a transparent and widely adopted system. The training system for audit of company classifiers is also much praised. The consensus and industry/political buy-in is the result of a long-negotiated outcome typical of Dutch politics. This is not necessarily replicable but the system is used elsewhere and NICAM assisted in the creation of pan-European games rating system PEGI. In this case study, the scope and replicability of NICAM are the primary focus.

The explosion of the supply of audiovisual media through video cassettes and multichannel cable and satellite programming prompted the Television without Frontiers Directive 89/552/EC and encouraged discussion of Dutch self-regulation. A 1997 government policy document calling for an integrated effort towards tackling harmful content, argued for the establishment of an independent national support group for audiovisual self-regulation.[74] This led in 1999 to the establishment of NICAM. Director Bekkers claimed that the development of this initiative is in line with the 'Nordic school of thought' that proclaims awareness building and education to protect children from harmful content.[75] NICAM was set up in 1999 in close cooperation with government. NICAM developed 'Kijkwijzer', the classification system that warns parents and educators about a television programme or film which can be harmful to children of different ages. On 22 February 2001, the new legislation replaced the Film Censorship Act 1977, heralding the end of film censorship. Policy officer from the Ministry of OC&W, Mr van Dijk (2007) explained that sanctions for violation via the criminal law have been increased. Initially,

---

[72] Location: Media Centrum, Media Park, Hilversum, The Netherlands; NICAM Annual Report 2005.
[73] www.kijkwijzer.nl.
[74] 'Niet voor alle leeftijden' (1997 'Not for all ages'), at www.minvws.nl/kamerstukken/djb/ niet_voor_alle_leeftijden.asp.
[75] Bekkers (2005, 2007).

the intention was to slowly phase out the involvement of government, but after the first evaluation of NICAM, government concluded that a pure self-regulatory body was not desirable.

It was decided that the Commissariaat voor de Media (CvdM) would exert close (meta-)supervision and the Ministry would continue to contribute financially. CvdM is the independent regulatory authority which acts as a 'safety net' for NICAM's co-regulation initiative.[76] It supervises the absolute prohibition on broadcasting content that can cause serious damage to minors in Article 52d, paragraph 1 of the Media Act. CvdM stops non-NICAM members from broadcasting any programmes that could be harmful to minors. Every broadcaster that becomes a NICAM member submits a written declaration to CvdM, and NICAM informs the Commissariaat regularly on membership. CvdM performs 'meta-supervision' in which NICAM reports annually to CvdM on how it safeguards the quality of coders' classifications as reliable, valid, stable, consistent and precise. The process is laid down in a supplement to a covenant between both parties. As 'meta–supervisor', CvdM checks the quality of the classification system of NICAM (Betzel 2005): each year before 1 March NICAM submits all necessary data to CvdM, and before 1 July CvdM reports to the State Secretary.[77] NICAM is classified as co-regulation rather than pure self-regulation (Bekkers 2007).

Kijkwijzer expanded from TV and cinema to video and DVDs, and has now been applied to new media. For interactive games, the international PEGI system is applied, based on the Kijkwijzer classification (see www. pegi.info). NICAM, which is owner and the executing institution of the PEGI system, takes care of the daily activities involved with operating the PEGI scheme, including support via a helpdesk and monitoring adherence. In April 2005, NICAM signed a contract with mobile operators KPN Mobile, Orange, Telfort, T-Mobile and Vodafone. The initiative for this self-regulation came from MNOs who asked to join the Kijkwijzer system. Additionally, the publishing industry has also approached NICAM for potential application of the classification to print media. The Ministry does not want print media to be regulated through co-regulation for constitutional reasons, but it encourages exchange of information and expertise. Internet content is not yet classified by Kijkwijzer but NICAM

---

[76] For more information, see: www.cvdm.nl/pages/english.asp?.
[77] Commissariaat voor de Media (2007).

does closely monitor developments in this area, as member of Youth Protection Roundtable,[78] an international collaborative initiative for a safer internet that proclaims awareness building and education to protect children from harmful content. Furthermore, NICAM participants who offer online content that has been subject to classification use Kijkwijzer icons on their websites e.g., public TV, YouTube channels and the online theme channels (e.g., Nederland 4).

NICAM's responsibilities are: the setting up of and further development of the classification of audiovisual material of its members; drafting regulations for classification and the time of broadcasting on TV; audience research; supervising compliance including complaint handling; and imposing fines, if necessary. Secondary objectives include: maintaining and disseminating expertise in harmful media content; operating the classification system for interactive games; functioning as a contact point for new sectors interested in content classification; and maintaining a role in international policy-making. NICAM has both a general and an executive board plus a bureau; the boards consist of representatives of both public and commercial broadcasters, film distributors and cinema operators, distributors, video rental shops and retailers.[79] Implementation of Kijkwijzer is in the hands of the audiovisual institutions and companies. Three committees have specific responsibilities related to NICAM's mission: the members of the advisory committee include experts from the areas of media, youth, education and welfare, representatives of parents' organizations and other social organizations, as well as of the companies participating in NICAM. The two other committees are independent: the complaints committee, which handles complaints about classification from both individuals and organizations, and imposes sanctions ranging from warnings to substantial fines; and an appeals committee. NICAM's annual costs amount to approximately one million euros. The intention of government was to reduce its contribution from 73 per cent of the total in 2003, to 40 per cent of NICAM costs in 2006 (excluding funding of incidental projects). The Dutch Government commitment is de facto justified as NICAM fulfils certain functions that government would have to assume otherwise.

If other institutions meet the conditions set by CvdM, they are candidates for becoming a self-regulatory institute as well, an implicit incentive for NICAM to achieve and maintain a critical mass of participating

---

[78] Youth Protection Roundtable (2007), available at www.yprt.eu/yprt/content/sections, accessed 30 July 2007.
[79] Betzel (2005).

industry organizations. Although participation in NICAM is voluntary for organizations in the three media sectors (TV, film, DVD/video), those organizations that do not participate will fall under the CvdM regime: a strong incentive for the industry to collaborate. Umbrella organizations from the audiovisual sector that participate in NICAM include: Netherlands Association of Producers and Importers of Picture and Sound Carriers (NVPI), Netherlands Video Retailers Organization (NVDO), Netherlands Association of Gramophone Record Retailers (NVGD), Netherlands Cinematography Federation (NFC), Netherlands Broadcasting Corporation (NOS) representing all national public service broadcasting organizations, and the Association of Satellite Television and Radio Programme Suppliers (VESTRA) representing all commercial broadcasting organizations in the Netherlands.

The organizations affiliated with Kijkwijzer are responsible for the classification of the content, as well as the associated costs. NICAM's revenues through fines amount to tens of thousands of euros, sufficient to cover only a fraction of its costs. The remainder of the contributions are split equally between four sectors: public service broadcasting, commercial broadcasting, film distributors, and DVD distributors and rental agencies. The Ministry argues that NICAM has a strong reputation and is not influenced by industry interests; the institutional elements introduced to guarantee independence are functioning well.

Any citizen can complain and most complaints relate to incorrect classification of an audiovisual product or a programme broadcast too early in the day. Complaints are usually dealt with by the NICAM bureau on behalf of the chairman of the complaints committee; they are referred to the complaints committee; only in cases of serious doubts about the classification. The complainant and the involved broadcaster or other party are invited for the hearings but are not obliged to attend. The institutions 'charged' with the complaints that are upheld by the complaints committee have the opportunity to appeal to the appeals committee. If the complaints are upheld before the appeals committee, the complaints committee can enforce fines on the participating organizations. To 2007, the highest was €12,000 for a repeat offender. After the first evaluation of NICAM in 2003, the Ministry increased the maximum fine to €135,000, the same level as those used by CvdM.

Kijkwijzer is, in principle, applicable to any geopolitical scope, because of the evidence-based nature of its rating system. Kijkwijzer was implemented with government support in Turkey, and is also being implemented in Iceland (Bekkers 2007). NICAM will ask for compensation when other countries use Kijkwijzer but without compromising independence and not-for-profit status. An element of innovation is NICAM enabling the Kijkwijzer icons to be 'machine readable'. External evaluations of NICAM include:

(1) Every three years, the ministries involved are responsible for periodical evaluation of NICAM. This evaluation is usually outsourced to an external consultant.
(2) CvdM conducts an annual review of NICAM's functioning.[80]

Hoff states that: 'NICAM has done a wonderful job taking some power away from existing government-run ratings systems that couldn't hope to keep up with new media. In my opinion it's the one example that proves that self-regulation can work, with all its weaknesses.'[81]

Pan European Game Information (PEGI)

The model for self-regulation of the video game industry on the pan-European level is the PEGI rating system (Pan European Games Information), implemented in the spring of 2003 by the Interactive Software Federation of Europe (ISFE).[82] Self-regulatory institutions are well known and analyzed by Tambini, Leonardi and Marsden and Hans Bredow in the case of offline games.[83] Note that legal ratings and decisions not to rate (i.e., refuse licences to distribute) to games also exist, and PEGI has no legal force. A corpus of legal scholarship concentrates on the virtual world's relationship with the law, with the 'State of Play' conference an annual event.[84] The effect of violent gaming on youth has been recently much debated in the media.[85] Content rating is instituted in Australia under the co-regulatory schemes established by the National Classification Code of 1995, under the powers in the Broadcasting Services Act 1992, and in 2000, section 5 of the Act became operational, extending the co-regulatory system to the Internet.[86] Further co-regulatory measures have recently been introduced in China and South Korea (to prevent games players' obsessive playing resulting in harm to self and others offline). The video game market was the fastest-growing component of the entertainment industry, worth, in 2009, almost $55 billion.[87]

---

[80] Valkenburg *et al.* (2001), pp. 329–354.
[81] Hoff (2007).   [82] See Calvert (2002).
[83] Tambini, Leonardi and Marsden (2008), pp. 190–209; Hans Bredow Institute (2006).
[84] See www.nyls.edu/pages/2713.asp.
[85] American Psychological Association (2005).
[86] See Wright (2005).
[87] Price Waterhouse Coopers (2005). See also OECD (2005), pp. 53–54.

PEGI is an independent, non-profit organization, founded by the industry, which puts a high priority on protecting industry interests.[88] PEGI relies on the voluntary national character of self-regulation.[89] It has well-developed public outreach and publicity programmes designed to explain how the rating systems serve the public interest.[90] PEGI has developed programmes to address rating at point of production, and also in distribution and marketing. It provides guidance on application of rating icons on packaging, has an informal and internal procedure for evaluating and revising rating mechanisms, and a formal complaint and appeal procedure for settling disputes.

PEGI cooperates with government both in the formation of the two variants of PEGI (offline and the new PEGI Online) and in the Advisory Board on which government members sit. The presence of government officials on the Advisory Board of PEGI, with civil society representatives on the Complaints Board, makes for an interesting governance structure whose coordination can be seen as a type of 'co-regulatory policy- making with self-regulatory implementation'.[91] PEGI itself claims to be more co-regulatory and self-regulatory: 'One key feature of the PEGI system – probably the main driver of its success – is its unique combination of business and government input (on this ground, some would call it co-regulation rather than self-regulation).'[92] Its composition, with an advisory board made up almost entirely of government representatives supports that interpretation.[93]

Research commissioned by PEGI in 2004, fifteen months after launch, suggested that the pan-European system had resulted in greater player awareness of ratings than in Australia's system, which had been developed in 2000. Of respondents, 59 per cent said that they were aware of a game rating system in Europe against 42 per cent in Australia, despite PEGI's later introduction and larger community.[94] Without consumer awareness, and retailer education to actually enforce the ratings, the system is an empty vessel. Chazerand claims the system works for three specific reasons:

---

[88] PEGI Info newsletter No.7, at www.pegi.info/pegi/download.do?id=12.
[89] The three most prominent self-regulating bodies of the electronic game industry, on whose models PEGI was built, were the Entertainment Software Rating Board (ESRB, programme of the US Interactive Digital Software Association), the Video Standards Council (VSC, UK programme of the European Leisure Software Publishers Association) and Kijkwijzer (NICAM).
[90] Chazerand (2007).
[91] The PEGI age categories are three, seven, twelve, sixteen and eighteen, and all the games also receive up to six content descriptors, warning that games' content include discrimination, drugs, fear, bad language, sex or violence.
[92] Chazerand (2007). See also ISFE (2005a).
[93] See ISFE (2005b).   [94] See ISFE (2004).

(1) All the major industry players joined the system at its political inauguration in 2001–2, urged by the EC and Member States.

(2) It used the classification system expertise of NICAM and the appeals procedure expertise of VSC, using national expertise for comparative advantage.

(3) The initial success of the system produced a virtuous circle of improved procedures (for instance, appeal) and pan-sectoral impacts (for instance, mobile and online markets).

The ratings system has provided a model for IMCB. There is no separate Board representing consumer groups or civil society. The Complaint Board is composed partly also by psychologists and other experts in the field.[95] Reding states that: 'I believe the fact that PEGI has been designed to meet varying cultural standards across the participating countries and that representatives of society such as consumers, parents and religious groups were involved in the setting up of the PEGI system, is very important. Obviously, it must be ensured that this involvement of main societal groups remains.'[96] The European Parliament concerns with online computer games feature in Recital 12 of the 2006 Recommendation on the Protection of Minors and Human Dignity, which 'covers new technological developments and complements Recommendation 98/560/EC. Its scope, on account of technological advances, includes audiovisual and on-line information services, such as newspapers, magazines and, particularly, video games, made available to the public via fixed or mobile electronic networks.'[97]

The 2007 PEGI Online Safety Code (POSC) authorized those parties who agree to be bound by its rules to display the PEGI Online Logo once their games are registered with the PEGI system. The Code is available online.[98] In 2007 Commissioner Reding launched the new PEGI Online system, whose development had been co-funded by the SIAP,[99] explaining that since PEGI was founded in 2002:

> we have massively multi-player online role-playing games or MMORPGs; online communities such as SecondLife blur the border between games and community websites; and the European Union has twelve more Member States. [I will prepare a] Commission report … [on] progress on

---

[95] See Independent Mobile Classification Body (2005), p. 6.
[96] Reding (2007).
[97] COM (2004b).
[98] PEGI (2007).
[99] www.pegionline.eu/en/index/id/235.

the labelling of video and computer games according to age group since the adoption of Council Resolution 2002/952/EC.[100]

The fact that PEGI Online was part-funded by the EC SIAP was a move which strengthened PEGI links to the mobile and ISP communities. Chazerand explains that the EC involvement included meeting officials in January 2007– and in Rome the PEGI Advisory Board meeting discussed and invited the Commission to have an Advisory Board seat.[101] However, the EC did not sit on the drafting council until its review meeting. These proposals all clearly make PEGI co-regulation. The EC suggested in review of the project co-funding that the draft Code should be put out for consultation, as the code committee included only one civil society member. Advisory group member Isabelle Falque-Pierrotin in July said that code needed strengthening. However, PEGI's view was that to make that public during negotiation would be 'imprudent', that commercial sensitivity means that decisions have to be agreed first as it is important to get all members to join up. Chazerand suggested that mobile content providers were very much less politically pressurized in their code. Age verification was the key concern in both mobile and PEGI Online.

The European Parliament's January 2009 Resolution on Computer Games states that it:

> 21. Welcomes the PEGI Online system, which is a logical development of PEGI and which deals with video games made available over the internet, such as downloaded or online games; supports its continued co-financing by the Commission under the Safer Internet programme, the aim of which is to tackle issues relating to the safe use of the internet by children and to new online technologies; calls on the Commission, in connection with the Safer Internet programme, to promote a systematic study of the effects of video games on minors;
>
> ...
>
> 24. Takes the view that the PEGI system for rating games is an important tool which has improved transparency for consumers, especially parents[102]

It also 'urges the Member States to ensure that any national rating system is not developed in a way that leads to market fragmentation'.

In the UK, the VSC sanction mechanisms are reserved for repeat offenders, as the VSC's stated policy is first to seek industry's cooperation in improving practices to correct for the breaches of the Rules. Once it decides to impose sanctions, the VSC can terminate membership in the

[100] Reding (2007).   [101] Chazerand (2007).
[102] European Parliament (2008).

organization, which includes loss of benefits. VSC has all 18+ games referred to them, and they forward the rating to the BBFC when unsure of whether rating can be undertaken. In the case of *Manhunt 2*, it was refused a rating, so the BBFC effectively banned the game. Delays associated with previous government policy to use BBFC ratings for video games led the UK to only implement PEGI ratings in full from the implementation of the DEAct on 1 April 2011.[103] Having lost its powers over video games, the film censor BBFC begun inserting voluntary ratings into ISP filters, with the first such voluntary scheme implemented by Tibboh in April 2010.[104] In the Netherlands, NICAM can impose a warning or penalty as a result of a successful complaint before the NICAM Independent Complaints Committee. The fines and warnings are public. The complainant or a party subject to the complaint can appeal the decision of the Complaints Committee. The possibility of banning games across Europe was proposed by various countries in 2005. Denmark and Portugal claimed that this is impossible at a European level, as their constitutions or laws forbid such censorship.

PEGI is a best-practice model for other industries in search of a coordinated scheme of pan-EU self-regulation. Germany's 2003 laws on the protection of minors place video and computer games within the overall media 'co-regulatory' framework,[105] with a shared responsibility between a self-regulatory body on the federal level and Länder governments on the local level. Such a national scheme precludes Germany from relying on an entirely voluntary pan-European system of video ratings.[106] Germany's decision not to use the PEGI system serves as an important reminder that even the most successful 'pan-European' self-regulatory models may not live up to all the Member States' concerns or national legal requirements. France has a proposal to add language descriptors in French, but PEGI is avowedly non-lingual (let alone multilingual). If coders claim that cultural specificities are important, then a full PEGI Advisory Board panel is required to review the whole of the content for all cultures. France and Italy pressed for consumer association representation on the complaint board rather than advisory board. Chazerand explains that the danger of pan-European schemes is that Europe has different approaches between

---

[103] Hartley (2010a).   [104] Hartley (2010b).
[105] Interstate Treaty on the protection of minors – JMStV, English version available at www.kjm-online.de/public/kjm/downloads/JMStV2007-englisch.pdf. See further Hans Bredow Institute (2006).
[106] However, one could envisage a system where governments could delegate the rating responsibility to a pan-European self-regulatory agency.

the 'North-west' and the rest to content rating, meaning legal harmonization is less likely than approximation of rating standards. PEGI relies
to a large extent on national enforcement of regulation in addition to its
filtering system – it does not replace national co-regulation, but acts as a
harmonized European addition to that system.

Conclusion: towards pan-sectoral, pan-European self-rating?

It appears that PEGI and NICAM have proved that a co-regulatory system can suceed in a highly dynamic and rapidly converging industry,
though the 2007 travails of ICSTIS are salutory. Using the examples taken
from film classification and video classification, PEGI has formed a pan-
European system (absent Germany) that has itself been acclaimed by the
EC and adopted in part by the mobile industry. NICAM has also been
adopted on a pan-sectoral basis in the Netherlands as a more formally
co-regulatory scheme with legal enforcement powers. PEGI effects are
extending to online and mobile markets through the ratings system itself.
Its success may be more an exception than the rule, however, as the lack
of institutional inheritance and prior art in regulation in this field permitted computer gaming to take a more self-regulatory approach than
more established media. NICAM's consensus-forming may be a Dutch
exception. The lessons adopted by IMCB and pan-European mobile content self-regulation are striking, but the differences compared to many
more established industries mean that the view of PEGI or NICAM as
blueprints for all content regulation online is simplistic.

The continued co-regulatory trend is summarized well in a case study
by Dorbeck-Jung *et al.* of preventing access to harmful content by minors
(as opposed to illegal content depicting minors) in the Netherlands, where
the authors conclude that: 'it is still unclear whether combinations of hard
law and soft law, co-regulation, and legally enforced self-regulation really
make regulation more effective'.[107] Given the lack of effectiveness in protecting minors from harmful content, they argue that this arises from
eight causes:

(1) poorly informed staff members,
(2) lack of internal and external controls,
(3) low rule enforcement,

---

[107] Dorbeck-Jung *et al.* (2010), pp. 154–174.

(4) insufficient overlap between public and private interests,
(5) poor social responsibility in the Dutch media sector,
(6) deficiencies in the institutional framework,
(7) an inconsistent regulatory strategy, and
(8) inadequate responses from responsible regulators.

State intervention for child protection from harmful content was limited in the Netherlands, and one could argue the same applies to the UK and indeed across the world. The paradigm which continues to hold is that parents and schools must take responsibility via filters, as we saw in Chapter 4. The authors argue that audit is needed of co-regulatory forms, as 'Ongoing "regulatory care" through control, corrective responses, and rule enforcement seems to be crucial for a hybrid regulatory system to perform well.'

Microsoft solves its security problems via the world's largest coordinated download system, in which 400 million computers automatically update their software monthly and reboot to install the updates. If child protection were really taken as seriously by industry and politicians that it was held to trump individual autonomy, such a filtering system would long ago have been introduced, as it was in television broadcasting. As it has not, the system is as much gesture politics and shadow-puppetry as it is an effective solution to the problems of children accessing adult content depicting sex, violence, substance abuse and suicide. The following chapter examines the political attempts to prevent 'accidental' viewing of child pornography on the Internet through a self-regulatory system, rather than remove the content at source.[108]

---

[108] Edwards (2009).

6

Private ISP censorship

Introducing Internet filtering and website blocking

This chapter explores the private filtering and censorship of the Internet that already takes place, its murky legal stature and government attempts to substantially increase the levels of censorship that take place, by encouraging private ISPs to censor their own customers.[1] The information is largely culled from the 2008 EC study.[2] I am particularly grateful to the interviewees and relevant team members of the study, for their degree of candour in discussing Internet censorship and government pressures.[3]

Where there is no direct contractual relationship between ISP and content provider, no explicit possibility to enforce mass media-type regulation applies, and the ISP is only responsible for content when it has been given notice of its potential harmful or illegal nature, at which point it may take down such content prior to investigating the complaint – the so-called 'Notice and Take Down' (NTD) regime under ECD. This regime has been criticized as a 'shoot first, ask questions later' approach in which ISPs have little incentive to investigate the complaints of alleged pornographic, defaming or copyright-infringing content (to name the three most 'popular' categories for NTD). The role, effectiveness and impact on ISP competitiveness of filtering is also essential to the roles of NTD regimes under ECD. The suggestion that other interlocutors, notably search engines and p2p systems, provide alternative routes for users to share potentially illegal or harmful content, raises the issue of the reform or amendment of the ECD to embrace these categories of content intermediaries.[4]

---

[1] See the most recent and comprehensive analyses, McIntyre (2010a, pp. 209–221; 2010c); McIntyre and Scott (2008); Akdeniz (2004, 2008); Edwards (2008); Clayton (2008).
[2] Marsden *et al.* (2008).
[3] In particular, team members Lorna Woods and Ian Brown, and interviewees John Carr, Peter Robbins, Malcolm Hutty, Cormac Callanan, Ola Kristian Hoff and Richard Clayton. Details extracted from Marsden *et al.* (2008).
[4] Sutter (2000), pp. 338–378.

Table 6.1. *Regulatory schemes for filtering*

Regulatory scheme	Self-Co	Scale	Government involvement
Co-founded self	FOSI#	6	Prior negotiation of body; no outcome role
Sanctioned self	PEGI# Euro mobile	7	Recognition of body – formal policy role (contact committee/ process)
Approved self	Hotline#	8	Prior principled less-formal discussion with government – with recognition/approval

Hash tag indicates government-funded in whole or part

The types of self-regulatory regime I examine in this chapter are all EC- and/or Member State-supported, and in the case of hotlines part-funded, which places them in a hybrid category. ISP filtering has emerged from directly EU-funded labelling and anti-paedophile sexual image reporting hotlines. European funding for hotlines to remove suspected child pornography via reports to the police in each Member State continue, with multi-year EU funding. The best-known and oldest example is the UK Internet Watch Foundation (IWF), but these institutions exist across Europe. Other European governments have instituted a more formal co-regulatory structure with direct reporting to the police.

Given the bottleneck control over the user experience provided by ISPs,[5] co- and self-regulatory initiatives populated by these critical actors are central in Internet content regulation.[6] Kreimer restated government's dilemma in regulating Internet content: 'Even where speakers are theoretically subject to sanctions, the exponential increase in the number of speakers with potential access to broad audiences multiplies the challenge for censors seeking to suppress a message.'[7]

There are various procedures to ensure filtering, all relying on a combination of:

• upstream labelling applied by content creator;
• protecting content from unauthorized use with technological 'locks';
• filtering out insecure or potentially unwanted content ('blacklisting');
• only accessing trusted content ('whitelisting'); or

---

[5] Frieden (2010).   [6] Braman with Lynch (2003), pp. 422–448.
[7] Kreimer (2006), p. 13. See further Stalla-Bourdillon (2010), pp. 492–501.

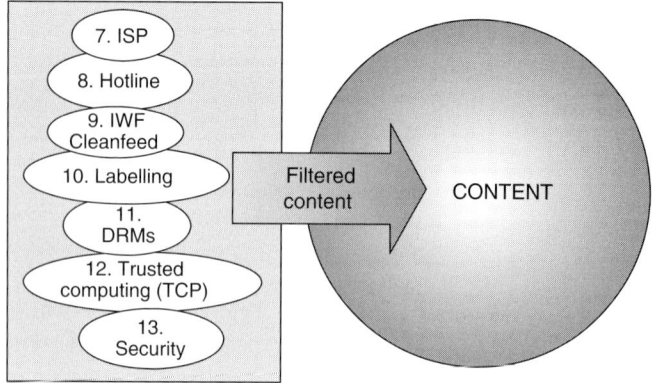

Figure 6.1.   Machine-labelled content filtering

- flagging of potentially harmful sites by users and ISPs,
- with users of the ISP contacting a 'hotline' (a contact centre designed to report and investigate the complaint).

Note in Figure 6.1 the various means by which content can be labelled to ensure its filtration prior to the user accessing the content onscreen. The types of institutions to assess and interview in the fixed ISP field include the following:

- ISP groups including the European Internet Service Provider Association (EuroISPA) and multinational ISPs (7);
- Hotlines (8, e.g., INHOPE: European hotlines association);
- ISP blocking technologies (9, e.g., IWF and BT 'Cleanfeed');
- Labelling experts (10, e.g., ICRA[8]) and W3C for the PICS process;
- User groups including those contributing to European networks;
- Co- and self-regulatory organizations, for instance KJM (Germany);[9]
- User representatives including child safety and awareness networks;[10] and
- Anti-censorship groups.[11]

---

[8] Internet Content Rating Association is part of the Family Online Safety Institute (FOSI), see www.fosi.org/.
[9] Kommission für Jugendmedienschutz, at www.kjm-online.de/public/kjm/index.php?show_1=54.
[10] Many funded in part by governments and the SIAP, see http://ec.europa.eu/information_society/activities/sip/projects/index_en.htm.
[11] Such as chillingeffects.org, EDRi and Bits Of Freedom.

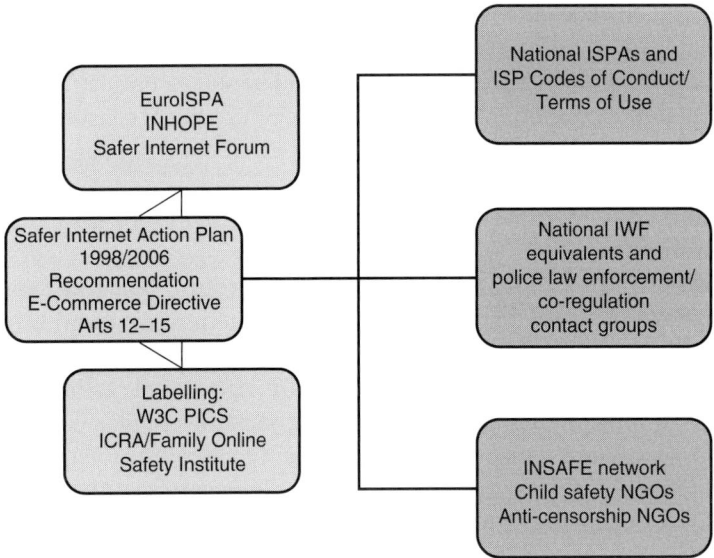

Figure 6.2.   European policy and local implementation of ISP codes, hotlines, and civil society

A European process map of illegal content co-regulation is shown in Figure 6.2. Support for the development of website quality labels became part of the Internet Action Plan 1999–2002.[12] By voting on the extension to 2003–4 of the Internet Action Plan on 11 March 2003, the European Parliament committed the Commission to give further support to encourage the development of website quality labels.[13] Note the importance of coordination mechanisms such as the EC Safer Internet Forum, together with European organizations representing hotlines, national ISP associations, user awareness nodes (INSAFE) and ICRA. The formation of FOSI strengthens this coordination, both within Europe and elsewhere. Note also that freedom of speech/anti-censorship civil society organizations play a role in trying to prevent over-zealous censorship of sites considered harmful. Empirical studies of ISP blocking of content (in the claim of breach of copyright) suggest such a danger is real. Conventional labelling and rating methods may not be easily applicable to inappropriate user-

---

[12] See Oxford University (2003).
[13] For the full text of the decision of the European Parliament please view: http://www3.europarl.eu.int/omk/omnsapir.so/pv2?PRG=CALDOC&FILE=981117&LANGUE=EN&TPV=DEF&LASTCHAP=6&SDOCTA=2&TXTLST=1&Type_Doc=FIRST&POS=1.

generated and posted content. However, the legitimacy and acceptability of intervention raises ethical as well as practical questions. Who has the right to judge whether particular content should be shown or not? When does the intervention amount to inappropriate or unethical censorship? European funding for hotlines to remove suspected child pornography via reports to the police in each Member State continue. McIntyre has considered the UK example alongside Ireland's,[14] which has a similarly free-standing body.

Technology and social standardization are two-edged. Blocking systems established to inhibit access to content (and communication) can be used to serve the interests of censorship as well as free expression, and that censorship can be subverted by determined technology-literate users. Against this complex background some companies emphasize that it is not possible (and even not desirable) for them to take over the role of 'Internet police'. This is particularly true when there is lack of clarity in the separation of functions between the:

- legislature (determining what is acceptable and expressing this in laws or norms),
- executive (enforcing acceptable behaviour through prevention or evidence collection) and
- judiciary (interpreting laws and norms in light of evidence and acting to impose sanctions),
- or where functions overlap across technological, market and jurisdictional boundaries.

An example of this overlap or lack of clarity and transparency between SRO and police is the blocking of claimed illegal images. Figure 6.3 shows a map of stakeholders in the UK ISP community.

Internet Watch Foundation (IWF)

The IWF was founded in 1996 as the UK ISP industry charitable hotline for the removal of child pornographic content.[15] Hotlines are exemplars of user reporting and ISP removal of illegal content. It is claimed

---

[14] McIntyre (2010b).
[15] Correspondence address: 5 Coles Lane, Oakington, Cambridge, CB4 5BA, UK. IWF is a company limited by guarantee and has acquired charitable status since December 2005. IWF holds the shares in Internet Watch Limited and is obliged to run the company according to its articles and memorandum. IWL contributes to the income of IWF.

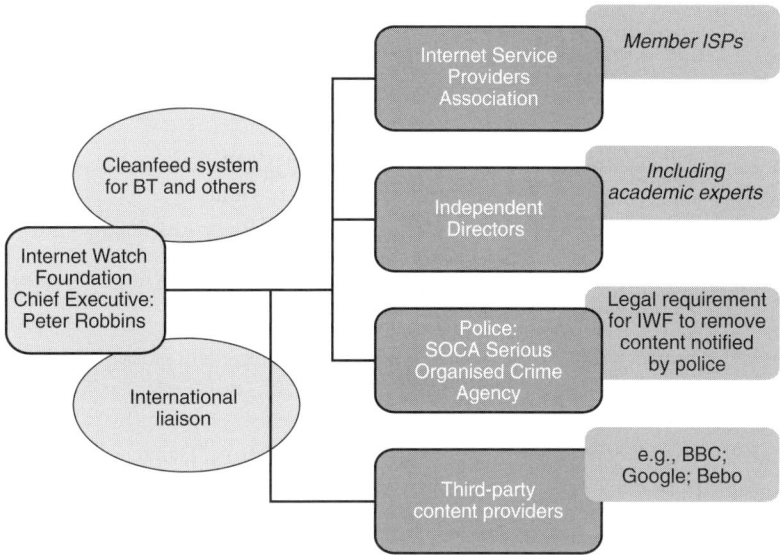

Figure 6.3.   Stakeholder map of IWF as UK fixed ISP self-regulator

as a success in its core remit: an increased number of cases of reported illegal content; driving child pornography out of the UK; involvement in UK government and police initiatives; and international support for INHOPE and coordinated police activities. Nonetheless there are serious recurring issues about freedom of expression and access to justice, with the original case-by-case take-down notices replaced by the total removal of newsgroups in 2002 and the 2007 initiative, the CAIC blocklist. The implementation of automated filtering based on this list by British Telecom and others encompasses over 90 per cent of consumer Internet users, and the police minister tried to insist in 2007–8 that if not voluntarily adopted, it be made mandatory. IWF has broadened its funding base to include mobile networks and search engines, among others, and there is tension between supporters of its original mission and an increasingly independent executive management. IWF has undergone a number of governance reviews during its first ten years, both internally and by government.

As Internet use developed, it became apparent that in addition to the positive aspects of Internet use, there was a potential for misuse. In particular, although child pornography has always existed, the Internet was perceived as giving greater opportunities for the dissemination of this type of

Table 6.2. *Summary of IWF case study*

Was there a government mandate initially?	Yes, Home Office and DTI sanctioning
What kind of government involvement is there?	Continued Home Office intense liaison, EC partial funding
Which other stakeholders are involved and how?	Advisory board – note funding council plays vital role
How is transparency ensured?	Web publication of all proceedings
What is the enforcement mechanism; is it effective; at what cost?	Blocklist for all members, excellent liaison with police and INHOPE
What is the relative size of administrative burdens?	Very low for chosen community. Danger of over-blocking evident in 'class' blocking of e.g., Usenet groups.
Is financial independence assured and how?	Continued dependence on key ISPs and EU.
Which internal factor most impacts success?	Expanded mandate suits newer members more, except BT
Which external conditions impact success/failure (e.g., competitive situation, technology, etc.)?	Governmental: relationship with Home Office, INHOPE. Market: adoption of 'Cleanfeed' type system. Technology: development of new filtering standards in e.g., ETSI.
Lessons for European policy	Widening membership approach effective, significant new efforts to address user community with blocklist. Danger of market fragmentation in new filter approach and pan-European proposals.

material.[16] The Metropolitan Police sent a letter to all ISPs on 9 August 1996 requesting them to censor Usenet newsgroups, threatening otherwise the prosecution of ISPs in relation to illegal material therein. Facilitated by the Department of Trade and Industry (DTI) certain ISPs, the Metropolitan Police, the Home Office and a body called the Safety-Net Foundation (formed by the Dawe Charitable Trust) agreed the R3 Safety-Net Agreement, where 'R3' referred to the triple approach of rating, reporting and responsibility.[17]

[16] www.iwf.org.uk/public/page.29.htm.
[17] Internet Service Providers Association, LINX and Safety-Net Foundation (1996) R3 – Rating, Reporting, Responsibility for Child Pornography and Illegal Material on the Internet, at www.mit.edu/activities/safe/labeling/r3.htm.

In September 1996, this agreement was made between the Internet Service Providers Association (ISPA), the London Internet Exchange (LINX) and the Safety-Net Foundation which was subsequently renamed IWF. From the perspective of industry, consumer protection issues (or the public benefit generally) were seen as a side benefit though not the driving force for the establishment of IWF.

IWF, a charity in the form of a corporation limited by guarantee, was founded by industry to provide an online reporting mechanism for content that was alleged to be illegal, a system now recognized by legislation. IWF's governing document is its Memorandum and Articles, amended 30 October 1998, 13 January 2005 and 16 September 2005. It states that IWF objectives are:

(a) The promotion of the care and protection of the health and welfare of the public in particular children and young people by working to minimize the availability of potentially illegal or otherwise harmful content on the Internet. (b) The prevention of crimes relating to offences involving exposure to illegal content on the internet in particular by: (i) operating a hotline enabling the public to report such instances; (ii) operating a notice and take-down service to alert hosting service providers of such criminal content found on their servers; and (iii) alerting relevant law enforcement agencies to the content. (c) To further such purposes as are recognized as exclusively charitable under the law of England and Wales.

IWF set up a subsidiary company, to run in line with IWF's main objectives and IWF itself obtained charitably status, registered on 5 December 2005. Charitable status suggests a change of emphasis, as to be registered as a charity a body must meet a charitable purpose and have that charitable purpose exclusively, subject to the Charities Commission.[18] Its mission is:

To work in partnership with Internet service providers, telecommunication companies, mobile operators, software providers, the police, Government and the public to minimize the availability of online illegal content, particularly child sexual abuse images.

[18] Preamble to the Charitable Uses Act 1601 contains a list of purposes which courts have developed by analogy, see *Income Tax Special Purpose Commissioners* v. *Pemsel* [1891] AC 531. The courts have stressed that the definition of charitable purpose is not static. It is generally accepted now that there are four main charitable purposes: relief of poverty; advancement of education; advancement of religion; and other purposes of benefit to the community. In determining whether a purpose falls in the fourth head, the Charity Commission adopts a two-step test: is the purpose analogous to a purpose previously accepted as charitable; does the purpose benefit the public? Charities Act 2006 changes can be found at www.charity-commission.gov.uk/enhancingcharities/pbanalysis.asp.

IWF coordinates with the police and a number of government agencies (such as the Home Office Task Force) and service providers (such as the CAIC list initiative). The core of its activities is an NTD system relating to child pornography, and other criminally obscene or criminally racist content hosted in the UK. The scope of IWF activities is limited, concerning limited types of content (essentially child pornography, obscenity and hate speech).[19] It does not cover issues such as paedophile conversations intended to persuade children to engage in illegal sexual acts, a process known as 'grooming' (an offence under the Sexual Offences 2003). Nor do its activities include p2p services, online games, 'happyslapping'[20] and torture websites.[21] Further, although originally the IWF was going to develop a labelling and rating system this became the responsibility of ICRA.

IWF underwent a governance review commissioned by the DTI in 1998 and carried out by KPMG and Denton Hall.[22] Carr (2007) states that following the 1997 election, Minister Barbara Roche called for the review, on which Carr was a government appointee.[23] The review endorsed the notion of self-regulation, so confirmed IWF in its role. The KPMG/ Denton Hall Review revealed that only 6 per cent of the public had heard of IWF.[24] The White Paper, 'A New Future For Communications' summarized – in paragraphs 6.10.1–6.10.8 – the UK self-regulatory model for the Internet based on the work of IWF and described IWF as 'a model internationally'. Carr notes that the Home Office became more and more responsible for self-regulation after this review,[25] creating the Home Office Task Force since 2001, and the Internet Crime Forum, which had a subgroup on chatrooms. In the view of Carr (2007), Clayton (2007), Hutty (2007b) and Robbins (2007), the major regulatory battle on the board of the IWF was around attitudes to blocking of entire newsgroups and Usenet in 1999/2000. Peter Robbins was appointed CEO in April 2002.

---

[19] Note guidance on the scope of this at www.iwf.org.uk/corporate/page.49.232.htm, and changes in UK law which might affect it.
[20] The term used for mobile phone-captured videos of assaults on victims posted on the Internet.
[21] Grooming, peer-to-peer services and such like fall within the responsibility of CEOP: see www.ceop.gov.uk/.
[22] KPMG Peat Marwick and Denton Hall (1999).
[23] Carr was also a member of the Policy Board of IWF from 1996, and appointed as Director until 2003.
[24] http://networks.silicon.com/webwatch/0,39024667,11008420,00.htm.
[25] Antelope Consulting, Regulation and the Internet, available at www.communications-act.gov.uk/responses/Antelope%20Consulting.doc.

As he puts it, he 'joined when the IWF was in crisis' with 'about a dozen major funders – ISPs'. At this point it began taking down whole groups rather than individual posts, against the preferred option of many ISP policy-makers who viewed this as a step towards wider censorship of the Internet. In their view, each individual piece of illegal content should be judged on its own merits. By taking down entire newsgroups, the IWF was removing many legitimate posts alongside the offending messages. Newsgroups complaints were near zero. As a result, IWF analysts were now freed up to deal with web-based content. That decision to take down newsgroups is now seen by Robbins as a 'resource-intensive futile exercise in view of newsgroup postings going through the roof'. In parallel with the change in policy towards newsgroups, there were new constituencies with more diverse interests than the original fixed ISPs. Together with five major mobile operators joining, search providers also joined.[26]

IWF is one of several co-regulatory bodies involved in the control of Internet content within the UK, with ICSTIS and IMCB. IWF recognized the need for cooperation with Ofcom, though during the passage of the Communications Act 2003, it strenuously opposed Ofcom's involvement with the regulation of the Internet.[27] IWF is funded by industry members[28] whose numbers have grown from twelve in 2001 to fifty-five in the 2005–7 Business Plan and seventy-six in the 2006 Annual Report. IWF also receives funding under SIAP as well as specific project funding.[29]

Following the Sex Offences Act 2003, which amends the protection awarded to children under the Protection of Children Act 1978,[30]

[26] An example of service providers extending the remit beyond IWF powers is in search: Google blocks child porn from search results though this is unofficial filtering; see chillingeffects.org which shows the notice in the UK. Sites that complain were apparently accused of 'gaming' Google: see Wikipedia. Also note Google issues instructions on how to 'delist' from being blocked.
[27] Internet Watch Foundation (2002).
[28] A full list of donors is listed at www.iwf.org.uk/funding/page.64.htm.
[29] The Annual Report is available on the IWF webpage: www.iwf.org.uk/corporate/page.173.htm.
[30] Section 45 amends the Protection of Children Act 1978 so that the offences under that Act of taking, making, permitting to take, distributing, showing, possessing with intent to distribute, and advertising indecent photographs or pseudo-photographs of children will now also be applicable where the photographs concerned are of children of 16 or 17 years of age. The same change applies to the offence of possessing an indecent photograph or pseudo-photograph of a child at section 160 of the Criminal Justice Act 1988 (section 160(4) applies the 1978 Act definition of 'child'). Section 46 provides a defence in that an individual will not have committed the offence where it was necessary for him to make the photograph or pseudo-photograph for the purposes of the prevention, detection or

the Chief Constables' Association and the Crown Prosecution Service entered into a Memorandum of Understanding about the reporting of such offences which, inter alia, recognizes the role of the IWF and states that reports made to the IWF in line with its procedures will be accepted as a report to the relevant authority for the purposes of the Sex Offences Act 2003.[31] According to the IWF this was significant in clarifying the legal status (legal exposure) of IWF and its employees under UK criminal legislation.

IWF is controlled by a single board of trustees of ten members, comprising six non-industry members, three industry members appointed by an open selection process, and an independent chair. The board may set up any such subcommittees as it may think appropriate. In general, there is an executive committee comprising the chair and two vice chairs of the board. The responsibilities and conduct of all IWF board members are governed by the provisions of the board members' handbook, available on the IWF website.[32] This constitution can be amended by decision of the board, provided that the changes do not conflict with the Memorandum and Articles of Association. Industry members are determined by the funding council, which determines its own rules and procedures.

According to the IWF 2006 Annual Report, its team receives training from the police and applies criteria for the categorization of material in accordance with those set by the UK Sentencing Advisory Council. These decisions are made independent of the board, though within the scope of policies made by the board. Woods reports that: 'Decisions on content are made by the hotline team, who are salaried individuals, and who act in accordance with the policies determined by the Board, although in many instances the role of the IWF is that of passing information on to law enforcement agencies.'[33] IWF offers specific services in addition to the core activity of providing a hotline. These services are in general available to its members and are aimed at supporting ISPs in identifying illegal material. The services are: CAIC list; keyword service; newsgroup service

---

investigation of crime, or for the purposes of criminal proceedings, in any part of the world.
[31] www.iwf.org.uk/police/page.22.213.htm.
[32] www.iwf.org.uk/corporate/page.49.207.htm.
[33] Woods (2006), Ch. 25, available at www.epsiplus.net/epsiplus/media/files/coregul_final_report_en.

designed to combat paedophilic content; spam alert; and a best practice guide.

IWF would seem to influence government policy in this area. Civil liberties groups have expressed concerns about the openness and accountability of this process. The hotline depends on individual reports of potentially illegal material being made. Cooperation and compliance with IWF is mandatory for members of ISPA by virtue of its code of practice. Membership of ISPA is not mandatory, though in practice most UK ISPs are ISPA members. Members may make representations to explain why a notice has not been complied with, specifically if they believe that there has been an error in the notice. The code makes clear that the final determination of whether or not content is illegal remains a decision for the law enforcement authorities. It is not clear how individuals affected by IWF determinations may make representations, nor did the infamous 'Virgin Killers' case make that any less obscure.[34]

Chief Executive Peter Robbins (2007) states that it is 'difficult to quantify [effectiveness], complaints are not always of the best quality but provide leads'.[35] Furthermore, there is a clear problem with repeat complainants who keep finding illegal sites: 'We try to deter people that are reporting regularly to us quality sites because obviously they are breaking the law – ethically that's the wrong thing to do.' Of the 14,300 reports of suspected child abuse sites made to IWF in the first six months of 2006, 4,908 were found to have potentially illegal content. According to the 2006 Annual Report, IWF processed 31,776 reports leading to 10,656 URLs being added to the CAIC. On its website, IWF comments that the percentage of potentially illegal content assessed by itself and hosted in the UK has been reduced from 18 per cent in 1997 to 1 per cent or less from 2003 onwards. The Annual Report for 2006 shows that the 1 per cent level for the UK remains broadly steady.[36] The report notes that many of the abuse sites have been long-lived, moved domain and consequently changed jurisdiction to avoid prosecution. The 2003 figures show that child abuse content traced to the US rose by 55 per cent on the previous year and that in relation to Russia, by 5 per cent. The location of much child abuse content in domains found in the USA and Russia was also a constant, as according to IWF's more recent Annual Report over 82 per cent of content constituting child abuse content were found in these two countries.

[34] See Edwards (2009); MacSíthigh (2009); McIntyre (2010c).
[35] Gringras (2003), p. 328.
[36] Details can be found at www.iwf.org.uk/police/tools.5.20.htm.

IWF is involved in international matters, both through funding from SIAP and, indirectly, through the Child Exploitation and Online Protection Centre (CEOP) and its initiatives such as the Virtual Global Taskforce (VGT).[37] CEOP is a much larger enterprise than the self-regulated IWF,[38] with a total budget of about £8m.[39] It is part of VGT,[40] made up of law enforcement agencies with the aim of building an effective, international partnership to protect children from online child abuse.[41] Jim Gamble, when Chief Executive of CEOP, was the chair of the VGT. The VGT claims it 'delivers low-cost, high impact initiatives that prevent and deter pae-dophiles from exploiting children online'. Within the UK, the IWF now works with several ministries. Robbins explains that the IWF talks to many policy research bodies internationally, which are typically interested in the co-regulatory partnership. He also reports much US interest.

ISPs were concerned at Home Office proposals for anti-terrorist and anti-hate censorship by ISPs. In Carr's view, IWF 'is now representative of the consumer and industry but wasn't always'. IWF has to pay close atten-tion to industry's needs and sensibilities, which creates problems regarding conflicts of interest, despite which it seems to work. Moreover, Carr sees that the advantage in the UK is that all industry meets on the Home Office Task Force, which creates a co-regulatory forum to exchange information. In his view, part of a US coordination problem on child protection is based on geography, part on antitrust, but the coordination of the UK Task Force pushed the debate beyond adversarial relations, by which he character-izes government–ISP relations in the US. As noted in the work plan for 2008, the IWF has undergone a form of governance review. Charitable and operational organization are now separate. The reform of governance has, according to Clayton (2007), meant the IWF is now less in control of ISPs and more in the charge of the 'child protection lobby', with which Robbins and Carr agree, though from the opposite perspective (they implemented

---

[37] Internet Task Force for Child Protection on the Internet, at www.virtualglobaltaskforce. com/.

[38] CEOP (2007a).

[39] Its annual review details contributions as: core operating budget (Home Office) £4,500,000; value of partnership resources £3,098,783; self-generated resources (profes-sional training revenue) £300,000; additional government funding streams (FCO, Home Office) £169,000.

[40] http://police.homeoffice.gov.uk/operational-policing/crime-disorder/child-protection-taskforce.

[41] The VGT is made up of: the Australian High Tech Crime Centre, the Child Exploitation and Online Protection Centre in the UK, the Royal Canadian Mounted Police, the US Department of Homeland Security and Interpol.

or supported this policy change). The addition of funding from mobile providers and search engines has somewhat changed the funding model. The funding council stop any move for IWF to change its mandate to distasteful as well as illegal material. The ISP blocking majority there is apparently firm – even with some mobile providers on the council.

It would be simple but persuasive to characterize a deliberate and quite transparent change during Robbins's years as CEO from a self-regulatory ISP-based body to a more co-regulatory police cooperation body. Robbins sees 'it as a partnership approach' with government. Clayton (2007) argues that: 'Arguably IWF has done what it was set up to do, eliminate child porn from the UK. Now they're trying to save the world instead of winding the organisation up … Any right-thinking person would want the sites taken down as soon as possible, but IWF wanted to get them prosecuted' which involves reporting sites to the police directly, not to ISPs. He reports that many ISPs were very upset at this unilateral action by IWF. There is a very sharp difference of opinion between Carr and Robbins on the extension of the hotline model of IWF to other countries.[42] Carr (2007) states that: 'Government is still very strongly wedded to the principle of self-regulation … [it] has worked because of the political culture and traditions of the UK … a product of necessity as much as choice, if you haven't got civil servants who knew what the Internet is … if it's not broken, don't fix it – so far people trust the IWF.' The conflict of interest is clear – governments have initially to ask industry to explain how Internet self-regulation works, from value chain to technology and points in between. Carr's view is that the model is not transferable to many other European countries where 'self-regulation is not part of their vocabulary', and instead more legally bound relations between government, police and ISPs are to be found. In answer to the charge that IWF is a 'gold-plated' regulator suitable only for the UK, Robbins (2007) respond that: 'On both counts (finance and technical ability) that's rubbish – IWF can be replicated across Europe … There's nothing particularly technical about any of this.' He believes that training can be done by INHOPE, Europol, etc., supported by EC money and CERT/ISP expertise, and that combating child pornography more effectively needs a pan-European non-governmental body – a type of super-INHOPE (see below).

Judicial review is possible of IWF procedures and the IWF board asked legal counsel to confirm that IWF is at those times acting in a

---

[42] Two directors otherwise notably in favour of greater intervention in the Usenet debates of 1999–2002.

quasi-judicial capacity. Further, although there is an appeal procedure, is it entirely independent as required by the Human Rights Act and by Article 6 ECHR; There are questions about whether an individual who wished to challenge a take-down notice would be able to bring an action for judicial review; it is not clear whether an individual affected by a take-down notice (and not the ISP itself) could challenge that decision within the IWF. There have been comments by NGOs about the problems of using ISPs to enforce the criminal law and the impact not only on access to the courts but also freedom of expression.[43] While the UK Government suggested in its 2000 White Paper that industry regulation is an improvement on traditional regulation, this assumes that industry interests and those of the citizen coincide exactly, which is not the case. 2009 legislation outlaws cartoon image viewing of child porn.[44] There must be an open question as to whether this increases the scale and scope of IWF activities. Robbins states that: 'Generally speaking there is huge consensus that this is wrong, but when it comes to privacy, copyright, terrorist material, it's very difficult to argue (if it's legal to look at it) that it should be blocked by government. That's why we've had no remit creep in our work.' It can be argued that enforced self-censorship is more insidious than traditional censorship, as it is more difficult to detect and challenge. Given both these points, the need for rights of access to the courts for those whose rights have been affected by the IWF is an important point to clarify. I examine the CAIC list later in the chapter.

International Association of Internet Hotlines (INHOPE)

INHOPE is the pan-European hotline association, officially founded in 1996, but established as an ongoing concern in 1999, based in Dublin and expanding rapidly to twenty-eight members across Europe and worldwide,[45] although it has never represented hotlines from all EU Member States. Its primary role is in training and coordination, and the majority of its funding is guaranteed by the SIAP, as well as Microsoft. It follows previous best practice developed in, for instance, the UK (IWF), Germany (FSM) and the Netherlands (a hotline which became part of

---

[43] Freedom of expression and Internet regulation background paper, which aims to draw out the most important questions with regard to Internet regulation and freedom of expression, including access issues, content regulation and monitoring and surveillance, 19 October 2001. See also submission to House of Lords: www.cyber-rights.org/reports/crcl-hl.htm.

[44] Coroners and Justice Act 2009, Part 2, Chapter 2.

[45] See www.inhope.org for details.

Table 6.3. *Summary of INHOPE case study*

Government mandate initially?	Yes, EC funding
Continuing government involvement?	Continued EC partial funding
Which other stakeholders are involved and how?	General assembly of members
How is transparency ensured?	Web publication of proceedings – website sparsely updated
What is the enforcement mechanism; is it effective; at what cost?	None currently except expulsion for non-paying members and vetting of new members
What is the relative size of administrative burdens?	Low membership fee, no practical administration currently
Is financial independence assured and how?	Continued dependence on EU
Which internal factor most impacts success?	Expanding mandate to create pan-European blocklist critical move towards regulatory impact
Which external conditions impact success/failure (e.g., competitive situation, technology, etc.)?	Governmental: relationship with EU and national police forces. Market: adoption of 'Cleanfeeed' type system. Technology: development of new filtering standards in e.g., ETSI.
Lessons for European policy	Widening membership approach effective, significant new efforts to address user community with blocklist. Danger of loss of extra-European focus in new filter approach and pan-European proposals.

NICAM), and acts as a coordinating mechanism for national hotlines to report and take down child pornography on the Internet. The use of EC funding for both partial funding of national hotlines and INHOPE is an example of the 'soft power' that can be exerted by the EC.

Stakeholder involvement works as follows:

(1) Member associations have wide relations with government/law enforcement/industry and others. INHOPE staff make two to three field visits to meet with stakeholders of potential members.
(2) INHOPE in 2004 signed a Memorandum of Understanding with EuroISPA – which is an example of international outreach.

(3) There is no direct outreach with consumer groups as such.
(4) Microsoft gives free software and otherwise supports INHOPE.
(5) INHOPE has direct relations as observers in the Interpol 'Crimes against Children' subgroup – as also with the Council of Europe and OSCE. Sustainability in these groups is difficult with such a small policy staff.

INHOPE has published three activities reports, available at its website.[46] It has fully audited reports from auditors in the Netherlands, which are filed and distributed to members. Its 2005 income was €533,692; 2006 income was €397,175 with €157,992 due to be paid revealing a slight increade in overall income.[47] It conducts the following activities: hotlines; training – e.g., for Europol and Interpol; publications; lobbying; and advice.

'Enforcement' is essentially by expulsion from membership if members fail to renew and pay their fees. Callanan explains that 'Brazil and Lithuania both withdrew, as they didn't pay their fees. In Sweden, the hotline collapsed and the new replacement hotline chose not to join.' Fees were €6,000 until 2006 – half of which could be reclaimed from the EC for European hotlines. Within INHOPE and its members, there are obviously minimalist and maximalist camps: should it help set up pan-European systems? Callanan explains that:

> I am of the opinion that self-regulation has failed, not because it doesn't work but because no one believes in it anymore. One, because governments see it as a stop gap until they get their own systems in place. Second, and more dramatically, because it's now a commercial advantage to be a self-regulatory organization – Bebo, Microsoft, Vodafone. It's become a competitive differentiator.

He outlines the fact that the broadening of the number of key interlocutors in the citizen's use of the Internet means that filtering and censoring of the Internet could become widespread with 'systems that have a dramatic impact on free expression in the Information Society', which he submits applies to content and application providers such as Google, AOL, Yahoo! and Microsoft, as well as incumbent ISPs. The lack of enforcement for hotline activities, and INHOPE's role as coordinator of hotlines but not enforcer, is a source of obvious tension between governments and industry.

---

[46] INHOPE (2006).
[47] Source: supplied to RAND Europe by INHOPE; Accounts of Horlings, Brouwer and Horlings, of Amsterdam (2006).

INHOPE contributes to the EC Safer Internet Forum with all the SIAP-funded programmes. There is little industry involvement in the Forum, except UK-based Vodafone, BT, Yahoo!, all of whom have suggested rolling out their best practices across Europe. The third INHOPE report states the difficulties in applying common standards in different countries, even the then-nineteen members from the European Economic Area: 'In Europe alone, the age of a "child" ranges from fourteen to eighteen years of age. In some countries knowingly possessing child pornography is also a criminal offence. Sometimes the definition of child pornography includes computer-generated or altered images and even cartoon characters.[48] The September 2007 INHOPE survey states: 'This report is the first step towards a global action plan to eradicate illegal activity from the Internet. It is a landmark publication for policy makers, governments and Industry.[49] Its statistics for the period September 2004–December 2006 show that INHOPE members received 900,000 reports from the general public, and in total members processed 1.9 million reports. Only 8 per cent (160,000 reports) were forwarded to law enforcement agencies for action – an average of 5,800 per month. Of all processed reports, 21 per cent were about illegal or harmful content (20,000 per month). As a result, based solely on reports received, the report claims that child pornography grew by 15 per cent per year; and racism and xenophobia websites grew by 33 per cent per year. It is not clear to what extent this crime reporting reflects the wider population using the Internet and to what extent it reflects the greater success of hotlines in attracting visibility among Internet users.

The total number of INHOPE members is rising fast, and the diversity of views, subjects and language skills create a potential danger of sclerotic decision-making, according to Callanan. Interviewees expressed the belief that INHOPE provides excellent value for money, but should be more committed than ever to transparency, outreach and accountability, and not just to its EC funders but also to its stakeholders. It has had substantial and consistent backing, but also some organizational frustration:

(1) Unique commitment by the SIAP has provided regular funding over ten years.
(2) INHOPE as an NGO, not a company, creates some unique difficulties in its audit submissions for that funding.
(3) Netherlands rules mean only €7,500 per annum can be retained.

---

[48] INHOPE (2006) at p. 10.   [49] Callanan and Frydas (2007).

(4) Computer equipment for people is not allowed by the funding, but servers are.

(5) The remaining 20 per cent of budget is raised from membership fees – also some training donations from Microsoft.

ISPs and their content-hosting partners are the key link between content and end-users, and hence their position as the only feasible point of control for governments who wish to block or filter content that is considered unsuitable for end-users. This places both national and European ISP lobbies in a pivotal policy position. EuroISPA recognized the development of a European network of hotlines to remove illegal content in its 2004 Memorandum of Understanding with INHOPE.[50] Then-President of EuroISPA Michael Rotert announced the memorandum as a 'formal statement of support' for hotlines, and 'a further significant step in this cooperation' with international bodies in combating illegal content. EuroISPA is the largest ISP association in the world (approximately 1000 ISPs). Nash states its self-regulatory position: 'EuroISPA considers that the most effective solutions to protect users should be as close to the end-user as possible. This underlines the importance of awareness raising to promote, above all, media literacy.'[51] It is clear that regulation drawn broadly does raise different standards of public scrutiny and inclusiveness/transparency from such a closed lobbying body. A question for any new public role for EuroISPA would be: how do you decide between an industry closed body versus an open SRO with multistakeholders and discussions? Obviously different types of purpose will determine the design, and there are hybrids between the fully-fledged regulatory body of the KJM, PEGI or IWF type, and the closed lobbying body of the EuroISPA type. While a vital stakeholder group in European Internet regulation, one cannot see EuroISPA as a regulatory group.

UK and European blocklists

The Internet was designed to allow the efficient transmission of information between networks around the world. As Brown explains, ISPs required to block access to specific websites have therefore relied on three crude mechanisms: IP address filtering, DNS poisoning and keyword searching.[52] A fourth possibility is to use a hybrid which combines two or more of these systems. The simplest filtering mechanism is for ISPs to block traffic

---

[50] EuroISPA–INHOPE (2004).   [51] Nash (2007).
[52] Brown (2008), pp. 74–91.

to and from lists of websites specified by their IP addresses. Any packets of data with a destination or source address on this list will be dropped by the routers within ISP networks, especially those that exchange traffic with overseas networks. Less advanced and motivated users find their access curtailed by IP address filtering. Because Web servers typically host many (sometimes many thousands) of individual sites, a block on one of those sites will mean none of the other sites hosted on that server will be accessible. Kulawiec states the common perspective among network architects:

> You can't block by protocol, because those same protocols are used for lots of other things. (And even if you did, someone would just invent another protocol.) You can't block by content, because no software method is even remotely close to reliable enough and all the ones involving humans are either biased, slow, or both. Besides, it's easy enough to encrypt traffic. And so on. [Blocking] will have a temporary, minor effect. It might even help authorities find a few of the stupider criminals. These arrests will be announced as 'proving' the success of the measures.[53]

Web users' access to information will be most affected by filtering systems. Some governments have accepted this, and claim that their aim is merely to stop users 'accidentally' viewing blocked information. In the US, former Attorney General Richard Thornburgh headed a study committee sponsored by the National Academy of Sciences that produced a report that concluded that a combination of media literacy and the use of voluntary filtering tools was the best approach to protecting users from undesired content.[54] There is a danger that states with a commitment to freedom of expression are putting in place an unwieldy and ineffective censorship infrastructure that could easily be abused by future governments and repressive regimes. Evaluation of such systems should be encouraged.

UK 'Cleanfeed' and CAIC

British Telecom in 2003 developed a system called 'Cleanfeed' which blocks end-users' access to pages containing illegal child pornography images;[55] it was implemented in 2004.[56] The CAIC list is a more general version of BT's 'Cleanfeed';[57] it is the UK Child Abuse Database Service: a list of URLs which have been reported to the police so that an ISP can block the website (the website owner does have a right of appeal but this

---

[53] Kulawiec (2007).   [54] Thornburgh and Lin (2004).
[55] See IWF (2004) 7 June announcement at http://web.archive.org/web/20090224191202/ http://www.iwf.org.uk/media/news.archive-2004.39.htm
[56] Truman (2009).   [57] Hutty (2004).

is uncertain in effect as it is often difficult for the retail ISP to determine whether the wholesale ISP has blocked the site).[58] These services are in general available to its members and are aimed at facilitating ISPs in identifying illegal material. In the UK, British Telecom and other large ISPs block customer access to sites that have been identified as containing child pornography by IWF.[59] Similar schemes (including coordination between police forces to improve and extend databases of websites for blocking) have been implemented in Denmark, Norway, Sweden and other countries, causing significant controversy in view of their potential for application of the ECD where ISPs typically also host content, and the lack of transparency and appeal for content providers so blocked.[60]

In May 2006 a Home Office minister told Parliament that ISPs would be required to implement CAIC:

> Currently, all the 3G mobile network operators block their mobile customers from accessing these sites and the biggest ISPs (who between them provide over 90 per cent of domestic broadband connections) are either currently blocking or have plans to by the end of 2006 ... If it appears that we are not going to meet our target through co-operation, we will review the options for stopping UK residents accessing websites on the IWF list.[61]

The Home Office has stated that filters could be extended to other topics such as the 'glorification' of terrorism: 'our policy is to pursue a self-regulatory approach wherever possible. However, our legislation as drafted provides the flexibility to accommodate a change in Government policy should the need ever arise.'[62] It has been argued that the requirement of cooperation between IWF and police has made IWF into a co- rather than self-regulator.[63]

In 2007 IWF committed to: 'deliver a quality CAIC service and prepare a discussion document on options for a verification and validation process for members deploying the list'. It also stated that it would:

(a) Work closely with members and licensees to deliver a robust and secure CAIC service upgrading in the light of experience and best practice.
(b) Develop policies and procedures to underpin the delivery of the service.

---

[58] Internet Watch Foundation (2008).   [59] Clayton (2005).
[60] See EDRI representatives' concerns expressed in the 2006 Safer Internet Forum, at http://ec.europa.eu/information_society/activities/sip/docs/prog_decision_2009/decision_en.pdf
[61] Hansard (2006).   [62] Hutty (2006, 2007a).
[63] Crown Prosecution Service and Association of Chief Police Officers (2004).

(c) Work with IWF Audit committee and external 'experts' to audit the processes and policies within the hotline and the CAIC service by 31 December 2007.

(d) Devise and deliver options and budgets for consideration for the delivery of a validation and verification of the CAIC service with its licensees by 31 May 2007.

It plans to: 'consider options for a new membership funding model for consultation with funding council to take account of the diversity of current membership, potential future members and the broader base of our catchment, which includes, ISPs, telcos, filtering companies, search companies etc.' This would enable it to offer lower-priced CAIC listing to ISPs who claim not to afford the current cost-oriented price ('supply of CAIC data to "small" ISPs free of charge or modest contribution viable') which will be particularly the case should the UK Government make CAIC filtering compulsory.

Robbins states that the UK CAIC database 'list is a dynamic add-removal system at a rate of about fifty a day'. He argues that the blocklist does not stop paedophiles but stops the general public stumbling upon sites: 'Well over 90 per cent of domestic consumers are covered by the list ... We would say that there's approximately 10 per cent of the population that has got alternative ISPs, but the majority of them are covered upstream'[64] by, in particular, BT Wholesale. IWF attempted to assuage criticisms of the blocklist based in inadequacy of appeal against incorrect banning of sites, by developing a self-certifying validation and auditing programme for use by ISPs – to confirm deployment of the system. Compliance managers report to IWF that they have checked the list for errors, and a contractual requirement to audit was to be introduced. Blocking by ISPs in the manner of Cleanfeed should be as objective and transparent in process as possible.

Clayton claims the reason for continued extension of the blocking system despite technical, legal and natural justice concerns is the media climate surrounding child pornography, hence little or no pressure is exerted to independently examine whether blocking can work – or how it might be extended. ISPs do not want to block, except the big incumbents who can afford it, and want to be seen to be conforming, not least to conform to the expected regime under the AVMS Directive. Clayton explains that: 'The mobiles of this world do a lot of blocking, IWF is only a part'

[64] Robbins (2007).

and that mobile users until now have not expected to access the whole Internet.[65] Clayton also notes that the SIAP co-funding of hotlines means less financial control lies with ISPs. He contends that the 'IWF has a lot of money and not much more to do' though of course a pan-European and UK-compulsory CAIC list would require more resources.

IWF's 2008 work plan details its outreach activities including 'Work with INHOPE to deliver a European CAIC database and then extend its activities to include two-way reporting functionality.' This last item is particularly controversial, as a European CAIC database has been opposed by EuroISPA and ISPA UK over a long period. It demonstrates the degree to which the IWF executive has separated in policy terms from its original fixed ISP constituency in favour of greater intervention and co-regulatory approaches. Robbins (2007) analyzes the problems for pan-European hotline cooperation as:

- Resource and in particular finance gaps, often solved by Microsoft and the SIAP supplying 50 per cent funding each.
- Legal status for different private organizations to share information. UK is pragmatic but others worry about the constitutional position in sharing child porn information across borders, particularly between police forces and civilian bodies.
- Cultural attitude towards civilian hotlines differ – many countries prefer to have statutory law enforcement bodies involved. So that becomes a non-starter, particularly where hotlines are very small and somewhat distrusted by law enforcement: credibility gaps exist between professional police officers and civilian hotline staff.

Robbins' analysis is that this is due to the scale of the problem – research can be undertaken into total reports, but duplication must be removed: 'We need a European database of these URLs, to check if it's been reported or actioned' as hotlines have more data than the police, and there is substantial duplication currently between hotlines. He strongly believes the national hotline effectiveness cannot be accurately measured without pan-European cooperation, and that the metric for effectiveness should be 'put down' of damaging content: 'That is meaningful information – but what it requires is international coordination – they're creating skeleton websites and waiting for people to join … The only way to cope with the sophisticated criminals is to strip out the quantity and get after the quality.'

---

[65] Clayton (2007).

European CAIC

ISPs self-regulate in an environment conditioned by the 1998 settlement of the Recommendation on the Protection of Minors, which recommended governments to ensure they individually or collectively adopt codes of conduct on illegal and harmful content. This was supported in the settlement of the ECD. While several major pan-European ISPs as well as incumbent cable/telecoms operators have the resources to develop their own policies individually on a bespoke basis tailored to their market needs (for example, Microsoft, AOL, Yahoo!, France Telecom, T-Online, British Telecom, Tiscali), where there are many small ISPs, an ISPA formation can make sense in achieving scale and scope economies in designing best practice documents for the industry membership. As codes of conduct are in general widely available, it is not a major expense to adapt previous designs for current practice. To this extent, one can describe ISPAs as helping members' self-regulatory policies.[66]

Brown states that: 'In a piecemeal fashion, courts and governments in France, Germany, Switzerland, Finland, the UK and Italy have ordered ISPs to filter their users' access … However, the application of such restrictions to [ISPs] has yet to be tested against [ECD].'[67] Düsseldorf in Germany in 2002 ordered seventy-eight Internet Service Providers in North Rhine-Westphalia to block access to two US-hosted Nazi websites. The Finnish Government has encouraged ISPs to implement a 'voluntary' system that blocks access to a secret list maintained by the police of IP addresses hosting websites suspected to contain child pornography. Unlike similar systems in neighbouring Sweden and Norway, users will not have any choice whether their access is filtered; but the Finnish constitution would make it difficult for an openly mandatory system to be imposed by the Government. Save the Children, ISPs and the Danish police have cooperated to set up a blacklist of sites which are 'voluntarily' blocked once police validate that a site should be on the list and notify this fact to ISPs.

A Norwegian legislative study group decided against a proposed solution, to have filtering supported by the legal system, so every domain or computer to be filtered will have a fair trial in a public court. One of the members in the study group said: '[If we pass this as law], we will send a signal that Norway want to be outside the information society, and not

---

[66]   See Tambini *et al.* (2008), Chapters 6–7, pp. 112–189
[67]   Brown (2008) at p. 75. See further van Eijk *et al.* (2010).

take part in the Internet economy.'[68] Sandberg states: 'This is a volunteer solution that some of the large ISPs are using. This filter is maintained by the police (Kripos) and is mainly targeted at sites that accept money for material that shows maltreatment of children. The proposal will actually make this filter less intrusive, as the courts, not the police, will decide what to filter.'[69] The study group reached consensus that total effectiveness is not possible nor expected: 'a measure of this type will not give 100 per cent effect, as there exists technical by-passing possibilities. Still, at the same time, this is the case for most measures in the struggle against computer criminality … If one can stop most of the illegal traffic with a filter, a lot will be achieved.' Norway in 2007 tried to introduce filtering of suicide sites, sites which are actually NOT illegal under Norwegian law. (This refers to the media-described practices of 'suicide predators' – aiding and abetting suicide). Hoff suggests that: 'What is really needed is a White Paper on what to block, best practice in filtering, and freedom of speech standards … We are basically eroding freedom of speech from within at a very very disturbing rate if we expand beyond child pornography into sites that display racism, suicide and so on.' France, Portugal and Australia have specific laws against suicide advocacy which is symbolic legislation with no prosecutions/case law. However, websites have been closed down in Australia.[70]

In France, Law n° 2004–575 relating to trust in the digital economy, Article 6 paragraph I – 1 states that: 'Persons whose activity consists in providing public access to online communication services must inform their subscribers of the existence of technical means to limit access to certain services or must select and provide their subscribers with at least one of these means.'[71] Benhamou (2007) states that self-regulation is not possible sometimes from a French Government perspective, and the public interest has to be protected, but the Internet itself does not have to be regulated. He notes the difference between transparency, multistakeholder activism and independence in democratic and non-democratic states. He states

---

[68] Norwegian Parliament study group on Internet filtering law proposal, at NOU-2007–2: www.regjeringen.no/nb/dep/jd/dok/NOUer/2007/NOU-2007-2/6/13.html.
[69] Sandberg (2007).
[70] He refers to the cycle of media-induced legislative excitement which is emerging in Norway, with a recent conference on suicide and new media (Internet suicide pacts, etc.). He was recently commissioned to write a legal opinion for University of Oslo, in which he states that it is impossible to stop pro-euthanasia information from being published on the Internet.
[71] Naudin (2007).

that 'we must avoid Chinese attempts to censor in advance using Western technologies, and even reinventing technologies that can be re-exported back to the West'. He believes that an end-to-end interoperable and neutral Internet must be the aim. A major problem with end-to-end is filtering by ISPs not by end-users. To Benhamou: 'That's censorship.'

Several European states have laws against Holocaust denial, while many ban materials promoting racial hatred. These prohibitions have been harmonized in a 2003 protocol to the Council of Europe Cybercrime Treaty of 2001.[72] Signatories must criminalize the making available of:

> any written material, any image or any other representation of ideas or theories, which advocates, promotes or incites hatred, discrimination or violence, against any individual or group of individuals, based on race, colour, descent or national or ethnic origin, as well as religion if used as pretext for any of these factors ... [and] ... material which denies, minimizes, approves of or justifies crimes of genocide or crimes against humanity.

One of the key decisions for pan-European harmonization of a CAIC-type hotlist is the differing interpretations of 'child' for child pornography purposes, and the nature of any crime committed, whether simply by viewing, by purchasing or only by creating child pornography. Christiansen (2007) suggests that AOL would be an ideal candidate for a pan-national code of conduct: with particular contribution to the regulatory interface between France and Germany. He observes that there used to be big cultural differences on anti-piracy e.g., in France, a very different policy existed to elsewhere. By contrast, the UK has very strong lobbies on child pornography (shared with Scandinavia), but in Germany there is 'almost no pressure' politically on child pornography as compared with the hot issue of racism and xenophobia. Framework conditions are therefore very different in these countries. AOL used to have local decisions on national markets but now is increasingly pan-European in approach. The fact that it is a content provider, an ISP without access business, helps create this new policy. Callanan also points out the very different moral standards in different countries: in the UK, about child chat room 'grooming'; in Spain, adolescent anorexia/bulimia; in Germany, Nazi and hate speech; in Ireland, stricter pornography rules than the UK; in Norway, suicide

---

[72] Additional Protocol to the Convention on cybercrime, concerning the criminalisation of acts of a racist and xenophobic nature committed through computer systems, ETS No. 189, made at Strasbourg, 28 January 2003.

sites. He therefore believes that 'Homogenization is not an option, best practices are.' He notes the differences between Scandinavia and the UK, in that UK filtering systems do not currently allow for police intervention, but Scandinavian models do.

The UK model is regarded as the most technologically advanced, where much of the rest of the world uses DNS filtering (including in China). Filtering to block access to child pornography is a debate that's not properly been had in Ireland. Callanan states that filtering: 'creates its own accountability and transparency issues. It demonstrates a crying need for audit. Filtering is such an enormous policy and social decision in individual countries.' This concern is shared with other experts Hoff, Clayton and Carr, despite different policy perspectives. Clayton explains that different national legislation affecting child pornography includes that the IWF will list 'photo realistic' material (realistic fakes) as illegal – but different countries have different rules. This is a problem that continues from previous harmonizations, for instance on the age of sexual consent when drafting the Cybercrime Convention – differences between fourteen and eighteen existed in Europe.[73] He argues that: 'If anything the IWF is underblocking in order to maintain legality and its role as honest broker.'

The advisory board to INHOPE provides industry input and most recently pressure to provide a pan-European URL list modelled on the UK CAIC list and Scandinavian equivalents, and give search engines a list of banned terms in all European languages. Mobile providers and ISPs appear to be pressurizing INHOPE more than governments directly, according to Callanan (2007). He argues that as INHOPE is not an operational organization but a coordinating organization, if it took such systems and put them in place, it would fundamentally change. Since 2004–5 and the BT Cleanfeed/Scandinavian blocklist launches, concerted attempts have been made to persuade EuroISPA of this change of policy, and for as long EuroISPA has resisted such proposals. There are three major reasons:

[73] See CETS No. 185 Council of Europe Convention on Cybercrime of 23 November 2001, entered into force 1 July 2004, at http://conventions.coe.int/Treaty/EN/Treaties/Html/185.htm; Council Framework Decision on combating the sexual exploitation of children and child pornography, 2004/68/JHA, available at: http://eurlex.europa.eu/LexUriServ/site/en/oj/2004/l_013/l_01320040120en00440048.pdf.

(1) Principled objection on the grounds that EuroISPA is not a regulatory body, nor are national ISPAs, and therefore they will not take on such a changed role;
(2) Objection to the censoring of content both on freedom of expression grounds and, interrelated but more narrowly, on ECD Article 15 which requires that governments not introduce general ISP censorship laws;
(3) Technical concern that such attempts do not achieve their purpose with sufficient focus and can easily be extended to block other content, while failing to discourage users from adopting technical circumvention of the blocking.

Blocks on access to child pornography can be trivially extended to restrictions on 'hate speech' and 'glorification' of terrorism, and from there to political debate and information on minority rights, alleged defamation, purported copyright infringement and the texts of cults such as Scientology.[74] A proposal for a pan-European ISP Code of Conduct proposed in 2004–5 to be co-funded by the SIAP and national ISPA members of EuroISPA failed due to a combination of financial concerns and principled objections to such a scheme and the formal introduction (via funding, evaluation and policy discussion) of the SIAP into ISPA policy deliberations. The idea was revised in 2006 as 'ISPNet' with more than 50 per cent SIAP funding. EuroISPA would probably have accepted a policy forum even though it would be expensive and time-consuming but not with the additional measure to control membership of the body and offer it to all SIAP members. The overall plan was seen by EuroISPA to have a rather co- and not its traditional self-regulatory approach, as well as being strongly partisan to EC sponsors with norms that would be likely to be disagreeable to ISP associations (Hutty 2007a). This contrasts with PEGI's embrace of such an SIAP role.

These three arguments are well rehearsed and have applied for the entire public policy history of the Internet. ECD entrenches them, and *LICRA* v. *Yahoo!* (2000)[75] may have created a precedent for ISP blocking on court orders and in accordance with national law, but not for industry-wide schemes absent such clear illegality. What has changed more recently is:

• the strengthening role of ISP hotlines and the wide public and political acceptance of the strength of their procedures;

[74] See Brown (2008).   [75] See Reidenberg (2001).

- the technical solutions offered by BT and others as well as the vendors of filtering systems; and
- the political impetus towards filtering and surveillance of content created since 2000 by both:
  - police and anti-terrorist legal requirements; and
  - the continual litigation against Internet content hosts and their users (primarily on copyright and defamation grounds).

Callanan (2007) states: 'Governments have completely abdicated their responsibilities for regulating the Internet, in favour of instructing private companies that can breach the human rights[76] that governments would not do publicly' [footnote added].[77] EuroISPA continues to defend its principled objections in the face of these pressures, as do national ISP associations. EuroISPA is opposed to regulation of illegal content via compulsory blocklists for ISPs. What follows is an analysis of national enforcement schemes, industry self-regulation schemes, and their costs and benefits. Clayton, Callanan and Hoff note that ETSI is attempting standardization on child protection services. Callanan suggests that: 'Everyone saw the glory that BT got for their solo run on Cleanfeed – and decided to follow as a marketing tool.' ETSI is following this lead, but as major incumbents have already invested and got a lead in technology, there may be resistance. Auditing the outcome of this technological development may well be essential in determining the success (and indeed overextension) of audit in this area.

Towards a pan-European CAIC fudge?

The move towards either national or ultimately pan-European lists of blocked content to be filtered by ISPs, before end-users can receive the content, is the key to policy-making controversy and any potential regulatory role for ISP associations. It is possible to imagine two circumstances which would make ISP associations part of a co-regulatory scheme:

- national ISP associations introduce a binding requirement on their members to conform to an industry code of conduct on filtering, and

---

[76] Convention for the Protection of Human Rights and Fundamental Freedoms (European Convention on Human Rights or ECHR), signed in Rome on 4 November 1950 and entered into force on 3 September 1953, summary at http://conventions.coe.int/Treaty/en/Summaries/Html/005.htm.
[77] See All Party Parliamentary Communications Group (2009); Callanan et al. (2009).

- government make membership of such an association a legal requirement to permit ISPs to operate inside their boundaries.

The first part of such a move could be seen as a form of self-regulation
without government intervention except in a potential policy partner role,
and this is seen for instance in the UK ISPA requirement that its members
join the IWF and support the operation of its child pornography hotline.
Arguably, the extension of this hotline function into new areas, as proposed by both the UK government and the IWF executive management,
could involve ISPA in an (unbidden) role as part of a wider co-regulatory
scheme. Nevertheless, absent any compulsion for ISPs to join ISPA, that
would be a very weak form of co-regulation. It is the case that virtually without exception, UK ISPs join ISPA, LINX (the London Internet
Exchange) and Nominet, as a matter of commercial common sense, and
which act as introductions to the industry and an almost de rigeur mark of
minimum good faith in inter-ISP negotiations, to the extent that it would
be very difficult to imagine an ISP not joining both ISPA and NOMINET.

This example is by no means universal in Europe. ISP associations in
the majority of European countries have not joined EuroISPA and serve
no wider policy function. Where police impose a direct duty on ISPs to
filter according to hotlines funded only by non-ISP partners (typically
in Eastern Europe joint funding by the SIAP and Microsoft), then direct
regulation would be in place. Where no such duty exists, Internet users
could report directly to hotlines, and of course ISPs are still under a duty
to report potentially illegal sites either to the police directly or to such a
hotline. Nevertheless, without a well-funded and widely accepted hotline
supported by industry, the need for an ISP association is a lobbying need.
Furthermore, in countries with relatively fewer ISPs than the UK or the
Netherlands,[78] it may be that those few large ISPs either represent themselves to government and policy-makers directly, or through national
telecoms and cable associations. Therefore it is not possible to generalize
regarding the state of ISP relations with government. We can note these
three models:

(1) ISPs funds national hotline and lobbies government on behalf of
wider industry;
(2) Self-regulatory hotline funded by SIAP and/or individual multinationals with little local ISP management involvement; and

---

[78] Wouter *et al.* (2009), p. 254.

(3) ISPs required to directly filter through police/hotline resources regulated by law.

There may be other hybrid arrangements but these three models capture the main flavours of ISP–government regulatory arrangements.

The new management of INHOPE, the renewed SIAP and the moves by larger ISPs and their national governments in northern Europe towards blocking systems is likely to put ever greater strain on and pressure for pan-European systems, despite the objection of EuroISPA. The Council of Europe has recently provided support for EuroISPA's resistance to compulsory blocklists.[79] EuroISPA accepts that classic regulatory capture with raised barriers can result from larger companies introducing filtering and content regulation, in that it makes ISP operations more expensive for all smaller ISPs, and puts large ISPs in a position of potentially greater competitiveness (as they can design the system and have greater policy and technical resources to shape it in their favour). EuroISPA asks why should 'free-riding' (refusal to filter) by smaller ISPs be a problem? Why does the Home Office want a single universal approach to filtering, for instance? This may form the basis for a European policy evaluation similar to that conducted by Hoff in Norway.

COM (2010) 94[80] is a proposal whose Impact Assessment focused wholly on criminology and child protection rather than including wider free expression and cost-benefit impacts,[81] admitting that Article 21 on 'blocking access to child pornography on the Internet'[82] is not within the Council of Europe Convention[83] which the remainder of the proposal is meant to fully implement. It is this blocking which is the main cause of controversy, critics claiming it is expensive, pointless and diverts from the main item of prosecuting offenders. Recital 13 of the proposed Directive states in part:

> … mechanisms should also be put in place to block access from the Union's territory to Internet pages identified as containing or disseminating child pornography. For that purpose, different mechanisms can

---

[79] Council of Europe (2008); Recommendation No. CM/Rec (2008) 6 on measures to promote the respect for freedom of expression and information with regard to Internet filters).

[80] COM (2010), p. 14.

[81] Impact Assessment SEC (2009a) and Impact Assessment summary SEC (2009b).

[82] COM (2010) at p. 8.

[83] CETS No. 201. Also note on a global scale, the main international standard is the Optional Protocol to the Convention on the Rights of the Child on the sale of children, child prostitution and child pornography, of 2000.

be used as appropriate, including facilitating the competent judicial or police authorities to order such blocking, or supporting and stimulating Internet Service Providers on a voluntary basis to develop codes of conduct and guidelines for blocking access to such Internet pages. Both with a view to the removal and the blocking of child abuse content, cooperation between public authorities should be established and strengthened, particularly in the interest of ensuring that national lists of websites containing child pornography material are as complete as possible and of avoiding duplication of work.[84]

It specifically cites the SIAP-funded network of hotlines. Article 21 'Blocking access to websites containing child pornography' as drafted states:

> 1. Member States shall take the necessary measures to obtain the blocking of access by Internet users in their territory to Internet pages containing or disseminating child pornography. The blocking of access shall be subject to adequate safeguards, in particular to ensure that the blocking is limited to what is necessary, that users are informed of the reason for the blocking and that content providers, as far as possible, are informed of the possibility of challenging it.
>
> 2. Without prejudice to the above, Member States shall take the necessary measures to obtain the removal of Internet pages containing or disseminating child pornography.

However, such adequate safeguards are not detailed at all – a worrying lacuna in view of state privatization of censorship and known previous inaccuracies and errors in blocking lists.

Filtering software imposed by government appears to have run into both practical and financial difficulties in 2010, with the Australian mandatory filter abandoned by government until after a General Election held in late 2010,[85] and Chinese attempts to impose mandatory filtering by 1 July 2009 also abandoned in favour of a public institution filter for schools and cybercafés. The latter 'Green Dam' technology appears to have seen its funding cut in 2010 and its prospects are uncertain.[86]

Both Europe and Canada have also recently debated whether ISPs can be required to filter Internet video content with updated audiovisual laws. While in Europe, the situation is confused as the implementation of the 2007 AVMS Directive takes shape, in Canada, a ruling in the Federal Court of Appeal on a referral by the Canadian Radio-television and Telecommunications Commission decided that ISPs which act as mere

---

[84] COM (2009a).
[85] Moses (2010).   [86] BBC (2010c).

conduits cannot be reclassified as video broadcasters and thus required to contribute to Canada's cultural fund:

> Because ISPs' sole involvement is to provide the mode of transmission, they have no control or input over the content made available to internet users by content producers and as a result, they are unable to take any steps to promote the policy described in the Broadcasting Act or its supporting provisions. Only those who 'transmit' the 'program' can contribute to the policy objectives.[87]

Conclusion: is co-regulation emerging and is it durable?

Individual companies are choosing to go further than EuroISPA's position of supporting only self-regulation for illegal content removal. The most popular search engines have in certain circumstances changed their rankings under public and government scrutiny. In Germany, where particular importance has been placed on the potential for harm resulting from unadulterated search engine results,[88] a new form of self-regulation for search engines has been developed since 2005, in coordination with the SRO FSM. The search engine self-regulation scheme was formally instituted in April 2006.[89] Though this self-regulatory form is very new, its implications are profound given the importance of search engines and their place as the largest market in Europe for Internet usage. It is a unique experiment in co-regulation across content types, and therefore continues to develop and refine its processes. Christiansen states: 'My belief is that every provider says they don't do things, but they do secretly – to avoid liability [under ECD] and for fundamental PR reasons' and suggests the EC should give Member States more freedom on liability rules when they revise the ECD: 'Liability rules are clearly a counter-incentive to achieving more.'[90] The overwhelming case presented is that government favours more private censorship with loose – and therefore largely unenforceable – links to government, but very strong policy and informal bonds.

The engagement of multiple stakeholders can also institutionalize a failure of collective will, as in the compliance by Internet content providers

---

[87] CBC (2010).   [88] Machill and Welp (2003).
[89] See Brehm (2006). In Leipzig in 2007 at the European Presidency conference, the representative of the FSM indicated that the 'Verhaltungskodex Suchmaschinen' was the only remaining purely self-regulatory initiative by the FSM, dating from 2004. However, they may have been forced into this by the KJM.
[90] Christiensen (2007).

with the Chinese Government's demand to block a range of websites hosting political as well as sexual content.[91] I emphasise the need for all stakeholders to be engaged in the discussion to encourage legitimacy in the final decision and its observance. Such pressures impose devolved law enforcement responsibilities on hosts and/or providers in much the same way as government censorship demands impose political enforcement liabilities. While such stakeholders do not have standing to accept these responsibilities, they may not have the power to resist them. There is a clear need to develop a fundamental and explicit strategy in response to such pressures to avoid the inconsistencies and ultimate failure of case-by-case approaches whereby the parties can be played off against each other. Testing the market structure and regulatory commitment of fixed ISPs, with widely varying resources, against those of mobile ISPs, where all companies are of significant size, would be a useful case study result.

---

[91] Although the most prominent example, China is not by far the only country censoring the Internet; see Deibert *et al.* (2010). In such cases, ISPs (in effect) enforce host country standards, and the weakness of the collective derives in part from commercial pressures, reinforced by a hope that such restraints will eventually become untenable as the Information Society unfolds. Of course, the limits of such 'soft-power' approaches are not limited to socially beneficial content.

7

Analyzing case studies

Analysis across case studies

In this chapter, I first summarize and compare the case studies in the earlier chapters across SROs, discovering the factors which led to success or failure, sustainability or ossification. I explore path dependence, then funding and resources, reform processes, expansion of scale and scope, enforcement powers and practices, reporting, public engagement and media literacy efforts among users. This leads to a summary of governance mechanisms, focused on independence of directors from industry and the representation of civil society stakeholders. The second section examines the failure of self-regulation in the case of copyright enforcement under the Digital Economy Act 2010 ('DEAct'), introduced in order to broker an enforced settlement between ISPs and copyright holders. It demonstrates many of the conditions that need to be present for co-regulation to succeed and that intractable industry stakeholders combined with political will for action may veto such arrangements and force a regulatory solution. Such is the contemporary importance of the ISP challenge to the legality of the regulatory solution adopted by Parliament, that I devote the third section to exploring the prospects for judicial review of the relevant provisions of the DEAct. The fourth and concluding section summarizes the type of problems that prevent the successful adoption of co-regulatory solutions. In the final chapter, I will go on to draw general principles for co-regulation taken from the case study analysis.

Case studies were based on previously observed SRO practice, and the path dependence is clear. I represent this in Figure 7.1. Figure 7.2 illustrates the year of foundation and budget of SROs – in constructing the Figure, I estimated budgets for those organizations which declared staff numbers but not annual budgets. It reveals that the year of foundation of the SRO is not significant in its later budget, but its relationship to government and the degree to which it could be considered to be performing a vital function in the operation of markets were very important. How is financing

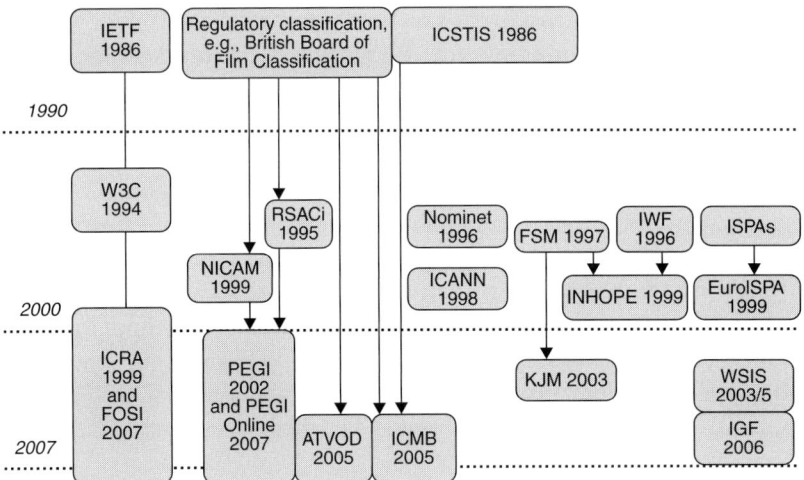

Figure 7.1.   SROs' year of foundation, development and associations

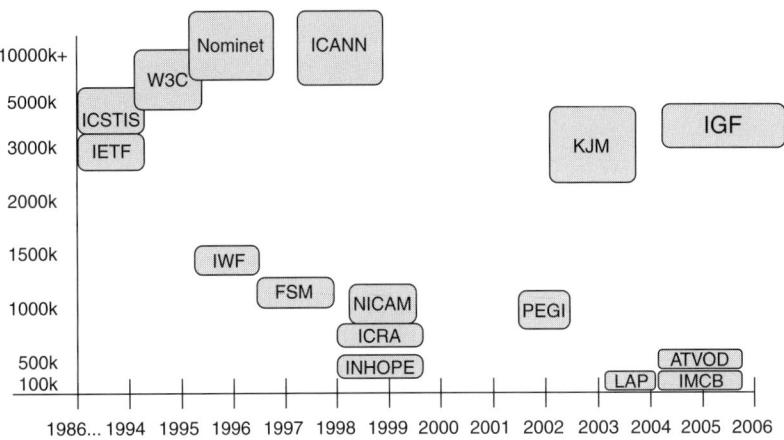

Figure 7.2.   Budget of SROs by year of foundation

secured? Typically, the main source of income is membership fees. These are supplemented by government (including EC) and corporate funders beyond fees, as for instance in hotline funding. In addition, sponsorships of events and other activities of SROs can form a major part of funding, as for instance in IETF meeting fees. Operational funding is an important item for SROs including PEGI, Nominet and NICAM, where their classification and other activities are charged on a per item basis.

Two caveats apply to an overall picture of underfunded SROs. Market makers are SROs producing critical resources for markets, or those assumed to deliver a necessary function (historically) for that market to gain consumer acceptance, and appeared better resourced. Examples included Nominet and ICANN, but also the IWF, as well as the standards bodies. Co-regulatory schemes received statutory backing for their resource demands on industry and therefore form a special category, but one might count these as a subcategory of market makers declared essential to market formation by government: NICAM, ATVOD and ICSTIS are examples. Market-funded SROs are paid for volume of output in growing markets and also secured resources based on market growth rather than membership fees, for instance Nominet as above, also ICSTIS, FOSI, PEGI and standards bodies W3C and IETF where membership increases with market participation.

Additionally, a strong theme is that 'hidden resources' play a powerful role in SROs, greater in relation to the formal resources than in direct state regulation. These hidden resources come in three forms: direct member resources, self-implementation activities by individual members, and third-party pro bono activities. Member resources devoted to self-implementation under SRO protocols include, for instance, BT's Cleanfeed initiative, AOL's hotlines and anti-abuse teams, and Bebo's activities (the latter unregulated). Third-party resources devoted through pro bono activities included initial university and independent funding for IETF, W3C and Creative Commons. Corporate interviewees for case studies all represented successful companies, either start-up or established businesses. Therefore, they represent the 'leading edge' of Internet businesses rather than the broad membership of the thousands of companies involved in, for instance, Nominet membership. Interviewees with substantial experience of these environments stressed that many Internet companies have neither the resources nor the incentive to perform compliance functions beyond the bare minimum required. In particular, companies with no interest in users avoiding harmful content (and especially companies who have incentives to ensure wide viewership of content that may be offensive to some), will have no incentive to contribute to SROs whose mission this is. The range of funding of SROs is very broad, with several SROs essentially skeleton activities. The focus for evaluation in examining SRO funding is to establish whether the SRO is fully resourced, and also the vital question of the extent to which funding dictates form and function. In the examination of corporate governance below, I explore the extent to which the SRO is 'captured' by the design of an independent funding council, or takes measures to widen its corporate governance to include non-executives who are also not corporate members, via advisory boards or government participation in some form.

Many Internet SROs have founding 'myths'. I therefore noted in the case studies the references to the histories of the SROs and focused in the empirical interviews on what reform could reveal for the reconsideration of the foundation settlement of the SRO's mission and form, and gained access to some of those who were present at foundation or at the key moments of reform of the organization.[1] The lessons of regime formation can be divided into two classes, the emergency response and the market-forming. Given the usual incentive problems in formation of SROs, why would anyone but the incumbent choose to be 'first-mover' and why would the incumbent run the risk of accusations of anti-competitive regime formation? Despite the risks of being considered anti-competitive (as expressed particularly in the IMCB and INHOPE case studies), the market-forming motive tends to dominate.

How is reform undertaken? SROs themselves identified via internal consultations and self-evaluation many requirements for reform during the study period. Substantial reform was observed in the SROs under examination, ranging from:

- the very public (PEGI, Nominet, FOSI and European mobiles) to
- the very political (ATVOD, ICSTIS, ICANN, IWF, INHOPE) to
- the private (Second Life, Bebo).

The choice of method was very deliberately selected by the SRO executive and membership, with regard to exogenous forces where these were felt particularly relevant – as in the public or political arenas chosen for reform discussion. The extent to which reform was undertaken with publicity of various kinds reflects the responsiveness of SROs to their wider policy environment: in general, the more the publicity, the greater a policy impact intended. Some SROs saw no pressing need for structural reform, notably the standards organizations W3C and IETF. Others are of such recent vintage that reform could be seen as

---

[1] Weitzner (W3C), Clark (IETF), Boyle (Nominet and ICANN), Benhamou (ICANN and IGF), Swetenham and Hoff (ICRA and INHOPE), Clayton, Hutty and Carr (IWF and EuroISPA), Callanan (INHOPE), Christiensen (KJM, FSM), Borthwick and Whiteing (IMCB), van Dijk and Bekkers (NICAM), Bekkers and Chazerand (PEGI), Millwood-Hargrave (ATVOD), Ondrejka (Second Life). I also interviewed those associated with SNS formation. The notable exception is ICSTIS as 'old' co-regulator, which published an 'official' history to mark its anniversary (ICSTIS 2006).

presumptuous without an opportunity for governance arrangements to 'bed in' – notably IMCB. In these cases, the pressing requirement appears to be increased legitimacy and stakeholder acceptance through activity. Where reform was taking place during 2007, I identified types of reform relating to: scope, stakeholders, governance structure, reporting, media literacy, government relations, and external evaluations. These relate to the evaluation framework used for the individual case studies and the summary notes those items which the SROs themselves considered important factors in their reform. To reiterate the methodology, the examination of reform during the survey period was intended to revisit the issue of regime formation, in that reform begs the question of prior institutional design.

Expansion of the scope of SROs included those of PEGI, IWF and Creative Commons. Where reform took place, the scope extension was largely undertaken through existing resources or on the basis of projected resource increases associated with the new activities (membership increases). Expansion of scale (internationalization) was seen in the PEGI and Euro-mobile examples. Reform to better encompass 'third-sector' (charity, consumer, volunteer, user) input was seen in the new formal arrangements undertaken by FOSI, Nominet, ICANN and IWF, but was explicitly rejected by PEGI, in which the end-users' input was assumed to be included in the Government and member companies' activities. For standards bodies such activities remained a matter of activity-based inclusion. In general, multistakeholderism was a matter of ad hoc consultation and web-based input rather than formal management structures. Where SROs decided on board structures with a majority of non-industry members, such as ICSTIS and IMCB, multistakeholderism could be considered to be institutionalized in the method of governance chosen. However, given the 'chameleon' nature of many individuals in this area, with commercial, voluntary, academic and even government roles in their portfolio of interests, I caution that even the apparent exclusion or alternately the 'hard-wired' multistakeholder governance models may conceal a range of practices that are much more inclusive or exclusive respectively. Note in particular the use of the SROs' websites, listservs and other discussion lists to encourage a pluralistic response to consultations and ongoing activities as well as the use of instant reporting tools (hotlines, abuse buttons, etc.).

Paradigms for innovative regulation supplanting earlier classes of scheme include:

- NICAM as a paradigm of cross-sectoral schemes, which has been widely followed;
- IETF for its open method of setting standards;
- Nominet as a business-oriented but non-profit infrastructure provider;
- IWF as a hotline which, in co-operation with police and ISPs, produced significant results in 'offshoring' child pornography;
- ICSTIS as an effective co-regulatory mechanism which concentrates on 'following the money' in its regulation of the premium content value chain; and
- Creative Commons as an innovative international not-for-profit approach to legal protection of content.

Note that the pioneering efforts of these organizations have been followed or adapted in many other schemata studied. Though I do not consider that these case studies can in themselves provide any example of geographical clustering, it is the case that there are concentrations that may reveal skills and human capital that make certain regulatory schemes decide on particular locations – this is more likely to be the case where those schemes are not established simply in their regional or national capital. Technical skills explain the locations of W3C and IWF, for instance. Also note the 'paradigms' of apparently unsuccessful SROs, where a scheme has not been sufficiently adopted by industry or attracted sufficient confidence from consumers to be successful. Examples include ICANN and ICRA/FOSI schemes. Many schemes are close to invisible to end-users and therefore are on the brink of failure or at least unproven in their effectiveness, though in the case of new schemes that is perhaps inevitable.

Membership structures affected the pace and direction of reforms. Therefore the 'veto' on IWF reform posed by its funding council, or the need for a poll of the entire membership for fundamental Nominet reforms, affect any change to their original mission. By contrast, W3C features a particularly direct form of leadership which favours rapid reform. Note the particular case of 'Government Advisory Committees' of some form for PEGI and ICANN, and the difficulty in such a formal role translating into understanding the true influence of such committees. Typically the government members believe that their real influence is overblown by non-members while civil society observers believe that it is greater than theirs – a case of mutual mistrust.

Enforcement of the rules demands continued scrutiny. Given the subtlety and flexibility of application of norms to SROs, enforcement often amounts to moral censure, expulsion or suspension of membership, or market refusal to adopt the standard/filter. None of these techniques should be under-estimated: a reputation of bad faith attached to a researcher or organization in a standards body can entirely undermine their effectiveness, as much work relies on building alliances and persuading others of one's cause. Expelling a member, suspending or terminating membership of a social network or virtual world, loses that person the 'reputational capital' developed in friendship networks, recommendations and so on. Finally markets that do not adopt standards, distributors who ignore filtering guidelines, and consumers who do not trust the regulatory technique, make such SROs entirely redundant, a danger admitted by standards bodies and filtering organizations alike. The case studies and previous empirical research guide these findings. More extensive quantitative and qualitative research is needed into the methods and techniques used by SROs to maximize market and consumer knowledge and adoption of the proposed SRO solution.

Reporting by SROs appears to be gaining greater importance in their reform agendas. SROs held public meetings, including webcast meetings, to report on their work and discuss and receive views from the interested constituency often including the general public.[2] It is clear that Internet SROs are paradigms of reporting and public engagement, unsurprisingly using the Internet as a major source of distant communication without excluding the need for 'live' personal meeting opportunities. Where criticisms were made, they often related more to the overload of information available than the lack thereof. In particular, civil society stakeholders often claimed that simply keeping up with the volume of work produced by an SRO was a full-time job, and it was impossible for many developing country and smaller country experts to stay informed of the vital activities of, for instance, ICANN. This is an obvious resource gap that some SROs are attempting to cover by use of summaries, monthly bulletins and annual activities reports, recognizing that many interested parties cannot keep up to date with the entirety of SRO activities.

Media literacy is an element of SRO activity which was continually stressed by interviewees. Thus notable efforts to engage with the public were stressed by SROs varying from standards-based (W3C) to labelling (PEGI, FOSI, NICAM) to hotline (INHOPE, IWF) to self-organizing

---

[2] Marsden in 2007–8 attended public meetings held by ICSTIS, Nominet, ISPA UK, PEGI, ICANN and FOSI in person during or immediately before the project, and invitation expert meetings with Second Life, Creative Commons, W3C, ICSTIS, IMCB, TRUSTe, ATVOD, FSM, KJM and NICAM (the final four all at the German Presidency media self-regulation meeting in Leipzig, May 2007).

(Bebo, Second Life, Creative Commons). These activities are dedicated resourced activities in addition to those of their members and
the reporting-type expert/stakeholder meetings referred to above.
Public knowledge of these bodies is extremely poor, and of the overall framework itself weak. The Eurobarometer surveys are an essential
evidential contribution to public perceptions and knowledge of SROs.[3]
The long-established standards (IETF, W3C) and technical infrastructure (ICANN) bodies are accused by critics of being captured by their
industry supporters, but can claim significant mandates from industry, government and users, acclaim for their technical expertise and
widespread market adoption of their interoperable standards. Rating
schemes are not well known by the public or widely adopted by industry,
except where compulsory.

With regard to SRO engagement with government, note the formal
reviews of NICAM, ICSTIS and ATVOD, and requirements to appear
before Parliament, as well as deliberate and extensive outreach by various bodies (e.g., Nominet, IWF, PEGI) to both politician and government
audiences. Many SROs in case studies were partially funded by SIAP and
formal reviews (as well as financial and project reporting and continued
informal engagement) took place.

Table 7.1 shows board composition and governance for the SROs.
Note that this Table cannot capture the complexity of ICANN, while
several of the firm-level SROs are simply directors of private companies,
and therefore there is no requirement to grant independent directorships
nor any level of representation for user civil society groups. In any case,
the boards should exercise good corporate citizenship, and corporate
social responsibility can exercise a level of good governance and environmental (social and sustainable) consideration absent any acknowledgement of the regulatory agenda.

Evaluation of SROs was limited to those that I class as co-regulatory,
notably NICAM's ongoing evaluation,[4] the UK system for media self-
regulation by Latzer, Price and Verhulst for Ofcom,[5] and evaluation of
ICANN. Several UK reform proposals referred to:

- the UK 'Better Regulation' framework (Nominet, ICSTIS) and
- the Cadbury corporate governance reform proposals (IWF,
  Nominet).

---

[3] See Eurobarometer (2007).   [4] See van Stoel *et al.* (2005).
[5] Latzer M., Price, M. E., Saurwein, F. and Verhulst, S. G. (2007).

Table 7.1. *Types of managing instrument in each SRO (1 January 2008)*

SRO	Board directors	Non-executives	Independent funding	Advisory board	Executives on board
ICANN	15 plus 6 non-voting	Appointed by nominating committee	No	Yes	President / CEO *ex-officio*
Nominet	2 execs and 4 non-execs	Sit on board	Executive set budget for board	Policy and advisory body	CEO
IETF	Administrative Oversight Committee (AOC)	IETF Chair appointed by IAB (also sits on AOC)		Internet society board of trustees	Administrative director appointed by AOC
W3C			No	Advisory board elected by members	Director sits on board
FOSI/ICRA	16	Majority	No	Advisory council: 9 members	Yes – CEO sits on board
IWF	10	Yes	Funding council	Board of trustees	CEO: executive committee of chair and 2 members

INHOPE	4 – including President and Vice	Board is executive	No	General assembly of 30 members	No
ICSTIS	10		Budget approval Ofcom	15 on Industry Liaison Panel	Chair on board; also Chief Exec.
IMCB	4	3	No	Board co-opted from ICSTIS	Chair and director
NICAM	10 General and executive board		No	Advisory comm. 27 members	Chair independent of board
PEGI	15			Government advisory board	Yes

ICANN continued its experiment with an ombudsman and appointed a public participation manager to encourage outreach to its constituency. The analysis of the case studies has shown that the lack of compulsion or state involvement has led to significant private or non-profit innovation in several sectors: social networks; virtual worlds; copyright. Sharing of global best practice between governments and other stakeholders has been seen from both top-down and more heterarchical initiatives. The problems of illegal and inappropriate content have led to significant private sector initiative on both individual company (i.e., BT Cleanfeed) and more sectoral levels (IMCB in mobiles, ATVOD in video on demand). ISP regulation of broadband Web2.0 content has been highlighted by several leading authoritative analysts of Internet regulation.[6] Though 'net neutrality' and the contractual relations between content providers and network owners is outside the scope of this book, it is evident that significant tensions exist based on divergent business models and regulatory inheritances.[7] Whereas network owners are active in building self-regulatory organizations, such as ATVOD, IMCB, IWF and others, content providers from a more 'start-up' culture continue to rely on their distinctive use based and mediated self-organization forms: this is true of Second Life, Bebo, Creative Commons and others.

The primary substantive concerns that arise from the regulation perspective remain those of the balancing of interests, a primarily political equation.[8] These include the rights of intellectual property holders and the interest in innovation, and the right balance to strike for copyright and other rights in an evolving UGC environment. The second such trade-off is between the public interests in unfettered freedom of expression for Internet users versus the various public safety concerns including inappropriate and harmful content and 'malware' (spam, viruses, etc.), as well as criminal content or

---

[6] Frieden (2007); Faratin *et al.* (2007); Bauer and Bohlin (2007).
[7] See Marsden (2010), Ch. 3.
[8] Benhamou (2007) offers a considered analysis of three problems: there is a need for transparency at technical interfaces. Anti-competitive dominance is a real concern – especially over scarce resources such as spectrum, numbering space and APIs for dominant search engines. Search engine regulation must be transparent. A particular problem to him is vertical integration of mobile devices with networks (e.g., lack of WiFi or 3G functionaliy in the iPhone). Another concern he has is for 'the need for a citizen-centric approach, which does not exist as there is no global view of the rights of the citizen online'. An example is privacy and control of information. He takes Spock.com as an example of new meta-search people sites – using LinkedIn public information. He also considers Open ID: a new form of federated identity creates possibilities for interoperability to create 'big brothers' on a federated data level.

that promoting criminal activity. Further concerns arise in regards to entrepreneurial attempts to adapt their services to new commercial opportunities versus the interests of many users in maintaining a privacy opt-out from exposure of their personal information to either strangers or commercial presence. These policy fields cannot be left to self-regulation without continually refreshed impact assessment (IA) and review of the public interest.

I identify significant innovations but also increasing resource constraints on SROs. Adoption of the multistakeholder paradigm and the inclusion of user interests is increasing from a low base, encouraged by the minimal co-regulation involved in government monitoring and oversight of such multistakeholder discussions, as well as more formal policy tools including funding and support for such activities. The introduction of formal appeal mechanisms, ombudsmen and formal opportunities for dialogue, as well as open consultations, is increasing. As expected, the use of online discussion fora is well developed and public participation via this means (short of e-voting) is flourishing. Both government and civil society have a role here in ensuring maximum transparency and effectiveness of decision-making, while maintaining high standards of efficiency in implementation of the SRO goals. Budgets for SROs are often extremely low by government regulatory standards, which may prove:

- the greater efficiency of the private sector,
- resource gaps to ensure maximum transparency and good governance or
- that the true costs of SROs lie in the individual and combined members' activities (both in serving the SRO directly and in the policies adopted at the individual company/service level).

Only detailed researched and audited examination can explain the functioning of SROs. The more informal surveys of participant behaviour evidenced in chat fora run by, for instance, the standards organizations (as well as best practice in ICANN, IGF, Creative Commons, Second Life, SNS and so on) can give a better indication of activist opinion on present issues. For a representative user sample, one would need the resources of Eurobarometer. A programme of impacts has been carried out via independent research in several countries,[9] in addition to the independent evaluations carried out on behalf of SIAP and other DG INFSO activities (including for privacy and standard-setting policy). Several institutions have carried out evaluations of their processes or commissioned research

---

[9] For instance, Austria by Latzer *et al.* (2006); Germany by Hans Bredow (2007), UK by Latzer *et al.* (2007) for Ofcom; France by the Forum des Droits sur l'Internet on ongoing basis.

to evaluate processes (notably ICANN and ICSTIS in our survey). The multi-sectoral and interdisciplinary approach taken in this survey showed the connections in labelling between ICRA, NICAM, IMCB and PEGI on one hand, and ICRA with ICANN (through FOSI's interaction with .xxx), W3C and ultimately IETF on the other. The interconnectedness of the various SROs was very much a feature that emerged from the elite interviews conducted. Aggregated analysis produces meaningful evaluation of Information Society SROs.

Co-regulation failure in practice: Digital Economy Act 2010

Co-regulation has been brought into UK law via the implementation of Directives, but also as a result of the internalization of co-regulation by communications regulator Ofcom. A case study in the difficulties of primary legislation empowering self-regulation or regulation in the absence of industry agreement is the Digital Economy Act 2010 (DEAct).[10] The provisions of the DEAct that are the particular cause of controversy arose as a result of the decade-long 'stand-off' between copyright holders, notably music companies, and the ISP industry, a global phenomenon.

In order to chase illegal file sharing, the music industry needs the IP addresses (a string of numbers e.g. 168.168.234.231) of the sharers to be identified by the ISPs against the actual subscriber. This process needs repeating as IP addresses are dynamic and can be shared and reallocated with each session of Internet use. The government was by 2008 applying severe pressure on ISPs to cooperate, largely against their own commercial interests, as they stated:

> ISPs were strongly encouraged by the government to endorse a memorandum of understanding with the British Phonographic Industry and other rights' owners in July 2008 … ISPs undertook to work together with other signatories on a process whereby Internet service customers were informed when their accounts were being used unlawfully to share copyright material and pointed towards legal alternatives. The claimants participated in a three month trial to send notifications to subscribers identified to them by music rights holders, as having been engaged in illicit uploading or downloading … The MOU three-month trial period expired in January 2009.[11]

---

[10] Digital Economy Act 2010 (c. 24) received royal assent 8 April 2010.
[11] R. v. *Secretary Of State For Business, Innovation And Skills Ex parte (1) British Telecommunications Plc (2) Talktalk Telecom Group Plc Claimants* [2010] Statement Of Facts And Grounds, at pp. 10–11. Henceforth 'Statement of Facts and Grounds'.

This was the attempt to achieve a solution via self-regulation, though ISP involvement was less than voluntary. It was followed by a government draft policy paper 'Digital Britain',[12] which led the music industry to lobby government to introduce legislation forcing ISP cooperation. In fact, the entire drafting period of 'Digital Britain' paralleled the ISP discussions with music companies, and one could characterize the latter as a dialogue intended to demonstrate the minimum of good faith alongside lobbying for 'Digital Britain' to lead to each side's preferred outcome. The final 'Digital Britain' report ended this phony war in June 2009,[13] and both sides then focused on persuading ministers during the summer drafting of what became the Digital Economy Bill (DEBill) of their preferred option. 'Digital Britain' states:

> Ofcom will be placed under a duty to take steps aimed at reducing online copyright infringement. Specifically they will be required to place obligations on ISPs to require them: to notify alleged infringers of rights (subject to reasonable levels of proof from rights-holders) that their conduct is unlawful; and to collect anonymized information on serious repeat infringers (derived from their notification activities), to be made available to rights-holders together with personal details on receipt of a court order.[14]

> Ofcom will also be given the power to specify, by Statutory Instrument, other conditions to be imposed on ISPs aimed at preventing, deterring or reducing online copyright infringement, such as: Blocking (Site, IP, URL); Protocol blocking; Port blocking; Bandwidth capping (capping the speed of a subscriber's Internet connection and/or capping the volume of data traffic which a subscriber can access); Bandwidth shaping (limiting the speed of a subscriber's access to selected protocols/services and/or capping the volume of data to selected protocols/services); and Content identification and filtering.[15]

This power would be triggered if the notification process has not been successful after a year in reducing infringement by 70 per cent.[16] The specific consultation on file sharing states: 'a duty will be placed on Ofcom to take steps aimed at reducing online copyright infringement. Specifically

---

[12] Digital Britain (2009b) Interim Report (Cm 7548) proposed legislation which would require ISPs given reasonable proof of infringement to notify alleged copyright infringers that their conduct is unlawful; coupled with a requirement on ISPs to collect anonymized information on serious repeat infringers. This information could be made available to rights holders upon production of a court order.

[13] Digital Britain: (2009a) Final Report (Cm 7650) was published in June 2009.

[14] Digital Britain: (2009a) Final Report at para. 24/28.

[15] Digital Britain: (2009a) Final Report at Chapter 4.

[16] Digital Britain: (2009a) Final Report at para. 31.

they will be required to impose the two obligations on ISPs set out in the Digital Britain Interim Report … they will be required to put in place a code to support any obligations that are in place.'[17]

The document at paragraph 4.39 sets out an indicative timeline, with no technical measures taken against subscribers until 'zero+28 months', zero being the date of Royal Assent to any order instructing Ofcom to set up the mechanism. The DEBill confirmed Secretary of State Mandelson's plan; it was published on 16 November 2009 and introduced into the House of Lords six months before the final date by which Parliament would have to be prorogued for a General Election. Government issued an outline Initial Obligations Code (IOC) to give some detailed guidance to add to the DEBill in January 2010.[18] Ofcom would need to draft a detailed IOC rapidly in order to give effect to the provisions. ISPs, unlike copyright owners, are regulated by Ofcom and may be directed to comply by sections 45 and 49 Communications Act 2003; penalties may be imposed for non-compliance by Ofcom under section 96 Communications Act 2003 of up to £250,000, under section 124L(2) Communications Act 2003.

The change that occurred in 2009 in response to copyright industry lobbying was to introduce much more expensive and invasive monitoring of suspected pirates, with ISPs required to introduce a 'three-strikes' regime to cut off connections of alleged infringers, amending section 124 of the Communications Act 2003. This was a major victory for the copyright lobby, a major defeat for ISPs and a potential kangaroo court for 'pirates'. A similar piece of legislation had just been passed, struck down by the *Conseil Constitutionel* and then revised by the French Senate (the HADOPI laws, as this is the name of the authority set up to hear appeals by three-strikers). The French constitutional court found that only judges could make decisions on Internet access,[19] citing the Declaration of the Rights of Man of 1789.[20] This was in response to a law promulgated in order to cut off those Internet subscribers suspected of repeated copyright

---

[17] Department of Business, Innovation and Skills (2009), para. 1.3 stating: 'This takes forward recommendation 39 of the Gowers Review of Intellectual Property, the recent BIS consultation on possible regulatory options and Action 13 of the Digital Britain Interim Report.'

[18] Department of Business, Innovation and Skills (2010).

[19] Decision n° 2009–580 DC of 10 June 2009, J.O.R.F. of 13 June 2009, p. 9675, § 16, decision available in English at www.conseil-constitutionnel.fr/conseilconstitutionnel/root/bank/download/2009–580DC-2009_580dc.pdf.

[20] Human and Citizens Rights Declaration of 1789, at Constitutional Council website: www.conseil-constitutionnel.fr/conseilconstitutionnel/root/bank_mm/anglais/cst2.pdf.

violation, similar to the proposal in the DEAct. The Council of Europe Conference of Ministers responded to the prospect of special copyright tribunals by stating that: 'Only a judge should be able to decide whether to cut or not Internet access or to ask for a specific action on the Internet in full respect of fundamental rights and freedoms.'[21]

The DEAct's use of the 'wash-up' provisions that end a Parliament meant the increasing control of parliamentary business by the political parties' front-bench teams,[22] with Conservative official opposition acquiescence vital to DEAct passage through all of its House of Commons readings in just two days. A brief listing of relevant sections of the DEAct is:

3. Obligation to notify subscribers of reported infringements.
4. Obligation to provide infringement lists to copyright owners.
5. Approval of code about the initial obligations.
6. Initial Obligations code by Ofcom in the absence of an approved code.
7. Contents of Initial Obligations Code.
8. Progress reports.
9. Obligations to limit Internet access: assessment and preparation.
10. Obligations to limit Internet access.
11. Code by Ofcom about obligations to limit Internet access.
12. Contents of code about obligations to limit Internet access.
13. Subscriber appeals.
14. Enforcement of obligations.
15. Sharing of costs.
16. Interpretation and consequential provision.
17. Power to make provision about injunctions preventing access to locations on the Internet.
18. Consultation and parliamentary scrutiny.

The debate was notable for the lack of technical and market expertise exhibited by politicians on both sides of the House of Commons. In contrast to the development of railways, canals and turnpikes, each of which required Acts of Parliament on a regular basis, essentially to secure and maintain access to land, the development of the Internet has largely relied on regulated cable franchises and regulated access to British Telecom

---

[21] MCM (2009) 021, p. 5.
[22] On the legislative process within its public law and policy setting, see Le Sueur *et al.* (2010).

or British Rail (now Railtrack) infrastructure. Therefore, since the 1982 Telecommunications Act and 1984 Cable and Broadcasting Act, there have only been occasional recourses to Parliament. Most telecoms legislation implements European legislative decisions, meaning that Parliament has very little discussion of telecommunications, and since the beginning of the commercial Internet, almost no legislative scrutiny of Internet regulation (though there were Broadcasting Acts in 1990 and 1996). The exceptions have been the 2003 Communications Act and the DEAct. In both cases, the ignorance of Parliamentarians on telecoms – as opposed to broadcasting – issues were exposed. An early day motion in the new Parliament, calling for repeal of the sections 9–18 that had caused particular controversy, only attracted thirty seven signatures in four months.[23] Parliament may revisit the DEAct in 2011 to approve Ofcom's IOC.[24]

DEAct sections 3–8 require a warning letter to be sent to subscribers explaining that their Internet subscription is being used to download copyrighted material illegally. These provisions are less controversial than sections 9–18 which cut off subscribers, which are considered particularly egregious. Doctorow states that the main practical objection is that it will not work as intended and actually encourages evasion:

> Once non-anonymous, non-encrypted downloading bears a significant risk, downloaders will simple switch to anonymized, encrypted alternatives … the naive user who only downloads occasionally will still be in harm's way, as will his family or housemates if his connection is disconnected by an entertainment bully … Once the Act drives downloaders to use SSL-encrypted services that are harder to monitor, watch for the entertainment lobby to ask for great swaths of the Internet to be blocked by the Great Firewall of Britain that the Act also provides for.[25]

It can only catch the ignorant Internet user.

Ofcom set out in May–July 2010 on its consultation on a draft IOC, which it published in May.[26] This is in line with a timetable which obliges Ofcom to present its IOC to Parliament via the relevant minister within a

---

[23] Early Day Motion 17 (2010): 'That this House believes that sections 9 to 18 of the Digital Economy Act 2010 should not have been rushed through in the dying days of the last Parliament; further believes that these sections have large repercussions for consumers, civil liberties, freedom of information and access to the Internet; and calls on the Government to introduce early legislation to repeal those provisions.'

[24] *ISP Review* stated that the DEAct is: 'already a prime candidate for a second review by the House of Lords next year, assuming a proposal to give Lords the power of post-legislative scrutiny is passed'. See Mark (2010).

[25] Doctorow (2010).   [26] Ofcom (2010c).

year of the passage of the Act, a brief timetable given the Better Regulation practice of permitting twelve weeks for each consultation. ISP criticisms of Ofcom's draft IOC consultation in their responses to the first consultation, which closed in July 2010, were in part practical, with others based on administrative law. The ISPs argued that the draft IOC contains requirements which entail changes to their business models, and will create a market-distorting effect. Ofcom's proposed 400,000 subscriber threshold was designed to prevent the full costs being passed on to small, niche and regional ISPs, as well as excluding MNOs for technical reasons. ISPs claim that they will have to develop, install and implement new large-scale systems for the benefit of rights holders, with significant engineering implications.[27]

The response by Joint Academic Network (JANET) identifies exactly the 'mere conduit' problem that reclassification of ISPs as active filtering participants will cause.[28] Ofcom's most controversial consumer proposal in its consultation was that users of public Internet access (libraries, pay-as-you-go WiFi and mobile providers) would need to identify themselves, for copyright infringement liability to be established, and is accused by JANET of going beyond the will of Parliament:

> In effect it would no longer be possible to access the Internet in the UK without first proving one's identity. This major policy change (in direct contradiction of other Government policies on widening Internet access) does not seem to have been considered either in the Bill's IA or in the Parliamentary debate. The idea was debated, and strongly resisted, in Parliament when Data Retention proposals were being discussed in the context of terrorism and serious crime. It therefore seems surprising for it to be introduced, with no Parliamentary debate, in an Act dealing with copyright infringement at or below the level of a civil wrong.

JANET argues that Ofcom erred in its interpretation of 'ISP', 'communications provider' and 'subscriber': 'Paragraph 3.22's statement that a provider of open wifi (sic) must be either an ISP or a subscriber does not match the definitions in the Act: a business that provides open wifi is clearly a communications provider (and therefore not a subscriber) as defined in the Communications Act 2003 and referenced in [DEAct]. If it does not have an agreement with its users then it cannot be an ISP.' JANET argues that a business subscriber to an ISP should be classified as a 'communications provider' rather than a 'subscriber' (under section 124N Communications Act 2003), because businesses provide connectivity

[27] See further Horten (2010).   [28] JANET (2010).

to individuals, any of whom might access copyrighted material illegally. This would risk cutting off Internet access for many large businesses. At the time of writing, the IOC consultation had not moved on to a final draft. However, it may be outflanked by the BT–TalkTalk joint application for judicial review.

ISP judicial review of DEAct

BT and TalkTalk claimed DEAct to be unconstitutional under a judicial review application they made in early July 2010.[29] The claimants argued that the DEAct is a disproportionate response to unlawful p2p file sharing, due to the significant impact on 'innocent' Internet users, as well as an infringement of the privacy of Internet users and the confidentiality expected by subscribers. Their declaratory relief claim is that DEAct is contrary to European law on four grounds:

> 10.1. The contested provisions constitute a technical regulation and/ or a rule on services within the meaning of the Technical Standards Directive.[30] They should have been notified to the EU Commission, but have not been. The provisions are accordingly unenforceable;
> 10.2. The contested provisions are incompatible with the [ECD];[31]
> 10.3. The contested provisions are incompatible with the Privacy and Electronic Communications Directive (PEC Directive) and with the requirement that the measures in issue should be proportionate.[32] [footnotes added]

The final ground refers to human rights of their subscribers and is detailed below. They 'are also disconcerted at the prospect of their being required to discharge an enforcement function on behalf of copyright owners'.[33] BT and TalkTalk argue an incorrect use of terminology in the 'appeal' process, as subscribers will be contesting an 'allegation', not an appeal against conviction. An appeal can only be made following a decision by a legally competent tribunal, which in law neither rights holders nor ISPs actions are. The appeals procedure was the Government's method of ensuring compliance with EU law.

---

[29] Statement of Facts and Grounds (2010) at pp. 1–14.
[30] Directive 98/34/EC laying down a procedure for the provision of information in the field of technical standards and regulations, OJ [1998] L No 204, 21.7.98, p. 37, as amended by Directive 98/48/EC, OJ [1998] L No 217, 5.8.98, p. 18.
[31] Directive 2000/31/EC.
[32] Directive 2002/58/EC concerning the processing of personal data and the protection of privacy in the electronic communications sector, OJ [2002] L No 201, p. 37.
[33] Statement of Facts and Grounds (2010) at p. 2.

On the first ground, the EC clearly should have been notified at the time of publication of the draft DEBill. Indeed, the EC had in 2009 commissioned a law firm to produce a study on the national divergences in enforcing copyright online,[34] itself clearly a topic of pan-European interest, both due to the nature of the technology and the number of major pan-European ISPs and copyright owners. It is worth noting that, whatever the merits, the Technical Standards Directive and ECD are not always obeyed to the letter by national governments (in fact, officials have privately informed me that very few governments bother to conform).[35] The Government was already subject to enforcement action by the EC for failure to fully implement PEC Directive Article 5 (which covers illegal interception of communications) in the case of the behavioural advertising company PHORM together with BT itself.[36] On all these grounds, one could attempt judicial review of any government telecoms regulation. That is not to state that these are spurious or trivial grounds, simply that the Directives are obeyed as much in the breach. It will be interesting to observe the court's decision on these more technical grounds, but the final ground is more substantial.

Finally, as DEAct is disproportionate in impact on ISPs, business and consumers, they claim it infringes:

- Article 56 TFEU (ex-Article 49 EC) coupled with Article 61 TFEU (ex-Article 55 EC) and Article 52 TFEU (ex-Article 46 EC), as a disproportionate restriction on ISP activities;
- Article 3(4) of the ECD;
- Article 15(1) of the PEC Directive;
- Articles 8 and/or 10 of the European Convention on Human Rights, as given effect to through: Article 6(3) TEU;[37] general principles of

---

[34] Hunton & Williams, Brussels (2008).
[35] However, the Grounds cite Case C-42/07 *Liga Portuguesa de Futebol Profissional* v. *Departmento de Jogos* [2009] ECR I-0000, [2010] 1 CMLR 1, ECJ per Advocate General Bot at [53]: 'Therefore Directive 98/34 provides for a system whereby each Member State must notify the Commission of its proposed technical regulations so as to enable the Commission and the other Member States to inform it of their viewpoint and to propose a standardization which is less restrictive of trade. This system also gives the Commission the necessary time to propose, if necessary, a binding standardisation measure.' The effect of such a strict interpretation in the case of the DEAct would be a delay of between three months and two years before the measures are implemented.
[36] See further Marsden (2010), Ch. 3 – noting that the breach of the Regulation of Investigatory Powers Act 2000 is more substantial, but that the Commission action was in respect of a failure to ensure adequate enforcement powers were given.
[37] Treaty of European Union, OJ [2000] C No. 364, p. 1.

European Union law; the requirements of the Framework Directive, as amended;[38] equivalent rights conferred by Articles 7, 8, 11 and 52 of the Charter of Fundamental Rights of the European Union and Article 6(1) TEU; and/or the Human Rights Act 1998.[39]

The claim here is that the DEAct acts against the very interests it claims to pursue, notably those of UK citizens using the Internet, and the ISPs' freedom to provide those services. In particular, it is the 'see no evil, hear no evil, speak no evil' role of ISPs that has given them what I term the 'Three Wise Monkeys' defence against copyright infringement, defamation and so on committed by their subscribers.[40] As the claim puts it: 'The overall regime recognises the neutral and essentially passive role played by ISPs. ISPs ... are mere conduits for the communications data conveyed over the Internet ... This passive role has been recognised by the Courts at common law, in such areas as defamation.'[41] On 9 November 2010, the leave to apply was granted on all four grounds, and the case will be heard between February and April 2011.[42]

The DEAct judicial review will be an essential element in deciding the future of regulation of the Internet, but we should note that the stakeholders here are ISPs and copyright holders, as well as government. Therefore it is a type of regulation that entirely ignores the requirements of the Inter-Institutional Agreement (IIA) as regards co-regulation. Consumers, whether individually or as groups, are able to respond to Ofcom's consultation on its code of practice, as they were to respond to the 'Digital Britain' review, but the sense remains that consumers' real involvement is only in the possibility of having their Internet connection suspended for violation of copyright rules – without the luxury of appeal to a court, only to a tribunal whose rules are yet to be established.

---

[38] Directive 2009/140/EC amending Directives 2002/12/EC on a common regulatory framework for electronic communications networks and services, 2002/19/EC on access to, and interconnection of, electronic communications networks and associated facilities, and 2002/20/EC on the authorization of electronic communications networks and services, OJ [2009] L No 337, p. 37.

[39] Statement of Facts and Grounds (2010) at p. 3.

[40] See Marsden (2010) at Ch. 4.

[41] Statement of Facts and Grounds (2010) at p. 7, citing the case of *Metropolitan International Schools v. Designtechnica Corporation and Google UK Ltd* [2009] EWHC 1765 (QB); [2009] EMLR 27 per Eady J.

[42] BBC (2010b).

Conclusion: better regulation and co-regulation

The analysis of the case studies showed that the lack of compulsion or state involvement has led to significant private or non-profit innovation in several sectors: social networks; virtual worlds; and copyright. Sharing of global best practice between governments and other stakeholders was seen from both top-down and more heterarchical initiatives. The problems of illegal and inappropriate content have led to significant private sector initiative on both individual company and more sectoral levels. The case studies appear to produce a dilemma: there are private organizations and firm-level governance arrangements which do not suit the classic model of an independent SRO. The questions asked of SROs and experts appear to reveal significant and often constructive tensions in the role and reform of the SROs, and government intervention. It is clear that the necessity for IA of SROs must include the interaction between national, European and global initiatives, and the multi-sectoral and interdisciplinary approach taken in this survey is necessary.

As the DEAct example has shown, there is very little involvement of consumers in the workings of many co-regulatory arrangements, and zero formal involvement in self-regulation. This is observing the Mandelkern Report and IIA in the breach and it suggests greater government involvement in the formation of co-regulation is required to make industry take consumer and other stakeholder rights seriously, as I have argued elsewhere.[43] Nominet's reforms of 2010 as well as those rushed through by ATVOD might prove models to follow, though they lag far behind the example set by NICAM of best practice. A better UK example might be that of PhonepayPlus, as reformed in 2007–8. In all cases, however, there is a very strong argument for formal auditing of regulatory arrangements. The 2001 Governance White Paper states that: 'The Union must reform itself in order to fill the democratic deficit of its institutions. This governance should lie in the framing and implementation of better and more consistent policies associating civil society organisations and the European institutions.'[44] I gave EC-commissioned advice in 2004:

> [EC] should develop and publish clear benchmarks for acceptable levels of transparency, accountability and due process and appeal, particularly with regard to communications regulation that may impact upon freedom of expression. Co-regulatory institutions should follow the guidelines for transparency and access to information that are followed by public and

---

[43] Marsden (2008).   [44] EC (2001).

government bodies according to international best practice. At the very least self-regulators should provide summaries of complaints by clause of code of conduct, numbers of adjudications, findings of adjudications on their website. Failure to conform to these baseline standards of transparency should be viewed as a failure of co-regulation.[45]

I maintain that view. In the final chapter, I explore further the medium-term development of co-regulation, focusing on the question of constitutional legitimacy of Internet regulation.

[45] Marsden (2004a), p. 195. See also Marsden (2004b), pp. 76–100.

8

Internet co-regulation as part of the broader regulatory debate

Polycentric or just eccentric?

I have described in this book an increasingly polycentric regulatory environment, in which networked government agencies interact with networked private sector actors, with networked NGOs and other civil society actors actively intervening in processes, negotiations and ultimately regulatory activities. It is because online activity offers so much freedom and risk to individual users that it is a paradigm of polycentric regulation, as Black terms it.[1] The Internet has always been regulated in this manner, with increasingly comfortable accommodation between the needs of these various actors, adding venture capital to the mix as start-up companies and financiers have been vitally important to Internet entrepreneurship. The route to this intermingled co-regulatory environment has also been somewhat novel in that it owes as much to bottom-up as top-down co-regulation. Bottom-up can be seen in many standards organizations, content (especially print journalism) and technical regulatory bodies, and top-down in other more traditional standards bodies, and regulatory arrangements inherited from telecoms and broadcasting inheritances. The direction of travel is in almost all cases towards co-regulation, no matter what the basis from which each arrangement starts. I use the term 'arrangement' carefully, as in several environments there is no agency or SRO that one can identify, and regulatory activities rely on a mix of user-generated self-regulation (which genuinely exists in many places), self-organization and contractual rules imposed by the dominant service provider on its customers, and technical architectures which determine the enclosed space within which regulatory actors must operate (noting that those architectures may be changed by regulation as well as vice versa).[2]

Attempting to view Internet regulation through the lens of offline child protection, broadcast regulation or gambling regulation is an exercise

---

[1] Black (2008, 2009).   [2] Dommering (2006), pp. 6–17.

in incompatible wish fulfillment – online regulation does not intend to achieve the same outcomes, effectiveness or legitimacy. It is made up of largely 'Potemkin regulators'.[3] Superficially, they look like 'real' regulators, with offices, supervisory boards, appeals mechanisms, constitutions, charitable status and the like, but in reality they are a film set, a series of gaily painted facades without substance or foundation. One might go further in the cinematic analogy and compare them to 'The Wizard of Oz', with the academic critic placed in the position of Dorothy believing she could tap her heels together and return to a more regulated pre-Internet world of monochrome safety. I do not seek to reassert the solution of a paradise lost (broadcast regulation was no such thing), but Cherry correctly points out that we abandon wholesale our previous communications policies, such as common carriage, at society's cost.[4] Black asserts: 'The role of the institutional environment in the construction of legitimacy, the dialectical nature of accountability relationships, and the communicative structures through which accountability occurs and legitimacy is constructed.'[5] I agree, and stress that I am taking no normative position, but rather a pragmatic view that it is unhelpful to criticize an orange for not being an apple. Black argues that we need to make 'an attempt to build a more realistic foundation on which grander "how to" proposals can be built. For until we understand these dynamics, the grander, normative arguments risk being simply pipe dreams – diverting, but in the end making little difference.'[6] In arguing from a constitutional position for a reversion to offline standards of regulation and accountability, many are making the 'pipe dream' mistake of arguing for a position that is simply not recognized by the major multinational actors and the governments that control their operations. In this book, I do not do so. I argue for examining the role of these 'Potemkin' and other regulators on their own merits, as Black describes. Nor is this Potemkin examination unique to Internet regulation, as Bowman and Hodge describe very similar outcomes from codes of practice developed in the nanotechnology field (which shares its technical dynamism and ethically critical role with some Internet regulatory debate).[7] They state that 'voluntary nano-codes have weaknesses including a lack of explicit standards on which to base independent monitoring, as well as no sanctions for poor compliance'.[8] However, paper tigers though these codes are, they

---

[3] Cave *et al.* (2008).
[4] Cherry (2008), p. 274.   [5] Black (2008), p. 137.   [6] Black (2008), p. 138.
[7] Bowman and Hodge (2009), pp. 145–164.
[8] Bowman and Hodge (2009), p. 145.

'highlight the potential power of these governance mechanisms under conditions of uncertainty and co-regulation with government. It is likely that nano-codes will become the "first cut" of a new governance regime for nanotechnologies'.[9] Observed in the breach though such codes are, they become the first cut at governance of such technologies, for the Internet as well as nanotechnology.[10] We might add for traditional regulatory analysts: 'You're not in Kansas anymore, Dorothy.'

Kingma argues that the tendency towards re-regulatory policy extends beyond child protection into online gambling, among other areas, where it is felt that risk regulation has over-liberalized controls on gambling markets.[11] Scott examines case studies of the US attempts to prohibit gambling,[12] and the UK acceptance in the Gambling Act 2005 of the Gibraltar-based offshore status of many key corporate actors.[13] He states: 'Achieving compliance with regulatory objectives is challenging enough within domestic regimes where behavioural responses are difficult to predict. But, where that regime involves cross-border business activities, the complex relationships between regulators, businesses and consumers may conspire to frustrate the intentions of the policy makers ... the near impossibility of preventing determined punters from engaging in internet gaming.' He notes, 'The opportunistic arrest of the in-transit chief executive of the UK-based internet gambling company *Betonsports* in Texas in July 2006 is reported to have triggered the company's withdrawal from the US online market and the chief executive's dismissal.'[14] The US signalled that it was closed for gambling to non-US actors.[15] In as contested and complex an environment as online child protection or gambling, where realistic solutions involve a great deal of interference and state regulatory control over individual behaviour, it is unsurprising that the types of legitimacy and effectiveness that have long been the norm offline have been abandoned in favour of stylistic and superficial calls for self-regulation, in the knowledge that the problems are insoluble. Kay explains: 'the most common form of capture is honest and may be characterized as intellectual

[9] Bowman and Hodge (2009), p. 145.
[10] Tambini *et al.* (2008).
[11] Kingma (2008), pp. 445–458. See also Mikler (2008), pp. 383–404.
[12] Scott (2007).
[13] See previously Scott (2005).
[14] This airport transit arrest reminds Internet scholars of the Felix Somm Munich airport arrest in 1998. See Bender (1998).
[15] For the world trade law of Internet gambling, see WT/DS285/AB/R [2005] Gambling Services – WTO Appellate Panel Decision and Wu (2006).

capture … the regulator with the best intentions comes to see issues in much the same way as the corporate officers he deals with every day'.[16] This is not unique to Internet regulation, and Baldwin points to emissions trading as an example of 'lite' regulation that produces no short-term losers and in consequence no longer-term solution.[17]

Does it matter that Potemkin regulators are providing a false view of activity to curb the Internet's wilder excesses? The EC has always taken a far more relaxed view than the European Parliament, as one would expect of a technocracy rather than political arena, though it is becoming clear that its IAs are at least theoretically now taking self- and co-regulation more seriously than previously.[18] As Zuckerman states: 'So long as it continues to be possible for for-profit [I]SPs to terminate difficult clients for arbitrary reasons, it is likely that we will see providers "optimizing" their client base, providing services to [low-risk] customers.'[19] He cites the work of Nas in assessing Dutch ISP take-down of sites.[20] It is common sense that ISPs do not want to deal with 'awkward customers' who induce regulatory liabilities, or take rights seriously, except in the most public-spirited of cases. High individual moral standards are not, and never have been, a basis for regulation.

SROs are not constitutional, in fact their very existence is a constitutional affront in the view of many free speech and communications scholars. It is a safe but fruitless pursuit to explain that they fail to stand up to scrutiny as legitimate and accountable guardians of free speech and other basic constitutional rights. On that, we can probably all agree, though I am shouting outside the tent of Internet regulatory discussion and my views have been repeated ad nauseam. Nevertheless, these regulators exist. My view is that they must be examined on their own merits, and having exposed their flaws on their own terms, useful reform can be suggested which also begins to achieve an increased accountability alongside that efficiency. Potemkin regulators are dangerous not only because they perform a function that government has abdicated responsibility for, but also because they perform that function inadequately, incompetently and at cost to themselves, governments and the consumer. There is

---

[16] Kay (2010).   [17] Baldwin (2008), pp. 193–215.

[18] See Cave *et al.* (2008). See also Cecot *et al.* (2008), pp. 405–424, stating unsurprisingly that the more contentious and important a European policy initiative the greater the attention paid to IA, and that 'the quality of EU IA increases with the expected cost of a proposal'. Further, see Pelkmans (2009).

[19] Zuckerman (2010), p. 81.

[20] Nas (2004).

a reason why these functions are still claimed to be performed, and it is not appeasement to go into the (rather skeletal) belly of the beast to examine why it cannot perform even the reduced functions for which it claims responsibility and competence.

Governments already have cartel investigations into SROs that act as oligopolies, yet it is precisely these market actors who are most likely to form stable SROs without a government stick of compulsory membership. Whether it is PEGI or mobile networks in various countries with content rating, these stable oligopoly structures suit both regulator and regulatees very well. These SROs are also of course the very worst competitive position for the market. Hiding behind oligopoly is a well-known government tactic, condemned from Adam Smith to John Kay to Vince Cable. Yet in an environment of dynamic market entry, SROs are unlikely to avoid free-riders and gaps in compliance. Thus government is caught in the central dilemma of Internet governance – the more dynamism, the worse regulation. This is the same dilemma that confronts those who would regulate merchant banks or hedge funds, the former an oligopoly that has captured its regulators in New York and London, the latter an offshore and loose group of billionaire adventurers based in Bermuda and other tax havens, and infamously 'non-domiciled' in the UK. In similar fashion, Internet entrepreneurs have been footloose investors using favourable tax regimes in, for instance, Luxembourg (Amazon S.A. is an example) or the Channel Islands (from whence Tesco has avoided sales taxes on products shipped to the UK). Gambling cases show the loose grip of the nation state on its offshoring Internet companies. But the answer of regulating the increasingly oligopolistic environment of ISPs and other intermediaries (such as Google or Facebook) is to create new approved choke points in the Internet's food chain.

Changing regulatory agendas

This book demonstrated the need to survey the range of regulatory or governance structures arising outside government and to assess their implications for future regulatory strategy as:[21]

- part of the *overall context* within which regulation takes place;
- a potentially *more efficient agent* of the public interest; and
- an *active partner* in responding to rapid change.

---

[21] This section of analysis draws heavily on my previous work with Dr Jonathan Cave, notably in Cave and Marsden (2008).

These needs find concrete expression in a variety of policy initiatives responding to new and emergent challenges, which recognize the importance of self- and co-regulatory solutions.[22]

It is important to note that, while the focus of the book is on *ex ante* assessment of alternatives, there are clear implications for both the *ex post* monitoring and evaluation of regulatory performance delivered by SROs, and the progressive development of information sources and analytic tools relating to such assessments. While many sectors have developed strong traditions of self-regulation (including many professions, financial services and environmental management), Internet self-regulation has developed perhaps the richest variety of forms and tackled the largest range of policy concerns.

Institutional design classification schemes in self-regulation are needed just as they have been undertaken in government regulation,[23] and the Beaufort Scale is my contribution. The scale relates to the 'wind' blowing from government to influence the SRO, from flat calm (0) to strong gale verging on hurricane (11), though the extremes amount to paradigms that are infrequently found in practice – pure self-regulation with no prior or later approval amounts to a self-regulatory body that is close to invisible in practice, and it is certainly the case that only the very 'early-stage' hybrid of self-regulation can be viewed in this space. These approximate classifications do not relate to degree of government funding – the relationship between direct or indirect government funding is not consistent with policy involvement. For instance, government financial support or co-funding is a policy approached vigorously by the SIAP since 1998. I investigated whether such approaches are consistent with policy support via proposed policy interventions which sought to extend the role of such bodies (see especially PEGI, IMCB and INHOPE, Chapters 5–6).

In addition to the obvious option of strengthened European levels of regulation, I identify SRO options suggested by the analysis that always should be considered for inclusion in IA at EC level, corresponding approximately to: '*laissez-faire*', self-regulation and co-regulation. The options relate to the 'Beaufort Scale'. While the twelve ideal types of SRO identified may suggest a microscopic granular approach to classification

---

[22] E.g., Recommendation for Protection of Minors and Human Dignity 2005, SIAP, Electronic Communications Framework 2009, E-Commerce Directive review 2010, AVMS Directive 2007.

[23] See Hood (1978), pp. 30–46; Jordana and Levi-Faur (2004); Priest (1997), p. 233.

Table 8.1. *The Beaufort scale of self- and co-regulation*

Regulatory scheme	Self-Co	Scale	Government involvement
'Pure' unenforced self-organization	Second Life	0	Informal interchange only – evolving partial industry forum building on players' own terms
Acknowledged self	Bebo Creative Commons	1	Discussion but no formal recognition/approval
Ex post standardized self	W3C#	2	*Ex post* approval of standards
Standardized self	IETF	3	Formal approval of standards
Discussed self	IMCB	4	*Ex ante* informal consultation – but no sanction/approval/process audit
Recognized self	ISP Associations	5	Recognition of body – informal policy role
Co-founded self	FOSI#	6	*Ex ante* negotiation of body; no outcome role
Sanctioned self	PEGI# Euro mobile	7	Recognition of body – formal policy role (contact committee/process)
Approved self	Hotline#	8	*Ex ante* informal negotiation with government – with recognition/approval
Approved compulsory co-regulatory	ICANN	9	*Ex ante* negotiation with government – with sanction/approval/process audit
Scrutinized co-regulatory	NICAM# ATVOD	10	As 9 with annual budget/process approval
Independent Body (with stakeholder forum)	ICSTIS#	11	Government imposed and co-regulated with taxation/compulsory levy

Hash tag indicates government-funded in whole or part
Modified from: Cave *et al.* (2008) at p. xii.

of SROs, I consider this to be work in progress with a level of detail that will need to be tested in individual IAs.

Option zero is no option

Government in setting out IA options typically offers a three-card trick: no more regulation (option 0), their preferred regulatory option 1 and highly prescriptive over-regulation (option 2). While the last option can be easily ruled out as 'twentieth-century thinking' or overly prescriptive command-and-control, option zero (no regulation) needs unpacking, and greatly expanding.[24] There is no 'no regulation'. There is the minimal generic regulation that all sectors of society face, there is self-regulation by industry and there are forms of more or less coerced co-regulation. This section explains my approach to 'no regulation' and tries to offer options for what lies between option zero and option 1. This will fill in what many IAs previously treated as a 'black box', failing to recognize that in the absence of regulation, either market/social failure or self-regulation will develop. This dynamic evolution of impacts is self-evident, yet IA has previously often been characterized as a static zero-sum game, reflecting the binary nature of many regulatory proposals and the confrontational gatekeeper function perceived in IA. Consider how very few IAs actually result in a reversed decision, not to regulate but to encourage self-regulation. This section briefly describes four possible scenarios, and note the first two are inside option zero. These need not describe developments exactly or exclusively, and should be used both to test assumptions and to draw out likely contributions of SROs to overall governance.

Option zero

The 'do nothing' or 'laissez-faire' option always should be included in regulatory IA. As SROs are dynamic, it is not a stable option, and must be explored.

'Self-organization 2.0': status quo with increased zuser-generated controls

The 'direction of travel' in SROs towards more co-regulation may be counteracted by user-generated deregulation or 'self-organization', in

---

[24]   See generally Torriti (2007), pp. 239–276.

which the ability to report abuse or switch between applications and services (e.g., social networking sites, virtual worlds) is heightened by new technologies and applications. Governments can monitor new developments while maintaining current regimes. Many new businesses depend on relatively lax control of content copyrights, user privacy and child safety. We can contrast Facebook and Second Life with Bebo. Are terms of use sufficient? Is there legitimacy in user-rated content? Youtube and Bebo can be compared to self-regulators such as PEGI/IMCB/ICRA. An important EC trade-off is innovation in Web2.0 versus legal certainty/ protection for rights of creators and users.

New self-regulation

A more proactive approach is to encourage the establishment or further development of SROs. This can include engagement with various SRO functions, including membership/participation, organization and procedures, rule-making, monitoring, enforcement, sanctions and evaluation. Support can take the form of delegation of powers, financial resources, recognition of the SRO in policy formation or implementation bodies, or recognition of SRO decisions (e.g., by endorsing SRO-generated standards for public procurement, accepting standards compliance as evidence of associated regulatory compliance, allowing evidence of non-compliance to be used in court proceedings, etc.), and informally taking part in policy fora.

Option 1: regulation2.0

This represents a movement towards formally recognized co-regulation, backed by audits to ensure that SROs adequately enforce rules, reform their activities and represent the interests of all stakeholders. For example, movements towards this can be seen in a social networking 'Bill of Rights'. It would involve delegation of powers to SROs, with financial and/ or administrative support, as well as supporting SRO membership (e.g., compulsory membership, as well as endorsing standards for public procurement or accepting standards compliance). It would formally involve inclusion of government officials in policy and/or implementation fora.

Option 2: legislation2.0

This is a more co-regulatory or even formal regulatory pattern to managing or preventing harm. Without EU harmonization, there could be potentially diverging national outcomes in such areas as Internet video, suicide sites, social networking, copyright, privacy and so on. Note here the role of the ECD, constraining national differences by the common EC legal basis in liability of content providers. This might involve:

- explicit division of powers between the SRO and government in some domains;
- explicit enforcement support;
- positive criteria for supporting exogenous or autonomously arising SRO proposals (with resources, information, delegated or agency enforcement power); and
- negative criteria for restricting, supplanting or pre-empting SROs (e.g., on competition policy, single market or other grounds).

Is legislation2.0 not already seen in the DEAct 2010 and the AVMS 2007 as implemented in the UK? That legislation2.0 arrived in the form of the DEAct, for ISPs, for Nominet and for PEGI. Legislation2.0 involves government officials in policy and/or implementation fora, as with PEGI Online. New co-regulation can take either a formal and explicit division of powers along policy area or domain lines, or a separate allocation of roles. An example of the latter form of differentiated roles is where either the public or the co-regulatory body takes explicit responsibility for enforcing the rules or decisions of the other, based on sovereign power (state enforcement) or informational advantage (SRO enforcement). A more flexible and adaptive arrangement is to base co-regulation on an undertaking to support proposals arising from SROs under *positive* conditions, or to combine SROs to address existing or emerging problems with control of other risks by the use of *negative* conditions: active restrictions and pre-emptions. Such conditions could be derived from competition policy, general regulatory or good governance principles. When flexible co-regulation is implemented by either positive or negative conditions, IA should attempt to gauge whether – and to what extent – the conditions are likely to be met. In addition, it is necessary to assess the legal and policy scope and implications of government activity to support or restrict SROs.

These options can be implemented in various ways. Where suitably representative, effective and informed SROs exist, new powers can be added to their existing portfolio of activities, with the support or encouragement of the government entity (or entities) best placed to engage them (as in extending the roles of hotlines or classification schemes). This will often be the EU as a whole, where the SROs or their key members have a strong European base or where self- or co-regulation can be 'decentralized'

from the global to the European level. In other cases, where the necessary engagement, powers and information are divided among existing SROs – and where the policy issue would be better served by their
cooperation than by their competition – government can encourage or
facilitate their merger, as with the NICAM or the German Kommission
für Jugendmedienschutz (KJM).[25] Where a full merger of SROs or their
powers is not desirable (e.g., on competition grounds), the appropriate
governmental entity can create a suitable framework contract for stakeholders to encourage best practice, to combine organizational and legal
certainty with flexibility.

There may be circumstances where SRO options should not be implemented at European level, with implementation pushed downstream to
the Member State or regional level, closer to the market, as with mobile or
ATVOD content regulation. In other cases, global institutions may have
more traction, either through intergovernmental negotiations or through
partnership with and/or support for global SROs, such as ICANN. This
may be more effective in the case of issues such as Internet security
rather than culturally divergent issues dealing with content regulation.
Outstanding examples of more local self-regulation include examples
from filtering (IMCB, FOSI), hotlines (IWF) and standards (W3C, IETF).
If we require public law standards of efficiency, representation, transparency and consultation, costs may grow exponentially. Put simply, con-
ducting a hierarchical committee structure and secretariat with 1.3 people
is not possible. Durable oligopoly is the most stable answer, as in IMCB
mobile classification and PEGI games rating. To exclude free-riders, the
government response is compulsory membership of the scheme. Barriers
to entry will arise, and co-regulation may prevent YouTube-type gar-
age start-ups. The price of social concern in a globalized world may be
too high, as with Bebo, which has lost out to Facebook. The European
Information Society model may have trouble competing. It would be
appropriate to include privacy IAs and audits of self-organizing schemata
such as YouTube, Google Street View and Facebook.

Risk and regulation

The importance of risk assessment is well understood. In relation to self-
regulation and IA, it is as important to get a sense of the range of possible
impacts as it is to generate a 'central' estimate of likely impacts. This can

---

[25] See Hans Bredow Institute (2007).

inform the design of compensatory or hedging strategies, coordination with other forms of policy activity, and the assignment of liability and responsibility. These considerations arise in general with IA, but are particularly germane to the Better Regulation agenda[26] and self-regulation, where government control is weaker. In this respect, it is useful to mention two broad classes of risk assessment. The first is concerned with how SROs are likely to respond to risks and uncertainty, and the degree to which this differs from the way formal regulation handles risk. The balance will vary with the particular IA context. The second concerns risks that are created by policies that accept, sanction, constrain or inhibit SROs. The areas considered in this study combine complex high-technology social problems with regulation in the public interest. This creates risks around:

- sustainability – the possibility that the regulation may outlive its purpose, or that the development and continuation of progress may be imperilled by SRO activities;
- efficiency – the possibility that market distortions may arise, or that the transfer of costs from public to private parties may lead to increased overall burdens, even while the burden on public institutions diminishes; and
- participation – the possibility that key players will opt out or be excluded, or the inverse risk that wide participation will result in a loss of focus, institutional 'bloat' and ossification.

Further, it should be noted that sectoral differences extend to risks as well as benefits. These differences should be taken into account for both policy formulation and *ex ante* assessment.

Recent failures of accountability, transparency and risk management in the financial sector derive in part from the failure of key assumptions, e.g., that risk-spreading provided diversification and thus minimized the extent or damage due to uncertainty. They also highlight the problem of complexity when the mechanisms through which effects are produced become so intricate that they cannot be managed effectively, or the patterns of risk measured and understood. A factor has been the ability of key parties to by-pass self-regulatory constraints by delisting (going into private equity control) or 'going dark' (retreating from listed exchanges). The key finding for SROs is not that it is possible to evade control, but that significant volumes of business did so quite suddenly, creating a situation

---

[26] The UK Government replaced the Better Regulation Commission with the Risk and Regulation Advisory Council. See Cabinet Office (2008).

from which it is difficult to return either to effective self-regulation, or even to effective formal regulation (note Scott's gambling case). Thus, the risks may have long-term as well as short-term consequences. Finally, even strong action in relation to failures of accountability (such as the US Sarbanes–Oxley Act of 2002)[27] may have perverse consequences, as some businesses suffer extra compliance burdens while others flee the jurisdiction.

In high-technology, high-risk areas such as nuclear power and biotechnology, rapid change and complex potential risks cast doubt on both the power of innovation to produce sustainable progress and the acceptance by the public of SROs as efficacious and effective mechanisms for managing technological or implementation risk. Here, the fundamental issue is one of alignment – whether industry, consumer broader public interests, understanding and risk tolerance coincide. Indeed, in some cases (e.g., genetically modified foods) there has been a perceived failure of self-regulation of trade-borne risks, due not only to the misalignment of commercial and other interests, but also to the different weights attached to these interests and objectives by sovereign governments. The idea of engaging experts with citizens directly in such cases has been broadly evaluated.[28] In other cases (notably stem-cell research, assisted reproduction, etc.) regulation is complicated by the sheer range and difference in objectives spanning religious and ethical concerns, strong economic interests and 'hot' issues relating to child safety, for example. In some sectors, other approaches were taken, including citizen juries, discourse-orientated civil society involvement, charitable foundations and innovation partnerships, to obviate the need for regulation. There is also a range of other specific structures for 'responsibility sharing' such as non-ministerial departments (executive or advisory), non-departmental public bodies, quasi-non-governmental organizations and public corporations (including chartered bodies). While these possibilities are associated with a range of sectors far beyond the Internet, the fundamental challenges they pose have arisen already in relation to the areas covered in the case studies, albeit with different pace, historical context and intensity. They remain relevant reference points.

---

[27] Sarbanes–Oxley Act of 2002, Pub. L. 107–204, 116 Stat. 745, enacted 30 July 2002.
[28] See National Audit Office (2002); National Consumer Council (2003); Office of Fair Trading (2007); Porter and Ronit (2006), pp. 41–72; Schulz and Held (2004); Grajzl and Murrell (2007), pp. 520–545; Bartle and Vass (2007), pp. 885–905.

The framework developed here may need to be extended to a much wider variety of risks and institutional arrangements for managing risk. The fundamental principles of risk management are as follows.

- Are all relevant risks identified?
- Are they properly assessed as to the likelihood and severity of, and amenability to, control?
- Do institutional arrangements strike an appropriate balance between placing risk on those best able to bear it and those best able to address it (reduce its likelihood or severity)?

This should guide risk assessment in relation to self-regulation. To the extent that risks are best managed collectively, the question of whether new regulatory innovations can prevent 'free-riding' is as germane to risk assessment as it is to accountability and compliance analysis.

Human rights and communications

It is important to make the distinction between negative and positive rights.[29] Positive rights oblige action (usually from a government) whereas negative rights oblige inaction. Rights listed in the Universal Declaration of Human Rights are generally negative rights – that governments do not restrict freedom of expression or peaceful assembly.[30] Positive rights place obligations on governments, and the International Covenant on Economic, Social and Cultural Rights places obligations on governments to provide their citizens with social security, employment, food, water, housing, health care, education and more.[31] The positive right of note is the right to communicate. It is frequently said that negative rights promote freedom whereas positive rights promote equality and fraternity. At the time of the signature of the Universal Declaration, Mrs. Franklin D. Roosevelt stated: 'It is not a treaty; it is not an international agreement. It is not and does not purport to be a statement of law or of legal obligation. It is a declaration of basic principles of human rights and freedoms ... to serve as a common standard of achievement for all peoples of all nations.'[32] Glendon points out that: 'Though the Declaration as such is not binding, most of its rights had already received a significant degree of

---

[29] Berlin (1969).   [30] Hannum (1995).
[31] International Covenant on Economic, Social and Cultural Rights (ICESCR) adopted by the United Nations General Assembly on 16 December 1966, and in force from 3 January 1976.
[32] Roosevelt (1948).

recognition by 1948 in the constitutions of many nations, if not in their practices. Since that time, most of its rights have been incorporated into the domestic legal systems of most countries.'[33]

Talk is cheap in asserting freedom of expression on the Internet, and it is the restrictions imposed by private and public actors that matter.[34] A cautionary tale is necessary at the prospect of global governance solutions. In 1998, the ITU was threatened by the unilateral actions of its largest, most powerful member. The US had first unilaterally abandoned the rules on international interconnection, privatized the Internet domain name system as ICANN, and approved what to most members was a new notion of private sector governance and self-regulation for Internet standards in IETF. ITU recommended to the UN Secretary-General that he hold a World Summit on the Information Society as a means of resolving its issues with the US and the Internet. US chief negotiator David Gross considers this a sideshow to real Internet regulation concerns:

> … with all of the focus on the internet governance, we the US together with very close allies, were able to get the paragraph 4 in to the Tunis Declaration, that enshrines the right to free-flow of freedom of expression over the Internet in an unfettered way. Where in 2003, when we had tried to hit it sort of head-on, we ended up restating the Universal Declaration of Human Rights paragraphs 19 and 29. So we were actually able to get something by a bit of a misdirection play. Bottom line, no change after the world summit, by the world summit. In a nutshell: A lot of work, no change … Ultimately the result, in my view, was extraordinarily positive.[35]

There is a great divide between US views of freedom of expression's limits and those of China, as Secretary Clinton outlined in Chapter 1. China has made a great play of its adherence to the Universal Declaration, and has published a white paper on its citizens' freedom to use the Internet, in which it declares: 'Chinese citizens fully enjoy freedom of speech on the Internet. The Constitution of the People's Republic of China confers on Chinese citizens the right to free speech … Vigorous online ideas exchange is a major characteristic of China's Internet development, and the huge quantity of BBS posts and blog articles is far beyond that of any other country.'[36]

[33] Glendon (2004), p. 2.   [34] MacKinnon (2010).
[35] Wu *et al.* (2007), p. 3.   [36] People's Republic of China (2010).

Rawls' work on natural justice[37] is authority for invoking human rights in communications regulation,[38] reinforcing the trend towards a critique of regulators as captured by market economics[39] to the disadvantage of weaker members of society. Rawls' 'justice as fairness' argument is that blind justice would force all to consider their original position given the chance of being in a disadvantaged group. Of course, it is clear that we cannot entirely adopt such an original position, and that therefore we are obliged to forecast what options such a position might create in policy terms.[40] The mental process is particularly helpful in removing vested interests from policy-making, especially given the growing invasiveness of lobbies from all sectors of society into policy-making processes. Moreover, by factoring increasing uncertainty into policy-making, we can replace formerly fixed and reliable models by models that allow for greater flexibility – in both technological and market structures, but also our place within them, as Walker, Rahman and Cave pointed out: 'Assumptions about the nature of the world can simply prove to be untrue, other actors may take actions in response to the policy that undermine its utility, or exogenous events may critically change the conditions under which the policy must operate.'[41] This helps us place the corporate chief executive who cannot type or use a computer in the place of the digital outcast.[42]

Those in relatively affluent societies are expected to show higher regard for freedom than for some marginal improvement in economic or social position: 'as the conditions of civilization improve, the marginal significance for our good of further economic and social advantages diminishes relative to the interests of liberty, which become stronger as the conditions for the exercise of the equal freedoms are more fully realized'.[43] Further, justice would be administered so as to ensure marginal benefits most clearly accrue to the most disadvantaged. From the perspective of communications regulation, these principles obviously support both universal service and the provision of reduced rates for low users, especially the elderly and handicapped. They also arguably support subsidy

---

[37] Rawls (1971). See further Kukathas and Pettit (1990); Sen (2009).
[38] See Collins (2007), pp. 1–23; Kariyawasam (2007); Schejter and Yemini (2007).
[39] Prosser (2010).   [40] See discussion in Jull and Schmidt (2010).
[41] Walker *et al.* (2001), p. 283.
[42] Famously, Tony Blair when Prime Minister admitted he had never used a computer and took lessons in digital literacy: see Blair (2010).
[43] Rawls (1971), p. 542.

for organizations that prevent the distribution and viewing of harmful images that otherwise minors could access.

This Rawlsian justice has many forms, but at base is anticipated to lead to a greater weighting of fairness than exists in usual game theoretic positions. In fact, one could describe it as an alternate to a 'weak Pareto optimal' position,[44] in which not only must all members of society have neutral or advantaged positions from economic developments, but also all must acknowledge that the outcome is both favourable to some and not disadvantageous to others. In which circumstances could such an outcome of either Rawlsian fairness or weak Pareto optimality result?[45] Clearly, both prospects for very substantial economies and very strong network or contagion effects with low entry barriers would be required. Consider the vast decrease in the price of personal computing and Internet access: this is only weak Pareto optimal if everybody can get online, or if offline equivalents are not phased out in order to protect the decreasing minority of non-Internet citizens. This suggests a response to the growth of digital goods and services that applies a handbrake to fast adoption in the interests of the more vulnerable and slower adoptive members of a society,[46] an outcome that has been at least partially rejected in most developed economies. However, it is politically compelling especially for those representing constituencies with disproportionately disadvantaged groups, as well as those societies with a stronger commitment to social justice, for instance, Scandinavia as opposed to the US.

Is this rational interpretation necessary more than ever in view of the critical failure of neo-liberal economic regulatory policies in the past decade, as evidenced by the banking collapse of 2007–9? As Nourse and Shaffer claim, 'the world has shown us the folly of some of legal scholarship's most powerful intellectual assumptions. The sudden collapse of our world economy has led to economists' open confessions that markets are not self-regulating and that they can be skewed by systematic irrational behavior, oppugning frequent assumptions of neoclassical law and economics.'[47] Sen argues that Rawls must be adapted to the acknowledgement that there are plenty of irrational actors who will always argue against change, and that we cannot therefore fully adopt a perspective

---

[44] Greenwald and Stiglitz (1986), pp. 229–264; Sen (1993), pp. 519–541.
[45] Pareto (1935).
[46] See Kariyawasam (2007) for a developing country and international economic law perspective.
[47] Nourse and Shaffer (2009), p. 63.

that places us rationally in the position of all sectors of society: we must choose the disadvantaged but rational actor if we are to stop deduction becoming nonsensical.

The Internet Governance Forum has organized major annual conferences in 2006–10 in Athens, Rio de Janeiro, Hyderabad, Sharm El Sheikh and Vilnius, Lithuania, and has tried to identify the core values, or principles, of the Internet that should be protected and regulated. The 'Charter of Human Rights and Principles for the Internet'[48] is not meant to establish new rights, but rather to apply existing human rights standards and principles to the Internet. The Charter states in article 2B: 'Everyone has the equal right to access the Internet. Where appropriate, this includes the right to broadband access.' This places the obligation on the state to provide Internet access to its citizens, such as Finland's decision to make broadband Internet access a legal right. Article 6A claims 'everyone has the right to express one's opinions on the Internet without interference' but article 7B insists 'any advocacy of national, racial or religious hatred on the Internet that constitutes incitement to discrimination, hostility or violence should be prohibited by law'. One person's opinion is another person's incitement to discrimination and/or hostility. These two rights are in clear tension if not contradiction. Article 9D reads: 'No one and no community shall be subjected to unlawful attacks on their/its honour and reputation on the Internet.' However, libel tourism has a major negative impact on freedom of expression and critical journalism, both for British-based writers and those whose overseas utterances are sued in the UK. The inherent copyright tension of article 12B should be self-explanatory: 'Creators should be remunerated and acknowledged for their work in ways that do not restrict innovation or access to public, educational knowledge and resources.' Payment suggests limiting access or targeting advertising, each of which poses threats to open access.

European Parliamentary pressure on 'soft law' measures and their democratic and human rights accountability deficit is reinforced by recent case law at national and European levels. While the EC settled its non-transparent and less than democratic international trade treaty on anti-counterfeiting,[49] the European Court of Justice found in November

---

[48] Internet Rights and Principles Coalition (2010). The Internet Rights and Principles Coalition from the 2005 World Summit on the Information Society is an attempt to collectively draft a document that articulates the rights of Internet users.

[49] Anti-Counterfeiting Trade Agreement (2010). See Joint Statement from all the Negotiating Parties to ACTA (2010).

2010 that the new Charter of Fundamental Rights, which incorporates the European Convention on Human Rights into European Union law, could be used to strike down secondary legislation which fails to respect the rights of individuals to privacy.[50] The ECJ refused to consider a broader question about the implementation of the controversial Data Retention Directive, 2006/24/EC,[51] which would have set a much broader precedent for national courts to consider European law against Charter rights. This may come back to the ECJ in a Swedish Supreme Court referral (*Perfect Communication AB*) to be heard in 2011–12.[52]

The Charter of Fundamental Rights serves up a web of conflicting rights for citizens and responsibilities on governments, with these articles especially relevant to the Internet:[53]

Article 8: Protection of personal data
(1) Everyone has the right to the protection of personal data concerning him or her.
(2) Such data must be processed fairly for specified purposes and on the basis of the consent of the person concerned or some other legitimate basis laid down by law. Everyone has the right of access to data which has been collected concerning him or her, and the right to have it rectified.
(3) Compliance with these rules shall be subject to control by an independent authority.

Article 11: Freedom of expression and information
(1) Everyone has the right to freedom of expression. This right shall include freedom to hold opinions and to receive and impart information and ideas without interference by public authority and regardless of frontiers.
(2) The freedom and pluralism of the media shall be respected.

---

[50] C-92/09 and C-93/09 [2010] 9 November Joined Cases *Volker und Markus Schecke GbR* (C-92/09), *Hartmut Eifert* (C-93/09) v. *Land Hessen*. For commentary see Content and Carrier (2010).

[51] C-92/09 *Volker und Markus Schecke GbR* v. *Land Hessen*, para. 38: 'the referring court asks the Court to rule on the validity of Directive 2006/24 and on the interpretation of Article 7(e) of Directive 95/46, so as to enable it to assess whether the retention of certain data relating to the users of the internet sites, laid down by European Union and German legislation, is lawful'.

[52] See McIntyre (2010d). Note the Swedish case was only referred in August 2010 and therefore timing of any hearing is unclear as I write.

[53] Charter Of Fundamental Rights Of The European Union (2010/C 83/02), at http://eur-lex.europa.eu/LexUriServ/LexUriServ.do?uri=OJ:C:2010:083:0389:0403:EN:PDF

It is clear that Articles 8 and 11 must be in constant tension, and the European Court of Human Rights has voluminous case law on these issues. However, Article 11 claims freedom of expression and this is reinforced by Article 24 on children's rights. Would compulsory filtering as suggested by the EC (see Chapter 6) not offend both articles?

> Article 24: The rights of the child
> (1) Children shall have the right to such protection and care as is necessary for their wellbeing. They may express their views freely. Such views shall be taken into consideration on matters which concern them in accordance with their age and maturity.
> (2) In all actions relating to children, whether taken by public authorities or private institutions, the child's best interests must be a primary consideration.

Rights to services of general economic interest also include communication, and the EC is consulting on a broadband universal service obligation. The right to access information also suggests the right to access online documents ('whatever their medium'). Jakubowicz suggests that not only should there be a right to public expression, a problematic but ambitious goal in the Web2.0 era, but also the 'user-generated' state.[54] The Charter recognizes the right to access documents, if not yet a right to be listened to – though the IIA states that multistakeholder co-regulation is meant to provide 'representativeness' of civil society.

> Article 36: Access to services of general economic interest
> The Union recognizes and respects access to services of general economic interest as provided for in national laws and practices, in accordance with the Treaties, in order to promote the social and territorial cohesion of the Union.

> Article 42: Right of access to documents
> Any citizen of the Union, and any natural or legal person residing or having its registered office in a Member State, has a right of access to documents of the institutions, bodies, offices and agencies of the Union, whatever their medium.

Furthermore, the threats to Internet connectivity outlined in the copyright tribunals we saw in Chapter 7, may offend against two separate rights.

> Article 47: Right to an effective remedy and to a fair trial
> Everyone whose rights and freedoms guaranteed by the law of the Union are violated has the right to an effective remedy before a tribunal

---

[54] Jakubowicz (2010), pp. 37–39. See further Akester (2010).

in compliance with the conditions laid down in this Article. Everyone is entitled to a fair and public hearing within a reasonable time by an independent and impartial tribunal previously established by law. Everyone shall have the possibility of being advised, defended and represented. Legal aid shall be made available to those who lack sufficient resources in so far as such aid is necessary to ensure effective access to justice.

Article 48: Presumption of innocence and right of defence
(1) Everyone who has been charged shall be presumed innocent until proved guilty according to law.
(2) Respect for the rights of the defence of anyone who has been charged shall be guaranteed.

The use of the Charter of Fundamental Rights as in *Schecke*, the forthcoming *Perfect Communication* referral and the judicial review of the DEAct, may be the most effective legal means for citizens to gain greater representation in co-regulatory activities.

Conclusion: co-regulation and constitutionalism

The space within which the Commission, Member States and corporations have been able to establish their Internet regulation arrangements without much parliamentary or judicial interference may be drawing to an end.[55] If greater scrutiny results, this is likely to lead to greater use of co-regulation with real accountability and legitimacy, as well as increasing costs of regulation and hence market entry barriers. However, the loss of dynamism that this heralds should not be the cause of great regret: as Wu has suggested,[56] the early dynamic period of Internet market entry has drawn to an end (with incumbent network operators, mobile networks and content behemoths such as Facebook and Google), and the innovation that does take place is in the flourishing standards for self-regulation, which takes place in the successful and fully functioning IETF and W3C. The increasing co-regulation of content that is taking place through institutions such as PhonepayPlus, ATVOD and IWF has been postponed for longer than many observers thought likely or credible.

---

[55] See generally Black (1998).
[56] Wu (2010) discusses the calcification and ossification of previous communications markets and applies this to the Internet.

I argued in this book, based on the 2008 study and further reinforced by the direction of travel in European and English law in the period since 2008, that co-regulation is becoming the defining feature of Internet regulation in Europe. It may prove the most appropriate model to respond to other dynamic technologically led and globalized fields of regulatory activity, such as biotechnology, nuclear and energy regulation, and environmental regulation. Scholars and policy-makers in those fields may engage with the co-regulatory model in an inter-sectoral conversation which has been sadly absent for much of the first twenty years of Internet regulation scholarship. Co-regulation offers the state a route back into questions of legitimacy, governance and human rights in the digital environment, and therefore opens up more interesting conversations than a static no-regulation versus state-regulation binary choice. I hope to have persuaded regulation and governance scholars that ignoring this critical element in the regulation that controls our digital destinies is akin to failing to grasp the importance of ethical regulation of research into the double helix that controls our biological destinies.

BIBLIOGRAPHY

AAP (Australian Associated Press) (2010) Facebook adviser critical of mandatory ISP filter, 11 June 2010

Abbott, K. and Snidal, D. (2004) Hard and soft law in international governance, *International Organization* 54, pp. 421–422

(2009) The governance triangle: regulatory standards institutions and the shadow of the state, in W. Mattli and N. Woods (eds.) *The Politics of Global Regulation*, Princeton University Press, Ch. 2, pp. 44–88

ACCC (Australian Competition and Consumer Commission) (2007) Authorisation no.: A91054 – A91055 Applications for authorisation in respect of a proposed retailer alert scheme, 31 October 2007

Ahlert, C., Marsden, C. and Nash, V. (2005) Implications of the mobile internet for the protection of minors. Report of the OII-led working group on mobile phones and child protection

Akdeniz, Y. (2004) Who watches the watchmen? The role of filtering software in Internet content regulation, in *The Media Freedom Internet Cookbook*, Vienna,Organization for Security and Co-operation in Europe, at www.osce.org/publications/rfm/2004/12/12239_89_en.pdf

(2008) *Internet Child Pornography and the Law: National and International Responses*, Aldershot, Ashgate Publishing,

Akester, P. (2010) The new challenges of striking the right balance between copyright protection and access to knowledge, information and culture, IGC(1971)XIV/4, 8 March, Paris, UNESCO.

All Party Parliamentary Communications Group (2009) Can we keep our hands off the net? Final report, October, at www.apcomms.org.uk/uploads/apComms_Final_Report.pdf

Almunia, J. (2010) SPEECH 10/365 Competition in digital media and the Internet, UCL Jevons Lecture, London, 7 July 2010

American Psychological Association (2005) *Resolution on Violence in Video Games and Interactive Media*, released 17 August 2005

Anonymous (2009) Our thinking about drinking, at www.ourthinkingabout-drinking.com/marketing-access-issues.aspx?id=258

Anti-Counterfeiting Trade Agreement (2010) Subject to legal review: 15 November 2010, text at www.dfat.gov.au/trade/acta/Finalized-Text-of-the-Agreement-subject-to-Legal-Review.pdf

Archer, P. (2007) CTO, ICRA-FOSI, interviewer: Chris Marsden, 13 September

Archon Fung, Graham, M., Weil, D. and Fargatto, E. (2004) The political economy of transparency: what makes disclosure policies effective? Ash Institute for Democratic Governance and Innovation, John F. Kennedy School of Government, Harvard University, OP-03–04, pp. 1–49

Archon Fung, et al. (2004) The Political Economy of Transparency: What Makes Disclosure Policies Effective? Ash Institute for Democratic Governance and Innovation John F. Kennedy School of Government Harvard University OP-03-04, pp. 1–49

Arrington, M. (2007) Second Life goes open source – should it be non-profit too? *Tech Crunch*, at www.techcrunch.com/2007/01/08/second-life-goes-open-source-should-it-be-non-profit-too

ATVOD (2010a) Announcing the new ATVOD – VoD regulator confirms new chair and CEO, news release, 24 March 2010

(2010b) Minutes of a meeting of the board of ATVOD held at the offices of Five, Thursday, 22 July 2010, 14.30pm

(2010c) Procedure for complaints about editorial content on VoD services (1st edn.), 15 September 2010

Ayres, I. and Braithwaite, J. (1992) *Responsive Regulation: Transcending the Deregulation Debate*, Oxford University Press

Baird, Z. (2002) Governing the Internet: engaging government, business, and non-profits, *Foreign Affairs* 81:6, p. 81

Baldwin, R. (2008) Regulation lite: the rise of emissions trading, *Regulation & Governance* 2:2, pp. 193–215

Baldwin, R. and Black, J. (2007) Really responsive regulation. LSE Legal Studies Working Paper No. 15/2007

(2010) Really responsive risk-based regulation, *Law & Policy* 32:2, pp. 181–213

Baldwin, R., Hood, C. and Scott, C. (eds.) (1998) *Socio-Legal Reader on Regulation*, Oxford University Press

Balkin, J. M. (2010) Information power: the information society from an anti-humanist perspective, in J. E. Katz and R. Subramanian (eds.) *The Global Flow of Information*, NYU Press, at http://papers.ssrn.com/sol3/papers.cfm?abstract_id=1648624

Balkin, J. M. and Noveck, B. S. (eds.) (2006) *The State of Play: Law and Virtual Worlds*, New York University Press

Banks, K. (2007) Association for Progressive Communications, London, interviewer: Chris Marsden, 28 August 2007

Barendt, E. (2003) Free speech and abortion, *Public Law*, pp. 580–591

Baron, D. (2006) More W3C controversy, Friday, 18 August 2006, at http://dbaron. org/log/2006–08#e20060818a

Bartle, I. and Vass, P. (2007) Self-regulation within the regulatory state: towards a new regulatory paradigm? *Public Administration* 85:4, pp. 885–905

Bauer, J. M. and Bohlin, E. (2007) Dynamic regulation: conceptual foundations, implementation, effects. Paper presented at 35th Research Conference on Communication, Information and Internet Policy, 29 September 2007

BBC (2010a) Bebo sold by AOL after just two years, 17 June, at www.bbc.co.uk/ news/10341413

(2010b) Net providers get Digital Economy Act judicial review: plans to monitor illegal file-sharers will be scrutinised by a judge, at www.bbc.co.uk/news/ technology-11724760

(2010c) China Green Dam web filter teams 'face funding crisis', 13 July, at www. bbc.co.uk/2/hi/world/asia_pacific/10614674.stm

Beaufort International (2003) Premium SMS services research, at www.icstis. org.uk/icstis2002/pdf/SMS_RESEARCH_REPORT_MAY03.PDF

Beck, U. (1992) *Risk Society: Towards a New Modernity*, trans. M. Ritter, London, Sage

Bekkers, W. (2005) *Child Safety and Mobile Phones*, at http://ec.europa.eu/ information_society/activities/sip/docs/mobile_2005/wim_bekkers.ppt#

(2007) Director of NICAM, interviewer: Stijn Hoorens, 18 July 2007

Bender, G. (1998) *Bavaria v. Felix Somm*, the pornography conviction of the former CompuServe manager, *Int. J. Communications L. Pol.*

Bendrath, R. (2009) Global technology trends and national regulation: explaining variation in the governance of deep packet inspection. Paper presented at the International Studies Annual Convention in New York

Bendrath, R. and Mueller, M. (2010) The end of the net as we know it? Deep packet inspection and internet governance, at http://ssrn.com/abstract=1653259

Benhamou, B. (2007) Senior Lecturer, Paris Pantheon Sorbonne University, interviewer: Chris Marsden, 31 August 2007

Benkler, Y. (1998a) Communications infrastructure regulation and the distribution of control over content, *Telecommunications Policy* 22:3, pp. 183–196

(1998b) Overcoming agoraphobia: building the commons of the digitally networked environment, *Harvard Journal of Law and Technology* 11, pp. 287–400

(2002) Coase's penguin: or Linux and the nature of the firm, *Yale Law Journal* 112, p. 369

(2006) *The Wealth of Networks*, Yale University Press

Beresford Ponsonby Peacocke, G. (1989) Discussion paper on industry co-regulation, New South Wales: Business and Consumer Affairs

Berlin, I. (1969) *Four Essays on Liberty*, Oxford University Press

Berman, J. and Weitzner, D. J. (1995) Abundance and user control: renewing the democratic heart of the First Amendment in the age of interactive media, *Yale Law Journal* 104, p. 1619

Berners-Lee, T. (with M. Fischetti) (2000) *Weaving the Web: The Original Design and Ultimate Destiny of the World Wide Web*, New York, HarperCollins

Berry, D. M. and Moss, G. (2006) On the 'Creative Commons': a critique of the commons without commonalty – Is the Creative Commons missing something? at www.freesoftwaremagazine.com/

Best, J. (2006) Vodafone users to chat through Second Life avatars, *Silicon.com*, at http://networks.silicon.com/mobile/0,39024665,39163702,00.htm?r=1

Better Regulation Executive (2005) Routes to better regulation: a guide to alternatives to classic regulation Annex B: case study 2, non-broadcast advertising, at http://archive.cabinetoffice.gov.uk/brc/upload/assets/www.brc.gov.uk/routes.pdf

Betzel, M. (2005) Co-operative regulatory systems in the media sector of the Netherlands, for Hans Bredow Institute (2006)

Black, J. (1996) Constitutionalising self-regulation, *Modern Law Review* 59:1, pp. 24–55

(1998) Reviewing regulatory rules: responding to hybridisation, in J. Black, P. Muchlinski and P. Walker (eds.) *Commercial Regulation and Judicial Review*, Oxford, Hart Publishing

(2008) Constructing and contesting legitimacy and accountability in polycentric regulatory regimes, *Regulation & Governance* 2:2, pp. 137–164

(2009) Legitimacy and the competition for regulatory share. LSE Legal Studies Working Paper No. 14/2009, at http://ssrn.com/abstract=1424654

(2010) Managing the financial crisis – the constitutional dimension. LSE Legal Studies Working Paper No. 12/2010

Blair, A. (2010) *The Journey*, New York, Random House

Bledsoe, E., Coates, J. and Fitzgerald, B. (2007) Unlocking the potential through Creative Commons, at http://creativecommons.org.au/learn-more/publications/unlockingthepotential

Blind, K., Gauch, S. and Hawkins, R. (2010) How stakeholders view the impacts of international ICT standards, *Telecommunications Policy* 34:3, pp. 162–174

Bonnici, J. P. M. (2008) *Self-Regulation in Cyberspace*, The Hague, TMC Asser Press, pp. 199–200

Borthwick, R. (2007) Vodafone, UK, telephone interviewer: Chris Marsden, 10 August 2007

Börzel, T. A. (2000) *Private Actors on the Rise? The Role of Non-State Actors in Compliance with International Institutions*, July, Max-Planck-Projektgruppe Recht der Gemeinschaftsgüter

Boston Consulting Group/Colin Carter & Associates (2008) Independent reviewer's report on the ICANN Board, 2 November 2008

Bowman, D. and Hodge, G. (2009) Counting on codes: an examination of transnational codes as a regulatory governance mechanism for nanotechnologies, *Regulation & Governance* 3:2, pp. 145–164

Boyle, K. (2001) Hate speech – The United States versus the rest of the world, *Maine Law Review* 53:2, pp. 487–521

(2008) Twenty-five years of human rights at Essex, *Essex Human Rights Review* 5:1 (July), pp. 1–15

Boyle, K. and D'Souza, F. (1992) Striking a balance: hate speech, freedom of expression, and non-discrimination, London, Article XIX (Organization)

Boyle, K. and Simonsen, S. (2004) Human security, human rights and disarmament, *Disarmament Forum* 3, pp. 1–14

Boyle, M. (2007) Department for Business Enterprise Regulatory Reform, interviewer: Chris Marsden, 6 September

Braithwaite, J. (2008) *Regulatory Capitalism: How It Works, Ideas for Making It Better*, Cheltenham, Edward Elgar

Braithwaite, T. (2006) Old media goes in pursuit of youth, *Financial Times*, 7 August 2006

Braman, S. (2004) *The Emergent Global Information Policy Regime*, New York, Palgrave Macmillan

Braman, S. (with S. Lynch) (2003) Advantage ISP: Terms of service as media law, *New Media & Society* 5:3, pp. 422–448

Brehm, M. (2006) Self-regulation of search engines in Germany, *Insafe Newsletter Issue 15*, 26 April, at www.saferinternet.org/ww/en/pub/insafe/news/articles/0506/de3

Brown, I. (2008) Internet filtering – be careful what you ask for, in S. Kirca and L. Hanson (eds.) *Freedom and Prejudice: Approaches to Media and Culture*, Istanbul, Bahcesehir University Press, pp. 74–91

Brown, I. and Marsden, C. (in press) *Regulating Code*, Cambridge, MA, MIT Press

Burri-Nenova, M. (2007), The new Audiovisual Media Services Directive: television without frontiers, television without cultural diversity, *Common Market Law Review* 44:6, pp. 1689–1725

Bussani, M. and Mattei, U. (eds.) (2002) *The Common Core in European Private Law*, Amsterdam, Kluwer

Cabinet Office (2008) Public risk – the next frontier for better regulation, at http://archive.cabinetoffice.gov.uk/brc/upload/assets/www.brc.gov.uk/public_risk_report_070108.pdf

Cafaggi, F. (2006) Rethinking private regulation in the European regulatory space. EUI Working Paper LAW No. 2006/13

Callanan, C. (2007) Managing Director, INHOPE, telephone interviewer: Chris Marsden, 10 September 2007

Callanan, C. and Frydas, N. (2007) INHOPE global Internet trend report at www.saferinternet.org/ww/en/pub/insafe/news/articles/0907/2007_inhope.htm

Callanan, C., Gercke, M., De Marco, E. and Dries-Ziekenheiner, H. (2009) *Internet Blocking: Balancing Cybercrime Responses in Democratic Societies*, Dublin,

Aconite Internet Solutions, at www.aconite.com/sites/default/files/Internet_blocking_and_Democracy.pdf

Calvert, J. (2002) New age rating system for games in Europe, *Gamespot*, 25 October 2002

Campbell, A. (1999) Self-regulation and the media, *Federal Communications L. J.* 51, pp. 712–772

Carlberg, K. (2007) Science Applications International Corporation, interviewer: Ian Brown, 21 August 2007

Carr, J. (2007) Coordinator, UK children's charities, London, interviewer: Chris Marsden, 8 August

Castells, M. (1996) *The Networked Society*, Oxford University Press

Catacchio, C. (2010) Today Finland officially becomes first nation to make broad band a legal right, *The Next Web*, 1 July, 2010

Cave, J. and Marsden, C. (2008) *Quis custodiet ipsos custodies* in the Internet: self-regulation as a threat and a promise. Presented to 36th Telecoms Policy Research Conference, Alexandria, VA

Cave, J., Marsden C. and Simmons, S. (2008) Phase 3 (final) report options for and effectiveness of Internet self- and co-regulation, TR-566, Santa Monica, CA, RAND Corp

CBC (2010) ISPs not broadcasters, court finds, 7 July, at www.cbc.ca/arts/story/2010/07/07/isp-broadcasting-court-appeal.html#ixzz0tfyK8BdA

Cecil, A. (2007) Regulatory Affairs, Yahoo! Europe, telephone interviewer: Chris Marsden, 10 August 2007

Cecot, C., Hahn, R., Renda, A. and Schrefler, L. (2008) An evaluation of the quality of IA in the European Union with lessons for the US and the EU, *Regulation & Governance* 2:4, pp. 405–424

CEN, Cenelec and ETSI and the EC and the European Free Trade Association (2003) General Guidelines (2003) General guidelines for the cooperation between CEN, Cenelec and ETSI and the EC and the European Free Trade Association, 28 March 2003 (2003/C 91/04)

CEOP (Child Exploitation and Online Protection Centre) (2006) Understanding online social network services and risks to youth: preliminary report on the findings of CEOP's Social Network Seminar Series

(2007a) Annual Review 2007

(2007b) Strategic Review 2006–7

CFA Institute (2007) Self-regulation in today's securities markets: outdated system or work in progress? at www.cfapubs.org/doi/pdf/10.2469/ccb.v2007.n7.4819

Chazerand, P. (2007) Chief Executive PEGI Brussels, interviewer: Chris Marsden, 26 June 2007

Cheliotis, G., Chik, W., Gugliani, A. and Giri Kumar Tayi (2007) Taking stock of the Creative Commons experiment. 35th Research Conference on Communication, Information and Internet Policy

Cherry, B. (2008) Back to the future: how transportation deregulatory policies foreshadow evolution of communications policies, *The Information Society* 24:5, pp. 273–291

Children's Charities' Coalition on Internet Safety (2010) Briefing on the Internet, e-commerce, children and young people, 30 October 2010

China People's Daily (2006) Online video boom raises concerns, 13 July (2006)

Christiansen, Per (2007) AOL Deutschland, Regulatory Direction, telephone interviewer: Chris Marsden, 26 August 2007

Christou, G. and Simpson, S. (2009) New modes of regulatory governance for the Internet? Country code top-level domains in Europe, at http://regulation. upf.edu/ecpr-07-papers/ssimpson.pdf

CIC Regulator (2008) Guidance – Overview of a community interest company

Clark, D. D. (2007) Head, FINE programme, NSF Washington DC, interviewer: Chris Marsden, 29 September 2007

Clark, D. D. (1985) The design philosophy of the DARPA Internet protocols, Proc SIGCOMM 88, *ACM Computer Communications Review* 18:4, pp.106–114

Clayton, R. (2005) Failures in a hybrid content blocking system, presented at the Workshop on Privacy Enhancing Technologies, Dubrovnik, at www.cl.cam. ac.uk/~rnc1/cleanfeed.pdf

(2007) Research Fellow, Cambridge University Computer Laboratory, telephone interviewer: Chris Marsden, 28 August 2007

(2008) Technical aspects of the censoring of Wikipedia, Light Blue Touchpaper, 11 December 2008, at www.lightbluetouchpaper.org/2008/12/11/technical-aspects-of-the-censoring-of-wikipedia/

Clinton, H. R. (2010) Remarks on Internet freedom, The Newseum, Washington, DC, 21 January 2010

Clinton, W. J. and Gore, A. Jr. (1997) A framework for global electronic commerce, at http://itlaw.wikia.com/wiki/A_Framework_for_Global_ Electronic_Commerce

Coates, J. (2007) Creative Commons – the next generation: Creative Commons licence use five years on, 4:1 SCRIPT-ed 72, at www.law.ed.ac.uk/ahrc/ script-ed/vol4-1/coates.asp

Coglianese, C. and Kagan, R. A. (eds.) (2007) *Regulation and Regulatory Processes*, Aldershot, Ashgate Publishing

College of Europe (2005) *Report on ICANN*, at www.coleurop.be/content/rd/devof-fice/research/projects/ICANN/ICANN.htm#Participants;

Collins, H. (2004) EC regulation of unfair trading practices, in Bussani and Mattei (eds.), Chapter 1, pp. 1–41

Collins, R. (2007) Rawls, Fraser, redistribution, recognition and The World Summit on the Information Society, *International Journal of Communication* 1, pp. 1–23, reproduced in R. Collins (2010) *Three Myths of Cyberspace: Making*

Sense of Networks, Governance and Regulation, Bristol, Chapter 8, Intellect pp. 151–172

(2009) Misrecognitions: positive and negative freedom in EU media policy and regulation, From Television Without Frontiers to The Audiovisual Media Services Directive, in I. Bondebjerg and P. Madsen (eds.) *Media, Democracy and European Culture*, Bristol, Intellect, pp. 334–361

Collins, R. and Murroni C. (1995) *New Media, New Policies*, London, Institute of Public Policy Research

COM (2001) 690 Evaluation of SIAP 1999–2000

(2002a) 0278 Action plan simplifying and improving the regulatory environment

(2002b) 704 Towards a reinforced culture of consultation and dialogue – General principles and minimum standards for consultation of interested parties by the Commission, 11 December 2002

(2002c) 275 European governance: better lawmaking

(2003) 653 on the evaluation of the Safer Internet programme 1999–2002

(2004a) 674 on the role of European standardization in the framework of European policies and legislation, of 18 October 2004

(2004b) 0341 – C6–0029/2004 – 2004/0117(COD) on the proposal for a recommendation of the European Parliament and of the Council on the protection of minors and human dignity and the right of reply in relation to the competiveness of the European audiovisual and information services industry

(2005a) 97 Better regulation for growth and jobs in the EU

(2005b) 646 proposing revisions to Directive 89/552/EEC, as amended in Directive 97/36/EC, with proposals for further revisions

(2006) 663 on the final evaluation of the Safer Internet programme for the period 2003–4

(2009a) 135 Proposal for a Council Framework Decision on combating the sexual abuse, sexual exploitation of children and child pornography, repealing Framework Decision 2004/68/JHA

(2009b) 504 Report from The Commission on subsidiarity and proportionality (16th report on Better Lawmaking covering the year 2008)

(2009c) 8301 WORK PROGRAMME Safer Internet : a multi-annual community programme on protecting children using the Internet and other communication technologies, of 29 October 2009

(2010) 94 2010/0064 (COD) Brussels, 29.3.2010 Proposal for a Directive on combating the sexual abuse, sexual exploitation of children and child pornography, repealing Framework Decision 2004/68/JHA OJ L 13, 20.1.2004

Commissariaat voor de Media (2007) Commissariaat rapporteert over functioneren NICAM in 2006. Press release, 3 July 2007

Commission on Child Online Protection (2000) Final Report of the COPA Commission, Presented to Congress, 20 October 2000, at www.copacommission.org/report/

Constine, J. (2010) Facebook proposes minor changes to its governing documents, 17 September, at www.insidefacebook.com/2010/09/17/facebook-proposes-minor-changes-to-its-governing-documents/

Content and Carrier (2010) 'break no privilege nor charter'*: ECJ invalidates regulations for breaching Charter of Fundamental Rights, at www.contentand-carrier.eu/?p=413

Cornford, T. (2008) *Towards a Public Law of Tort*, Aldershot, Ashgate Publishing,

Cosma, H. and Whish, R. (2003) Soft law in the field of EU Competition Policy, *European Business Law Review* 141, pp. 25–56

Council of Europe (2007) Convention on the Protection of Children against Sexual Exploitation and Sexual Abuse, CETS No: 201, signed 25 October 2007 and entered into force 1 July 2010

   (2008) Human Rights Guidelines for Internet Service Providers, developed in cooperation with the European Internet Services Providers Association (EuroISPA)

Council of Europe: European Commission Against Racism and Intolerance CRI (2005) Third report on the United Kingdom, adopted on 17 December 2004 and made public on 14 June 2005

Cowhey, P. and Aronson, J. (2009) *Transforming Global Information and Communication Markets: The Political Economy of Innovation*, Cambridge, MA, MIT Press

Cowie, C. and Marsden, C. (1999) Convergence: navigating through digital pay-TV bottlenecks, *Info* 1:1, pp. 53–66

Craig, P. P. (2009) Shared administration and networks: global and EU perspectives, in G. Anthony, J.-B. Auby, J. Morison and T. Zwart (eds.) *Values in Global Administrative Law*, Oxford Legal Studies Research Paper No. 6/2009, at http://ssrn.com/abstract=1333557

Cranor, L. (2002) The role of privacy advocates and data protection authorities in the design and deployment of the platform for privacy preferences. Remarks for 'The Promise of Privacy Enhancing Technologies' panel at the Twelfth Conference on Computers, Freedom and Privacy conference, San Francisco, 16–19 April 2002, at www.cfp2002.org/proceedings/proceedings/cranor.pdf

Crown Prosecution Service and Association of Chief Police Officers (2004) Memorandum of Understanding between Crown Prosecution Service and the Association of Chief Police Officers concerning section 46 Sexual Offences Act 2003, 6 October 2004, at www.iwf.org.uk/documents/20041015_mou_final_oct_2004.pdf

Croxford, I. and Marsden, C. (2001) WLAN standards and regulation in Europe, *Re:Think!*, London

Currie, D. (2005) speech 21 September 2005, available at: www.ofcom.org.uk/media/speeches/2005/09/liverpool_conf

Dacko, S. and Hart, M. (2005) Critically examining theory and practice: implications for coregulation and coregulating broadcast advertising in the United Kingdom, *Int. J. on Media Management* 7:1 & 2, pp. 2–15

Darlin, D. (2010) Google settles suit over Buzz and privacy, *New York Times* Bits section, 3 November 2010

d'Aspremont, J. (2008) Softness in international law: a self-serving quest for new legal materials, *European Journal of International Law* 19:5, at www.ejil.org/pdfs/19/5/1700.pdf

Davidson, A., Morris, J. and Courtney, R. (2002) Strangers in a strange land: public interest advocacy and Internet standards, presented on 29 September 2002, at the 30th Telecommunications Policy Research Conference in Alexandria, VA

Davies, H. (2010) Don't bank on global reform, *Prospect* 174, 25 August 2010

Davies, T. and Noveck, B. (eds.) (2006) *Online Deliberation: Design, Research, and Practice*, CSLI Publications/University of Chicago Press

DCMS (Department for Culture, Media and Sport) and BIS (Department for Business, Innovation and Skills) (2009) Digital Britain: Final Report (Cm 7650), June 2009

Deibert, R. J., Palfrey, J. G., Rohozinski, R. and Zittrain, J. (eds.) (2010) *Access Denied: The Shaping of Power, Rights, and Rule in Cyberspace*, Cambridge, MA, MIT Press

Delgado, J. (2007) Yahoo! Europe search engine business unit, telephone interviewer: Chris Marsden, 26 July 2007

DeNardis, L. E. (2009) *Protocol Politics: The Globalization of Internet Governance*, Cambridge, MA, MIT Press,

  (2010) The privatization of Internet governance, Yale Information Society Project Working Paper Draft at Fifth Annual GigaNet Symposium, Vilnius, Lithuania, September 2010

Department of Business, Innovation and Skills (2009) Consultation on legislation to address illicit peer-to-peer (p2p) file-sharing, 16 June 2009

  (2010) Outline initial obligations code

Dicey, A. V. (1959) *Introduction to the Study of the Law of the Constitution* (10th edn.), London, Macmillan, p. 157

Digital Britain (2009a) Final Report (Cm 7650), 16 June 2009

Digital Britain (2009b) Interim Report (Cm 7548), 29 January 2009

DiPerna, P. (2006) The connector website model: new implications for social change, presented at Annual Meeting of the American Sociological Association, Internet and Society, Montreal, 11 August 2006

Doctorow, C. (2010) Why the Digital Economy Act simply won't work: disconnecting downloaders will alienate the entertainment industry's most loyal customers, 1 June at www.guardian.co.uk/technology/2010/jun/01/digital-economy-act-will-fail

Dommering, E. (2006) Regulating technology: code is not law, in E. Dommering and L. F. Asscher (eds.) *Coding Regulation: Essays on the Normative Role of Information Technology*, The Hague, TMC Asser Press, pp. 6–17

Dorbeck-Jung, B. R., Vrielink, M. J. O., Gosselt, J. F., van Hoof, J. J. and de Jong, M. D. T. (2010) Contested hybridization of regulation: failure of the Dutch regulatory system to protect minors from harmful media, *Regulation & Governance* 4:2, pp. 154–174

Drake, W. J. and Wilson III E. J. (eds.) (2008) *Governing Global Electronic Networks: International Perspectives On Policy And Power*, Cambridge, MA, MIT Press

Duina, F. G. (1999) *Harmonizing Europe: Nation States within the Common Market*, State University of New York Press

Early Day Motion 17 (2010) Effects of Digital Economy Act 2010 on use of the Internet, of 25 May 2010, at http://edmi.parliament.uk/EDMi/EDMDetails.aspx?EDMID=40931 Huppert, Julian

EC (2001) White Paper on European Governance, at http://ec.europa.eu/governance/white_paper/en.pdf

(2002) Better regulation action plan

(2006) Definitions in the proposal for an Audiovisual Media Services Directive, February, mimeo

(2007) Summary of results of the public consultation (to October 2006) 'Child safety and mobile phone services'

Economic and Social Committee (2008) INT/SMO – R/CESE 708/2008 Proceedings of the public hearing on The Current State of European Self- and Co-Regulation held at the European Economic and Social Committee on Monday, 31 March, 2008

Edwards, L. (2008) IWF v Wikipedia and the rest of the world (except OUT-LAW), panGloss, at http://blogscript.blogspot.com/2008/12/iwf-v-wikipedia-and-rest-of-world.html

(2009) Pornography, censorship and the Internet, in L. Edwards and C. Waelde (eds.) *Law and the Internet* (3rd edn.) Oxford, Hart Publishing, pp. 667–696

Ellickson, R. C. (1991) *Order Without Law – How Neighbors Settle Disputes*, Harvard University Press

Emerson, J. and Twersky, F. (1996) *New Social Entrepreneurs: The Success, Challenge and Lessons of Non-profit Enterprise Creation*,California, Roberts Foundation

Espiner, T. (2010) Government proposes ISP mediation for web take-downs, *ZDNet UK*, 1 November, at www.zdnet.co.uk/news/business-of-it/2010/11/01/governmentproposes-isp-mediation-for-web-takedowns-40090709/

EU Network of Independent Experts on Fundamental Rights (2005) Combating racism and xenophobia through criminal legislation: the situation in the EU Member States, Opinion No. 5–2005, 28 November, p. 5

Eurobarometer (2007) Safer Internet for children: qualitative study in 29 European countries – summary report

EuroISPA–INHOPE (2004) EuroISPA and INHOPE lay foundations for cooperation, 28 January

European Interactive Advertising Association (2007) survey by Synovate/Aegis of 7,000 users in ten EU Member States, 12 November 2007, reported by R. Wray, Young networkers turn off TV and log onto the web, *The Guardian Online*, at www.guardian.co.uk/technology/2007/nov/12/internet

European Network Information Security Agency (2007) Security issues and recommendations for online social networks, ENISA Position Paper No.1

European Parliament (2007) Resolution INI/2007/2028 Institutional and legal implications of the use of 'soft law' instruments, of 4 September, adopted as text P6_TA(2007)0366

  (2008) Resolution INI/2008/2173 on the protection of consumers, in particular minors, in respect of the use of video games PE 416.256v02–00 A6–0051/2009, of 16 February

Facebook (2010) Statement of rights and responsibilities update, requesting comments by 30 September, at www.facebook.com/fbsitegovernance?v=app_49 49752878

Faratin, P., Clark, D. D., Gilmore P. *et al.* (2007) Complexity of Internet interconnections: technology, incentives and implications for policy. Paper presented at 35th Research Conference on Communication, Information and Internet Policy, 30 September 2007

Federal Trade Commission (2007) *Online Behavioral Advertising: Moving the Discussion Forward to Possible Self-Regulatory Principles*, Washington, DC, FTC

Feintuck, M. and Varney, C. (2006) *Media Regulation, Public Interest and the Law* (2nd edn.), Edinburgh University Press

Fenn, J. and Raskino, M. (2008) *Mastering The Hype Cycle: How to Choose the Right Innovation at the Right Time*, Harvard Business Press

Forrester, I. (2004) Where law meets competition: is *Wouters* like a *Cassis de Dijon* or a platypus? in C. D. Ehlermann and I. Atanasiu (eds.) (2006) *European Competition Law Annual 2004*, Oxford, Hart Publishing, pp. 271–294. *et seq.*

FOSI (2010) FOSI commemorates tenth anniversary of COPA Commission Report, 20 October, at www.fosi.org/pr2010.html

Frieden, R. (2007) Neither fish nor fowl: new strategies for selective regulation of information services. Paper presented at 35th Research Conference on Communication, Information and Internet Policy, 29 September 2007

  (2010) *Winning the Silicon Sweepstakes: Can the United States Compete in Global Telecommunications?* Yale University Press

Froomkin, A. M. (2003a) Habermas@discourse.net: toward a critical theory of cyberspace, *Harvard Law Review* 116:3, p. 749

(2003b) ICANN 2.0: Meet the new boss, *Loyola of Los Angeles Law Review* 36:3, pp. 1087–1102

Gaines, S. E. and Kimber, C. (2001) Redirecting self-regulation, *Env. Law* 13, p. 157

Garratt, R. and Garrett, S. (2010) Nominet governance review 2008/9, Oxford, Nominet

Gibson, O. and Wray, R. (2007) ITV faces £70m fine after viewers cheated out of millions on premium phone-ins, *The Guardian*, 19 October 2007

Giddens, A. (1998) *The Third Way: The Renewal of Social Democracy*, Cambridge, Polity Press

Gill, R. and James, P. (2009) *Crown Copyright User Testing Report*, Office of Public Sector Information, UK, at http://perspectives.opsi.gov.uk/crown-copyright-user-testing.pdf

Glendon, M. A. (2004) The rule of law in The Universal Declaration of Human Rights, *Nw. U. J. Int'l Hum. Rts.* 2:5, pp. 1–18, at www.law.northwestern.edu/journals/jihr/v2/5

Goldman, E. (2006) Search engine bias and the demise of search engine utopianism, *Yale Journal of Law and Technology*, at http://papers.ssrn.com/sol3/papers.cfm?abstract_id=893892

Goldsmith, J. (1998) What internet gambling legislation teaches about internet regulation, *Int'l Lawy.* 32, p. 1115

Goldsmith, J. and Wu, T. (2006) *Who Controls the Internet? Illusions of a Borderless World*, Oxford University Press

Gould, M. (2000) Locating internet governance: lessons from the standards process, in C. Marsden (ed.) Ch. 10

Graham, A. (2007) Chair, ICSTIS, London, interviewer: Chris Marsden, 25 June 2007

Grajzl, P. and Murrell, M. (2007) Allocating lawmaking powers: self-regulation v. government regulation, *Journal of Comparative Economics* 35, pp. 520–545

Greenstein, S. (2006) Letters 'Re: open standards, open source and open innovation' by Elliot Maxwell, *Innovations* 1:4, pp. 3–4

Greenstein, S. and Stango V. (eds.) (2008) *Standards and Public Policy*, Cambridge University Press

Greenwald, B. and Stiglitz, J. E. (1986) Externalities in economies with imperfect information and incomplete markets, *Quarterly Journal of Economics* 101:2, pp. 229–264

Grewlich, K. (1999) *Governance in 'Cyberspace': Access and Public Interest in Communications*, Amsterdam, Kluwer

Grimmelmann, J. (2007) The structure of search engine law, *Iowa Law Review* 93:1

Grindley, P., Salant, D. J. and Waverman, L. (1999) Standards wars: the use of standard setting as a means of facilitating cartels in third-generation wireless telecommunications, *International Journal of Communications Law and Policy* 3:2, at www.ijclp.org/3_1999/ijclp_webdoc_2_3_19999.html

Gringras, C. (2003) *The Laws of the Internet*, London, Butterworths,

Guadamuz, A. (2007) Edinburgh Law School, Edinburgh, interviewer: Chris Marsden, 26 October 2007

(2010) Belgian court recognises CC licences, 2 November, at www.technollama. co.uk/

Gunningham, N. and Grabosky, P. (1998) *Smart Regulation: Designing Environmental Policy*, Oxford University Press

Gunningham, N. and Rees, J. (1997) Industry self-regulation: an institutional perspective, *Law & Policy* 19:4

Haddadi, H., Fay, D., Uhlig S. *et al.* (2009) *Analysis of the Internet's Structural Evolution*, Technical Report 756, University of Cambridge, UCAM-CL-TR-756, September 2009

Hafner, K. and Lyon, M. (1996) *Where Wizards Stay Up Late: The Origins of the Internet,,* New York, Simon & Schuster

Hannum, H. (1995) The status of the universal declaration in national law, 25 *Ga. J. Int'l & Comp. L.* p. 287

Hans Bredow Institute (2006) Final report: study on co-regulation measures in the media sector. Study for the European Commission, Directorate Information Society and Media Unit A1 Audiovisual and Media Policies (Tender DG EAC 03/04; Contract No.: 2004–5091/001–001 DAVBST)

(2007) Analyse des Jugendmedienschutzsystems: Jugendschutzgesetz und Jugendmedienschutz-Staatsvertrag, Hans Bredow Institut, Hamburg, at www.hans-bredowinstitut.de/forschung/recht/071030Jugendschutz-Endbericht.pdf and www.hans-bredowinstitut.de/forschung/recht/jugendmedienschutz-games.htm

Hansard (2006) Written answers for 15 May 2006 (pt 0107) col. 715W, 15 May 2006, at www.publications.parliament.uk/pa/cm200506/cmhansrd/cm060515/text/60515w0111.htm#06051532000085

Hansard Westminster Hall (2010a) col. 178WH, 28 October 2010

(2010b) column 143WH-180WH, The Internet and privacy, 28 October 2010

Hart, H. L. A. (1961) *The Concept of Law*, Oxford, Clarendon Press

Hartley, A. (2010a) New UK games age-ratings delayed: revamped PEGI system starts next April, *Tech Radar*, 16 July 2010

(2010b) Facebook and Google given BBFC '12' rating: ISP offers web filtering with BBFC age-ratings, *Tech Radar*, 22 April 2010

Hatziz, N. (2005) Giving privacy its due: private activities of public figures in *Von Hannover v Germany*, *King's College Law Journal* 16, p. 143

Helin, S. and Sandström, J. (2007) An inquiry into the study of corporate codes of ethics, *Journal of Business Ethics* 75, pp. 253–271

Hendon, D. (2010) Letter to Bob Gilbert, Chair, Nominet, 2 February 2010

Heronymi, R. (2006) Working paper on AVMS definitions, at www.europarl. europa.eu/meetdocs/2004_2009/documents/dt/618/618091/618091en.pdf

Higgs-Kleyn, N. and Kapelianis, D. (1999) The role of professional codes in regulating ethical conduct, *Journal of Business Ethics* 19, pp. 363–374

Hilary, G. and Lenox, C. (2005) The credibility of self-regulation: evidence from the accounting profession's peer review program, *Journal of Accounting and Economics* 40, pp. 211–229

Hodson, D. and Maher, I. (2004) Soft law and sanctions: economic policy co-ordination and reform of the Stability and Growth Pact, *Journal of European Public Policy* 11:5, pp. 798–813

Hof, R. (2006) Second Life's first millionaire, *Business Week*, at www.businessweek. com/the_thread/techbeat/archives/2006/11/second_lifes_fi.html

Hoff, O. K. (2007) Norway-based independent legal advocate, telephone interviewer: Chris Marsden, 14 September 2007

Hoffmann-Riem, W. (2001) *Modernisierung in Recht und Kultur*, Frankfurt, Suhrkamp

Holoubek, M. and Damjanovic, D. (2006) Part III, in M. Holoubek and D. Damjanovic (eds.) (2006) *European Content Regulation: A Survey of the Legal Framework*, Institute for Austrian and European Public Law/Vienna University of Economics and Business Administration for Austrian Federal Chancellery

Hood, C. (1978) Keeping the centre small: explanations of agency type, *Political Studies* 26:1, pp. 30–46

Horlings, Brouwer and Horlings, of Amsterdam (2006) Annual accounts of INHOPE Association, Amsterdam, Horlings, Brouwer and Horlings

Horlings, E., Marsden, C., Van Oranje, C. and Botterman, M. (2006) Contribution to impact assessment of the revision of the Television without Frontiers Directive, TR-334-EC DG, submitted 1 November 2005, published February 2006, at www.europa.eu.int/comm/dgs/information_society/evaluation/studies/

Horten, M. (2010) DE Act unjustified: Internet industry hits out at Ofcom, at www.iptegrity.com, 8 September 2010

Hovey, R. and Bradner, S. (1996) The organizations involved in the IETF standards process, RFC 2028, October 1996, at www.ietf.org/rfc/rfc2028.txt

Howells, G. (2004) Co-regulation's role in the development of European fair trading laws, in Bussani and Mattei (eds.) Ch. 5, pp. 119–130

Huizer, E. and Crocker, D. (1994) RFC 1603 IETF Working Group Guidelines and Procedures

Hulme, K. and Ong, D. (in press) The challenge of global environmental change for international law: an overview, in P. S. Low (ed.), *Global Change and Sustainable Development: Asia-Pacific Perspectives*, Cambridge University Press

Hunton & Williams, Brussels (2008) Study on online enforcement for EC, at http://ec.europa.eu/internal_market/iprenforcement/docs/study-online-enforcement_en.pdf

Hutty, M. (2004) Cleanfeed: the facts, London Internet Exchange Public Affairsblog, 10 September 2004, at https://publicaffairs.linx.net/news/?p=154

(2006) Government sets deadline for universal network-level content blocking, London Internet Exchange Public Affairs blog, 17 May 2006, at https://publicaffairs.linx.net/news/?p=497

(2007a) Italian law mandates content blocking, London Internet Exchange Public Affairs blog, 5 January 2007, at http://publicaffairs.linx.net/news/?p=622

(2007b) Policy Officer, LINX, telephone interviewer: Chris Marsden, 30 August 2007

Huyse, L. and Parmentier, S. (1990) Decoding codes: the dialogue between consumers and suppliers through codes of conduct in the European community, *Journal of Consumer Policy* 13, pp. 253–272

Ibáñez Colomo, P. (2009) Ofcom's proposal to regulate access to premium television content: some thoughts. Paper presented to TILEC Media Workshop on Competition Policy and Regulation in Media Markets: Bridging Law and Economics, 4–5 June 2009

ICANN (2010) Final report of the board review working group, 26 January 2010

ICSTIS (2003) Annual activity report 2002

(2006) ICSTIS 1986–2006, a celebration

(2007) Annual report

IDATE–TNO–IViR (2008) User created content: supporting a participative information society, at http://ec.europa.eu/information_society/eeurope/i2010/docs/studies/ucc-annexes.pdf

IETF (1995) RFC 1792, Not all RFCs are standards

RFC 2028, The organizations involved in the IETF standards process, Hovey, R. and Bradner, S.

(1998a) RFC 2396, Uniform resource identifiers (URI): generic syntax, Berners-Lee, T., Fielding, R. and L. Masinter

(1998b) RFC 2418, Working group guidelines

(2001) RFC 3160, The Tao of the IETF

Imperial Gazetteer of India (1908) *The Indian Empire, vol. II, Historical*, Oxford, Clarendon Press

Independent Mobile Classification Body (2005) IMCB guide and classification framework for UK mobile operator commercial content services

INHOPE (2006) Towards online safety: taking action today, ready for tomorrow, Third Report, January 2006

Inter-Institutional Agreement on Better Law-Making (IIA), OJ EU 2003/C 321/01, at http://eur-lex.europa.eu/LexUriServ/LexUriServ.do?uri=OJ:C:2003:321:0001:0005:EN:PDF

International Standards Organization (2009) Guidance on social responsibility. Draft International Standard ISO/DIS 26000 (14/09/2009)

International Telecommunication Union (2010) RESOLUTION WGPL/8 Facilitating the transition from IPv4 to IPv6, Final Acts Of The Plenipotentiary Conference, Guadalajara, 2010

Internet Rights and Principles Coalition (2010) Draft 1.0 of the Charter of Human Rights and Principles for the Internet, September, at http://internetright-sandprinciples.org/node/367

Internet Service Providers Association, LINX and Safety-Net Foundation (1996) *R3* – Rating, reporting, responsibility for child pornography and illegal material on the Internet, at www.mit.edu/activities/safe/labeling/r3.htm

Internet Watch Foundation (2002) Memorandum submitted to the Joint Committee on the draft Communications Bill, 06 June 2002

(2008) Child sexual abuse content URL list, at www.iwf.org.uk/corporate/page.49.233.htm

ISFE (2004) PEGI celebrates its first two years of operations, press release, 14 December 2004

(2005a) Position paper on the communication from the Commission 'Challenges for the European Information Society beyond 2005'

(2005b) Appendix to ISFE's comments on Issue 6: Protection of Minors and Human Dignity, September 2005

Jacobs, C. (2005) Improving the quality of regulatory impact assessments in the UK, Centre on Regulation and Competition Working Paper 102

(2006) Current trends in regulatory impact analysis: the challenges of main-streaming RIA into policy-making, Jacobs & Associates, at www.regula-toryreform.com/pdfs/Current%20Trends%20and%20Processes%20in%20RIA%20-%20May%202006%20Jacobs%20and%20Associates.pdf

Jakubowicz, K (2010) *The Right to Public Expression: A Modest Proposal for an Important Human Right*, Open Society Institute Media program, London, Open Society Institute

JANET (2010) JANET response to Ofcom consultation on copyright infringement and the Digital Economy, July 2010

Joerges, C., Meny, Y. and Weiler, J. H. H. (2001) *Responses to the European Commission's White Paper on Governance*, Florence, European University Institute

Johnson, D. R. and Post, D. (1996) Law and borders: the rise of law in cyberspace, *Stanford Law Review* 48:5, pp. 1367–1402

Joint Statement from all the Negotiating Parties to ACTA (2010) press release Tokyo – Japan, 2 October 2010, at http://trade.ec.europa.eu/doclib/press/index.cfm?id=623, text of Informal Predecisional/Deliberative Draft at http://trade.ec.europa.eu/doclib/docs/2010/october/tradoc_146699.pdf

Jones, C. and Hesterly, W. S. (1993) *Network Organization: an Alternative Governance Form or a Glorified Market?* Atlanta, Georgia, Academy of Management Meetings

Jordana, J. and Levi-Faur, D (eds.) (2004) *The Politics of Regulation: Institutions and Regulatory Reforms for the Age of Governance*, Cheltenham, Edward Elgar

Joskow, P. L. and Noll, R. G. (1999) The Bell Doctrine: applications in telecommunications, electricity, and other network industries, *Stan. L. Rev.* 51, p. 1249

Jull, K. and Schmidt, S. (2010) From behind the veil of the unknown: justice and innovation in telecommunications, at http://ssrn.com/abstract=1648951

Kahan, D. (2002) The logic of reciprocity: trust, collective action, and law. John M. Olin Center for Studies in Law, Economics, and Public Policy Working Papers, p. 281

Kahin, B. and Abbate, J. (eds.) (1995) *Standards Policy for Information Infrastructure*, Cambridge, MA, MIT Press

Kahin, B. and Nesson C. (eds.) (1997) *Borders in Cyberspace: Information Policy and the Global Information Infrastructure,* Cambridge, MA, MIT Press

Kariyawasam, R. (2007) *International Economic Law and the Digital Divide: A New Silk Road?* Cheltenham, Edward Elgar

Kay, J. (2010) Better a distant judge than a pliant regulator, 3 November 2010, *Financial Times*, at www.johnkay.com/2010/11/03/better-a-distant-judge-than-a-pliant-regulator/

Kelly, G., Mulgan, G. and Muers, S. (2002) *Creating Public Value: An Analytical Framework for Public Service*, London, Cabinet Office, UK Government

Kelsen, H. (1967) *Pure Theory of Law*, trans. M. Knight., Berkeley, University of California Press

Kempf, J. and Austein, R. (2004) The rise of the middle and the future of end-to-end: reflections on the future of the internet architecture, IETF (2004) RFC 3724

Kerwer, D. (2005) Rules that many use: standards and global regulation, *Governance* 18:4, pp. 611–632

Kiedrowski, T. (2007) Ofcom Strategy Manager, London, interviewer: Chris Marsden, 20 September 2007

Kingdon, J. W. (1984) *Agendas, Alternatives, and Public Policies*, Boston, Little Brown and Company

Kingma, S. (2008) The liberalization and (re)regulation of Dutch gambling markets: national consequences of the changing European context, *Regulation & Governance* 2:4, pp. 445–458

Klang, M. and Murray, A. (eds.) (2005) *Human Rights in the Digital Age*, London, Glasshouse Press

Klein, H. (2001) Global democracy and the ICANN elections, *Info* 3:4, pp. 255–257

Kleinstuber, W. (2004) The Internet between regulation and governance, in *The Media Freedom Internet Cookbook*, Vienna, Organization for Security and Co-operation in Europe, pp. 61–100

Kohler-Koch, B. and Eising, R. (eds.) (1999) *The Transformation of Governance in the European Union*, London, Routledge

Komaitis, K. (2010) *The Current State of Domain Name Regulation: Domain Names as Second Class Citizens in a Mark-dominated World*, London, Routledge

Koppell, J. G. S. (2005) Pathologies of accountability: ICANN and the challenge of 'multiple accountabilities disorder', *Public Administration Review* 65:1, pp. 94–108

KPMG Peat Marwick and Denton Hall (1999) Review of the Internet Watch Foundation, London, KPMG

Kreimer, S. (2006) Censorship by proxy: the First Amendment, internet intermediaries, and the problem of the weakest link, *U. Penn. Law Rev.* 155, p. 13, at http://papers.ssrn.com/abstract=948226

Kroes, N. (2010) SPEECH 10/300 Openness at the heart of the EU Digital agenda, Open Forum Europe 2010 Summit, Brussels, 10 June 2010

Kukathas, C. and Pettit, P. (1990) *Rawls: A Theory of Justice and its Critics*, Stanford University Press

Kulawiec, R. (2007) Re: The great firewall of Norway? Interesting People discussion list, 13 February 2007

Latzer, M. (2007) Regulatory choice in communications governance, *European Journal of Communication* 22:3, pp. 399–405

Latzer, M. and Saurwein, F. (2007) trust in the industry – trust in the users: self-regulation and self-help in the context of digital media content in the EU. Report for Working Group 3 of the Conference of Experts for European Media Policy, More Trust in Content – The Potential of Co- and Self-Regulation in Digital Media, Leipzig, 9–11 May 2007

Latzer, M., Just, N., Saurwein, F. and Slominski, P. (2003) Regulation remixed: institutional change through self- and co-regulation in the mediamatics sector, *Communications and Strategies* 50:2, pp. 127–157

(2006) Institutional variety in communications regulation. Classification scheme and empirical evidence from Austria, *Telecommunications Policy* 30:3–4, pp. 152–170

Latzer, M., Price, M. E., Saurwein, F. and Verhulst, S. G. (2007) Comparative analysis of international co- and self-regulation in communications markets. Research report commissioned by Ofcom, September, Vienna, ITA

Laurie, B. (2000) An expert's apology, at www.apache-ssl.org/apology.html

Le Sueur, A., Sunkin, M. and Murkens, J. (2010) *Public Law: Text, Cases, and Materials*, Oxford University Press

Leadbeater, C. (1997) *The Rise of the Social Entrepreneur*, London, Demos

Lemley, M. A. (2006) Terms of use, *Minnesota Law Review* 91, p. 459

Lenox, M. (2006) The role of private decentralized institutions in sustaining industry self-regulation, *Organization Science* 17:6, pp. 677–690

Lessig, L. (1999) *Code and Other Laws of Cyberspace*, New York, Basic Books

(2001) *The Future of Ideas: The Fate of the Commons in a Connected World*, New York, Random House

(2004) *Free Culture: The Nature and Future of Creativity*, New York, Penguin Press

(2006) *Code 2.0*, New York, Basic Books

(2007) Creative Commons @ 5 Years, [cc-lessigletter] at www.creativecommons. org

(2008) *Remix*, New York, Penguin

(2010) Guest blog post: *Lawrence Lessig, For The Record II*, at http://blogs.law. harvard.edu/palfrey/2010/07/11/guest-blog-post-lawrence-lessig/

Levy, D. A. L. (1997) The regulation of digital conditional access systems, a case study in European policy making, *Telecommunications Policy* 21:7, pp. 662–676

Lewis, J. (2007) The European cciling on human rights, *Public Law*, p. 720

(2009) *In re P* and others: an exception to the 'no more and certainly no less' rule, *Public Law*, p. 43

Lewis, T. and Cumper, P. (2009) Balancing freedom of political expression against equality of political opportunity: the courts and the UK's broadcasting ban on political advertising, *Public Law*, pp. 89–111

Linksvayer, M. (2008) Toward useful Creative Commons adoption metrics. Presentation at ACIA, at www.slideshare.net/mlinksva/acia-2008-toward-useful-creative-commons-adoption-metrics

Livingstone, S., Haddon, L., Görzig, A. and Ólafsson, K. (2010) *Risks and Safety on the Internet: The Perspective of European Children, Initial Findings*, London School of Economics

LSE Public Policy Group and Enterprise (2006) A review of the generic names supporting organization for the Internet Corporation for Assigned Names and Numbers, September 2006, at http://icann.org/announcements/gnso-review-report-sep06.pdf

Lynn, S. (2002) President's report: ICANN – The case for reform, 24 February 2002, at www.icann.org/general/lynn-reform-proposal-24feb02.htm

McCarthy, K. (2007) *Sex.com: One Domain, Two Men, Twelve Years and the Brutal Battle for the Jewel in the Internet's Crown*, London, Quercus

(2009) Leaving report, 25 November, at www.icann.org/en/participate/gmpp-leaving-report-25nov09-en.pdf

(2010a) Response to: questions to the community on accountability and transparency within ICANN, Wednesday, 14 July 2010, at http://forum.icann. org/lists/atrt-questions-2010/msg00012.html

(2010b) New Nominet chair: I'll start by listening: Baroness Rennie Fritchie opens up, *The Register*, 11 June 2010

Machill, M. and Welp, C. (2003) *Wegweiser im Netz. Qualität und Nutzung von Suchmaschinen*, Gutersloh, Bertelsmann Foundation

McIntyre, T. J. (2010a) Blocking child pornography on the Internet: European Union developments, *International Review of Law, Computers and Technology* 24:3, pp. 209–221

(2010b) Hotline.ie 2009 Annual Report, at www.tjmcintyre.com/2010/07/hotli-neie-2009-annual-report.html

(2010c) Balancing regulatory effectiveness and legitimacy? An examination of internet filtering in the United Kingdom. Paper presented to Third Biennial Conference of the European Consortium on Political Research Standing Group on Regulatory Governance, Dublin, 19 June 2010

(2010d) Are Norwich Pharmacal orders compatible with the Data Retention Directive? 9 November 2010, at www.tjmcintyre.com/2010/11/are-norwich-pharmacal-orders-compatible.html

McIntyre, T. J. and Scott, C. (2008) Internet filtering: rhetoric, legitimacy, accountability and responsibility, in R. Brownsword and K. Yeung (eds.) *Regulating Technologies*, Oxford, Hart Publishing, at: http://ssrn.com/abstract=1103030

MacKinnon, R. (2010) China's Internet White Paper: networked authoritarianism in action, 15 June 2010, at http://rconversation.blogs.com/rconversation/2010/06/chinas-internet-white-paper-networked-authoritarianism.html

MacSíthigh, D. (2008) The massage of internet law, *Information and Communication Technology Law* 17:2, pp. 79–94

(2009) Datafin to virgin killer: self-regulation and public law. Norwich Law School Working Paper No. NLSWP 09/02, at p. 3

(2010) More than words: the introduction of internationalised domain names and the reform of generic top-level domains at ICANN, *Int J. Law Info Tech* 18:3, pp. 274–300

Majone, G. (1999) The regulatory state and its legitimacy problems, *West European Politics* 22:1, pp.1–24

Maldonado, E. A. and Tapia, A. H. (2007) Government-mandated open source development: the case study of Venezuela. Paper presented at 35th Research Conference on Communication, Information and Internet Policy, 30 September 2007

Maney, K. (2007) The king of alter egos is surprisingly humble guy: creator of Second Life's goal? Just to reach people, *USA Today.Com*, available at: www.usatoday.com/printedition/money/20070205/SecondLife_cover.art.htm

Mark, J. (2010) UK Liberal Democrat MP rallying support to tackle Digital Economy Act, 20 September, *ISP Review*

Marsden, C. (1996) Structural and behavioral regulation in UK, European and US digital pay-TV, *Utilities Law Review* 8:4, p. 114

(2000) The pantomime Trojan horse: US–EU state–firm relations in Internet governance. Paper presented at 28th Telecom Policy Research Conference, 24 September 2000, at tprc.si.umich.edu/Agenda00.htm

(2001) Cyberlaw and international political economy: towards regulation of the global information society, 2000 *L. Rev. M.S.U.-D.C.L.* 1, pp. 253–285

(2004a) Co- and self-regulation in European media and Internet sectors, *Tolley's Communications Law* 9:5, pp. 187–195

(2004b) Co- and self-regulation in European media and Internet sectors: the results of Oxford University's study, in *The Media Freedom Internet Cookbook*, Vienna, Organization for Security and Co-operation in Europe, pp. 76–100

(2008) Beyond Europe: the internet, regulation, and multi-stakeholder governance – representing the consumer interest? *Journal of Consumer Policy* 31:1, pp. 115–132

(2010) *Net Neutrality: Towards a Co-Regulatory Solution*, London, Bloomsbury Academic

Marsden, C. (ed.) (2000b) *Regulating the Global Information Society*, London, Routledge

Marsden, C. and Verhulst, S. (eds.) (1999) *Convergence in European Digital Television Regulation*, London, Blackstone

Marsden, C., Cave, J. and Hoorens S. (2006) *Better Re-use of Public Sector Information: Evaluating the Proposal for a Government Data Mashing Lab*, Cambridge, RAND Corporation

Marsden, C., Simmons, S., Brown, I., Woods, L., Peake, A., Robinson, N., Hoorens, S. and Klautzer, L. (2008) *Options for and Effectiveness of Internet Self- and Co-Regulation: Phase 2 Case Study Report*, Cambridge, RAND Europe for EC

Mayer-Schönberger, V. (2003) *Crouching Tiger, Hidden Dragon: Proxy Battles over P2P Movie Sharing*, mimeo

Mayer-Schönberger, V. and Crowley, J. (2006) Napster's Second Life? The regulatory challenges of virtual worlds, *Northwestern University Law Review*, 100:4, at www.vmsweb.net/attachments/pdf/NWLR100n4.pdf

Mayer-Schönberger, V. and Ziewitz, M. (2007) Jefferson rebuffed, *Columbia Science and Technology Law Review* 8, pp.188–238

Mayo, E. and Steinberg, T. (2007) The Power of information: an independent review, available at www.opsi.gov.uk/advice/poi/power-of-informationreview.pdf

MCM (2009), 021, First Council of Europe Conference of Ministers responsible for Media and New Communication Services, A new notion of media? 21 April 2009

Media Council of Australia (1992) A review by the Media Council of Australia of the co-regulatory system of advertising insofar as it relates to the advertising of alcoholic beverages, Media Council of Australia

(1993) Australian advertising co-regulation: procedures, structures and codes: effective 1 October 1993, Media Council of Australia

Michael, D. C. (1995) Federal agency use of audited self-regulation as a regulatory technique, *Admin. L. Rev.* 47, pp. 171–178

Mikler, J. (2008) Sharing sovereignty for global regulation: the cases of fuel economy and online gambling, *Regulation & Governance* 2:4, pp. 383–404

Millwood-Hargrave, M. (2007a) Report for Working Group 3 of the Conference of Experts for European Media Policy, More Trust in Content – The Potential of Co- and Self-Regulation in Digital Media, Leipzig 9–11 May, 2007

(2007b) Secretary, ATVOD, London, interviewer: Chris Marsden, 26 September 2007

Ministry of Justice (2007) Consultation Paper CP 27/07

Moglen, E. (2000) When Code isn't law, at http://emoglen.law.columbia.edu/publications/lu-01.pdf

Moreham, N. (2006) Privacy in public places, *Cambridge Law Journal* 65, p. 606

Mosco, V. (2004) *The Digital Sublime: Myth, Power and Cyberspace*, Cambridge, MA, MIT Press

Moses, A. (2010) Conroy backs down on net filters, *Sydney Morning Herald*, 9 July 2010, at www.smh.com.au/technology/technology-news/conroy-backs-down-on-net-filters-20100709-10381.html

Mueller, M. L. (2002) *Ruling the Root: Internet Governance and the Taming of Cyberspace*, Cambridge, MA, MIT Press

(2010a) *Networks and States: The Global Politics of Internet Governance*, Cambridge, MA, MIT Press

(2010b) ICANN, Inc.: accountability and participation in the governance of critical Internet resources, Internet Governance Project

Mueller, M. L., Mathiason, J. and Klein, H. (2007) The internet and global governance: principles and norms for a new regime, *Global Governance* 13:2

Mulgan, G. and Landry, C. (1995) *The Other Invisible Hand: Remaking Charity for the 21st Century*, London, Demos

Murray, A. (2006) *Regulatory Webs and Webs of Regulation: Regulating the Digital Environment*, London, Glasshouse Press

Nas, S. (2004) The Multatuli Project: ISP Notice and Takedown, 1 October 2004, http://74.125.45.132/search?q=cache:lKhZFWp5TkcJ:www.bof.nl/docs/researchpaperSANE.pdf

Nash, R. (2007) INSAFE Newsletter, September 2007, www.saferinternet.org/ww/en/pub/insafe/news/newsletter/newsltr_archives/2007_september.htm

National Audit Office (2002) Alternatives to state-imposed regulation. Report to the Ninth Meeting of INTOSAI Working Group on the Audit of Privatisation, Oslo, June 2002

National Consumer Council (2003) Three steps to credible self-regulation, at www.ncc.org

Naudin, F. (2007) French internet service providers (ISP) obliged to offer free parental control software, INSAFE Newsletter, 28 September, at www.saferinternet.org/ww/en/pub/insafe/news/articles/0907/fr.htm

Nelson, M. and Francis, C. (2007) The 3D Internet and its policy implications. 35th Research Conference on Communication, Information and Internet Policy, Alexandria, VA, 30 September 2007

Newman, A. L. and Bach, D. (2004) Self-regulatory trajectories in the shadow of public power: resolving digital dilemmas in Europe and the United States, *Governance: An International Journal of Policy, Administration, and Institutions* 17:3 (July 2004), pp. 387–413

NGO and Academic ICANN Study (2001) ICANN, legitimacy, and the public voice: making global participation and representation work. Report of the NGO and Academic ICANN Study, August 2001, New York, Markle Foundation

Nicholls, A. (2007) What is the future of social enterprise in ethical markets? London, Office of the Third Sector

(2010) What gives fair trade its right to operate? Organisational legitimacy and strategic management, in K. Macdonald and S. Marshall (eds.) *Fair Trade, Corporate Accountability and Beyond: Experiments in Global Justice Governance Mechanisms*, Aldershot, Ashgate Publishing

Nicholls, A. and Albert Hyun Bae Cho (2006) Social entrepreneurship: the structuration of a field, in A. Nicholls (ed.) *Social Entrepreneurship*, Oxford University Press, p. 102

Noll, R. G. and Owen, B. M. (1983) *The Political Economy of Deregulation: Interest Groups in the Regulatory Process*, Washington, DC, AEI Studies

Nominet (2010) Nominet hosts W3C office for UK and Ireland, 30 September 2010

NOU-2007–2: Norwegian Parliament study group on Internet filtering law proposal, at www.regjeringen.no/nb/dep/jd/dok/NOUer/2007/NOU-2007–2/6/13.html

Nourse, V. and Shaffer, G. (2009) Varieties of new legal realism: can a new world order prompt a new legal theory? *Cornell Law Review* 95:61, p. 63

Noveck, B. (2006) Architecture, law and virtual worlds, *First Monday* 10:11, at www.firstmonday.org/issues/issue10_11/noveck/

O'Connell, R. (2007) Chief Safety Officer, Bebo, London, interviewer: Chris Marsden, 30 August 2007

OECD (2005) Digital broadband content: the online computer and video game industry DSTI/ICCP/IE(2004)13/FINAL, 12 May 2005, pp. 53–54

(2006a) Interim report on alternatives to traditional regulation: self-regulation and co-regulation. Working party on regulatory management and reform, Paris, OECD

(2006b) Open educational resources at OECD, at http://oer.wsis-edu.org/oecdoer.html

(2006c) Next generation networks: evolution and policy considerations, 3 October, Paris, OECD at www.oecd.org/document/12/0,2340,en_2649_34223_37392780_1_1_1_1,00.html

OECD Centre for Educational Research and Innovation (2007) Giving knowledge for free: the emergence of open educational resources, at http://213.253.134.43/oecd/pdfs/browseit/9607041E.pdf

Ofcom (2004) Criteria for promoting effective co- and self-regulation, at http://stakeholders.ofcom.org.uk/binaries/consultations/co-reg/statement/co_self_reg.pdf

(2005) Ofcom approves amendment to ICSTIS Code of Practice, 4 August 2005

(2006a) Approval of the ICSTIS Code of Practice (11th edn.), a statement and notification on approval of the ICSTIS Code of Practice (11th edn.)

(2006b) Online protection: a survey of consumer, industry and regulatory mechanisms and systems, 21 June, at: www.ofcom.org.uk/research/telecoms/reports/onlineprotection/report.pdf

(2007) *Initial Assessments of When to Adopt Self- or Co-Regulation*, London, Ofcom

(2008) Identifying appropriate regulatory solutions: principles for analysing self- and co-regulation, 10 December 2008, at http://stakeholders.ofcom.org.uk/consultations/coregulation/

(2009a) Proposals for the regulation of video on-demand services, 14 September, at www.ofcom.org.uk/consult/condocs/vod/vod.pdf

(2009b) The regulation of video on-demand services, 18 December, at www.ofcom.org.uk/consult/condocs/vod/statement/vodstatement.pdf

(2010a) Designation pursuant to section 368B of the Communications Act 2003 of functions to the Association for Television On-Demand in relation to the regulation of on-demand programme services, at http://stakeholders.ofcom.org.uk/binaries/broadcast/tv-ops/designation180310.pdf

(2010b) Proposals for the setting of regulatory fees for video on-demand services for the period up to 31 March 2011, 26 March, at www.ofcom.org.uk/consult/condocs/vod_proposals/vod_proposal.pdf

(2010c) Consultation on 'Online infringement of copyright and the Digital Economy Act 2010: Draft Initial Obligations Code', at http://stakeholders.ofcom.org.uk/consultations/copyright-infringement/

Ofcom and ICSTIS (2005) Memorandum of Understanding of August 2005 between Ofcom and premium rate co-regulator ICSTIS

(2007) Joint Ofcom and ICSTIS response to Culture, Media & Sport Committee report on call TV quiz shows, 23 March 2007

Office of Fair Trading (2007) Review of impact on business of the consumer codes approval scheme, at www.oft.gov.uk

Office of Regulation Review (1998) *A Guide to Regulation* (2nd edn.), December 1998

Oftel (2001) The benefits of self- and co-regulation to consumers and industry, at www.oftel.gov.uk/publications/about_oftel/2001/self0701.htm

Ogus, A. (1994) *Regulation: Legal Form and Economic Theory*, Oxford, Clarendon Press

(2004) Corruption and regulatory structures, *Law & Policy* 26:3 & 4, pp. 329–346

Ondrejka, C. (2004) *Aviators, Moguls, Fashionistas and Barons: Economics and Ownership in Second Life*, at http://ssrn.com/abstract=614663

(2007) Chief Technology Officer, Second Life, telephone interviewer: Chris Marsden, 8 August 2007

One World Trust (2007) Independent assessment of standards of accountability and transparency within ICANN, at www.icann.org/transparency/owt-report-final-2007.pdf

Oxford University (2003) Website quality labelling: support for cooperation and coordination projects in Europe, 2 April 2004, at http://pcmlp.socleg.ox.ac.uk/sites/pcmlp.socleg.ox.ac.uk/files/IAPCODEfinal.pdf

Palfrey, J. G. (2004) The end of the experiment: how ICANN'S foray into global Internet democracy failed, *Harvard Journal of Law & Technology* 17:2, p. 425

Pam, A. (2002) Hyperdistribution, *Serious Cybernetics*, at www.sericyb.com.au/hyperdistribution.html

Pareto, V. (1935) *The Mind and Society* [Trattato Di Sociologia Generale], New York, Harcourt Brace

Pasquale, F. A. (2006) Rankings, reductionism, and responsibility, *Seton Hall Public Law Research Paper*, at http://ssrn.com/abstract=888327

Pattberg, P. (2005) The institutionalization of private governance: how business and nonprofit organizations agree on transnational rules, *Governance: An International Journal of Policy, Administration, and Institutions* 18:4, pp. 589–610

Peake, A. (2004) Internet governance and the World Summit on the Information Society (WSIS). Prepared for the Association for Progressive Communications (APC)

Peers, S. and Ward, A. (eds.) (2004) *The EU Charter of Fundamental Rights: Politics, Law and Policy*, Oxford, Hart Publishing

PEGI (2007) PEGI Online Safety Code ('POSC'): a code of conduct for the European interactive software industry, at www.pegionline.eu/en/index/id/235/media/pdf/197.pdf

PEGI Info newsletter No.7 (2007), at http://web.archive.org/web/20070301050356/http://www.pegi.info/pegi/download.do?id=12

Pelkmans, J. (2009) Who drafts better EU regulation? Regulatory Policy CEPS Commentaries, 14 December, at www.ceps.eu/book/who-drafts-better-eu-regulation

People's Republic of China (2010) The Internet in China, Information Office of the State Council of the People's Republic of China, Beijing, 8 June 2010, section III, at http://china.org.cn/government/whitepaper/2010–06/08/content_20207994.htm

Pessach, G. (2010) International comparative perspective on peer-to-peer file-sharing and third-party liability in copyright law – framing past, present and next-generation's questions, *Vanderbilt Journal of Transnational Law*, available at http://ssrn.com/abstract=924527

Phillipson, G. (1999) The Human Rights Act, 'Horizontal Effect' and the common law: a bang or a whimper? *Modern Law Review* 62, p. 824

(2007) Clarity postponed: horizontal effect after *Campbell*, in H. Fenwick, R. Masterman and G. Phillipson (eds.) *Judicial Reasoning under the UK Human Rights Act*, Cambridge University Press, p. 143

Pierre, J. (2000) Introduction: understanding governance, in J. Pierre (ed.) *Debating Governance: Authority, Steering and Democracy*, Oxford University Press

Pitofsky, R. (1998) Self-regulation and antitrust. Prepared remarks of Chairman, Federal Trade Commission, D. C. Bar Association Symposium, February 18, Washington, DC, at www.ftc.gov/speeches/pitofsky/self4.shtm

Popularis Ltd (2010) Nominet UK extraordinary general meeting, 24 February 2010, votes cast on resolutions

Porter, M. and Kramer, M. (2006) Strategy and society: the link between competitive advantage and corporate social responsibility, *Harvard Business Review*, December, pp. 78–93

Porter, T. and Ronit, K. (2006) Self-regulation as policy process: the multiple and criss-crossing stages of private rule-making, *Policy Sciences* 39, pp. 41–72

Posner, E. A. (2000) Law and social norms: the case of tax compliance, *Virginia Law Review* 86:8, pp. 1781–1819

Posner, E. A. and Posner, R. A. (1971) Taxation by regulation, *Bell J. Econ.* 2, p. 22

(2007) *Economic Analysis of Law* (7th edn.), New York, Wolters Kluwer

Prakash, A. and Gugerty, M. (2010) Trust but verify? Voluntary regulation programs in the nonprofit sector, *Regulation & Governance* 4:1, pp. 22–47

Price, M. (1995) *Television, The Public Sphere and National Identity*, Oxford University Press

Price, M. and Verhulst, S. (2000) In search of the self: charting the course of self-regulation on the Internet in a global environment, in Marsden (ed.), Ch. 3

(2005) *Self-Regulation and the Internet*, Amsterdam, Kluwer

Price Waterhouse Coopers (2005) Global entertainment and media outlook 2005–9, at www.pwcglobal.com/extweb/industry.nsf/docid/8CF0A9E0848 94A5A85256CE8006

Priest, M. (1997) The privatisation of regulation: five models of self-regulation, *Ottawa Law Review* 29, pp. 233–301

Prime Minister's Strategy Unit (2004) Alcohol harm reduction strategy for England, March 2004, cited at www.publications.parliament.uk/pa/cm200910/cmselect/cmhealth/151/15108.htm

Prosser, T. (2008) Self-regulation, co-regulation and the Audio-Visual Media Services Directive, *Journal of Consumer Policy* 31, pp. 99–113

(2010) *The Regulatory Enterprise: Government, Regulation, and Legitimacy*, Oxford University Press

R. v. *Secretary Of State For Business, Innovation And Skills Ex parte (1) British Telecommunications Plc (2) TalkTalk Telecom Group Plc Claimants* [2010] Statement Of Facts And Grounds

Raphael, T. (2000) The problem of horizontal effect, *European Human Rights Law Review*, p. 493

Rappeport, A. (2007) When virtual crises turn real, cfo.com at www.cfo.com/article.cfm/9670900/1/c_2984312?f=gm

Rawls, J. (1971) *A Theory of Justice*, Harvard University Press

Reding, V. (2007) SPEECH 07/429, Self regulation applied to interactive games: success and challenges, ISFE Expert Conference, Brussels, 26 June 2007

Reidenberg, J. (1999) Restoring Americans' privacy in electronic commerce, *Berkeley Technology Law Journal* 14:2, pp. 771–792

(2001) The Yahoo! case and the international democratization of the Internet. Fordham University School of Law Research Paper 11

(2004) States and law enforcement, *Uni. Ottawa L.& Tech. J.* 1, p. 213

(2005) Technology and internet jurisdiction, *Univ. of Penn. L. Rev.*, p. 1951, at http://ssrn.com/abstract=691501

Resnick, P. and Miller, J. (1996) PICS: Internet access controls without censorship, *Communications of the ACM* 39, pp. 87–93, at www.w3.org.PICS.iacwcv2.htm

Rhodes, R. A. W. (2007) Understanding governance: ten years on, *Organization Studies* 28:8, pp. 1243–1264

Richter, W. (2010) 'Better' regulation through social entrepreneurship? Innovative and market-based approaches to address the digital challenge to copyright regulation. Thesis submitted for the Degree of Doctor of Philosophy, Oxford Internet Institute, Oxford University

Robbins, P. (2007) Chief Executive, Internet Watch Foundation, interviewer: Chris Marsden, 17 August

Robinson, J. (2006) Navigating social and institutional barriers to markets: how social entrepreneurs identify and evaluate opportunities, in J. Mair, J. Robinson and K. Hockerts (eds.) *Social Entrepreneurship*, New York, Hampshire, p. 95

Roosevelt, E. (1948) statement by Mrs. Franklin D. Roosevelt, *Department Of State Bulletin* 751, 19 December 1948

Rosedale, P. (2007) interview available at http://SecondLife.reuters.com/stories/2007/08/25/exclusive-philip-rosedale-interview-from-slcc

Ross, A. (2009) Innovation in the Office of Secretary of State, Hillary Clinton, senior adviser, date of appointment, 6 April 2009

Rudolf, B. (2006) Case comment: *Von Hannover v. Germany, International Journal of Constitutional Law* 4, p. 533

Sahel, J.-J. (2007) Department for Business Enterprise Regulatory Reform, London, interviewer: Chris Marsden, 24 August 2007

Saltzer, J., Reed, D. and Clark, D. (1984) End-to-end arguments in system design, *ACM Transactions in Computer Systems* 2:4, pp. 277–288

Samuelson, P. (1999) A new kind of privacy? Regulating uses of personal data in the global information economy, *Calif. L. Rev.*, 87 p. 751

Sandberg, S. E. (2007) Re: [IP] The great firewall of Norway, Interesting People discussion list, 13 February 2007

Sarkozy, N. (2010) Speech to the Embassy of France to the Holy See, reported in J. Moya (2010) French Pres: Increased Net Regulation is 'Moral Imperative', *Zeropaid*, 11 October, at www.zeropaid.com/news/90997/french-pres-increased-inet-regulation-is-moral-imperative/?utm_source=twitterfeed&utm_medium=twitter

Saurwein, F. and Latzer, M. (2010) Regulatory choice in communications: the case of content-rating schemes in the audiovisual industry, *Journal of Broadcasting & Electronic Media* 54:3, pp. 463–484

Schejter, A. M. and Yemini, M. (2007) Justice, and only justice, you shall pursue: network neutrality, the First Amendment and John Rawls' Theory of Justice, *Mich. Telecomm. & Tech. L. Rev.* 14

Schneider, M. and Teske, P. (1992) Toward a theory of the political entrepreneur: evidence from local government, *American Political Science Review* 86:3, pp. 737–747

Schulz, W. and Held, T. (2001) *Regulated Self-Regulation as a Form of Modern Government*, Hamburg, Hans Bredow Institute

(2004) *Regulated Self-Regulation as a Form of Modern Government: A Comparative Analysis with Case Studies from Media and Telecommunications Law*, University of Luton Press

Science Daily (2009) *Australian Alcohol Advertising Self-regulation Not Working, As Ads Target Younger Drinkers, According To Experts*, 9 June, Wiley-Blackwell

Scott, C. (2004) Regulation in the age of governance: the rise of the post-regulatory state, in Jordana and Levi-Faur (eds.)

(2005) Between the old and the new: innovation in the regulation of internet gaming, in J. Black, M. Lodge and M. Thatcher, *Regulatory Innovation: A Comparative Analysis*, Cheltenham, Edward Elgar

(2007) Innovative regulatory responses, *Risk And Regulation Magazine*, (summer), at www.lse.ac.uk/resources/riskAndRegulationMagazine/magazine/summer2007/innovativeRegulatoryResponses.htm

Scott, J. and Trubek, D. M. (2002) Mind the gap: law and new approaches to governance in the European Union, *European Law Journal* 8:1

Screen Digest Ltd, CMS Hasche Sigle, Goldmedia GmbH, Rightscom Ltd (2006) Interactive content and convergence: implications for the information society. A study for the European Commission

SEC (2005) 791 IA Guidelines

(2009a) 355 Impact assessment for COM (2010) 94 2010/0064 (COD) Brussels

(2009b) 356 Impact Assessment summary for COM (2010) 94 2010/0064 (COD) Brussels

Sen, A. (1993) Markets and freedom: achievements and limitations of the market mechanism in promoting individual freedoms, *Oxford Economic Papers* 45:4, pp. 519–541

(2009) *The Idea of Justice*, The Belknap Press of Harvard University Press

Senden, L. (2005) Soft law, self-regulation and co-regulation in European law: where do they meet? *Electronic Journal of Comparative Law* 9:1

Shah, R. C. and Kesan, J. P. (2003) Manipulating the governance characteristics of code, *Info* 5:4, pp. 3–9, and also Illinois Public Law and Legal Theory Research Papers Series, Research Paper No. 03–18 of 18 December 2003, at p. 5

Short, J. and Toffel, M. W. (2007) The causes and consequences of industry self-policing. HBS Technology & Operations Mgt. Unit Research Paper No. 08–021, pp. 1–16

Sinclair, D. (1997) Self-regulation versus command and control? Beyond false dichotomies. *Law & Policy* 19:4, pp. 529–559

Spar, D. (2001a) *Pirates, Prophets and Pioneers: Business and Politics Along The Technological Frontier*, London, Random House

(2001b) When the anarchy has to stop, 15 October, *The New Statesman*

Spear, R. and Bidet, E. (2003) The role of social enterprise in European labour markets, EMES working paper series 3/10, p. 8

Spinello, R. A. (2002) *Regulating Cyberspace: The Policies and Technologies of Control*, Westport, London, Greenwood Publishing

Stalla-Bourdillon, S. (2010) The flip side of ISP's liability regimes: the ambiguous protection of fundamental rights and liberties in private digital spaces, *Computer Law & Security Rev.* 26, pp. 492–501

Stigler, G. J. (1971) The theory of economic regulation, *RAND J. Economics* 2:1, pp. 3–21

Stol, W. *et al.* (2009) Governmental filtering of websites: the Dutch case, *Computer Law & Security Review* 25, pp. 251–254

Stol, W.Ph., H.W.K. Kaspersen, J. Kerstens, E.R. Leukfeldt and A.R. Lodder (2009) 'Governmental filtering of websites: the Dutch case'. *Computer Law & Security Review* 25 (3): pp.251–262

Sunstein, C. R. (2002a) *The Cost-Benefit State: The Future Of Regulatory Protection*, Section of Administrative Law and Regulatory Practice, American Bar Association

(2002b) Switching the default rule, *New York University Law Review* 77, pp. 106–134

Sutter, G. (2000) 'Nothing new under the Sun': old fears and new media, *International Journal of Law and Information Technology* 8:3, pp. 338–378

Suzor, N. (in press) The role of the rule of law in virtual communities, *Berkley Tech. L.J.*

Swetenham, R. (2007) DG INFSO, telephone interviewer: Chris Marsden, 4 July 2007

Tambini, D., Leonardi, D. and Marsden, C. (2008) *Codifying Cyberspace Self Regulation of Converging Media*, London, Cavendish Books, Routledge

Taylor, E. (2007) Legal and Public Policy Director, NOMINET, London: interviewer, Chris Marsden, 30 June

Teubner, G. (1986) The transformation of law in the welfare state, in G. Teubner (ed.) *Dilemmas of Law in the Welfare State*, Berlin, W. de Gruyter

Thierer, A. (2007) *Social Networking and Age Verification: Many Hard Questions; No Easy Solutions*, Progress on Point 14.5, The Progress and Freedom Foundation

Thierer, A. (ed.) (2004) *Who Rules the Net?* Washington, DC, Cato Institute

Thompson, J. (2002) The world of the social entrepreneur, *International Journal of Public Sector Management* 15:5, pp. 412–431

Thornburgh, R. and Lin, H. S. (2004) *Youth, Pornography and the Internet*, available at http://books.nap.edu/html/youth_internet/

Torriti, J. (2007) Impact assessment in the EU – a tool for better regulation, less regulation or less bad regulation, *Journal of Risk Research* 10:2, pp. 239–276

Truman, N. (2009) The experience of BT in online child protection. Presented at the Effective Strategies for the Prevention of Child Online Trafficking Pornography and Abuse, Bahrain, at www.befreecenter.org/Upload/Conference/papers/BT.ppt

Tryhorn, C. (2007) Purnell: TV may face tougher regime, *Guardian Unlimited*, 25 October 2007

Unnamed (2010) If you are a Gmail user who was presented with the opportunity to use Google Buzz, you could be part of a class action settlement, at www.buzzclassaction.com/docs/notice.pdf p. 3

US Government (1998) White Paper, Federal Register, 20 February 1998

Vaizey, E. (2010) The Open Internet, Speech to FT World Telecoms 2010 Conference, 18 November 2010

Valcke, P. and Stevens, D. (2007) Graduated regulation of 'regulatable' content and the European Audiovisual Media Services Directive, *Telematics & Informatics* 24, pp. 285–302

Valkenburg, P. M., Beentjes, H., Nikken, P. and Tan, E. (2001) *De Kijkwijzer als classificatiesysteem voor audiovisuele producties: een verantwoording*, in Tijdschrift voor communicatiewetenschap, Jaargang 29, n° 4, pp. 329–354

van der Stoel, A.L., van Eijk, N., Hoogland, D., van Noorduyn, E. and Wermuth, M., (2005) Self-regulation in audiovisual products. Final Report commissioned by the Youth Policy Directorate of the Ministry of Health, Welfare & Sport

van Eijk, N. A. N. M., van Engers, T. M., Wiersma, C., Jasserand, C. A. and Abel, W. (2010) Moving towards balance: a study into duties of care on the Internet, University of Amsterdam/WODC (Research and Documentation Centre of the Ministry of Security and Justice), at www.ivir.nl/publications/vaneijk/ Moving_Towards_Balance.pdf

Van Schewick, B. (2010) *Internet Architecture and Innovation*, Cambridge, MA, MIT Press

Van Scooten, H. and Verschuuren, J. (2008) *International Governance and Law: State regulation and Non-state Law*, Cheltenham, Edward Elgar

Vance, A. (2007) Meet Mark Radcliffe: the man who rules open source law – 'The most inefficient conspirator in the world', *The Register*, 30 August 2007

Verhulst, S. (2007) Head of Research, Markle Foundation, New York, interviewer: Chris Marsden, 26 July 2007

Vrielink, M. O., van Montfort, C. and Bokhorst, M. (2010) Codes as hybrid regulation. ECPR Standing Group on Regulatory Governance, 17–19 June 2010, Dublin

Walker, W. E., Rahman, S. A. and Cave, J. (2001) Adaptive policies, policy analysis, and policy-making, *European Journal of Operational Research* 128, pp. 282–289

Weber, R. H. (2009) *Shaping Internet Governance: Regulatory Challenges*, Zürich, Schultess Juristische Medien

Weinberg, J. (1997) Rating the net, *Hastings Comms & Ent. L. J.* 19, pp. 453–482

Weiser, P. (2001) Internet governance, standard setting, and self-regulation, *Northern Kentucky Law Review* 28, pp. 822–846

   (2009) The future of internet regulation, *U.C. Davis L. Rev.* 43, pp. 529–590

Weiss, P. N. (2002) Borders in cyberspace: conflicting public sector information policies and their economic impacts, US Department of Commerce, National Oceanic and Atmospheric Administration, National Weather Service, www.weather.gov/sp/Borders_report.pdf

Weitzner, D. J. (2007a) Free speech and child protection on the Web, *IEEE Internet Computing* 11:3, pp. 86–89

   (2007b) General Counsel, World Wide Web Consortium, London, interviewer: Chris Marsden, 17 September 2007

Werbach, K. (2005) Federal computer commission, *North Carolina Law Review* 85, p. 1

WGIG (2005) *Report of the Working Group on Internet Governance* 05.41622, Chateau de Bossey, June 2005

Whiteing, P. (2007) Director, IMCB, London, interviewer: Chris Marsden, 31 August 2007

Wiley, D. (2005) Understanding the CC license selection behavior of Flickr users, available at http://web.archive.org/web/20051109024105/http://wiley. ed.usu.edu/docs/flickr_and_cc.html

Williams, C. (2008) UK.gov tells domain industry to get its house in order: Oh no! Here comes the government..., *The Register*, 20 November 2008

(2009a) Mandelson to get Nominet reform powers: just in case, *The Register*, 20 November 2008

(2009b) Nominet legal boss quits, *The Register*, 24 December, at www.theregister.co.uk/2010/03/30/nominet_gilbert/

(2010) Nominet chair quits, *The Register*, 30 March 2010

Williams, K. S. (2003) Child pornography and regulation on the Internet in the United Kingdom: the impact on fundamental rights and international relations, *Brandeis Law Journal* 41, pp. 463–469

Williamson, O. E. (1975) *Markets and Hierarchies: Analysis and Antitrust Implications*, New York, Free Press

(1985) *The Economic Institutions Of Capitalism: Firms, Markets And Relational Contracting*, New York, Free Press

(1994) Transaction cost economics and organization theory, in N. J. Smelser and R. Swedberg (eds.) *The Handbook of Economic Sociology*, Princeton University Press, pp. 77–107

Woods, L. (2006) Chapter 25: United Kingdom, in Hans Bredow Institute, June 2006

(2008) Internet protocol TV: ATVOD, in C. Marsden *et al*.

Wright, A. (2005) Coregulation of fixed and mobile internet content. Paper at Safety and Security in a Networked World: Balancing Cyber-Rights and Responsibilities conference, Oxford, September, at www.oii.ox.ac.uk/research/cybersafety/?view=papers;

WSIS Declaration of Principles (2005) (WSIS-03/GENEVA/DOC/0004)

Wu, T. (2003) When code isn't law, *Virginia Law Review* 89:4, pp. 679–751

(2006) The world trade law of internet filtering, *Chi. J. Intl. L.* 7, p. 263

(2010) *The Master Switch: The Rise and Fall of Digital Empires*, New York, Knopf

Wu, T., Dyson, E., Froomkin, A. M. and Gross, D. A. (2007) On the future of internet governance. *American Society of International Law, Proceedings of the Annual Meeting* 101:3

York, J. C. (2010) Policing content in the quasi-public sphere, Open Net Initiative Bulletin, at http://opennet.net/sites/opennet.net/files/PolicingContent.pdf

Young, A L. (2009) Human rights, horizontality and the public/private divide: towards a holistic approach, *University College London Human Rights Law Review* 1, pp. 159–187

Zittrain, J. (1999) ICANN: between the public and the private – comments before Congress, *Berkeley Law Technology Journal* 14, pp. 1070–1094

(2006a) The generative Internet, *Harvard Law Review* 119, p. 1174
(2006b) A history of online gatekeeping, *Harv. J. L. & Tech.* 19:2, pp. 254–298
(2008) *The Future of the Internet, and How to Stop It*, London, Penguin
Žižek, S. (2008) *Enjoy Your Symptom! Jacques Lacan in Hollywood and Out*, New York, Routledge Classics
Zuckerman, E. (2010) Intermediary censorship, in Deibert *et al.*, Ch. 5, pp. 72–85
Zysman, J. and Weber, S. (2000) Governance and politics of the internet economy – historical transformation or ordinary politics with a new vocabulary? BRIE Working Paper 141, E-conomy Project Working Paper 16 also in N. J. Smelser and P. B. Baltes (eds.) *International Encyclopedia of the Social & Behavioral Sciences*, Oxford, Elsevier Science Limited

INDEX

802.11x standards, 52

Advertising Standards Authority, 151
age verification
  Bebo, 78
  mobile phones, 144
Ahlert, Marsden and Nash, 140
Alcohol Beverages Advertising Code
  (Australia), 55
Allan, Richard, Lord Allan of Hallam,
  80
AOL, as candidate for a pan-national
  Code of Conduct, 189
Archer, Phil, 34
Association for Television On Demand
  (ATVOD), 42, 147–152
ATVOD (Association for Television
  On Demand), 42, 147–152
Australia
  blocking suicide sites, 188
  website filtering, 195
Ayres, Ian, 47

Baird, Z., 60
Baldwin, Robert, 224
Balkin, J. M., 12
Bangemann, Martin, 108
Banks, Karen, 34
Barlow, John Perry, 49, 90–91
BBC (British Broadcasting
  Corporation), CC-UK licence
  attempt, 92
BBFC (British Board of Film
  Classification), 161
Beaufort Scale, for self-regulation, 228
Bebo, 39, 71, 77–80, 84
Beck, U., 12

Bekkers, W., 153
Benhamou, Bernard, 34, 188–189
Berners-Lee, Sir Tim, 40, 107, 108, 111,
  115
Betonsports, CEO arrest, 223
Better Regulation, 5, 58–59, 205
Black, Julia, 52, 221, 222
Blair, Tony, 236
blogs, 73, 75
Borthwick, Rob, 34, 140, 142–143, 144,
  145, 146
Börzel, Tanja A., 72–73
Boyle, Martin, 34
Bradner, Scott O., 129
Braithwaite, J., 12, 47
Broadband Stakeholder Group (BSG),
  146
Brown, I., 182, 187
browser wars, 111
BSG (Broadband Stakeholder Group),
  146
BT
  INHOPE, 181
  judicial review of Digital Economy
    Act 2010, 216
Byron, Tanya, 138

Cafaggi, F., 52–53
CAIC list, 169, 174–175, 182–183
  European implementation,
    187–192
  future, 192–196
  UK implementation, 183–187
Callanan, Cormac, 34, 79–80, 180, 181,
  190, 192
Canada, filtering Internet video
  content, 195–196

277

Somm, Felix, 51
spam alert (IWF), 174–175
Spar, Debora, 49–50
SROs (self- and co-regulatory
    organizations)
  board composition and governance,
    205–210
  definitions, 2
  documents analyzed, 31–37
  enforcement of rules, 203–204
  engagement with government,
    205
  expansion of scope, 202–203
  expert interviews, 31, 32, 34
  funding, 200–201
  innovative paradigms, 203
  media literacy, 204–205
  membership structures, 203
  multistakeholder paradigm, 209
  oligopolies, 225
  regime reform, 202
  reporting by, 204
  resources, 200
  stakeholder survey, 37–38
Stallman, Richard, 39–40, 91, 96
subcontracting (regulation), 51–52
suicide sites, blocking when not illegal,
    188
Swetenham, Richard, 36, 145

TalkTalk, judicial review of Digital
    Economy Act 2010, 216
Tambini, D., 28, 53, 157
Taylor, Emily, 36
Teubner, G., 48
'Three Wise Monkeys' defence, 218

UGC (User Generated Content).
    see Web2.0
UK
  filtering Internet video content,
    195–196
  industry consolidation, 10
  influence of US regulatory policies,
    6–7, 10–11
  light touch, 10
UNESCO, OCL (Open Content
    Licensing) models, 94

US
  claiming Internet access as human
    right, 4
  less concern for child safety, 81
  unmetered local telephony, 6
Usenet censorship, newsgroups
    removal, 172–173

Vaizey, Ed, 80
van Eijk, Nico A.N.M., 35
Van Schewick, Barbara, 105
Verhulst, Stefaan, 36, 48, 59, 60, 99
VGT (Virtual Global Taskforce), 176
video sharing sites, 73
Video Standards Council (VSC),
    158, 160–161
Virgin Killer album cover case, 175
Virtual Global Taskforce (VGT), 176
virtual worlds, 73
  regulation scenarios, 82,
    see also Second Life
Vodafone, INHOPE, 181
voting frauds via text/phone, 133,
    137–138
VSC (Video Standards Council), 158,
    160–161

W3C (World Wide Web Consortium),
    107–113
  overview, 40, see also PICS
walled gardens, 71–72
Web2.0,
  content regulation, 73–77
  overview, 71–72, see also Bebo;
    Second Life
Weitzner, Daniel J., 36, 110, 111, 113, 114,
    115
WGIG (Working Group on Internet
    Governance), 14
  policy area categorization, 14–16
Whiteing, Paul, 36, 143, 145
Wilson, Ernest J., III, 11
Woods, L., 174
World of Warcraft, 83
World Summit on the Information
    Society (WSIS), 117
WorldCom, 7, 8
WorldOnline, 7